D0535487

American River College Library
4700 College Oak Drive
Sacramento, CA 95841

BECOMING NEW YORKERS

BECOMING NEW YORKERS

ETHNOGRAPHIES OF THE NEW
SECOND GENERATION

PHILIP KASINITZ,
JOHN H. MOLLENKOPF,
AND
MARY C. WATERS,
EDITORS

RUSSELL SAGE FOUNDATION, NEW YORK

The Russell Sage Foundation

The Russell Sage Foundation, one of the oldest of America's general purpose foundations, was established in 1907 by Mrs. Margaret Olivia Sage for "the improvement of social and living conditions in the United States." The Foundation seeks to fulfill this mandate by fostering the development and dissemination of knowledge about the country's political, social, and economic problems. While the Foundation endeavors to assure the accuracy and objectivity of each book it publishes, the conclusions and interpretations in Russell Sage Foundation publications are those of the authors and not of the Foundation, its Trustees, or its staff. Publication by Russell Sage, therefore, does not imply Foundation endorsement.

BOARD OF TRUSTEES
Robert E. Denham, Chair

Alan S. Blinder	Jennifer L. Hochschild	Cora B. Marrett
Christine K. Cassel	Timothy A. Hultquist	Eugene Smolensky
Thomas D. Cook	Kathleen Hall Jamieson	Eric Wanner
John A. Ferejohn	Melvin Konner	Mary C. Waters
Larry V. Hedges		

Library of Congress Cataloging-in-Publication Data

Becoming New Yorkers : ethnographies of the new second generation / edited by
  Philip Kasinitz, John H. Mollenkopf, and Mary C. Waters.
    p.   cm.
  Includes bibliographical references and index.
  ISBN 0-87154-436-9
    1. New York (N.Y.)—Ethnic relations.   2. New York (N.Y.)—Race
relations.   3. Ethnicity—New York (State)—New York.   4. Minorities—
New York (State)—New York—Social conditions.   5. Children of
immigrants—New York (State)—New York—Social conditions.
  6. Intergenerational relations—New York (State)—New York.   I. Kasinitz, Philip,
1957– II. Mollenkopf, John H., 1946–   III. Waters, Mary C.

F128.9.A1B33 2004
305.8'00974971—dc22   2004046633

Copyright © 2004 by Russell Sage Foundation. All rights reserved. Printed in the United States of America. No part of this publication may be reproduced, stored in a retrieval system, or transmitted in any form or by any means, electronic, mechanical, photocopying, recording, or otherwise, without the prior written permission of the publisher.

Reproduction by the United States Government in whole or in part is permitted for any purpose.

The paper used in this publication meets the minimum requirements of American National Standard for Information Sciences—Permanence of Paper for Printed Library Materials. ANSI Z39.48-1992.

Text design by Genna Patacsil.

RUSSELL SAGE FOUNDATION
112 East 64th Street, New York, New York 10021
10   9   8   7   6   5   4   3   2   1

For Basya Xiaoshan Kasinitz,
Katie Xiaorong Bayly,
Harry Quang Bayly,
Maggie Chun Ning Bayly,
and Mira Chun Kasinitz
—all "1.5 generation," albeit of an unusual sort—
and Emily Gerson Mollenkopf
—4th generation (more or less)—
and the very different America they will inherit.

CONTENTS

CONTRIBUTORS

PHILIP KASINITZ is professor of sociology at Hunter College and the Graduate Center of the City University of New York.

JOHN H. MOLLENKOPF is Distinguished Professor of Political Science and Sociology and director of the Center for Urban Research at the Graduate Center of the City University of New York.

MARY C. WATERS is professor of sociology and chair of the Sociology Department at Harvard University.

SHERRI-ANN P. BUTTERFIELD is assistant professor of sociology at Rutgers University.

AMY FOERSTER is assistant professor of sociology at Pace University.

DAE YOUNG KIM is assistant professor of sociology and Asian American studies at the University of Maryland, College Park.

KAREN CHAI KIM is assistant professor of sociology at the University of Houston.

SARA S. LEE is assistant professor of sociology at Kent State University.

NANCY LÓPEZ is assistant professor of sociology at the University of New Mexico in Albuquerque.

VIVIAN LOUIE is assistant professor of education at the Harvard Graduate School of Education.

VICTORIA MALKIN is a social anthropologist working at the Wenner Gren Foundation for Anthropological Research.

NICOLE P. MARWELL is assistant professor of sociology and Latina/o studies at Columbia University.

ALEX TRILLO is assistant professor of sociology and Latino studies at Saint Xavier University in Chicago.

NATASHA WARIKOO is a doctoral candidate in sociology at Harvard University.

AVIVA ZELTZER-ZUBIDA is assistant professor of sociology at Brooklyn College, City University of New York.

ACKNOWLEDGMENTS

The "Second Generation in Metropolitan New York Project," of which *Becoming New Yorkers* is one product, came about through the efforts of a large number of people, only some whose names appear in the present volume. The editors wish to thank some of those whose hard work and generosity helped make this and subsequent volumes possible.

Our greatest debt of gratitude is to the Russell Sage Foundation and its president, Eric Wanner. The idea of doing a study of the new second generation in New York City originally came from Eric and the Russell Sage Foundation Immigration Advisory Committee, which at that time—more years ago than we care to mention—consisted of Nancy Foner, Charles Hirschman, Douglas S. Massey, Alejandro Portes, and Marta Tienda. Throughout the years and the many twists and turns the project has taken, Dr. Wanner has been a generous and supportive research partner. Without him, this research would not have happened.

In addition to funding much of the "data-gathering" stage for the project, the Russell Sage Foundation hosted Philip Kasinitz and John H. Mollenkopf for a wonderful year as visiting scholars, during which time it sponsored the final meeting of the contributors to this book. Our work at the Foundation was greatly enriched and supported by the staff, particularly by program officer Stephanie Platz. When it came time to put the book together, the Russell Sage publications staff did a wonderful job. Three anonymous reviewers were extremely helpful to us by bringing some focus to what was originally a rich but diffuse collection. We particularly wish to thank the Russell Sage Foundation director of publications Suzanne Nichols, who helped shape the manuscript from the beginning, and production editor Genna Patacsil, who shepherded the work into its final form.

Support for the project also was provided by the National Institute for Child Health and Development, the Ford Foundation, Rockefeller Foundation, Mellon Foundation, and United Jewish Appeal-Federation of New York. We owe particular thanks to Katherine McFate at Rockefeller, Taryn Higashi at Ford, Harriet Zuckerman at Mellon, and Caroline Katz at United Jewish Appeal-Federation of New York. The inclusion of Russian Jews in the study—and the chapter by Aviva Zeltzer-Zubida in this volume—is due almost entirely to the efforts of the late Gary Rubin. For years one of the leading voices on immigration matters within the American Jewish community, Gary worked tirelessly to bring together academic researchers, policy makers, and social service providers. He was a great friend of the project—an enthusiastic supporter in public, a tough-minded but always constructive critic in private. A few months before the final draft of this manuscript was completed, Gary died suddenly at age fifty-three. He is missed.

Since its inception, the project has been based at the Center for Urban Research of the City University of New York, Graduate Center. The Center hosted six postdoctoral fellows whose year of ethnographic research forms the core of this volume. During that time, the project was managed by Jennifer Holdaway, then a member of the Center's staff. Ethnographers are notoriously independent spirits, and organizing a team of them often amounts to herding cats. Jennifer not only oversaw the organizational side of the project with skill and sensitivity, she became a vital contributor to the intellectual side as well. Now a program officer at the Social Science Research Council, we are thrilled that Dr. Holdaway has chosen to remain our partner in the second-generation enterprise.

Finally, no list of acknowledgments would be complete without mentioning our spouses: Lisa Jane Gibbs, Kathleen Gerson, and Ric Bayly. Intelligent, accomplished, and otherwise sensible individuals, they nevertheless continue to put up with us. Bless them.

Philip Kasinitz
John H. Mollenkopf
Mary C. Waters

CHAPTER 1

WORLDS OF THE SECOND GENERATION

PHILIP KASINITZ, JOHN H. MOLLENKOPF, AND MARY C. WATERS

IMMIGRATION has reshaped America since the mid-1960s. Today immigrants make up one-tenth of the U.S. population. Their U.S.-born children constitute nearly another tenth. In the nation's two largest cities, New York and Los Angeles, more than half of the population is now of immigrant stock. The number of immigrants in the country now rivals the number at any point in American history, and the diversity of contemporary immigration is unprecedented.

This dramatic demographic change has produced intense debate. Analysts, journalists, and politicians argue over whether immigration is having a positive or negative impact on the U.S. economy, the quality of neighborhood life, the labor market prospects of the native poor, intergroup relations, the cost of government services, the integrity of our civic culture, and even our national security. Yet ultimately these questions will be answered not by the immigrants themselves but by their ambivalently American children. This "second generation," now coming of age, is negotiating new and different ways of "being American." In so doing, they are reshaping American culture, economics, politics, and racial and ethnic relations—indeed, the character of American society.

This book is a collection of qualitative case studies about second- and "1.5"-generation immigrants in New York City–that is, people whose parents were immigrants but who themselves were born or substantially raised in the United States. The people in these studies come from a wide variety of backgrounds and now find themselves in a variety of circumstances. Yet they are all now young adults making their way in a complex and often very tough city. Most see themselves as very different from their immigrant parents. By and large they work in different types of jobs and have had different educational opportunities. They tend to think about race and ethnicity differently from their parents, and they often have very different ideas about love and marriage, relations with kin, and how to raise children. At the same time few of these young people truly see themselves as "mainstream" Americans. In their daily lives they balance notions of foreign-ness and native-born entitlement, of "insider" and "outsider" status—a tension that, as they often point out, makes them very much "New Yorkers."

And indeed, within their age group, their experience is, to a considerable degree, the quintessential New York experience. Together, the second and 1.5 generations make up over 29 percent of eighteen- to thirty-two-year-old New Yorkers—in contrast to only 14 percent of New Yorkers over thirty-two (many of whom are the now elderly children of pre-1924 immigrants). Another almost 29 percent of New Yorkers age eighteen to thirty-two are immigrants who arrived after age twelve. Of the city's native-stock population in this age group, 13.1 percent are African American and 6.6 percent Puerto Rican. So in the age group with which today's second generation generally goes to school, competes for jobs, recreates, and looks for love, only one New Yorker in five is a native white of native parentage. This is, however, only a preview of things to come: among New Yorkers under age eighteen, 62.4 percent are second- or 1.5-generation immigrants!

Of course, it would be wrong to glibly suggest that New York's future is America's future. In some ways the studies presented here are very much New York stories, reflecting the unique role that immigration and second-generation incorporation have historically played in the shaping of the city's institutions and political culture. In other respects the situations here may closely echo those of other "gateway cities" with similar numbers of immigrants. Although the ethnic particularities may be different, there is much here that is clearly comparable to Los Angeles, Miami, Chicago, San Francisco, and other major American cities. Twenty years ago these immigrant-receiving gateway cities seemed quite distinct from the rest of the country, but the out-migration of immigrants—and perhaps of natives fleeing immigrants—has now left few places in the country unaffected. If the incorporation of the second generation looks increasingly like the story of the coming decades in New York, it is also one of the most important stories to be told about early-twenty-first-century America.

This book is part of the Immigrant Second Generation in Metropolitan New York Study, a larger study of second- and 1.5-generation New Yorkers that we have been directing since 1998.[1] The project has had three stages. The first was a telephone survey of approximately four hundred eighteen- to thirty-two-year-olds from each of five of the largest second-generation groups: Chinese, Dominicans, Russian Jews, West Indians, and a synthetic

South American category of Colombians, Ecuadoreans, and Peruvians. All had at least one immigrant parent, and all were born in the United States or had arrived before age twelve. In addition, we surveyed equal numbers of native whites of native parentage, African Americans of native parentage, and mainland-born Puerto Ricans. These comparison groups proved vital in sorting out the second-generation experience from the experience of simply being a young New Yorker at this historical moment. In the second phase of the study we conducted loosely structured in-depth interviews with a 10 percent subsample of the original survey group. These interviews, which served as a basis for several of the chapters in this book, were wide-ranging and lasted two to four hours.[2]

The third phase was a series of ethnographic field projects that make up the bulk of the contributions to the present volume.[3] Although the case studies were all shaped and informed by the interests and questions posed by the project directors, each study was created by the individual researcher. The choice of field sites was the result of extensive discussions between the ethnographers—Alex Trillo, Victoria Malkin, Amy Foerster, Nicole Marwell, and Karen Chai Kim—and the project directors. In choosing the research sites, we deliberately avoided case studies of specific ethnic groups.[4] Although certain groups were likely to be more present in certain sites, our goal was to get a fuller picture of how second-generation young adults function in the contexts in which they live their lives. Sometimes these settings are mono-ethnic, and often, as the chapters make clear, they are not. Although the ethnographers faced different questions in their different research sites, they were also guided (or so the project directors flatter themselves in thinking) by the general questions underlying the project and by the discussions that took place at biweekly meetings.

We supplemented these case studies with related projects. Dae Young Kim, who had been an interviewer and project manager in an early phase of the project, undertook a parallel study of second-generation Koreans using instruments based in part on ours but using a different sampling method (see chapter 6). Since we had originally wanted to include Koreans for a variety of theoretical reasons, we supported this effort, and he worked closely with the group. We thus have comparable data for Koreans on many, but not all, survey items and in-depth interview topics, although the differences in sampling method require that we use caution when making direct comparisons. Nancy López and Aviva Zeltzer-Zubida, both of whom had worked as interviewers, wrote chapters for this volume based on the interviews they had done for the project, supplemented with their own ethnographic work.[5] Sherri-Ann Butterfield, Vivian Louie, Sara Lee, and Natasha Warikoo, all of whom had also worked as interviewers on the project, each contributed a chapter based on her own related work. Through extensive discussions, the insights gleaned from all of these projects has proved to be of invaluable help to the project directors in making sense of the survey and the in-depth interview data. However, we also feel that these chapters stand on their own as fascinating accounts of what it means to be a second-generation young adult in New York today.

What sort of Americans will these children of immigrants become? This question lurks just beneath the surface of the contemporary debate over immigration. There is a widely felt anxiety in many quarters, even among many of those who take a positive view of the economic effects of immigration, that this latest generation of huddled masses will not "assimilate" as the pre-1924 European immigrants are supposed to have done (and for the most part did). The question of what constitutes "American culture" and the role of immigrants in that culture are issues now being debated publicly in a way that has not happened since the Progressive Era.

These debates, whether it is explicitly stated or not, are always comparative. This is unfair, of course, but also probably inevitable. For Americans, and particularly for New Yorkers, the incorporation of immigrants from around the world has been one of our most celebrated achievements, and justifiably so. The Statue of Liberty and Ellis Island have become shrines to what makes America unique. More and more in the decades since World War II they have come to eclipse images of the Revolutionary War in American patriotic iconography. At the same time America's (and especially New York's) proud history of incorporating immigrants stands in sharp contrast to the more troubled history of America's native, racial minorities. This paradox is particularly stark for today's newcomers, most of whom are both immigrants and nonwhite.

Social scientific observers of the last great wave of immigrants to the United States, the largely European migration between the midnineteenth century and 1924, tended to assume that assimilation was both desirable and inevitable. Indeed, social scientists of the midtwentieth century, writing at the height of American self-confidence, saw assimilation as closely tied to upward mobility, and they often wrote as if assimilation, acculturation, and upward mobility were virtually the same thing. In the late 1960s, not surprisingly, these notions came under attack. This challenge was closely associated with a loss of confidence in America's ability to overcome its racial and ethnic problems with the waning of the civil rights movement. "Assimilation," we were reminded, had historically been for "whites only."

A key issue on which these debates turns is the extent to which "becoming American" means giving up ties to one's country of origin. During the nineteenth century and the first decades of the twentieth, nativist opponents of immigration frequently invoked the specter of "dual loyalties": Catholic schools, German American bilingualism, and Jewish distinctive dress, for instance, were all seen by some as threats to the unity of American society. On the other hand, those who welcomed immigration, as well as most social scientists, assumed that with time home-country ties would fade or at least mutate into an "ethnic" culture—one different from the mainstream perhaps, but nonetheless a distinctly American creation with less and less relationship to the cultural and political life of the home country. By and large, these predictions were borne out. By the midtwentieth century fears that the children of European immigrants would be anything less than 100 percent American seemed overblown, if not silly. To be sure, Irish immigrants and their American-born children remained concerned about Irish independence, and Jews remained active in efforts to create a Zionist homeland in Palestine. Yet efforts such as these were rarely seen as being at odds with loyalty to the United States.

When immigrant and American identities *did* come into sharp conflict—as happened with German Americans when the United States entered World War I—it was almost always the ethnic identity that disappeared. Thus, German American bilingualism, which had flourished for three generations, was dropped almost overnight as German newspapers shut their doors and thriving German American organizations were suddenly disbanded. By the Second World War few questioned the fact—or even noticed its irony—that the war against Germany was led by a general named Eisenhower. Of course, things were, to say the least, very different for the children of Japanese immigrants, who were suspected of congenital loyalty to Japan even after three generations. Assimilation meant becoming a *white* American, and those who could not do so remained in some ways "forever foreign" (Tuan 1999). Yet for the Europeans, who constituted the overwhelming majority of immigrants before the 1960s, ties to ancestral lands, while not forgotten, rarely played a central role in their daily lives after a generation or two.

Many argue that today's second generation will not follow this path. And they may have a point: low-cost travel and communication certainly make it possible for today's "transnational" immigrants and their children to remain active in more than one society, perhaps never fully committing to one or the other (Levitt and Waters 2002). Countless immigrants maintain social and political ties in anticipation of eventual return. New York's immigrant neighborhoods are jammed with businesses selling low-cost phone calls and instant money transfers to some of the most remote parts of the globe. Video- and audiotapes allow people in Brooklyn or Queens to "participate" vicariously in weddings and village festivals in the Andes, Iran, or West Africa only a few days after they take place. The Internet increasingly makes it possible to do so in "real time"!

In every group we talked to, there are at least some second-generation people who are strongly tied to their parents' homelands. They visit annually, send money, and even contemplate settling there. A surprising number of West Indians and Latinos are sent "back home" to live with relatives at some point during their teen years by parents who are terrified by the dangers of the New York streets or who suddenly experience a disruption of their child care arrangements. The governments of the sending societies have begun to recognize these realities. Until a few years ago most tended to ignore their communities abroad. Now they encourage them to participate socially and sometimes politically. Many grant dual citizenship rights to people living in the United States, and in a few cases to people *born* in the United States! Candidates for office in the Dominican Republic campaign on upper Broadway, and no Colombian presidential aspirant would neglect to put in an appearance on Roosevelt Avenue in Queens. South Korea and the People's Republic of China target cultural awareness tourism programs at second-generation youth, and Taiwan subsidizes tours for single young adults to visit Taiwan and get in touch with Taiwan's version of their Chinese heritage.

Yet the nickname this tour has acquired—"the love boat"—should caution against making too much of this new globalism. Most parents who send their children on the tour are probably less concerned about fostering ties to Taiwan than they are about making sure their single sons and daughters have the opportunity to meet eligible, middle-class Chinese Americans. While it no doubt helps foster ethnic ties, the "love boat" is likely to prove no greater a threat to assimilation than singles weekends at Grossinger's. In fact, the outmarriage rate for second-generation Chinese Americans is already higher than it was for Jews a generation ago.

It is by no means obvious, then, that transnational parents will produce transnational children. In their groundbreaking study of second-generation immigrants in San Diego and Miami, Alejandro Portes and Rubén Rumbaut (2001a) found that most young people prefer English to their parents' native languages, although they voice strong ethnic identities, which often intensify as they got older. Many are losing their parents' language altogether, particularly Asians, for whom fluent bilingualism appears extremely hard to sustain. Although most of the adult New Yorkers we surveyed report being able to *speak* their parents' language, far fewer report that they can read or write that language fluently. The drop-off, while particularly dramatic for the Asian groups, is seen across the board. The distinctions that members of the second generation make when describing themselves also tacitly concede the power of the American environment. Chinese young people are quick to differentiate between the "ABCs" (American-Born Chinese), the "ARCs" (American-Raised Chinese), and the much-maligned "FOBs" (Fresh Off the Boat). Koreans speak of the first, second, and "one-and-a-half" generations, which attests to the profound sense of "in-between-ness" of those "born there and raised here." Dominicans distinguish between young people raised on the island and the "Dominicanyorks" (New York-raised Dominicans), and Puerto Ricans between islanders and "Nuyoricans" (New York-raised Puerto Ricans).

Yet even if second-generation immigrants are, by and large, becoming ethnic Americans, many have asked whether this will be a good thing for them, and for the United States. In 1992 sociologist Herbert Gans (1992) turned traditional assimilation theory on its head by proposing what he termed the "second-generation decline" scenario. Gans speculates that those second-generation immigrants who are restricted by a lack of economic opportunities and by racial discrimination to poor inner-city schools, bad jobs, and shrinking economic niches will experience *downward* mobility relative to their immigrant parents. Like traditional observers of assimilation, Gans argues that substantial acculturation is taking place—the children of immigrants are indeed coming to share many of the values and outlooks of their American peers. Yet, lacking the economic opportunities of earlier immigrants, this outcome is often less than desirable. Further, if assimilation means joining the street culture of the urban ghetto, "becoming American" can be every immigrant parent's worst nightmare. Gans suggests that those children of immigrants who refuse to accept the low-level, poorly paid jobs that their parents hold will thus experience downward mobility. The other possibility is that the children of immigrants will refuse to "become American" and stay tied to their parents' ethnic community. This might lead to better economic outcomes, but less assimilation. Gans (1992, 188) writes: "The people who have secured an economically viable ethnic niche are acculturating less than did the European 2nd and 3rd generation and those without such a niche escaping condemnation to dead end immigrant and other jobs mainly by becoming very poor and persistently jobless Americans."

Alejandro Portes and Min Zhou (1993) make a similar argument in their frequently cited article on "segmented assimilation," a notion further elaborated by Portes and Rumbaut in *Legacies* (2001a). Perhaps the most influential of these "revisionist" perspectives, segmented assimilation describes the various outcomes of different groups of second-generation youth and argues that the mode of incorporation for the first generation gives the second generation access to different types of opportunities and social networks. Those groups who come with strong ethnic networks, access to capital, and fewer ties to U.S. minorities experience an ethnicity that creates networks of social ties and may provide access to job opportunities while reinforcing parental authority. Those who are socially closest to American minorities may adopt an "oppositional" or reactive ethnicity. They may become skeptical about the possibility of upward mobility and particularly about the value of education. No one feels these paradoxes more acutely than black immigrants, for whom assimilation means, literally, joining the ranks of America's most consistently downtrodden racial minority. As one West Indian young man we spoke to put it: "You can go to school for years to get your Ph.D., and after you graduate you'll come out with a regular job, probably in a supermarket or something. . . . A lot of people I've heard of, they went to school and got their master's, their Ph.D., whatever, and they are still working regular jobs just to survive. [Education] matters, but I think sometimes it is the connections. Who you know. . . . You see white people, they get hooked up like that because of their parents, who they know and how much money they have" (see also Kasinitz 1992; Vickerman 1999; Waters 1999).

Of course, the idea that assimilation has costs and "paradoxes" is hardly unprecedented, as Rumbaut has taken care to note (1999). Early-twentieth-century immigrants and those who wrote about them often expressed concern about intergenerational conflict and the heartache it produced (see in particular Thomas and Znaniecki 1927). Leonard Covello, a leading educator in New York's Italian American community in the midtwentieth century, famously recalled of his own second-generation childhood: "We were becoming Americans by learning how to be ashamed of our parents" (quoted in Iorizzo and Mondello 1980, 118). Years later, as principal of an East Harlem high school, Covello introduced the Italian language into the New York City public schools curriculum, specifically as a means of preserving ethnic heritage and keeping assimilation partially at bay. Nor is there anything new about the complaint that the children of immigrants become the "wrong kind" of Americans. As Bonnie Kahn (1987, 244) notes, as early as 1906, *The Outlook* magazine warned "against rushing Italian children into the 'streetiness' and 'cheap Americanism' which 'so overwhelms Italian youngsters in the cities.'" Even the notion that a dense "ethnic enclave" can provide a bulwark against the worst effects of the American street, a case made forcefully in Min Zhou and Carl Bankston's study of a Vietnamese community, *Growing Up American* (1998), is foreshadowed in studies of early-twentieth-century New York's Jewish community. These studies often made the case that juvenile delinquency among boys and sexual promiscuity among girls were both a direct result of Americanization and most common among the most assimilated youth in the community (for examples, see Landesman 1969; Prell 1999).

Yet if most of the arguments that would be made in the "segmented assimilation" literature were present as the last great migration produced New York's last large second generation, voices skeptical of the promise of assimilation were at that time still very much in the minority among intellectuals and social scientists and in the immigrant communities themselves. It was still, as Kahn (1987, 244) notes, "an age when people believed they could successfully become American." And it was a promise by and large made good in the mass upward mobility of postwar America. Today, against a background of falling real wages, rising income inequality, and continuing racial conflict, belief in both the possibility and value of assimilation seems considerably less pervasive.[6]

In contrast to these views of the corrosive side of incorporation into U.S. society, others have taken up the tattered banner of assimilation as an avenue of upward mobility. Richard Alba and Victor Nee (1999, 145) argue that "there is abundant evidence that assimilation is a process of major import, perhaps the master trend in fact, among whites in the U.S." (see also Alba and Nee 2003). They also argue that there is considerable reason to think that the factors working against assimilation among contemporary nonwhite immigrants have been exaggerated. Although they do not ignore the large volume of scholarship on the retention, resurgence, and even occasional wholesale revival of ethnicity among U.S. whites, they argue that, in retrospect, ethnicity researchers of the past several decades have often missed the forest for the trees. Ethnic occupational niches tend to diminish over time. Ethnic neighborhoods survive in some regions, but they account for a smaller and smaller portion of the population. Intermarriage continues to erode ethnic boundaries, not only among whites but increasingly among Asians and some Latino groups as well.

It is probably too early to say definitively whether the new second generation will assimilate—especially since it is not clear what "assimilation" means in today's world. After all, the "new immigration" is still less than four decades old. By the turn-of-the-century Russian-Jewish time clock, it is now about 1925. Yet this much seems clear: even if the new second generation lives in a world shaped by old and new ethnic and racial divisions, there is another, more creative side to what is going on among them. As in the past, assimilation surely means not only cultural loss but also cultural gains. It implies the reshuffling of boundaries and the making of connections across boundaries in new and complex ways. If at times this leads to conflict, it also creates new spheres of cooperation. The emergence of "Asian" identity symbolizes this process of invention and enrichment. In recent years churches catering specifically to the second generation have sprung up in both the Chinese and Korean communities: Chinese and Korean second-generation young people sometimes now worship together, live near each other, and join the same political groups. In fact, becoming an Asian (as opposed to Chinese, Filipino, or Korean) may be the most profound form of assimilation. To become Asian, in effect, is to internalize the racial definitions of the dominant society, to see oneself through the eyes of that society. Many Asian (and some Latino) respondents report that they first took up a pan-ethnic identity in college—another sign of its "made in America" quality. In groups like the New York Committee on Anti-Asian Violence, highly politicized, largely Korean American recent college graduates take up the cause of downtrodden Chinese factory workers and South Asian cab drivers. Of course, the "Asian" solidarity that underlies this stance often mystifies immigrant parents, for whom "Asian" is often a meaningless category.

Spending time with today's second-generation New Yorkers, one cannot help but be impressed by the sheer complexity of the business of constructing racial and ethnic identities. The second generation lives in a world of new and shifting ethnic divisions of which outsiders may be only barely aware. Latinos and Asians, whose swelling numbers and high rates of out-marriage are now complicating America's traditionally bimodal concept of race, are constructing new notions of ethnic identity, often influenced at least in part by the broader, hip-hop-influenced urban youth culture. Where the ethnic boundaries for these groups will be a few decades hence is impossible to predict. Recalling their experiences of discrimination in the multi-ethnic worlds in which they grew up, our respondents report that the greatest hostility occurs between groups that are relatively close to each other in residential space and the labor market. The narcissism of small differences abounds. One "Mountain Jew" from Central Asia reports the terrible discrimination he endured at the hands of Russian Jews and the pain he suffered when he was expelled from Yeshiva because his father became involved with "Jews for Jesus." English-speaking West Indians report conflicts with Haitians and African Americans; South Americans collide with Puerto Ricans and Dominicans. As one young West Indian man recalled of his high school days: "See, in Canarsie High School you had the [people from the] private houses, they was Caribbean, and the public housing, that was black Americans. And they used to have fights, on the bus and in the school and everywhere. People was getting hurt, getting stabbed, getting shot and stuff like that."

Chinese young people were quick to tell us of the tensions between the Cantonese (stereotyped as "rude" but also as simple, straightforward, and "open") and the Taiwanese (stereotyped as "polite" but also as officious and "wanting to have the upper hand"). Some Chinese respondents also resented what they saw as the chauvinistic style of Koreans: "Some Koreans, you know, act like they are a little bit higher than what you are." Others, particularly the upwardly mobile, voiced an admiration of Koreans that sometimes spilled over into identification. At least one second-generation Chinese respondent, married to an immigrant Korean woman, described himself as a "North East Asian." Sometimes ethnicity and class seemed to cross-cut: college-educated Chinese respondents had often gone to school with Koreans and now could be found in pan-Asian churches. Working-class Chinese respondents, by contrast, were less likely to be in pan-Asian institutions or neighborhoods and more likely to have ties to Chinatown. To the extent that they had contacts outside the ethnic enclave, it was more likely to be with Latinos.

As our respondents grew older, they often found themselves more likely to come into contact with—and sometimes conflict with—native whites. This had been particularly important for black and Latino youth. The most common encounters of this type were with store owners. A West Indian woman complained: "When you go to department stores to buy stuff, they constantly have people watching you. No matter what store you go to. . . . All of a sudden they have to fix what is in your aisle. I love that one. Sometimes we will make jokes. 'Did you put it in your pocket?' Jokes like that. It's not funny, but it is so true." Another middle-class West Indian woman recounted that "usually, if I go into a store in Jersey, they follow you around. One time we went into a store and it was owned by white people, so they didn't want to serve us. It turned into a big thing. . . . They were real rude. . . . I know I could not [live there], I probably would have been arrested because they discriminate against you a lot."

Ironically, this sort of experience of face-to-face prejudice seemed to be more common among better-off respondents, who shopped in more expensive stores, left their neighborhood more frequently, and were more likely to meet (and compete with) native whites on the job and in public. We were initially surprised at how few of the poorer and younger respondents, particularly the male respondents, reported having been the victims of discrimination. But as the interviews made clear, lack of discrimination was sometimes due to isolation from whites. For example, one nineteen-year-old West Indian reported that he had never felt discriminated against by taxi drivers, but he added that this was probably because he had never tried to hail a cab.

Asian respondents were less likely to report having experienced discrimination personally, although many believed that substantial anti-Asian discrimination existed. A few Chinese young men reported verbal encounters and sometimes fights with other ethnic groups: "Some teenagers, they curse at you in Spanish, and I understand a little Spanish—ethnic curses—like 'Chinos.'" While Asian respondents who had spent time outside of the New York metropolitan area sometimes reported having been discriminated against by whites, in the city they tended to be more concerned with discrimination at the hands of blacks and Latinos, particularly in school. On the other hand, some Chinese young people reported having benefited from the "positive stereotypes" of Asians, and one woman contrasted her experience to what she saw as the racism confronted by blacks. Some lighter-skinned Latinos may, in effect, stop being Latino, particularly if they marry whites or move to the suburbs. One fair-skinned Puerto Rican office worker made a point of removing stereotypically "ethnic" ornaments from his car when he moved to Long Island. While he had never lied about his origins, he said of his new suburban neighbors, "If they want to think I am Italian, I don't correct them."

The case studies in this book explore this complex and shifting terrain. Although the parts of the social world they explore are highly varied and distinct, the essays are linked by a number of themes that can be seen across the different settings. The first might be termed "the second generation between two worlds." This is perhaps obvious, but it nonetheless merits some examination. One of the things that defines the second- and 1.5-generation experience is growing up and becoming adult in a culture and social setting that is vastly different from the one in which their parents came of age. Of course, all modern people face something like this. The complaint that parents simply do not understand "things today" is the cri de coeur of teenagers the world over. Yet, for the children of immigrants, this is particularly true and often particularly poignant. The young people presented in this book do not share their immigrant parents' world or their worldview. But neither do they really share those of "mainstream" Americans. Some are self-consciously leaving their parents' world—sometimes over their parents' objections, sometimes with their blessing (for example, the young Korean Americans we meet in Dae Young Kim's chapter who were deliberately leaving the "ethnic economy"). Others are struggling with parental expectations that make little sense in their own lives. The outcomes of these situations are not always predictable. In Karen Chai Kim's chapter on Chinese American religious groups, we see young people who were on average more religious than their parents. For them, the embrace of conservative religious traditions became a source of autonomy from, and perhaps rebellion against, their secular families of origin.

It is often the members of the second generation, who have most successfully navigated the institutions of "mainstream" American society, who become the most acutely aware of their own marginality within that society. Yet when this realization leads them to seek stronger connections to their parents' community, they may, in turn, discover how "American" they truly are. The young, elite, college-educated activists studied by Nicole Marwell had chosen to "return" to the ethnic community and make it the site of their political work. Yet for all of their identification with the "authentic voices" of that community, they often found the endless speech-making, the elaborate rituals of deference, and the unconscious sexism of many of the veteran Dominican politicos tough to take. Similarly, several of Dae Young Kim's respondents had gone to work for South Korean companies only to be shocked by the blatant patriarchy and clannishness of Korean corporate life. In the end, having a foot in two worlds may make one unable to sit comfortably in either.

A second important theme is the fact that in most of these settings class and gender shape young people's lives at least as much as ethnicity. Indeed, class, gender, and ethnicity may cross-cut in unpredictable ways. Sara Lee, for example, examines what happens when a community, Korean Americans, is so heavily invested in defining itself as middle-class and upwardly mobile that the relatively worse-off members are virtually defined out of the group. Of course, Koreans *have* been highly successful in the United States. Even the least successful segments of the community (usually those of working-class origins in Korea) still show relatively high educational attainment and income compared to other immigrant groups. Yet Lee reminds us of the cost of being seen, and of seeing oneself, as a failure relative to other Koreans. The role of class and gender in shaping the educational expectations of Chinese college students and their parents is also clear in Louie's study of two four-year colleges, one public and working-class and one "Ivy League" and elite. The graduates of both institutions are well educated compared to most New Yorkers their age, yet the experiences of these college students seem worlds apart. Both kinds of graduates contrast sharply in turn with the South American community college students studied by Alex Trillo. The interaction of gender, education, and upward mobility is also a key factor in Nancy López's study of Dominican, West Indian, and Haitian high school students. Here we see partially Americanized girls chafing at the double standards that keep them at home, helping with housework and caring for younger siblings, while their brothers enjoy far greater freedom. Yet in the end, López argues, being shielded from the "freedom" to "sow some wild oats" on the streets of New York may turn out to be a blessing, as girls avoid many of the traps that ensnare the boys. What is more, the embrace of traditional notions of femininity may end up facilitating success in high school and beyond (despite the fact that in the Dominican case educational attainment is not traditionally seen as a female characteristic). Traditionally masculine behavior, by contrast, serves boys less well in American high schools. What teachers in a white middle-class setting might see as healthy, masculine, autonomous behavior is often perceived as aggressive, rebellious, and threatening coming from dark-skinned Caribbean students.

Finally, in Victoria Malkin's study of retail workers, we see workplace identities partially transcending ethnic ones. Many of these young people attended racially and ethnically segregated schools and were continuing to live in segregated neighborhoods. Working in midtown Manhattan, they found themselves in ethnically diverse settings, often for the first time in their lives. Of course, with only a few exceptions, the whites they encountered were either bosses or customers. Yet equally important is the fact that these Latino, West Indian, African American, Puerto Rican, Dominican, and Asian young workers were also encountering *each other*. The ethnically mixed workplace provided possibilities for acquaintance, friendship, romance, common conversation (often built around youth culture and popular music), and definitions of who "we" are that cut across ethnic lines in ways that residentially based notions of community usually do not. Yet this workplace identity will probably not create the type of class solidarity that an earlier "second generation" created on the shop floors of the mid-twentieth century (Montgomery 1989, Freeman 2000) or even that we see among the unionized professional workers in Amy Foerster's chapter. For the young workers Malkin studies, work was a problematic basis for an adult identity. Earning low wages and working erratic "part-time" schedules (even those who wanted to work full-time), few earned enough to form an independent household or even support themselves, in marked contrast to the largely unionized New York retail workers of earlier times.[7] Poised on the edge of adulthood, often living in their parents' households, many sought further training or education but had no clear direction or saw much real promise of improvement. Thus, Malkin argues, they sought an adult identity from the other side of the counter—as consumers. This common culture of consumption raises a number of issues: For young adults today, is it true that "you are what you buy"? (Or what you *can* buy?) Is "assimilation" today largely a marketplace transaction? And what does it mean that these young people are being socialized into adult roles primarily as consumers rather than as workers or citizens? (Zukin 2003).

A further theme we see clearly in many of the chapters is the role of educational institutions and other formal bureaucracies as sorting mechanisms. New York confronts the children of immigrants with a variety of large, impersonal bureaucratic institutions. Many of the young people we studied have ended up bitter and feeling that they have no control over their lives and that the game of opportunity is "fixed." Yet others manage to navigate this complex world by taking advantage of the substantial islands of excellence in a generally problematic public school system and by using New York's system of public colleges to seize "second chances." Part of the difference clearly comes down to differences in parental social capital and networks. Part of it may also be accounted for by differences in political strategies or by the existence of ethnic institutions. Russian Jewish immigrants, for example, clearly benefited from a well-financed network of Jewish social service agencies, and the advantages of this "helping hand" can still be seen in the second generation, even as many come to resent some of the attitudes that come with the help, as Aviva Zeltzer-Zubida's chapter shows. In a different way, the remarkably old-fashioned political machine in North Brooklyn that Marwell describes turns out be at least arguably as effective at reaching out to the Dominican second generation as are the more self-consciously ethnic community organizations of Washington Heights.

It is also important to note that many of the institutions encountered by today's children of immigrants were in fact reshaped by the historical context of their parents' arrival after the civil rights movement and the increased legitimation of ethnic difference in American society since the 1960s. In contrast to earlier "second generations," the people this book is about encounter institutions and a political culture in which the ways of negotiating difference were reshaped by the struggles of African Americans and (to an extent) Latinos during this period (Kasinitz 2004). The meaning of being a "minority" is now different than it was when the children of the early-twentieth-century European immigrants came of age. The struggles of the 1960s and 1970s also established institutions that sought to speak to the minority experience. Although the victories of the civil rights movement were partial at best, they did put a generation of Latino and African American leaders in the strange position of trying to manage ethnic succession in colleges, labor unions, political groups, and so on, while still seeing themselves as fundamentally outsiders to the larger power structures. Consider the situation faced by the predominantly African American leadership of the now largely West Indian labor union, as studied by Foerster, or the Cuban American instructor teaching "Puerto Rican studies" to a community college class made up largely of South Americans, as described by Trillo.

This is further complicated by the fact that second-generation racial and ethnic identities are themselves in flux. As Sherri-Ann Butterfield's chapter demonstrates, the children of West Indians *are* African Americans (to take perhaps the most extreme example) in some, perhaps most, contexts. Indeed, for the children of West Indians, Dominicans, Ecuadoreans, or Chinese, becoming American may mean becoming "black" or "Latino" or "Asian." And ironically, for the children of Russian Jews—a distinctly racialized minority in their homeland—becoming American may also entail becoming "white." Finally, as Natasha Warikoo demonstrates, some groups, like Indo-Caribbeans, may be poised between different ethnic identities. It is thus up to the second generation to figure out where they fit in the U.S. racial classification scheme.

Finally, many of the studies presented here come back to the question of the New York City context—many of the children of immigrants, whether or not they see themselves as becoming "American," are clearly already very much New Yorkers. Ironically, the children of immigrants, for all their transnational ties, are often more locally "attached" than the natives. In our larger survey, over one-third of the whites of native parentage had grown up outside the New York metropolitan area. Many had come to New York after college, often unattached, striking out on their own. About 8.5 percent of the African Americans of native parentage followed the same pattern. Yet, among the children of immigrants, only a handful—7 percent of the Chinese, fewer than 5 percent of the South Americans, 3.5 percent of the Russian Jews, 2.5 percent of the West Indians, and fewer than 1 percent of the Dominicans— had spent any significant amount of time growing up in a part of the United States outside of New York. Indeed, many continue to live in the neighborhoods where they grew up. The most internationally connected of New Yorkers are also the most locally attached, which perhaps accounts for some of the city's fabled combination of cosmopolitanism and parochialism.

Further, many of the children of immigrants in New York today interact with each other and native minorities far more than they do with native whites. This has important consequences, of course, for the patterns of prejudice and intergroup conflict experienced by different groups. But this intergroup contact also has positive dimensions. As the essays in this book make clear, the children of immigrants are creating a new kind of multiculturalism—not of balkanized groups huddled within their own enclaves but of hybrids and fluid exchanges across group boundaries. And the real cultural "action" may not be in the interplay of immigrant cultures with a homogenous and dominant American culture but in the interactions between first- and second-generation immigrant groups and native minorities. Today African American New Yorkers dance to Jamaican dance hall and imitate Jamaican patois, even as West Indian youngsters learn African American slang. Puerto Ricans can meringue and Dominicans can play salsa and rap in two languages, to say nothing of the second-generation youth growing up in an Indian–South American–Irish–Pakistani neighborhood like Jackson Heights, Queens, or in a Puerto Rican–Mexican–Chinese–Arabic neighborhood like Sunset Park (where the aging population of "real Americans" is Norwegian). Whether one looks at the music in the dance halls, the eclectic menus in the restaurants, or the inventive slang on the streets, one cannot help but be impressed by the creative contributions to New York of second-generation and minority young people.

In our larger study, we have seen this reflected in how respondents identify themselves. They use the term "American" in two different ways. One way is to describe themselves as American compared to the culture, values, and behaviors of their parents. They are not inclined, for example, to endorse the corporeal punishment of children, a practice, they often report, that their parents believe in and, according to some respondents, have enthusiastically practiced. They definitely think that the United States has influenced them to approach the world differently than their parents. But they also use "American" to refer to the native white Americans whom they sometimes encounter at the office or in public places but whom they know far better from television and the movies. They see these "Americans" as part of a different world that will never include them because of their race-ethnicity. As one of Butterfield's West Indian respondents noted:

> Do you know my cousins still had the nerve to call me an American?! I used to get so mad! I mean, now I sort of understand it, but they could never understand why I would get so angry. They meant that I lived here, and did and said things that were American, which was technically true . . . [but] somehow I always knew that the word "American" did not apply to me. I knew that my parents weren't American because they were not from here, but I was born here and still feel like I didn't belong. "American" was for the kids we used to see on TV, the little blond-haired, blue-eyed white girls playing with their Barbie and their Barbie playhouse in their big houses, not the little dark-skinned girl playing with some old doll in a small house while her parents are struggling to make it.

Many respondents sidestepped this ambivalent understanding of the meaning of being American by describing themselves as "New Yorkers." This term is open to them even as blacks or Hispanics or Asians, and it embraces them as second-generation immigrants. A New York identity reflects the dynamic cultural creativity familiar to them, but not necessarily the larger white society. "New Yorkers," for our respondents, can come from immigrant groups, native minority groups, and they can be Italians, Irish, Jews, and the like. The changes necessary to become a "New Yorker" are not nearly so large as those required to become an "American." And yet, as immigration continues to transform our nation, New York may serve as a positive model of creative multiculturalism and inclusion. Some skeptics might argue that New York is unique and not likely to be replicated other places, but we would counterargue that New York, being the quintessential immigrant city, is in fact at its core very American.

NOTES

1. The project has been supported by the Russell Sage Foundation, the Andrew J. Mellon Foundation, the Ford Foundation, the Rockefeller Foundation, the National Institute of Child Health and Welfare, and the UJA-Federation of Greater New York. All have our gratitude.
2. For further details on the sampling and methodology of the other phases of the project, see Kasinitz, Waters, and Mollenkopf (2002).
3. A fourth phase, reinterviewing selected respondents in the wake of the events of September 11, 2001, is under way as of this writing.

4. This approach had already been undertaken very successfully by Alejandro Portes and Rubén Rumbaut (2001b).
5. Nancy López's project, which was based on our pilot data—thus the inclusion of Haitians, who do not appear in the later study—and her own extensive field-work in upper Manhattan, has already appeared in book form (López 2003).
6. Although not necessarily among the immigrants themselves. See the strikingly optimistic results of the *New York Times*–CBS poll of Hispanic Americans, re-ported in the *New York Times*, August 6, 2003.
7. For a study of similar issues among New York fast-food workers, see Newman (1999).

REFERENCES

Alba, Richard, and Victor Nee. 1999. "Rethinking Assimilation Theory for a New Era of Immigration." In *The Handbook of International Migration*, edited by Charles Hirschman, Philip Kasinitz, and Josh DeWind. New York: Russell Sage Foundation.

———. 2003. *Remaking the American Mainstream: Assimilation and Contemporary Immigration*. Cambridge, Mass.: Harvard University Press.

Freeman, Joshua B. 2000. *Working Class New York: Life and Labor Since World War II*. New York: The Free Press.

Gans, Herbert. 1992. "Second-Generation Decline: Scenarios for the Economic and Ethnic Futures of the Post-1965 American Immigrants." *Ethnic and Racial Studies* 15(2): 173–93.

Iorizzo, Luciano J., and Salvatore Mondello. 1980. *The Italian Americans*. Boston: Twayne.

Kahn, Bonnie M. 1987. *Cosmopolitan Culture: The Gilt-edged Dream of the Tolerant City*. New York: Atheneum.

Kasinitz, Philip. 1992. *Caribbean New York: Black Immigrants and the Politics of Race*. Ithaca, N.Y.: Cornell University Press.

———. 2004. "Race, Assimilation, and Second Generations, Past and Present." In *Not Just Black and White: Historical and Contemporary Perspectives on Immigration, Race, and Ethnicity in the United States*, edited by Nancy Foner and George Fredrickson. New York: Russell Sage Foundation.

Kasinitz, Philip, Mary C. Waters, and John H. Mollenkopf. 2002. "Becoming American/Becoming New Yorkers: Immigrant Incorporation in a Majority Minority City." *International Migration Review* 36(4, Winter): 1020–36.

Landesman, Alter F. 1969. *Brownsville: The Birth, Development, and Passing of a Jewish Community*. New York: Bloch.

Levitt, Peggy, and Mary C. Waters, eds. 2002. *The Changing Face of Home: The Transnational Lives of the Second Generation*. New York: Russell Sage Foundation.

López, Nancy C. 2003. *Hopeful Girls, Troubled Boys: Race and Gender Disparity in Urban Education*. New York: Routledge.

Montgomery, David. 1989. *The Fall of the House of Labor: The Workplace, the State, and American Labor Activism, 1865–1925*. New York: Cambridge University Press.

Newman, Kathleen. 1999. *No Shame in My Game: The Working Poor in the Inner City*. New York: Alfred A. Knopf and Russell Sage Foundation.

Portes, Alejandro, and Rubén Rumbaut. 2001a. *Legacies: The Story of the New Second Generation*. Berkeley: University of California Press.

———. 2001b. *Ethnicities*. New York and Berkeley: Russell Sage Foundation and University of California Press.

Portes, Alejandro, and Min Zhou. 1993. "The New Second Generation: Segmented Assimilation and Its Variants." *Annals of the American Academy of Political and Social Science* 530(November): 73–96.

Prell, Riv-Ellen. 1999. *Fighting to Become American: Jews, Gender, and the Anxiety of Assimilation*. Boston: Beacon Press.

Rumbaut, Rubén. 1999. "Assimilation and Its Discontents: Ironies and Paradoxes." In *The Handbook of International Migration: The American Experience*, edited by Charles Hirschman, Philip Kasinitz, and Josh DeWind. New York: Russell Sage Foundation.

Thomas, William I., and Florian Znaniecki. 1927. *The Polish Peasant in Europe and America*. New York: Alfred A. Knopf.

Tuan, Mia. 1999. *Forever Foreigners or Honorary Whites: The Asian American Experience Today*. New Brunswick, N.J.: Rutgers University Press.

Vickerman, Milton. 1999. *Crosscurrents: West Indian Immigrants and Race*. New York: Oxford University Press.

Waters, Mary C. 1999. *Black Identities: West Indian Dreams and American Realities*. New York: Russell Sage Foundation.

Zhou, Min, and Carl L. Bankston III. 1998. *Growing Up American: The Adaptation of Vietnamese Adolescents in the United States*. New York: Russell Sage Foundation.

Zukin, Sharon. 2003. *Point of Purchase: How Shopping Changed American Culture*. New York: Routledge.

Part I

Education

Getting an education is both the biggest individual challenge facing children of immigrants as they grow up and the most important institutional sorting mechanism that will send them off into different life trajectories. Norman Nie, Jane Junn, and Kenneth Stehlik-Barry (1996) have underscored the paradox of education: that individual investment in education pays off in upward mobility, but that growing social investment in education has not produced a more equal social or political system. To the contrary, the educational system continues to be a defining element in our national patterns of social stratification. For the children of immigrants, just as for those with native parents, education thus represents both the most obvious path of upward mobility and a highly potent set of institutional barriers to that mobility.

Family background, school context, and individual talent and effort interact to shape the ways in which young people make their way through this system. Children from middle-class backgrounds with highly educated parents start with obvious advantages, while those whose parents have little education, difficulty speaking English, and low incomes are at a clear disadvantage. Family form also counts. Having more adult family members in the labor force provides more resources for each child. A nonworking mother seeking to support several children on her own can give each far fewer resources. Factors such as father's or mother's education and parental income also explain a good deal of the variation in children's educational experience, as do such closely related factors as the language spoken at home and the race of the household. But family resources, family strategies for investing in the children, and parental expectations are not the only significant factors. Not all children from better-off backgrounds succeed in reproducing their parents' level of education, nor are all children of poorly educated parents doomed to a similar educational position.

The kinds of schools to which young people have access are also vitally important. Good teachers, small classes, and performance norms count, but so do the mix of students, peer group pressures, and the surrounding neighborhood context. Parents of every class and ethnic group try hard to get their kids into "good" schools. Yet doing so is much easier for middle-class families, particularly white middle-class families, since residential segregation by race and class facilitates their access to better neighborhood schools, thus compounding already significant differences in parental resources. In New York an extensive system of private and parochial schools has become the favored option of the more educationally oriented and better-off parents in some groups. For others, seeking out special programs, enrolling children in magnet schools, and even moving the family into a new neighborhood with better schools are the favored strategies for finding islands of excellence in a public school system that in general is deeply troubled. School quality and parental efforts to gain access to better schools—often tied to one's neighborhood—have an important effect on outcomes. Schools—or rather, the teachers, administrators, and other students in them—set an example that can be bad or good.

Finally, individual choices count too. Some youngsters have more talent and apply themselves harder, while others are lured away from school by pursuits that are especially attractive in adolescence. To be sure, some families have an easier time and do a better job at insulating their children from bad influences, but these influences are pervasive even for middle-class families. Many young adults from immigrant families also have reason to doubt whether following the "straight and narrow" educational path urged on them by their parents will actually lead to a good outcome (though this connection is a lot clearer in upper-middle-class settings than in poor or working-class settings). Hanging out with girlfriends or boyfriends, experimenting with drugs and drinking, or developing a street hustle can be exciting, pleasurable, and even rewarding—as well as dangerous. Such options are particularly attractive when no other equally rewarding alternatives are in evidence.

These factors can be amply observed in the quantitative and qualitative data collected by the Immigrant Second Generation in Metropolitan New York Study. Initial family advantage clearly counts. The native white, Russian, and Korean respondents have the highest median levels of education—not surprising given the fact that they have the best-educated parents. Conversely, Hispanic respondents, whether South American, Dominican, or Puerto Rican, have the lowest median levels of education, in part because their parents are the poorest, the least well educated, and the least able to speak English. It should be noted, however, that of the Latino groups, South Americans, whose parents are somewhat more middle-class and more likely to live in white working-class neighborhoods in Queens and Brooklyn, tend to do somewhat better. Native African Americans and West Indians are in between: their parents have more education and income than the Hispanic parents and speak English, yet they are also more likely than Hispanic parents to live in highly segregated neighborhoods with the worst public schools and the least access to private schools. The fact that most native African Americans and West Indians are Protestant may also give even the most educationally oriented families among them fewer connections to parochial schools than are enjoyed by their largely Catholic Latino and Russian Jewish counterparts. Finally, we heard many stories from both those second-generation youth who reacted to their family and school environments by focusing on their schoolwork and avoiding the temptations or threats in their environment and those who succumbed to or were even pushed into life outside the classroom.

The educational outcomes for different groups of our respondents in the Second Generation Study are given in table P1.1, which looks at an age group, those age twenty-two and older, who are old enough to be well beyond high school and to have graduated from college if they went straight through their schooling. This table provides further support for many of the themes raised in the following chapters. It is not really surprising that Russian and Korean respondents—not to speak of native whites—have high rates of college attendance given their parents' similarly high levels of education. The Chinese second generation, however, shows a similarly high level of educational attainment despite the modest education of many of their parents. West Indians also show stronger levels of college attendance and graduation than African Americans, Puerto Ricans, and Dominicans, although their rate of college graduation remains only half that of whites, Russians, Koreans, and Chinese.

Even the lowest-performing groups, the Puerto Ricans and Dominicans, have generally become more educated than their parents, although the meaning of this fact is not always clear: parents with very modest educations by U.S. standards, for example, may have been relatively well educated by the standards of their poor rural village in the Dominican Republic. In contrast to predictions of "second-generation decline," it is noteworthy that "native" minority groups—African Americans and mainland-born Puerto Ricans—include a significant number who are downwardly mobile relative to their parents.

In almost every group it is also notable that women outperform men (see Stepick et al. 2001). As the chapters by López and Trillo make particularly clear, the young women in our study tend to be more insulated than the young men from the temptations of the street. Parental social control is stronger than for the boys, who may also face more challenges within their peer group to assert a macho personality that may be inconsistent with spending long hours doing homework. The gap between men and women is particularly sharp among Dominicans, a low-performing group, and Chinese, a

TABLE P1.1   EDUCATIONAL ATTAINMENT OF RESPONDENTS AGE
TWENTY-TWO TO THIRTY-TWO, BY GROUP AND GENDER

Sex Group	High School Dropout	GED or High School Diploma	Some College	B.A. Degree or More	Total
Males					
Colombian, Ecuadorean, and Peruvian	8.4%	17.5%	52.4%	21.7%	143
Dominican	17.0	20.8	43.4	18.9	106
Puerto Rican	16.2	29.7	39.6	14.4	111
West Indian	6.3	25.2	43.2	25.2	111
Native black	14.2	35.0	35.0	15.8	120
Chinese	2.8	5.6	34.1	57.5	179
Korean	0.0	2.0	15.0	88.2	98
Russian	4.7	8.1	34.9	52.3	86
Native white	2.0	10.6	17.9	69.5	151
Male total	8.3	18.2	37.0	36.4	1,007
Females					
Colombian, Ecuadorean, and Peruvian	7.6	16.8	47.3	28.2	131
Dominican	15.7	12.6	43.4	28.3	159
Puerto Rican	23.5	20.6	38.2	17.6	170
West Indian	7.1	7.1	54.8	31.0	126
Native black	13.3	18.7	48.8	19.2	203
Chinese	0.0	2.0	26.4	71.6	148
Korean	0.0	1.0	6.0	94.0	107
Russian	1.3	9.1	27.3	62.3	77
Native white	4.9	9.8	20.7	64.7	184
Female total	10.1	12.7	38.6	38.6	1,198

Source: Authors' compilation.

high-performing group. In the former, it may be that conservative social norms within Dominican families provide space for accomplishment in school. For the latter group, the difference is between high-achieving men and even higher-achieving women, perhaps owing to family pressure on the young men to enter the labor force (for a further exploration of this theme, see López 2003).

The various groups of young people also attend systematically different kinds of schools. Although a majority in all groups attended ordinary public high schools, table P1.2 shows that a significant minority of the youngsters in

Table P1.2   Type of High School Attended, by Group

	NYC Public	Magnet	Parochial	Private	Total
Colombian, Ecuadorean, and Peruvian	79.8%	1.5%	15.6%	3.2%	405
Dominican	87.6	0.0	11.0	1.4	419
Puerto Rican	86.4	1.4	11.0	1.2	419
West Indian	86.0	3.8	7.1	3.1	392
Native black	90.5	1.7	5.6	2.2	412
Chinese	76.2	18.0	3.0	2.9	596
Korean	N/A	N/A	N/A	N/A	N/A
Russian	75.3	7.2	16.4	1.0	304
Native white	67.1	1.7	19.2	12.0	401
Total	81.1	5.1	10.5	3.4	3,348

Source: Authors' compilation.

the most educationally successful groups used other options. Some 94 percent of the Chinese—the most upwardly mobile group in terms of education— attended public schools, but they were also far and away the most likely to attend New York's competitive public magnet schools. This also reflects the tendency of Chinese parents to move to areas with good local schools, an option less available to groups facing higher levels of discrimination in the housing market. (To a lesser extent, Russians and West Indians also found their way into these magnet schools, while many other groups, especially Spanish-speakers, did not.) Many educationally ambitious members of other groups found their avenues of opportunity outside the public schools. Whites attended private and parochial schools and made far heavier use of private schools than any other group. The Russians, who were in Jewish schools, and the Latino groups all made significant use of parochial schools.

The three ethnographic studies presented in the following pages present graphic snapshots of different parts of New York's educational terrain. Nancy López examines the bottom end of the system, a huge public high school in a predominantly Dominican neighborhood. Many of the teachers have low expectations of their students and do not offer them much. They and their administrators focus much of their effort on simply maintaining order. The students, especially the male students, respond to this treatment with hostility and cynicism. The authorities show more lenience toward the girls, perhaps because they fear them less, and the girls in return respond with higher aspirations and better school performance than the boys. This finding is particularly striking in light of the fact that most of their parents hail from places— chiefly the Dominican Republic—that do not have strong traditions of female education. Thus, López concludes, "the differing outlooks of men and women were not innate, but were the outgrowth of . . . different experiences . . . in the high school setting. In short, men's and women's understandings of the opportunity structure were shaped by their cumulative experiences with racialization and gender processes in the school setting."

Alex Trillo looks at a rung on the educational ladder that, while still relatively low, is much higher: a community college campus of the City University of New York. Located on a major transportation node in a mixed neighborhood, this community college attracts a largely 1.5- and second-generation student body, mostly from Hispanic backgrounds. He notes that, "on the one hand, community colleges must accommodate a precariously situated population with diverse needs, interests, and constraints. They must orchestrate a self-empowering discourse that speaks to the historical experiences of the student population. On the other hand, the colleges must deal with the reality that most of their students will not even graduate, much less go on to four-year universities. Therefore, they find ways to channel students into other reasonable opportunities." Here too the institution aims to channel groups toward opportunities that match their circumstances and manage their expectations. In contrast to López's high school, however, the community college does actually convey some useful skills and link many students, through its work-study program, to stable, if modest, jobs. Especially important is that this institution provides a second chance to people who have had negative school experiences of the kind described by López. One positive aspect of a system that may otherwise seem dismal is that such second-chance entry points are fairly plentiful in New York City. The community college is also a place where young people work out their identities and learn leadership skills. Trillo concludes that, although their career opportunities are still highly constrained, many students come away from their college experience feeling that they have made real progress.

Vivian Louie turns to the group that has made the most remarkable intergenerational progress from relatively modest beginnings: Chinese Americans. She examines young people from both working- and middle-class backgrounds—those whose families are "downtown" as opposed to "uptown" Chinese—in two settings: one of the better four-year colleges in the CUNY system, Hunter College, and one of the nation's elite universities, Columbia. Louie finds that Hunter students are mostly "downtown" Chinese, while Columbia students are "uptown." Regardless of family background, however, all the parents put strong pressure on their children to pursue "practical" majors that will lead to success in well-remunerated professions. Their motives for doing so are multiple: a need for the children to contribute to family incomes; the fear that whites will discriminate against their children in the absence of credentials and measurable performance; and a pervasive sense that a good professional job is their children's only defense against the privation experienced by the immigrant generation. Most of the children, regardless of family background or gender, conform to these expectations; if they make other choices, they do so with considerable guilt and against parental advice. At the same time, both family class background and choice of educational institution mediate their ability to reach this goal: with their more modest family backgrounds and attendance at an institution that lacks the prestige of Columbia, Hunter students are encouraged by their parents—as well as by Hunter—to move into "second-tier" professions like pharmacy or accounting. Though many Chinese American families and students see Hunter as a "last choice" rather than a "preferred option," it nonetheless facilitates a much wider range of options than the community college. At the same time, just as at the community college and the urban high school, managing expectations and adjusting them to realistic possibilities is an important part of the educational dynamic.

These three chapters thus provide a sampling of how second-generation young people are currently experiencing the New York City educational system, from the lowest stratum—"urban" high school—to one of the highest—Columbia University. One can sense in these chapters not only how family class background operates to limit and frame choices but how educational institutions and their students engage each other in matching and becoming reconciled to these choices. Finally, one sees some scope for individual choice. The lives of some of these respondents do not always work out according to plan—but sometimes with positive results.

REFERENCES

López, Nancy. 2003. *Hopeful Girls, Troubled Boys: Race and Gender Disparity in Urban Education*. New York: Routledge.

Nie, Norman, Jane Junn, and Kenneth Stehlik-Barry. 1996. *Education and Democratic Citizenship in America*. Chicago: University of Chicago Press.

Stepick, Alex, Carol Dutton Stepick, Emmanuel Eugene, Deborah Teed, and Yves Labissiere. 2001. "Shifting Identities and Intergenerational Conflicts: Growing Up Haitian in Miami." In *Ethnicities: Children of Immigrants in America*, edited by Rubén G. Rumbaut and Alejandro Portes. New York and Berkeley: Russell Sage Foundation and University of California Press.

Chapter 2

Unraveling the Race-Gender Gap in Education: Second-Generation Dominican Men's High School Experiences*

Nancy López

Poverty doesn't necessarily cause crime. . . . People come from New Jersey, buy their drugs, and what kind of life do they lead?
                                    —*Leo, second-generation Dominican high school student,*
                                                                      New York City

I read about a study in the newspaper that states that 40 percent of "weed-heads" are in the inner city, but 60 percent are from the suburbs!
                                    —*José, second-generation Dominican high school student,*
                                                                      New York City

THE SOCIAL critique articulated by Leo and José, both seniors at what I re-fer to as Urban High School in New York City, points to the ever-present awareness of racial stigma among Dominican youth, particularly young men. These social critiques are part and parcel of the race-gender gap in education that I witnessed at Urban High School's graduation in June 1998. At the end of the traditional graduation processional, rows of young women had to be paired with each other because they were graduating at greater rates than their male counterparts (López 2003; Sum et al. 2000; Kleinfeld 1998; Lewin 1998). While at the beginning of the twentieth century men attained higher levels of education than women, at the dawn of the twenty-first century we

*All names of individuals reported throughout the chapter are pseudonyms.

see the opposite pattern—women attaining higher levels of schooling than men. It is predicted that by 2007 the gender gap will reach 2.3 million, with 9.2 million women enrolled in college compared to 6.9 million men (Lewin 1998).

The race-gender gap in education is most pronounced among women from racially stigmatized groups. During the 1990s African American women were twice as likely as men to obtain a college degree (Dunn 1988). In the Boston public high school graduating class of 1998, it was estimated that 100 black and Hispanic males were going to a four-year college for every 180 black and Hispanic females (Sum et al. 1999). In New York City public high schools, where the majority of the student population is considered nonwhite (86 percent), more women graduate than men (New York Board of Education 2000). Even at the City University of New York (CUNY), the overwhelming majority of enrolled black and Latino undergraduates are women—up to 70 percent in graduate programs!

The race-gender gap is already discernible among the new second generation—the children of post-1965 immigrants from Latin America, the Caribbean, and Asia. Second-generation female students from diverse backgrounds in California and Florida outperform their male counterparts in educational attainment, grade point average, and educational aspirations (Rumbaut 1998; Portes 1996). This is also the case among second-generation Vietnamese students in New Orleans and Mexican-origin youth in California (Zhou and Bankston 1998; Matute-Bianchi 1991; Valenzuela 1999). In New York City, home to over one million public school students, the race-gender gap in education is already discernible among the children of immigrants from the Caribbean Basin—the largest new immigrant group in New York (Mollenkopf et al. 1998; Waters 1999; Hernandez and Rivera-Batiz 2003; López 2003).[1] Our own Immigrant Second Generation in Metropolitan New York Study revealed that across all groups women achieve higher educational attainment than their male counterparts. The targeted sample of second-generation Dominicans surveyed for the project uncovered that over twice as many of the male participants (31 percent) were still enrolled in high school or had dropped out as female participants (15 percent). Fifteen percent of males had graduated from either a two- or four-year college or had pursued graduate education, but 22 percent of females had done so. What accounts for the race-gender gap in education?

In explaining disparities in education among the second generation, the mainstream literature has focused on the ethnicity paradigm—namely, the assimilation process. Segmented assimilation theory posits that the second generation will experience upward or downward mobility depending on a number of characteristics of a given ethnic group: first, its mode of incorporation into U.S. society; second, the type of neighborhoods it lives in; third, the social and cultural capital available within the ethnic community; and finally, differences in its "color" (Portes and Zhou 1993; Portes 1996; Rumbaut 1998; Zhou and Bankston 1998; Kim 1999). Accordingly, ethnic groups experience upward mobility in one of two ways: either they assimilate into mainstream society or they draw on the resources of their ethnic community. However, those ethnic groups that, because of "color," are at risk of assimilating into the "oppositional" cultures of downtrodden native-born minority groups may experience downward social mobility.

In this study, I shift paradigms (see López 2003). In a departure from segmented assimilation theory's focus on the characteristics of a given ethnic group as predictors of educational success, I utilize a race-gender framework. A fundamental assumption is that racialization processes frame the very resources, neighborhoods, educational facilities, and social networks that are open to the second generation.

Another key dimension of my approach acknowledges that "race is gendered and gender is racialized" (Omi and Winant 1994, 68; Frankenberg 1993; Hill-Collins 1990; Roberts 1997; Hurtado 1996). This understanding of race and gender differs in fundamental ways from essentialist perspectives, which tend to present race and gender as givens—that is, as static and innate characteristics.[2]

Although race is incorporated as an independent variable into the segmented assimilation framework, it is operationalized as "color"—an unproblematic, static essence. Likewise, gender is not considered as a key variable that is central to the analysis.

Therefore, I bring race and gender processes from the margins of analysis to the center. Racialization and intersecting gendering processes can be examined at two levels: at the macro level, from the way in which funding is allocated to particular schools to the public discourse articulated by state officials and the way in which security measures are implemented in schools; and the micro level of pedagogical practices and teacher-student interactions in the classroom (Omi and Winant 1994; Feagin and Sikes 1994).

RESEARCH DESIGN

I chose to focus on second-generation Dominicans because although they were the single largest origin group in New York City during the 1980s and 1990s, there is a dearth of research on the education of Dominicans (Hernandez 1995; Torres-Saillant and Hernández 1998; Hernandez 2002; López 1998a, 1998b, 1999, 2003). To date, studies on the second generation have relied exclusively on surveys that attempt to capture differences in ethnic identity, but there are scarcely any qualitative portrayals of the actual lived experiences of youth in schools and in their classrooms that illustrate racialization as a process rather than an essence (skin color) (Lewis 2003; Fine 1991; Feagin and Sikes 1994).

To uncover race and gender processes in the lives of second-generation youth, particularly young men, I am guided by the following questions: How do race and gender processes intersect in large public high schools vis-à-vis the social relations between the school and the surrounding community, rules, policies, regulations, and institutional practices? How are ordinary, day-to-day social interactions among students, faculty, and staff, as well as classroom dynamics, racialized and gendered?

I conducted five months of participant-observation during the spring of 1998 at the New York City neighborhood public high school that I refer to as Urban High School. I chose this public high school because it was located in a neighborhood that has experienced extensive migration from the Dominican Republic. During three days of the week I regularly observed four mainstream classes in the social studies department: two senior economics classes taught by Mr. Green, a self-described biracial man in his early twenties who could "pass" for white in terms of phenotype; an American history course for juniors taught by Ms. Gutierrez, a Latina teacher in her early twenties who was from South America and could not "pass" for white; and a global studies course for sophomores taught by Mr. Hunter, a white man in his midtwenties. Each of these classes had between twenty-five and thirty students. Only Mr. Green's economics classes had unequal gender proportions. In his first class fewer than one-third of the students were female. Conversely, in the second class only one-third of the class was male. This skewed gender ratio proved quite useful for examining how race and gender intersect in classroom dynamics.

When I was not sitting in the back row of one of the four classes I was observing, I was floating around the school, sometimes visiting other classes, such as bilingual special education classes and the ninth-grade courses held in the trailer complex. I spent the afternoons hanging out with students in the lunchroom, college office, security office, hallways, and library. I also attended parent-teacher meetings, club activities, and other special events such as dances, guest speakers, and festivals. Since I lived in the neighborhood, I also attended community forums, parades, and political gatherings, and I often ran into students and teachers outside of the school setting.

Reactions to my presence in the field were varied. Depending on my attire, students and teachers alike sometimes mistook me for an older high school student. Since I was in my midtwenties and often wore jeans and a T-shirt, some of the older staff automatically assumed that I was a student. On one occasion an evaluator sitting in on Mr. Green's class asked me if he could see the previous day's class notes. Students, on the other hand, usually saw me as a co-ethnic and approached me in Spanish, sometimes inquiring about what part of "the DR" my family was from.[3] If I dressed in more professional clothing, students whom I encountered in the hallways and lunchroom, particularly young men, asked me in Spanish if I was a psychologist reporting on students who were "misbehaving."[4] Other students, particularly young women, simply saw me as a college student and asked me about getting into college.

My analysis of field notes centers on identifying how racialization and gendering processes intersect at Urban High School. I focus on two levels: first, the formal and informal institutional practices, in the form of rules, regulations, and policies; and second, the micro level of social relations and interactions among students, teachers, and other school personnel in the classroom setting. I find that although second-generation Dominican men and women are members of the same ethnic group, attend the same high schools, and come from the same socioeconomic background, they have fundamentally different *cumulative lived experiences* with the intersection of race and gender processes in the school setting. As we see in the discussion in this chapter, these processes are significant because they begin to frame the outlooks of these young men and women toward education and social mobility.

This chapter is part of a larger study on the origins of the race-gender gap that I conducted using focus groups and life history interviews with second-generation Dominicans, West Indians, and Haitians (see López 2003). This chapter focuses specifically on second-generation Dominican men's racialization at Urban High School (for an analysis of girls' experiences at Urban High School, see López 2003, ch. 5). Before delving into the dynamics of Urban High School, I briefly describe the neighborhood and institutional context in which it is embedded. Next, I bring into focus some of the "invisible" racialization and gendering processes that transpired at Urban High School in Mr. Green's classroom. I end with a discussion of the implications of my findings for future studies on the education of the second generation, particularly of racially stigmatized young men.

RACIALIZATION AND EDUCATIONAL OPPORTUNITIES

The de facto racial segregation of people of color, particularly those who are racialized as being of African ancestry, remains one of the most enduring "American dilemmas" of post-emancipation U.S. society (Myrdal 1944). Although racial segregation is no longer codified by law, it persists in federal redlining guidelines and practices among mortgage lending institutions (Massey and Denton 1994), and racial discrimination continues to play an important role in the housing conditions of immigrant and native-born communities of African phenotype (Myrdal 1944; Massey and Denton 1994;

Sanjek and Gregory 1994; Lieberson 1980). Specifically, in the 1990s, 34 percent of Dominicans, 22 percent of Africans and those from the Caribbean, and 27 percent of African Americans were living in New York City apartments that suffered from rat infestation, lack of water or heat, and no kitchen or bathroom (Schill, Friedman, and Rosenbaum 1998). In contrast, European immigrants from similar class backgrounds were able to obtain better housing.[5]

According to the 2000 census, among all Latino groups, Dominicans are the group with the largest number of members who marked "black" as their race (13 percent) (Logan 2003). Dominicans also have the lowest number of members who identify themselves as "white" (23.3 percent) and the largest number of members who reject the white-black binary and identify themselves as "other" (63 percent). Regardless of how Dominicans identify themselves on the census, the overwhelming majority of us would be classified as racially black because of our phenotype. For instance, over the last ten years of teaching undergraduate sociology courses at the City University of New York, the University of Massachusetts at Boston, and the University of New Mexico at Albuquerque, I begin my first day of class by asking students to anonymously guess what race I am. Anywhere from two-thirds to three-quarters of students define my race as black and African American, or black and Latino, again highlighting the permanence of the one-drop rule whereby any trace of discernible African ancestry is defined as "black" regardless of how a person identifies herself.

Owing to racial segregation, even the most successful blacks and Hispanics do not have the same quality of neighborhood amenities enjoyed by their white and Asian counterparts (Logan 2002b). Latinos who identify as black on the census are most segregated from whites and tend to live in predominantly black neighborhoods (Logan 2003). This reality has severe implications for the quality of schools available to racially stigmatized youth. In a study of racial imbalance in American public schools based on data from the National Center for Educational Statistics (NCES), John Logan (2002a) finds that the level of segregation in our schools did not improve over the decade of the 1990s. Indeed, racial segregation places the majority of black and Hispanic youth in the poorest schools.

Jean Anyon (1997) refers to the grossly inferior education that low-income Latinos and blacks are subjected to as "ghetto schooling." Urban High School is no exception to the de facto segregation that confronts racially stigmatized youth. Both inside and outside, the main building at Urban High School appeared to be falling apart and bursting at the seams when I was present in 1998 (New York Immigration Coalition 1999). Scaffolding enveloped the entire four-story, turn-of-the-century building. Sections of the roof regularly collapsed, and pigeons flew around in the auditorium and hallways, sometimes making their nests in the stairwells.

Originally intended to accommodate approximately 2,500 students, Urban High School had a student population of about 3,000. To accommodate the overflow of students, all incoming ninth-graders were housed in two dozen makeshift, neon-orange trailer classrooms that had been squeezed onto the crumbling baseball field located behind the main school building. Despite the fact that the trailer classrooms had only one toilet for about forty students, these facilities, ironically enough, appeared more hygienic than those in the main building.[6] Indeed, during the course of my fieldwork I could not locate a single working water faucet, so I always had to bring a water bottle with me. I dreaded using the bathrooms in the school: even the coveted, locked teachers' bathrooms in the main building were unsanitary, had missing doors and toilets that did not flush, and lacked toilet paper and working faucets.

Despite the fact that Urban High School is located in one of the city's most populated neighborhoods—one that has experienced intensive migration from the Caribbean—it is the only high school in a six- to eight-mile radius. While the election of Dominican representatives to local and state government has led to the creation of a handful of elementary and junior high schools to address the problems of overcrowding, the dire need for a new high school remains (Marwell, this volume). When queried about the possibility of moving to a habitable school building, Mr. Perez, the middle-aged Latino principal, lamented, "There is no public will to build new schools."[7]

Although the majority of teachers at Urban High School are white, the student population is officially designated as Latino (90 percent)—mostly Dominican, with a number of Puerto Ricans and Cubans and a sprinkling of Mexicans. The remaining students are categorized as black but include second-generation youth from Haiti, the Anglophone West Indies, and parts of Africa. The enrollment of Asian and white students is negligible (1 percent). During the entire course of my fieldwork, I did not see a single white or Asian student in the entire school. Although I did not attend a New York City neighborhood high school during the 1980s, I attended a school that was segregated. During my four years in high school I never saw a single "white" student.

The majority of students are from low-income families; three-quarters of them are eligible for the free school lunch program. One in four students are categorized as immigrants who entered the school system in the previous three years, and 39 percent of students are entitled to English Language Learner services. Over half of ninth- and tenth-graders are overage for their grade, and 7 percent of the students are classified as "special education." Only one-quarter of students graduate within the traditional four years that it usually takes to earn a diploma, and about one-quarter drop out, with over one-third of the cohort remaining enrolled beyond four years.

In part to deal with overcrowding and the growing number of students who were behind in their course work, Urban High School, like many other schools throughout the city, had adopted "p.m." school—extra after-school classes designed to deal with the large number of students who were behind in their classes but were too young or did not want to attend general equivalency diploma (GED) classes (López 1998a). Ironically, because more women graduate than men, it was men who were more likely to remain enrolled beyond the fourth year, making Urban High School's enrollment slightly more male than female (55 percent). I often overheard students, particularly young men, commenting that they had been at Urban High School for five to six years but had not been able to graduate.[8]

INSIDE URBAN HIGH SCHOOL

At our first meeting, Mr. Perez expressed enthusiasm about my research project because he had been observing the race-gender gap for quite some time during his eight-year tenure as principal and was curious to learn what I would find. Mr. Perez believed that the gender gap was present because boys seek independence through the streets. "The streets are more attractive to the men," Mr. Perez noted. "Girls in traditional Latino families are kept at home and seek independence through arming themselves with school." When I asked Mr. Perez about his position on single-sex schools, he replied that he supported them, but added, "More important than a single-sex school is having a facility that does not have the major infrastructure problems that we juggle on a daily basis."

Mr. Perez soon introduced me to Ms. Rivera, a middle-aged Latina teacher who was an assistant principal and chair of the social studies department. A vivacious veteran teacher of twenty years who could not remain still for a split-second, she gave me a whirlwind tour of the school. As we chatted in Spanish, Ms. Rivera commented that she was pleased to learn I was a Dominican graduate student who had been born and educated in New York City public schools; she hoped I could serve as a "role model" to Urban High School students. Ms. Rivera added that I should ignore all the stereotypical depictions of Urban as a dangerous school. The negative media representations of the neighborhood included images of drug wars, gang fights, and other criminal behavior at Urban. I noted, however, that Urban students were quite cordial toward each other. While changing classes and exchanging the latest gossip, students conversed in the hallways in a mixture of English and

Spanish. Young men usually greeted each other in Spanish by gliding, not shaking hands, while young women embraced and kissed each other on the cheek.

As Ms. Rivera and I made our way through the crowded hallways to the department office, I noticed that some classrooms were filled with students but had no teacher in sight. When I asked about this, Ms. Rivera lamented that at the beginning of every semester there was always a shortage of teachers. Close to one-third of the social studies teachers that spring were new recruits. Some of the veteran teachers in the social studies department informed me that in the fall the teacher turnover rate had been close to two-thirds of the department. Ms. Rivera later admitted that she had only recently joined the staff after teaching for over twenty years in another high school. Indeed, the need for teachers was so great that before the end of the semester Ms. Rivera tried to entice me into considering teaching at Urban High School, even though I had no prior experience with high school students and was not certified.

Every time I entered the social studies office I was struck by how dedicated and committed the teachers were to their jobs and their students despite the fact that they were neither treated nor compensated as professionals. Although Ms. Rivera was an assistant principal and the head of the social studies department, owing to lack of office space her office had been transformed into the makeshift headquarters for the two dozen teachers she supervised. This office was always abuzz with activity. During their "free" periods, these teachers were huddled elbow to elbow, crammed into a space designed to accommodate comfortably only a few people. Without access to a computer, teachers filled in attendance sheets, planned lessons, organized school trips, graded tests, advised students and, in the few minutes that remained, tried to eat their lunches. Since they did not have a place where they could sit down and do their grading, teachers had to walk around with all their class materials on their person. Since my official designation was "volunteer," before the end of my first day at Urban Ms. Rivera had me fixing billboards and distributing fliers to teachers for upcoming events.

I marveled over how teachers were able to perform their duties when they lacked the most basic supplies, such as books, chalk, or even a desk to sit at and prepare for their next lesson. Teachers improvised by sitting in the back row of their colleagues' classrooms to do class preparation. Remembering that the roof regularly collapsed, I always made it a point to sit away from the window in Mr. Hunter's class, where the ceiling was visibly patched up. I always sat through homeroom in Mr. Green's class, where announcements, sometimes bilingual, came over the outdated and barely audible intercom system; you were lucky if you could decipher every third word. Working under such dreadful conditions, even the most student-centered teachers receive the message that their job is not important to the bureaucrats who design "high standards," such as President Bush and his No Child Left Behind Act (2001), but fail to provide equitable funding. Likewise, even the most school-oriented students at Urban High School invariably learn that in the U.S. context their education is not important since they are not expected to amount to much.

In Ms. Gutierrez's American history class the electricity often went out. One time a young man named Julian remarked, "Mira, un apagon como en Santo Domingo" (Look, a blackout like in Santo Domingo)—an ironic reminder that poverty and lack of resources were present not only back home but here in the United States.

On Overcrowding, Policing, Racialization, and Gendering

Beyond the decrepit conditions of the school building and the lack of even the most rudimentary school supplies and basic resources, one of the most striking aspects of Urban High School is the ubiquitous security presence. All students have to enter the main building through a smaller side door because the main entrance is boarded up. Upon entering, students have to present their picture identification cards and pass through state-of-the-art, airport-style, full-body metal detectors monitored by video cameras staffed by black and Latino security personnel, including guards, peace officers, and an armed white police officer. The head of security was Mr. Castellanos, a Latino man in his fifties. I asked him whether the majority of students who were involved in fights were also involved in drugs or weapons possession. He responded that there were rarely any incidents over drugs—most of the fights were primarily squabbles over property. I queried Mr. Castellanos about why police officers had been introduced to Urban High School in the early 1990s, years before Mayor Rudolph Giuliani made it a citywide policy. He explained that police officers were brought in not because Urban High School was among the most violent schools in the city but because it was among the most overcrowded.

Crowd control is one of the major functions of the security personnel. During the five minutes that students are given to change their forty-minute-period classes, security guards with bullhorns are positioned at the corners of the hallways, yelling: "Move it!" Long after students are seated quietly in their classrooms, teachers often have to compete with the noise emanating from security guards' walkie-talkies as they patrol the corridors and stairwells. Students are also schooled against the backdrop of the eminent threat of violence from the security guards and the police officer permanently assigned to the school as they walk down the hallways (Pastor, McCormick, and Fine 1996; Rosenbaum and Binder 1997).

One afternoon while spending time in the security office, I asked a Latino security guard, who was in his thirties, about his interactions with female students. He assured me that young women were involved only in frivolous spats over jealousies, unlike male students, who were involved in more "serious" fights over property. Remembering my own experiences at the last all-girl New York City public high school, I pressed him to describe how he dealt with female students who had been involved in "real" fights. Before the guard had an opportunity to respond, another Latino male security guard interjected, joking that male security personnel were not allowed to make physical contact with female students; only female guards were allowed to do that. Since there were only two uniformed female security guards in the entire school, compared to over two dozen uniformed and plainclothes male security personnel, the informal institutional practice was to police the men but not the women.[9] Male security guards were allowed to chase, manhandle, and apprehend male students. Although the official discourse maintained that security guards were there to protect and supervise all students, in practice the only students under constant surveillance were young men. In due course, the problematic student was profiled as male.

Security measures in the trailer classrooms were even more extreme. Ninth-graders, all of whom were housed in the trailers, were required to wear school uniforms or face penalties, including having their identification card confiscated and losing their lunchroom privileges. Only students with swipeable identification cards were permitted access to the overcrowded lunchroom located in the main building. Not surprisingly, school administrators, students, and teachers colloquially referred to the gated trailer park complex located on the decaying baseball field behind the main building as "Riker's Island," a jail located in New York City.

During the late 1990s Mayor Giuliani insisted that crime could be reduced in the city if police officers had access to school yearbooks as a way of apprehending potential criminals (Van Gelder 1997). The memo issued by the Detective Bureau stated: "Every precinct detective squad must have the current yearbook for each secondary school [high school or junior high school] in their respective command" (Van Gelder 1997). Of course, police have always been able to examine yearbooks in individual cases, but this was the first attempt at making such access a citywide policy, thereby subjecting mostly low-income youth from racially stigmatized communities to the possibility of being mistakenly identified as suspects in criminal cases. Mayor Giuliani insisted, "I think maybe there's a certain level of discomfort because people aren't analyzing it correctly, *but* we do face an issue of youth crime in New York City" (Van Gelder 1997, emphasis added).

The mere suggestion that every student in public schools (not private schools) would be automatically included in police lineups was a powerful racialization. Given that the New York City public school system is predominantly Latino and black and most students are second-generation children from the Dominican Republic, the Anglophone West Indies, Haiti, and Puerto Rico, this demand can be interpreted as what Michael Omi and Howard Winant (1994) define as a racist racial project.[10] Regardless of intention, this discourse links dark-skinned (male) bodies to crime and simultaneously attempts to reallocate resources based on that definition. After much community organizing and protest, the policy was not instituted; nevertheless, the association of racially stigmatized youth as "suspects" in criminal investigations was accomplished. Not surprisingly, shortly after the controversy, in September 1998, police officers finally gained complete control of the security personnel at all New York City public schools. This is only one example of how racialization processes occur at the macrolevel without the need to directly refer to a given racial or ethnic group (Bonilla-Silva 2003).

These larger macrolevel racializations eventually trickle down to the high school level. I witnessed much physical and symbolic violence directed toward young men at Urban High School (see Herr and Anderson 2003). One morning, while making our way through the crowded hallways, Ms. Rivera and I bumped into Samuel, who was supposed to be on his way to her class but instead was walking in the opposite direction. When Ms. Rivera queried him in Spanish about where he was going, he explained that he was on his way to meet with his guidance counselor in order to change his program. Just as Samuel continued walking toward the guidance office, Ms. Rivera asked him to remove his hat, but he just kept on walking, ignoring her request. Ms. Rivera then pointed Samuel out to one of the security guards who happened to be patrolling the hallway and who quickly proceeded to chase him down. Overcrowding and the subsequent increase in security personnel is turning urban public high schools, which are supposed to be institutions of learning, into spaces in which urban, low-income, second-generation Dominican youth, particularly young men, are humiliated through searches and other demeaning encounters.

The prevailing assumption that low-income youth who are racialized as Latino and black, especially young men, are prone to aggression has resulted in the normalization of violence as well as the threat of violence against them in urban schools nationally (Stanton-Salazar 1997). In a study of single-sex, male-only classrooms, Kathryn Herr and Gary Anderson (2003) unpack multiple episodes of critical incidents of symbolic violence against male students, namely young Chicano and Latino, Native American, Vietnamese, and Cambodians. Herr and Anderson credit Bourdieu (1998, 2000, 2001; Bourdieu and Passeron 1990) with pointing out that the very invisibility of symbolic violence is what makes it so powerful. The proliferation of the punishment industry in the United States has made the criminalization of low-income youth from racially stigmatized communities who attend overcrowded, urban, public schools a "normal" occurrence (Davis 1997; Ayvazian 1995; Lewis 2003; Herr and Anderson 2003; López 2002a, 2002b, 2003).[11] It is not surprising, then, that young men who are racialized as black and Latino continue to be disproportionately arrested and convicted and are being absorbed by the burgeoning prison industrial complex in ever greater numbers (Davis 1997).

One of the worrisome by-products of school overcrowding that I witnessed at Urban High School was the forging of a pipeline between public urban schooling and the prison industrial complex (see Herr and Anderson 2003). While at Urban High School, I learned of one fight involving young men who were in the special education program. The Latino security guards involved in the incident spoke angrily about pressing charges against the students. On other occasions, I witnessed young men who had been engaged in scuffles being whisked away in handcuffs by the white police officer who was permanently assigned to the school.

Security measures are even more pronounced for special education students, most of whom are male. Originally destined for "Riker's Island," special education students were segregated on one section of the second floor, directly above the principal's office and the security headquarters. When asked why they were not placed in the gated and guarded trailer complex, security personnel answered that it was too risky to have them housed off of the main building. One afternoon I visited a ninth-grade special education global studies class taught by Mr. Jimenez, a bilingual Latino teacher in his thirties who was indistinguishable from the ubiquitous plainclothes security guards; he was equipped with a walkie-talkie that connected directly to the security office should any student require disciplining. The classroom was quite claustrophobic; it was really just part of a classroom that had been walled off. The chairs were pushed up against each other, and of the fourteen students in class that day, the four female students were seated farthest away from the entrance and closest to the window. As I entered the classroom, one young man jokingly announced, "Yo pongo las mujeres loca" (Women go crazy over me). The young men sitting beside me berated each other in Spanish for misbehaving in front of "la visita" (the visitor). While Mr. Jimenez drilled students on true or false questions about ancient civilizations, I noticed that the students struggled with reading and pronunciation. While Mr. Jimenez lectured, I was quite distracted by the teacher's aide assigned to the classroom, a Latina woman in her fifties who spent much of her time working on a one-to-one basis with a young man seated in the front row. I wondered whether "special education" was simply a dumping ground for bilingual young boys who did not have much formal schooling in their home countries, as well as for students who did not "behave."

UNEARTHING INVISIBLE RACE-GENDER PROCESSES IN THE CLASSROOM

Classrooms are not impervious to the social narratives and formal and informal institutional practices that "frame" youth who are from racially stigmatized groups, particularly young men, as "problems" (Fine 1991). Mr. Green's economics class for seniors provides a window to the invisible ways in which hegemonic race and gender narratives about racially stigmatized communities filter down to the classroom and ultimately affect the ways in which men and women from the same ethnic group experience racialization processes.

One morning, seconds after the bell rang, Mr. Green, who always wore a shirt and tie to his economics class, slammed the door shut and announced: "You will have exactly seven minutes to complete this quiz. Please take off your hats."[12] Since the doors were locked shut from the outside, all latecomers had to knock in order to be let in, and they were required to sign the late book.[13] While students were completing the quiz, Mr. Green inched his way down the crowded aisle, grasping his Delaney grade book as a shield, checking for homework; he often had to walk over desks just to get to the next row. Disappointed at the number of students who did not hand in their homework, Mr. Green remarked, "Students, this is unacceptable! Only a handful of you have submitted your homework. Many of you will lose points for not handing in homework."

One young man in the class called out: "How come you didn't used to give us homework last year?" Mr. Green retorted: "You guys quiet down! Do you want to be here? I suggest that you follow the rules," pointing to the blackboard. A large piece of cardboard stapled over the blackboard listed "Mr. Green's Rules for Success":

1. Be present every day.

2. Be in your seat when the bell rings.

3. Homework is due at the beginning of class.

4. Do not wear hats, walkmans, or beepers.

5. Be quiet and attentive when someone is speaking.

6. Do not bring food or drinks to the classroom.

7. Raise your hand and wait to be recognized before speaking.

8. Be prepared for school.

9. Treat faculty and other students with respect.

There was another rule that did not appear on Mr. Green's list but was strictly enforced, not only in his class but throughout Urban High School: English only. One time Mr. Green asked students about their favorite musicians, and a male student called out, "La Banda Loca" (the Crazy Band), a famous Dominican merengue band popular throughout the 1990s. Mr. Green ignored him—"Okay, no music artist"—and moved on to the next student, who answered in English.

At Urban High School the hegemonic understanding of Spanish was that it was a barrier that students had to overcome to become successful. At a day-long teachers' workshop held in the crumbling auditorium on the phasing in of the infamous statewide Regents examinations as a graduation requirement, many of the two hundred white teachers in attendance openly expressed their belief that students should speak *only* English in school. On a number of occasions some teachers, mostly whites, stopped students in the hallway and scolded them for speaking in Spanish. In one such instance a white, middle-aged, female teacher stopped a young man in the hallway and berated him for speaking his native tongue: "Pedro, you should never speak Spanish in my class. You know English. Speak English!" Understandably dejected about the informal prohibition of his native language in the school setting, Pedro just stared down at the floor while being scolded. During the course of my field-work, I, like Pedro, received a number of disapproving glances from some teachers and staff because I was speaking Spanish with students, personnel, and Latino teachers as well as some of the "white" teachers who did respect Spanish. Against this hostile background, it is not surprising that those still learning English feel humiliated, devalued, and symbolically violated throughout their schooling process (Herr and Anderson 2003; Ybarra 2000; Valenzuela 1999).

In an ethnography of Mexican-origin youth in a public high school in Houston, Texas, Angela Valenzuela (1999) finds that Mexican youth and their families value education. These families speak about having come to the United States not only to improve their socioeconomic status but also to provide their youth with the better educational and employment opportunities that are unavailable to them in their home country. However, schools as institutions are organized to undermine the cultural resources of Mexican and other Spanish-speaking youth by defining the language and cultural backgrounds of these youth as deficient and problematic, as something they must move beyond. The logic is that by subtracting Spanish and the cultural values of their Mexican families, students can assimilate and become successful. In the end Mexican students experience schooling as a subtractive process: their cultural and language backgrounds are defined as "problems" that need to be stripped away if they are to succeed (see also Gibson 1988). Likewise, Urban High School teachers all have "good intentions" in wanting their students to speak only English; however, despite their good intentions, the fact that some of them try to prohibit the culture and language of their students on the school premises gradually undermines the academic success of those students. Valenzuela finds that Mexican-origin students do not object to education per se, but rather that they may disinvest from a schooling system that consistently devalues their families and communities and chips away at their social and cultural resources.

Mr. Green was a dedicated teacher with many "good intentions," but he was working within the institutional confines of a school system that was grossly inadequate and resistant to change. The fact that Mr. Green had to cover a given amount of material within a forty-minute time block for each of the five classes he taught was not his doing; he simply worked to meet his obligations within the time blocks he was given as a teacher. For instance, the day when Mr. Green gave the quiz, exactly six minutes after the quiz had begun he warned, "Okay, students, you have one minute," and seconds later he added, "Okay, students, time is up. Put your pens down. Put your names on your papers, and pass them forward. If I see you writing, I will take points off." Mr. Green's classroom often felt like a very controlled environment with an inviolable time schedule that often gave priority to "coverage" over critical dialogue and meaningful learning.

Despite his "good intentions," during classroom discussions Mr. Green inadvertently "framed" young men from black and Latino communities as potential drug and crime statistics (Fine 1991). Another morning he began class by asking students to talk about the major problems in contemporary society. Male students called out, "Crime, drugs, pollution." Female students called out, "Poverty, homelessness."

Mr. Green continued: "Is crime directly or indirectly caused by poverty?" As reflected in the epigraphs to this chapter, Leo and José had a different read on the relationship between poverty and crime. Leo called out, "Drugs are a way to escape from reality; therefore we have a drug problem. But poverty doesn't necessarily cause crime. People come from New Jersey, buy their drugs, and what kind of life do they lead?" Leo's comment about New Jersey was a direct reference to white suburban youth who come to Latino neighborhoods in New York City to purchase drugs; in spite of the presence of white youth in these neighborhoods, Latinos, particularly those who are of African phenotype, are systematically racially profiled as drug dealers or targeted for criminal behavior. As discussed by Sherri-Ann Butterfield (this volume), young men of African phenotype in particular are subjected to the stereotype of the hoodlum or drug dealer, more so than young women. This racial stigmatization of the Dominican community was ever present in the minds of the second-generation Dominican youth, particularly young men, growing up in New York City during the 1980s and 1990s (López 1998a; Candelario and López 1995).[14] José chided: "I read about a study in the newspaper that states that 40 percent of 'weedheads' are in the inner city, but 60 percent are from the suburbs!" The rest of the young men clapped, made remarks in Spanish, and cheered Leo's and José's social critique and resistance to negative racialization. Noticeably upset, Mr. Green replied: "Students, I don't need the heckles! You need to raise your hands!"

Mr. Green continued in textbook fashion: "In an indirect way poverty can lead to drugs." Flustered by the "symbolic taint" that was cast on his community, Leo muttered under his breath, "Just because you're poor doesn't mean that you use drugs." Given that the majority of the students at Urban High School are from low-income Latino families and that the media has stigmatized Dominican young men as drug dealers, the young men in Mr. Green's class were understandably upset by his comments.

José continued the debate by saying, "Many of the people who engage in crime do not have drugs." Again, the rest of the class applauded and made remarks in Spanish. Oblivious to his students' social critique, Mr. Green continued to press them to agree with his class-based prescriptions: "What is the broad social goal of the minimum wage? Come up with alternative methods."

After a deafening silence, which could be interpreted as a form of resistance to the racialization processes that had taken place in the class thus far, Mr. Green offered another textbook solution: "Tax breaks to employers who create jobs." After another pause, Viscaino offered, "Train people for higher-skilled jobs." Other students clapped, and from his seat, Viscaino took a bow and looked at his friends. But José chided, "What good is job training if the jobs are not there?" Mr. Green reproached, "There is a demand for skilled workers, such as actuaries. They make over $100,000 a year." Lionel rejoined, "You have to understand that there are people out there who have an education but who still sell drugs because the jobs are already taken by people out there who have experience." Missing an opportunity to engage in a substantive dialogue on white-collar crime, racism, police brutality, and job ceilings,[15]

Mr. Green regurgitated the textbook answers and proceeded with the lesson for the day before the bell rang.

It is interesting to note that Mr. Green did succeed in getting the young men to participate in classroom dialogue, but the ways in which second-generation Dominican young men participated—speaking in Spanish, cheering each other when articulating counterhegemonic interpretations of the origins of racial and class inequality—were not palatable in the context of "banking education." Banking education, which conceives of students as empty receptacles to be filled with the knowledge of an omniscient teacher, is an instrument of oppression (Freire 1985, 1993; Hooks 1994). While the young men in Mr. Green's economics class were trying to participate in classroom discussion by making biting references to white-collar crime, job ceilings, racism, and police brutality, their social critique was often muffled by an institutional pedagogy fixated on "covering" a given amount of material and producing "official" responses. More important, the young men in Mr. Green's class were once again racialized as disruptive and experienced as problem students when in fact they were bright and engaged (Gilbert and Gilbert 1998).[16] In the end, Mr. Green's laudable attempts to encourage classroom discussion were undermined by his authoritarian pedagogy (Ybarra 2000).

As Alex Trillo discusses in this volume, the vast majority of Latino and black students who attend New York City public schools and are fortunate enough to graduate from high school or earn a GED do not end up in the top private schools or even the top four-year schools within the public university system; rather, they join a revolving door of community college students. In large part because of inadequate academic curricula in the secondary schools attended by the vast majority of racially stigmatized youth, many Latino and black undergraduates struggle with college-level work. Often they are placed on academic probation and forced to leave or are simply funneled into the low-paying jobs for which many community college vocational programs are preparing them (Trillo, this volume).

The gender balance of the class had a visible effect on Mr. Green's social interactions with the students. He was always on guard for his third-period class, which comprised mostly young men, some of whom looked only a few years younger than Mr. Green himself. However, his demeanor changed almost instantaneously for his fourth-period class, in which the majority of the students were women. Mr. Green described these two classes as being like night and day.

One morning, just as Mr. Green began to take attendance in his fourth-period class, Juan, who had arrived a few minutes late, knocked on the door in order to be let in. While Juan was signing the late book, Mr. Green demanded that he remove his hat. Juan refused and asked why Mr. Green had not asked the women in the class to remove their hats. Indeed, four women were wearing hats. Angrily, Mr. Green replied, "Ladies can wear it because it's fashion!" Unscathed by Mr. Green's insistence, Juan replied, "I'm fashion too, Mr. Green." Noticeably irate, Mr. Green threatened to send Juan to the principal's office, but Juan would not budge. After an uncomfortable silence, Mr. Green glanced at me, then back at Juan, and reluctantly asked the women to remove their hats. Juan then finally obliged. However, toward the end of the class the "ladies," but not Juan, had their hats back on, without a word from Mr. Green. Shortly thereafter, Juan stopped coming to class. Later that month I found Juan in the college office. When asked what happened, Juan said that he left because he had "problems" with Mr. Green. At Urban High School, school rules stipulate that no student may wear a hat in the school building. However, this rule was strictly enforced for young men but never for young women, who, unlike men, were not considered "threatening" by teachers, security, and other school staff and administrators.

The next month, in the same fourth-period class, a young woman who, just like Juan, was a class clown and often came in late wearing a baseball cap, greeted her classmates, joking about Mr. Green's resemblance to comedian Pee Wee Herman. Because of Mr. Green's likeness to the television personality, the entire class burst out laughing, including Mr. Green. In disbelief, a young man sitting beside me turned to another young man and whispered, "Imagine if we had said that—he would have kicked us out of the class!"

In part because some teachers appeared to feel intimidated by young men who were considered racial "others," they tended to respond more abrasively toward them. While I did note that young women "misbehaved" less often than men, teachers, regardless of gender and race, were generally more lenient toward young women who broke the same school rules for which their male counterparts were sanctioned. Even though it was against school rules to wear a hat on the school premises, I never witnessed a security guard chase down a young woman for wearing a hat, although this was a common occurrence for young men.

When their experience is compared to that of their female counterparts, men from groups that have been racialized as black and Latino have been more likely to believe that teachers did not encourage them to pursue their goals (Kleinfeld 1998). Valora Washington and Joanna Newman (1991) have found that black men are given less praise for their work in school and are more likely to be diagnosed as retarded or emotionally disturbed. Some research suggests that teachers tend to discriminate against young men who misbehave, particularly those from groups that are racialized as black and Latino, such that late-maturing boys are more likely to be tracked into low-level curriculum programs (Kleinfeld 1998; Ginorio and Huston 2001; Sadker and Sadker 2002; Newkirk 2002). Given the racialized and gendered ways in which school rules and policies are implemented at many low-income public urban schools, it is not surprising that men who are racialized as black and Latino make up a disproportionate number of the students who drop out or are discharged, expelled, or tracked into low-level curriculum tracks, including special education.

CONCLUSIONS

I began this study with the question of why more women attain higher levels of schooling than men. I examined the racial meanings that have been assigned to second-generation Dominicans in the setting of a large neighborhood public high school in New York City. This chapter focuses on men's racialization. I have found that both formal and informal institutional practices as well as pedagogical practices within schools, "racialize" and "gender" students in ways that significantly affect their outlooks toward education. While the intersecting and stigmatizing processes of racialization and gendering that second-generation Dominicans undergo in educational institutions can be seen at the micro level, such as in the interactions among students and teachers in the classroom setting, they are also emblematic of larger processes that occur at the institutional level. These latter processes are manifested in the dilapidated infrastructure problems at low-income and immigrant schools; the dearth of resources, such as books and computers; the absence of challenging curricula, as seen at Urban High School; and the framing of low-income youth of color as potential criminals, as seen in the New York City Police Department's abortive attempts to obtain every public high school and junior high school yearbook as a method of combating crime. Against a hostile backdrop that views them as hoodlums and drug dealers, men expressed social critiques about racism, job ceilings, and their prospects for social mobility (López 2003). Men's outlooks were the outgrowth of their experiences with race and gender processes.

What are the implications of these findings for teachers, policymakers, and other people concerned about eradicating race and gender disparities in education? What are the implications of these findings for the current debates on the education of the second generation? First and foremost, it is imperative to stress that teachers are not responsible for the race-gender gap. As previously mentioned, the majority of the staff and teachers at Urban High School were very caring professionals who went above and beyond their duties. Mr. Green is a perfect example of the sacrifices made by many teachers across the nation, particularly those in low-income, racially stigmatized communities. One cold and blustery February on my way to Urban, I bumped into Mr. Green at the bus stop; he was carrying a huge army duffel bag filled with student journals and fresh photocopies he had just picked up for distribution in class. Throughout the semester, none of the classes I observed had received textbooks, so they had relied on handouts and journal writing. Mr. Green, as well as many of the other teachers, often paid for basic school supplies for his students out of his own pocket. To Mr. Green's credit, students were engaged in his classroom; however, because of his fixation on maintaining order and producing "textbook" responses, students, particularly male students, were experienced as "problem boys" if they called out answers or challenged the "official" textbook definitions of the course work. To ameliorate this situation, schools should make an effort to incorporate teacher training that directly addresses issues of race, power, class, and gender as well as issues of student engagement and dialogic pedagogical strategies (Freire 1985, 1993; Aronowitz and Giroux 1993; Hooks 1994).

Second, it is imperative that school administrators and principals reexamine whether and how their security practices reproduce or challenge hegemonic racialization of youth, particularly young men from racially stigmatized communities as potential criminals. Are metal detectors more important than books? At Urban High School, because male security guards were not allowed to make physical contact with female students and the vast majority of security guards were male, in practice only young men were under constant surveillance. To redress this disparity, school administrators can make a conscious effort to employ representative proportions of male and female security guards that reflect the student population.

Third, participant-observation at Urban High School has led me to question segmented assimilation theory as a framework for unraveling the education of the second generation. Notwithstanding the differences in identity among members of the same ethnic group, it is the collective racialization of a given ethnic group that frames its educational opportunities. As they walk down the New York City streets, attend de facto segregated schools, and work in deplorable conditions, Dominican youth, particularly young men, are keenly aware of their racial stigmatization. Studying the assimilation process can provide interesting taxonomies about differences in ethnic identity, but racialization processes play a more significant role than ethnic differences in explaining the educational trajectories of the second generation. Given that the very neighborhoods, schools, jobs, resources, and networks that are open to the second generation are structured along racial lines, it is the racial meanings assigned to the second generation in the high school setting and beyond that influence their educational trajectories—not their ethnic identification and assimilation, as segmented assimilation theorists would suggest (Portes and Zhou 1993; Gans 1992).

Another shortcoming of the segmented assimilation theory is that it generally does not examine gendering processes as central to the schooling experience. Second-generation Dominicans are treated not as "genderless" ethnics, or "raceless" genders, but rather as racialized and gendered bodies in the school setting.[17] As seen at Urban High School, racialization and gendering processes produce quite different lived experiences among men and women from the same ethnic and class background in the school setting. It is not students' perceptions of racial stratification in the United States that influence the educational trajectories of the second generation, but their *actual lived experiences*— in public spaces, in their schools, in their homes, in their workplaces—that inform their view about the dynamics of social mobility and the role of education in their lives (for more on the race-gender gap, see López 2003).

If our goal is to eliminate the race-gender achievement gap in education from the experiences of the second generation, it is extremely important that we switch paradigms. Instead of asking, to what sector of American society are youth assimilating, there are several other questions we need to ask: What racial meanings have been assigned to a given ethnic group? How are racial meanings gendered, and gender meanings racialized? How are these meanings operationalized and enacted through the political-economic culture in a given neighborhood, city, or nation? In what ways are schools interrupting or reproducing these racial meanings? In this light, assimilation ceases to be the center of analysis, and instead racialization, conjointly with gendering processes, becomes the focus of analysis and action.

NOTES

1. John Smith (1999) found a similar pattern among Mexican-origin youth in New York.
2. I draw on the insights of critical theory and critical race theory, which seek to unveil processes of domination, oppression, and resistance (Gramsci 1971; Fine 1991; C. Delgado 1992; R. Delgado 1995; Crenshaw et al. 1995; Omi and Winant 1994; Hill-Collins 1990).
3. "The DR" is a colloquial term for the Dominican Republic used frequently by second-generation Dominican youth.
4. It is important to note that the race and gender of the researcher should always be a part of the data collection and analysis in all research, both qualitative and quantitative. As discussed by Jill Morawski (1997, 14, 15), a fundamental paradox of much social science research is that it is preoccupied with "the nature of otherness, all the while largely neglecting the meanings and implications of

whiteness." Morawski adds, "Many research programs harbor a dual model of persons: at least when the experimenter is white, the race of the experimenter is held to be unrelated to his or her cognition, whereas the race of the subject is held to possibly affect his or her cognition."

5. The process of residential segregation is a deliberate outcome of middle-class whites' institutionalized discriminatory practices: many formed neighborhood improvement associations whose purpose was the exclusion of blacks (Massey and Denton 1994, 25).

6. Not once during the course of fieldwork did I find a student smoking or doing drugs in the stairwells or in the bathroom.

7. While the majority of New York City public school students attend schools that are in the same deplorable state as Urban High School, new school buildings have been constructed for New York's elite public examination high schools.

8. Previously I found that second-generation Dominicans are reluctant to enroll in GED programs because they believe that if they obtain a GED instead of the traditional diploma, they will be stigmatized by potential employers and colleges (López 1998a). Therefore, many students choose to remain enrolled beyond the traditional four years of high school.

9. The occupational hierarchy of the security personnel also formed a racial pyramid: a white police officer on top, a layer of Latino or Puerto Rican uniformed security guards, and a bottom rung of plainclothes Dominican parasecurity guards and school aides who patrolled the hallways.

10. Omi and Winant (1994, 56, emphasis added) define a racial project as "*simultaneously an interpretation, representation, or explanation of racial dynamics and an effort to reorganize and redistribute resources along particular racial lines.* Racial projects connect what race *means* in a particular discursive practice and the ways in which both social structures and everyday experiences are racially *organized*, based upon that meaning."

11. Schools as institutions are not impervious to the racial constructions that occur in the wider society. In *Framing Dropouts*, Michelle Fine (1991) poignantly details how black and Latino students are "framed" as the cause of poor schools, while the structural inequities of society remain unquestioned. Fine argues that much of this "framing" is unintentional and occurs despite the "good intentions" of overworked and underpaid teachers and other school personnel, many of whom are also "framed" as lazy, unqualified, and deficient in their ability to teach students to pass standardized tests.

12. Students usually kept their coats on because they did not have lockers.

13. I was often a few minutes late for class myself: the five minutes that students are given to change classes is not enough time to get to their destinations because the hallways are so crowded.

14. Dominican women are regularly "framed" as welfare queens and perpetrators of welfare fraud, now known as Transitional Assistance to Needy Families (TANF) (see Candelario and López 1995; Sexton 1997). In prosecuting a case

of welfare fraud, federal judge Jack Weinstein said that the leadership of the Dominican community "must assume responsibility for dealing with unacceptable criminal behavior such as involved in these cases" (Fried 1993). Although Judge Weinstein said that the majority of Dominicans are law-abiding, his denunciation of the leadership insinuates that there is something missing in the moral fabric of the community. I wonder if similar comments would be made about the moral fabric of Russian immigrants, who are racialized as white and had the highest rate of welfare use of any immigrant group in New York City during the 1980s.

15. Logan's (2003) study also found that in spite of the fact that the educational attainment of Latinos who identify as black is higher than that of those who identify as white, those who identify as black have a lower average household income than those who identify as white.

16. Mr. Green was quite amicable toward young men outside of the classroom context. On another day, a young male student asked Mr. Green after class about the origins of an Asian landscape painting he used as a makeshift window shade. Mr. Green said he had acquired it on a recent trip to Asia. He further asked the male student to comment on any differences he saw between the Asian landscape painting and traditional European paintings. Mr. Green pointed out that while Asian paintings revere nature, traditional European paintings tend to focus on humans.

17. Second-generation students who are racialized as Asians, whether they are Chinese, Korean, or Japanese, are subjected to the "model minority" racial project, which, despite its seemingly benign appearance, is also oppressive and patronizing (Lee 1997; Dae Young Kim, this volume; Louie, this volume; Lee, this volume). Likewise, second-generation youth who are of European phenotype, such as Russians, are racialized as "white" and therefore are not subjected to the racial segregation and inferior schools that the vast majority of their African-phenotype counterparts are subjected to (Zeltzer-Zubida, this volume; Waters 1999; Alba, Logan, and Stults 2000). In contrast, ethnic groups that are predominantly of African phenotype, regardless of their cultural heritage, such as Dominicans, West Indians, and Haitians, are subjected to the same racial stigmatization and segregation that have historically plagued people of African phenotype in the U.S. context (Massey and Denton 1994; Butterfield, this volume; Trillo, this volume). Moreover, as members of a Spanish-speaking group that is predominantly of African phenotype, second-generation Dominican students are often seen through the lens of the deficit model: as racial others who are also "limited English proficient" and live in households where parents do not push education or have high career expectations for their children (Valenzuela 1999).

References

Alba, Richard, John Logan, and Brian Stults. 2000. "How Segregated Are Middle-class African Americans?" *Social Problems* 47(4): 543–58.

Anyon, Jean. 1997. *Ghetto Schooling: A Political Economy of Urban Educational Reform.* New York: Teachers College Press.

Aronowitz, Stanley, and Henry Giroux. 1993. *Education Still Under Siege.* Westport, Conn.: Bergin and Garvey.

Ayvazian, Andrea. 1995. "Interrupting the Cycle of Oppression: The Role of Allies as Agents of Social Change." *Fellowship* (January–February): 138–41.

Bonilla-Silva, Eduardo. 2003. *Racism Without Racists: Color-Blind Racism and the Persistence of Racial Inequality in the United States.* Lanham, Md.: Rowman & Littlefield.

Bourdieu, Pierre. 1998. *Acts of Resistance: Against the Tyranny of the Market.* New York: The New Press.

———. 2000. *Pascalian Meditations.* Stanford, Calif.: Stanford University Press.

———. 2001. *Masculine Domination.* Stanford, Calif.: Stanford University Press.

Bourdieu, Pierre, and Jean Claude Passeron. 1990. *Reproduction in Education, Society, and Culture.* 2nd ed. London: Sage Publications.

Candelario, Ginetta, and Nancy López. 1995. "The Latest Edition of the Welfare Queen Story: An Analysis of the Role of Dominican Immigrants in the New York City Political-Economic Culture." *Phoebe: An Interdisciplinary Journal of Feminist Scholarship: Theory and Aesthetics* 7(1/2): 7–22.

Crenshaw, Kimberlé, Neil Gotanda, Gary Peller, and Kendall Thomas, eds. 1995. *Critical Race Theory: The Key Writings That Formed the Movement.* New York: W. W. Norton.

Cummins, Jim. 1993. "Empowering Minority Students: A Framework for Intervention." In *Silenced Voices: Class, Race, and Gender in United States Schools,* edited by Lois Weis and Michelle Fine. Albany: State University of New York Press.

Davis, Angela. 1997. "Race and Criminalization: Black Americans and the Punishment Industry." In *The House That Race Built: Black Americans, U.S. Terrain,* edited by Wahneema Lubiano. New York: Pantheon.

Delgado, Concha. 1992. "School Matters in Mexican-American Home: Socializing to Education." *American Educational Research Journal* 29(3): 495–513.

Delgado, Richard. 1995. *Critical Race Theory: The Cutting Edge.* Philadelphia: Temple University Press.

Driver, Geoffrey. 1980. "How West Indians Do Better at School (Especially the Girls)." *New Society* 17: 111–14.

Dunn, James. 1988. "The Shortage of Black Male Students in the College Classroom: Consequences and Causes." *Western Journal of Black Studies* 12(2): 73–76.

Feagin, Joe, and Melvin Sikes. 1994. *Living with Racism: The Black Middle-class Experience.* Boston: Beacon Press.

Fine, Michelle. 1991. *Framing Dropouts: Notes on the Politics of an Urban Public High School.* Albany: State University of New York Press.

Frankenberg, Ruth. 1993. *White Women, Race Matters: The Social Construction of Whiteness.* Minneapolis: University of Minnesota.

Freire, Paulo. 1985. *The Politics of Education: Culture, Power, and Liberation.* South Hadley, Mass.: Bergin & Garvey.

————. 1993. *Pedagogy of the Oppressed*. New York: Continuum.

Fried, Joseph. 1993. "Prosecuting Welfare Fraud Ineffective, Judge Says," *New York Times*, June 24.

Gans, Herbert. 1992. "Second Generation Decline: Scenarios for the Economic and Ethnic Futures of the Post-1965 American Immigrants." *Ethnic and Racial Studies* 15(2): 173–93.

Gibson, Margaret. 1988. *Accommodation Without Assimilation: Sikh Immigrant in an American High School*. Ithaca, N.Y.: Cornell University Press.

Gilbert, Rob, and Pam Gilbert. 1998. *Masculinity Goes to School*. New York: Routledge.

Ginorio, Angela, and Michelle Huston. 2001. *Si Se Puede! Yes We Can! Latinas in School*. Washington: American Association of University Women.

Gramsci, Antonio. 1971. *Selections from The Prison Notebooks*, edited by Quentin Hore and Geoffrey Nowel Smith. New York: International.

Hernandez, Ramona. 1995. *Dominican New Yorkers: A Socioeconomic Profile, 1990*. New York: Dominican Studies Institute at City University of New York.

————. 2002. *The Mobility of Labor Under Advanced Capitalism: Dominican Migration to United States*. New York: Columbia University Press.

Hernandez, Ramona, and Francisco L. Rivera-Batiz. 2003. "Dominicans in the U.S.: A Socioeconomic Profile, 2000." New York: Dominican Research Monographs, The CUNY Dominican Studies Institute.

Herr, Kathryn, and Gary Anderson. 2003. "Violent Youth or Violent Schools? A Critical Analysis of Symbolic Violence." *Journal of Leadership in Education: Theory and Practice* 6(4): 415–33.

Hill-Collins, Patricia. 1990. *Black Feminist Thought: Knowledge, Consciousness, and the Politics of Empowerment*. Boston: Unwin Hyman.

Hooks, Bell. 1994. *Teaching to Transgress: Education as the Practice of Freedom*. New York: Routledge.

Hurtado, Aida. 1996. *The Color of Privilege: Three Blasphemies on Race and Feminism*. Ann Arbor, Mich.: University of Michigan.

Kim, Dae Young. 1999. "Beyond Co-ethnic Solidarity: Mexican and Ecuadorean Employment in Korean-Owned Businesses In New York City." *Ethnic and Racial Studies* 22(3): 581–605.

Kleinfeld, Judith. 1998. *The Myth That Schools Shortchange Girls*. Washington, D.C.: Women's Freedom Network.

Lee, Stacey. 1997. *Unraveling the "Model Minority" Stereotype: Listening to Asian American Youth*. New York: Teachers College Press.

Lewin, Tamar. 1998. "American Colleges Begin to Ask, Where Have All the Men Gone?" *New York Times*, December 6.

Lewis, Amanda. 2003. *Race in the Schoolyard: Negotiating the Color Line in Classrooms and Communities*. New Brunswick, N.J.: Rutgers University Press.

Lieberson, Stanley. 1980. *A Piece of the Pie: Black and White Immigration Since 1880*. Berkeley: University of California Press.

Logan, John. 2002a. *Choosing Segregation: Racial Imbalance in American Public Schools, 1990–2000*. Albany, N.Y.: Lewis Mumford Center.

———. 2002b. *Separate and Unequal: The Neighborhood Gap for Blacks and Hispanics in Metropolitan America*. Albany, N.Y.: Lewis Mumford Center.

———. 2003. "How Race Counts for Hispanic Americans." Report (July 14, 2003). Albany, N.Y.: Lewis Mumford Center for Comparative Urban and Regional Research, University at Albany. Available at: http://mumford1.dyndns.org/cen2000/BlackLatinoReport/BlackLatino01.htm (accessed April 29, 2004).

López, Nancy. 1998a. "The Structural Origins of Dominican High School Dropout." *Latino Studies Journal* (Long Island University) 9(3): 85–105.

———. 1998b. "Gender Matters." Paper presented to the annual meeting of the Eastern Sociological Association. Philadelphia, .

———. 1999. "Race-Gender Matters: Schooling Among Second-Generation Dominicans, West Indians, and Haitians in New York City." Ph.D. diss., City University of New York.

———. 2002a. "Race-Gender Experiences and Schooling: Second-Generation Dominican, West Indian, and Haitian Youth in New York City." *Race, Ethnicity, and Education* 5(1): 67–89.

———. 2002b. "Rewriting Race and Gender High School Lessons: Second-Generation Dominicans in New York City." *Teachers College Record* 104(6): 1187–1203.

———. 2003. *Hopeful Girls, Troubled Boys: Race and Gender Disparity in Urban Education*. New York: Routledge.

Massey, Douglas, and Nancy Denton. 1994. *American Apartheid: Segregation and the Making of the American Underclass*. Cambridge, Mass.: Harvard University Press.

Matute-Bianchi, Maria Eugenia. 1991. "Situational Identity and Patterns of School Performance Among Immigrant and Non-immigrant Mexican-Descent Students." In *Minority Status and Schooling: A Comparative Study of Immigrant and Involuntary Minorities*, edited by John Ogbu and Margaret Gibson. New York: Garland.

Mollenkopf, John, Philip Kasinitz, Mary Waters, Nancy López, and Dae Young Kim. 1998. "The School-to-Work Transition of Second-Generation Immigrants in Metropolitan New York: Some Preliminary Findings." Working paper 214. Annandale-on-Hudson, N.Y.: Bard College, Jerome Levy Economics Institute.

Morawski, Jill. 1997. "White Experimenters, White Blood, and Other White Conditions: Locating the Psychologist's Race." In *Off-White: Readings on Race, Power, and Society*, edited by Michelle Fine, Lois Weis, Linda C. Powell, and L. Mun Wong. New York: Routledge.

Myrdal, Gunnar. 1944. *An American Dilemma*. Vol. 1. New York: Harper and Brothers.

Newkirk, Thomas. 2002. "Misreading Masculinity: Speculations on the Great Gender Gap in Writing." In *The Jossey-Bass Reader on Gender in Education*, edited by Elisa Rassen. San Francisco: Jossey-Bass.

New York Board of Education. 2000. *Class of 1999 Four-Year Longitudinal Report and 1998–1999 Event Dropout Rates*. New York: New York Board of Education.

New York Immigration Coalition. 1999. *Immigrant and Refugee Students: How the New York City School System Fails Them and How to Make It Work*. New York: New York Immigration Coalition.

Omi, Michael, and Howard Winant. 1994. *Racial Formation in the United States: From the 1960s to the 1990s.* New York: Routledge.

Pastor, Jennifer, Jennifer McCormick, and Michelle Fine. 1996. "Makin' Homes: An Urban Girl Thing." In *Urban Girls: Resisting Stereotypes, Creating Identities*, edited by Bonnie Leadbeater and Niobe Way. New York: New York University Press.

Portes, Alejandro. 1996. "Introduction: Immigration and Its Aftermath." In *The New Second Generation*, edited by Alejandro Portes. New York: Russell Sage Foundation.

Portes, Alejandro, and Min Zhou. 1993. "The New Generation: Segmented Assimilation and Its Variants." *Annals of the American Academy of Political and Social Science* 530: 74–96.

Roberts, Dorothy. 1997. *Killing the Black Body: Race, Reproduction, and the Meaning of Liberty.* New York: Pantheon.

Rosenbaum, James, and Amy Binder. 1997. "Do Employers Really Need More Educated Youth?" *Sociology of Education* 70: 68–85.

Rumbaut, Rubén. 1998. "Transformations: The Post-immigrant Generation in an Age of Diversity." Paper presented to the annual meeting of the Eastern Sociological Society. Philadelphia, March 19–22.

Sadker, Myra, and David Sadker. 2002. "The Miseducation of Boys." In *The Jossey-Bass Reader on Gender in Education*, edited by Elisa Rassen. San Francisco: Jossey-Bass.

Sanjek, Roger, and Steven Gregory, eds. 1994. *Race.* New Brunswick, N.J.: Rutgers University.

Schill, Michael, Samantha Friedman, and Emily Rosenbaum. 1998. "The Housing of Immigrants in New York City." *Center for Real Estate and Urban Policy and New York University School of Law.* Working Paper 98(2). New York University.

Sexton, Joe. 1997. "Welfare Neighborhood: A Question of Honesty." *New York Times*, March 19.

Smith, Robert. 1999. "Mexican Second-Generation Youth in New York." Paper presented to the annual meeting of the American Sociological Association. Chicago, August.

Stanton-Salazar, Ricardo. 1997. "A Social Capital Framework for Understanding the Socialization of Racial Minority Children and Youths." *Harvard Educational Review* 67(1): 1–40.

Sum, Andrew, Julia Kroshko, Neeta Fogg, and Sheila Palma. 1999. *The College Enrollment and Employment Outcomes for the Class of 1998 Boston Public High School Graduates: Key Findings of the 1999 Follow-up Surveys.* Boston: Northeastern University, Center for Labor Market Studies.

Torres-Saillant, Silvio, and Ramina Hernández. 1998. *The Dominican Americans.* Westport, Conn.: Greenwood.

Valenzuela, Angela. 1999. *Subtractive Schooling: U.S.-Mexican Youth and the Politics of Caring.* Albany: State University of New York Press.

Van Gelder, Lawrence. 1997. "Police Use of Yearbooks Draws Protest from the Schools." *New York Times*, March 28, p. B7.

Washington, Valora, and Joanna Newman. 1991. "Setting Our Own Agenda: Ex-

ploring the Meaning of Gender Disparities Among Blacks in Higher Education."
Journal of Negro Education 60(1): 19–35.

Waters, Mary C. 1999. *Black Identities: West Indian Immigrant Dreams and American Realities.* New York and Cambridge, Mass.: Russell Sage Foundation and Harvard University Press.

Ybarra, Raul. 2000. "Latino Students and Anglo-Mainstream Instructors: A Study of Classroom Communities." *Journal of College Student Retention Research, Theory, and Practice* 2(2): 161–71.

Zhou, Min, and Carl L. Bankston. 1998. *Growing Up American: How Vietnamese Children Adapt to Life in the United States.* New York: Russell Sage Foundation.

CHAPTER 3

SOMEWHERE BETWEEN WALL STREET AND EL BARRIO:
COMMUNITY COLLEGE AS A SECOND CHANCE FOR
SECOND-GENERATION LATINO STUDENTS*

ALEX TRILLO

It is 11:30 P.M. on the last day of finals. Everyone is at Juan's basement apartment across from the college for the traditional end-of-the-semester bash. When classes are in session, they use this room for studying, hanging out, and getting away from college life. Scattered about are a chemistry chart, formulas scribbled on the chalkboard, a Gray's anatomy poster, and minutes from the last meeting of the Ecuadorean Club—one of many Latino organizations on campus. The dance floor is packed with students from a dozen Caribbean and Latin American backgrounds as well as a handful of Russian, Asian, and newly arrived Irish—all familiar parts of the Queens landscape in which the college is situated, and where most of the students live.

Out back, Miguel, 23, of Dominican and Puerto Rican heritage, and Ray, 24, a Colombian, talk about the jobs they have secured through the College's internship program. Ray says that he's just ready to move on . . . Miguel too. Later, both let it out that dropping out is really the only option. . . . Deflecting their disappointment, they joke about the raises they will get. "It's not so bad . . . we're doing better than our parents," Ray says.

—field notes, June 2000

LIKE OTHER Americans, the children of Latino immigrants in New York grow up hearing about the virtues of a formal education. But as Nancy López (this volume) reminds us, they often attend the city's least desirable schools. Add to this the many other challenges associated with the immigrant experience—newcomer communities, conflicts between the sending and re-

*All names of individuals reported throughout the chapter are pseudonyms.

ceiving cultures, and the like—and it seems painfully obvious why so many become demoralized or sidetracked and forgo a college education, and why only a handful get the opportunity for a traditional college experience.

Still, many students respond to such barriers by opting for a "second chance" at their educational goals, typically at a community college. Since their inception, two-year schools have provided immigrants and other less well-off populations with a second opportunity to get educational credentials after difficult initial experiences (Kasper 2002). Taken together, of the roughly half of the Latino participants in the Immigrant Second Generation in Metropolitan New York Study who had any college experience, 30 percent had attended a community college, mostly within the City University of New York system. Given the growing number of college-age children of Latino immigrants (Kasinitz, Mollenkopf, and Waters, this volume; Portes and Rumbaut 2001), the continuing quality deficit in the elementary and high school education received by Latinos (Anyon 1997), and the end of remedial courses given by the four-year campuses of the City University system (Schmidt et al. 1999), these numbers are likely to increase in the future.[1]

The goals of community colleges and their relative success at achieving them are commendable, but it is difficult to know exactly how much impact they have on the educational mobility of their students, and particularly on the immigrant adaptation process. Community colleges serve a vulnerable population with varying needs, interests, and constraints (Bailey 2003). They generally strive to provide a student-centered curriculum that acknowledges the historical experiences of the student population and creates a sense of community that encourages them to remain enrolled (Erkut and Mokros 1984; Castro-Abad 1995; Kirkpatrick 2001).[2] Yet in reality most community college students do not graduate or go on to four-year universities (Bailey 2003; Schneider and Stevenson 1999). As Kevin Dougherty (1994, 8, 186–87) notes in *The Contradictory College*:

> As a consequence of its diverse origins, the community college is a hybrid institution, combining many different and often contradictory purposes. It is a doorway to educational opportunity, a vendor of vocational training, a protector of university selectivity, and a defender of state higher education budgets (by providing an alternative to expanding the costly four-year colleges). Such eclecticism can breed synergy. But in the community college's case it has sown contradiction. The institution's desire to provide baccalaureate aspirants with educational opportunity has been undercut by its other purposes of providing vocational training and saving the state governments money.
>
> Because it is so strongly committed to vocational education, many baccalaureate aspirants are seduced away from their initial ambitions.

And . . . many fail to transfer or suffer an academic death in the middle of the passage.

THE STUDY

For fifteen months, I followed a group of second-generation Colombians, Ecuadoreans, Peruvians, and Dominicans who regularly encountered this bind at La Guardia Community College of the City University of New York. The college was a compelling site because of the growing population of second-generation students and because the community college experience crystallized many of the difficulties of the immigrant adaptation process. At bottom, the students of this process have debated about whether the children of immigrants will become more socially and economically "American" or whether discrimination and lack of opportunity will press them into a disenchanted urban underclass. It would seem that the community college experience would have some impact on such outcomes.

It was also a compelling research site because so little research had considered the experience of the children of immigrants in these settings. Scholars have assessed the impact of community colleges on the general student population (Brint and Karabel 1989; Dougherty 1994), and a few have noticed the presence of immigrant students on campus (Bailey and Weininger 2002). But no one has examined the specific experiences of the children of immigrants. Thus, it would provide new information about how the nuances of community college life shape the experiences of youngsters whom we expect to be upwardly mobile from their parents' positions as they face the challenges of immigrant adaptation.

The final reason I chose La Guardia was that it was the single most popular college choice among our second-generation Latino survey respondents (forty-three attended) and because the campus resembles the surrounding neighborhood, which includes many South American, Dominican, and Puerto Rican residents. According to the college's 1999 institutional data, 17 percent of its students identify as black non-Hispanic, 15 percent as Asian, and 15 percent as white (many are Russian or recently arrived Irish), while 35 percent identify as Hispanic. About 60 percent of La Guardia's students are foreign-born.

Faculty and staff helped me select four courses with significant Latino enrollment, many of whom could be categorized as 1.5- or second-generation.[3] These courses allowed me to befriend a variety of people, some of whom were kind enough to take me to social gatherings, places of employment, and even their homes.[4] They engaged in long conversations with me, gave me access to daily life on campus, and told me about how other aspects of their lives shaped their identities and college experiences. With the permission of students and the instructor, I also examined final exam essays from a Puerto Rican studies course. The assignment asked the students to comment on how the influx of other Latino groups—Colombians, Ecuadoreans, Peruvians, and Dominicans—was affecting the future of the Puerto Rican community.[5]

The study made it clear to me that the community college milieu plays a unique role in the adaptation processes of Latino immigrant children. The student-centered, diverse atmosphere did engage students and even fostered a pan-ethnic identity between second- (and some first-) generation Latinos of various nationalities, despite some generational and intergroup tensions. The location, student demographics, activities, curriculum, and even aesthetics of the college, which were grounded in earlier immigrant and minority communities, were all instrumental in this outcome. Although this type of consciousness-raising frustrated some, it also empowered these young people to want to overcome the barriers facing them and do better than previous generations.

Over time, however, it became apparent that actual outcomes contrasted starkly with student goals. Even the brightest, most persevering students had a hard time overcoming discrimination, bad schooling, low socioeconomic status, or some other life challenge, and they received only limited help from their families and the college with these challenges. That so many would succumb left one to ponder how the college rationalized its extremely low graduation rate and how students reacted to the limits on them.

Eventually the subtle ways in which the college channeled students into opportunities other than transferring or graduating became clearer to me. Facing day-to-day struggles with limited resources left students quite vulnerable to dropping out. Given that the college's mission was geared toward vocational training and preparing for the labor market, students reluctantly took advantage of more permanent opportunities that came to them through required internships and other campus job placements. The college experience helped others to advance in positions with their current employers. These jobs were somewhat better than those of their immigrant parents, but not nearly as good as those of native whites or any student graduating with a four-year college degree.

This limited mobility weighed on the students' sense of self and ethnic identity. It reminded them that, as Latinos, they occupy a precarious position in the racial hierarchy and must develop an explicit strategy for situating themselves in the larger society. For many of those who spoke to me, this strategy was not that of a hostile, oppositional underclass but rather one of becoming a "Latino." This does not mean that the experience of blocked mobility in community college did not matter. As they became more aware of their situation, the students did have to renegotiate their goals.[6] But the outcome was somewhere in between becoming fully American and adopting an oppositional culture. If we are to truly understand the second generation, we must investigate such "in-between" strategies further.

LATINO "IDENTITY WORK" IN NEW YORK CITY AND THE COMMUNITY COLLEGE

Early in the first semester, Mari, a twenty-two-year-old Colombian–Puerto Rican woman, and Yvette, a Dominican who was also twenty-two, talked with me:

Mari: Where are you from?"

Alex: I'm Cuban. . . .

Mari: Were you born there?

Alex: No. . . .

Mari: Yeah, I thought you were one of us . . . you know what I mean, a Latino brother, pero de aca. . . . You don't sound entirely from New York, but there's something about the way you talk. . . .

Yvette: Well, I'm Dominican, could you tell? A lot of people think I'm Puerto Rican—but you know, I tell them quick who I am. . . . But I was born here! You know? Like my uncle's always sayin', "Tu eres Americana!" *You are American!* Even though I'm deep in my culture, you know. I love merengue, bachata, I go to Dominican festivals and all that stuff. And when people ask, I let them know who I am. But he always tells me, *Ahhhhh*, tu eres Americana! I tell him I'm not American. . . . But it's true, you know, I am . . . compared to him!

Mari: Mira, so cuentame de ese research you're doing. Are you like a reporter?

Alex: Not exactly. . . . I just want to know what life is like for Latino community college students. . . .

Yvette: That's cool . . . there are so many of us here, it's like what you have to do. . . . But whatever. . . . Asi es la vida . . . Latinos have to invent their way, you know? Not like other people who get everything handed to them. . . .

Mari: So what do you think about this class? We just don't like our group [referring to the somewhat older, first-generation Dominican and Colombian women with whom she and Yvette had been working]. I mean, all these people won't speak English, it's like they don't realize where they are. I mean, I'm down with being proud and I like my Spanish, but come on, man.

This exchange demonstrates that the children of Latino immigrants identify themselves in complex ways that often push the boundaries of conventional social science categories. Situated between the traditions and expectations of their parents and American institutions and peers, they continuously adapt themselves depending on whom they are talking to and in what context. This "identity work" can be a practical strategy for figuring out where they fit in a diverse spectrum. It is also a way of holding on to their parents' ways without appearing to be "fresh off the boat."

In New York ethnic identity work is and always has been part of life in the city. Despite the folklore, most of New York's ethnic communities have consisted of more than one ethnic group (Massey and Denton 1994). While conflict was prevalent, cooperation and commingling among ethnic groups was also common and even necessary. Early on, it happened between Irish, German, Italian, and Central European Jews. By the 1960s, "the rapid growth of the city's black and Puerto Rican populations . . . resulted in growing minority activism, culminating in political alignments" between them, even as they maintained separate identities. Thus, more than in Los Angeles, Miami, or Chicago, group interactions occur "along an ethnic continuum, not a sharp boundary between nonwhite immigrants and native whites" (Kasinitz, Mollenkopf, and Waters 2002, 1024). Today the New York City population remains extremely diverse, and a large pool of foreign-born residents live in dense, overlapping neighborhoods knit together by a vast public transportation system and other public institutions that make group interaction and overlap unavoidable.

This is true of La Guardia Community College as well and provides a basis for identity politics there in least three ways. First, the intense racial and ethnic overlap in the college replicates that of the larger city around it. La Guardia Community College is located in one of the most racially and ethnically diverse areas of the United States. It is nestled between the Fifty-ninth Street/Queensborough Bridge into Manhattan and densely populated immigrant communities like Sunnyside, Woodside, Jackson Heights, Corona, and Flushing. The main corridors leading to the school—Queens Boulevard, Northern Avenue, and Roosevelt Avenue—are lined with small businesses operating in Spanish, Korean, Tagalog, Russian, Hebrew, and various Indian languages. Scattered throughout the back streets are ethnic corner stores, bakeries, lavanderias (laundromats), and multiservice offices specializing in travel, immigration, and legal services.

The campus has a similarly intense diversity. Although the majority of the faculty are white, the college has far more nonwhite instructors than the typical campus: 20 percent are African American, 10 percent are Latino, and 10 percent are Asian. The college does not distinguish between first- and second-generation immigrant students, but its Latino population clearly contains many of both:

> The accents I hear coming from classrooms, hallways, and the cafeteria indicate to me that there are many for whom English is not their native language. . . . Many others who speak English must be at least mildly fluent in Spanish. The words they use, the sentence structures, and even the accents on some words are Spanish-like. . . . It's the same way downstairs in the student government offices, the library, and at some of the restaurants across the street. (field notes, November 1999)

The physical layout of the college also has an important impact on how students interact with each other. Composed of several adjacent or nearby multistory buildings, the college is dense and compact. Its layout channels students into a common area that straddles two buildings and connects with a passage that includes a lounge area and access to an outdoor garden patio with benches. Several building entrances lead directly into this common area, which as a result was often congested:

> Walking from the cafeteria to the library, I sense a lot of social interaction. Several cliques of students are sitting around passing time between classes. . . . Some West Indian students play dominoes in the corner. Across the way, young women talk in Spanglish about what classes they will take next semester. Outside, a mix of students are enjoying the warmer weather and landscaping. . . . As I walk through the connector from one building to another, students are lounging everywhere, eating lunch, talking animatedly, or just dropping in to say hello. Recently added courses have been posted on the bulletin board, among them a music history course to be taught in Spanish. A young woman taping up a notice for the next meeting of the Ecuadorean Club asks her friend if she will register for that course. It would be hard to avoid people you know in such a confined space. The concentration of so many students has to prompt interaction. (field notes, October 1999)

Second, the aesthetics of the college—the symbolic messages that promote a hyperdiversity and recognize the unique historical challenges facing Latinos and other minorities—encourage awareness and discussion of these matters. The common area, connecting halls, and some outlying areas were decorated with photos, advertisements, and student information that further informed identity dynamics. The walls were covered with political memorabilia, famous quotes, and artwork from New York City history, including not only mainstream pieces but also quotes from Malcolm X, Frederick Douglass, and unnamed authors in Spanish, including a discussion of the bracero movement.

> It's hard to miss the intense symbolic content. Messages everywhere allude to the political and immigrant history of New York and the United

States. Flyers inviting students to meetings of various ethnic clubs fill the bulletin boards on all sides. On the far northeast corner of the library, a civil rights photo exhibit includes at least a hundred black-and-white prints, mostly informal shots of participants reflecting on their activities. These are not casual . . . they depict real grassroots participants, real riots, and real people who would lynch any one of the demonstrators in a second! And they are not concentrated into one or a few spaces . . . the messages of immigrant history and minority group struggle are everywhere. (field notes, September 1999)

Finally, the college's courses and pedagogy particularize these histories. For example, the Puerto Rican studies course uses the Puerto Rican example to help students learn about the larger immigrant experience. It apprises them of the challenges they face as immigrants but also provides ammunition for stressing the importance of perseverance and explains what they might become, under the right circumstances.

The identity work that emerges in this context was not hard to discern in the class on the Puerto Rican community. The first- and second-generation students mostly got along, although some conflicts did come up. The syllabus required three books by Puerto Rican authors living in New York.

It is late one evening in the fall term. . . . I am sitting in a Puerto Rican studies class filled with first- and second-generation Colombians, Ecuadoreans, Dominicans, and a few others all being taught by a Cuban professor. . . . Almost no one here is Puerto Rican. . . . They are discussing a book called *Family Installments*, a classic story of the Nuyorican diaspora. Students slide back and forth between identifying with and distancing themselves from the characters in the book. The content of the discussion, the shaking heads, and the passion with which many students state their positions indicate that they know exactly what is going on with the main characters. Still, there are moments of separation when they talk about the characters as "them," an "other" different from themselves. (field notes, February 15, 2000)

The professor's teaching style encouraged students to talk about the characters in the book and related news topics he would bring to class. The focus on the Puerto Rican immigrant and adaptation experience yielded moments in which Colombian, Ecuadorean, Peruvian, and Dominican students identified similarities with their own. As one student wrote in the final essay: "I think all our [Latino] parents have to go through this . . . and so do we [the children]."

Students did not abandon their nationalistic tendencies, nor did they forget that there were differences among them. On one occasion, the students discussed the Elian Gonzalez story taking place in south Florida. Josie, an older Dominican woman, argued, "If that little kid had been a Dominican, his ass would have been sent back on the raft!" Yet Latino solidarity dominated much of the conversation. One student commented on the media coverage of the protesters in Little Havana who favored keeping Elian in the United States: "Did you see all those flags? It was like the Spanish UN! All those people know it [Elian's situation] could happen to them. . . . They don't want that! All the Latinos were out there fighting for that kid!"

Late in the spring the class took a trip to East Harlem—El Barrio—to see some of the places described in the book. On the subway from Queens to 116th Street, students plotted what they would look for. For one of the few Puerto Ricans in the class, it was a trip back to the neighborhood that he had left many years before. It was also a trip home for a Dominican student.

While the students wandered the streets, the professor added life to the class material. He noted how a new wave of Mexican immigrants had transformed the neighborhood and many of the "monuments" in the book. Mexicans now operated the funeral home at the center of *Family Installments*, and they lived in most of the apartments along its main streets. Many local restaurants now employed and served Dominicans and Mexicans. Andre, who had spent his childhood at his abuela's house on 118th Street, reminisced about the pet store and his church, which now featured a statue of Our Lady of Guadalupe—the Mexican version of the Virgin Mary. When asked how he felt about these subtle changes—as we passed a Puerto Rican restaurant now staffed by Mexicans, Dominicans, and only one or two Puerto Ricans—he said: "Well, it's kind of strange, but at least it still has a Latino feel. . . . Everyone is still talking Spanish, and it's not like neighborhoods that have completely gentrified. . . . Puerto Ricans are still here."

The visit began with a tour of La Marqueta, the old market under the elevated Metro North train where earlier generations of Puerto Ricans had purchased foods and other necessities not readily available elsewhere. The stores had lost their appeal when larger ones moved into the area. Now La Marqueta was a mini-mall for items like those sold on Forty-second Street and throughout other tourist sections of the city, except cheaper in quality and price. Among the items were Mexican, Puerto Rican, and Dominican flags.

BECOMING A SECOND-CHANCE STUDENT

Earlier life experiences also shaped student careers. Miguel and Ray, who were both on the verge of dropping out to take jobs they had secured through internships, saw the difficulties they were having in passing certain classes as rooted in their high school experiences, if not before. Both described getting by, but rarely learning, in their earlier schooling:

> Miguel: Like in math . . . the teacher was an old man who didn't care too much. . . . I think he was counting the days to retirement. This guy was always talkin' about stuff nobody could understand. I just chilled in the back of the class . . . and he passed me! [*He gives a puzzled look.*]

> Ray: At least you had a math teacher. One time we had four different ones in the same year, and some of them didn't even know math. Those people didn't even know our names!

> Miguel: It wasn't like we didn't learn anything, or that we didn't care. . . . Sometimes you felt like none of this stuff mattered and that nobody really wanted to explain it to you. My parents wanted me to go to school, but they didn't really know the things we were being taught either. They had their own problems with work and learning the language.

Such negative school experiences lead many second-generation young people to became second-chance students at the community college, but other paths also lead to this destination. Immigrant families often rely on added incomes from their young adult children, who find that the need to work often severely limits how much time and energy they can put into making up for lost years at school. Ray discussed how his educational struggles were compounded by his parents' dependence on his financial contributions: "If I didn't have to work so much, man, forget it. . . . I could do all the things I need to pass that exam . . . but how can I be taking so many extra classes with no time? And I can't stop working."

Discrimination, or the perception of it, was another issue. Luisa, a twenty-five-year-old Ecuadorean woman, talked about her short-lived experience at a four-year college:

> I hated that place. Everybody was so uptight, and they always tried to make you feel so stupid . . . even all those stuck-up bougie Latinos . . . thinking it's an ivy freakin' school or something. . . . And the teachers just don't get it! I was having a hard time, but I still wanted to pass my classes. . . . I was working a lot. I went to one professor to ask what I could do to get caught up. That fool looked at me like I was crazy. He said, "I'm sorry, but this is not high school, and you can't expect to do work whenever you feel like it. Maybe you should think about the fact that some people are not cut out for college." What kind of shit was that? "Some people"? I was doing most of my work! I just didn't understand it! I'm not sayin' all teachers are like that, but some. . . . Finally, I just got too depressed to go.

Cultural differences between their immigrant parents and their native peers can also complicate matters. Parents seek to preserve cultural ways that they interpret as being helpful to survival in the new society. Their children may live at home, but they form their lives in the outside world of school, friendships, work, and other activities. They generally develop a bicultural savvy that satisfies their parents while trying to live up to expectations from peers, teachers, and other authority figures, but the outcome is not always simple. New social opportunities can conflict with familial expectations, especially for young women. College is a time when individuals are given (and expect to have) more freedoms. Social events, class schedules, and class assignments that require spending odd hours in the library or working with classmates often go against the grain of protective immigrant parents who are wary about their children being out alone—even en route from one location to another. The freedom afforded by going away to college also sometimes can lead to problems. On her way home from class one evening, Yvette summed up her journey to the community college:

> Yeah, I went to Baruch after high school, but I didn't make it past the first year. I never went! I couldn't take it; I just wanted to get out of the house and hang out. Cuz when I was young—you know how Spanish parents are [with girls]—I couldn't do anything, I couldn't even go to sleepovers where the parents were home. When I started college, forget it, I hardly ever went to class. I was enjoying my freedom. Then when [Baruch] kicked me out, I had to move out, go get a job, and take care of myself. No way was I gonna go back to that same old life. I love my parents, but . . . you know.

Maritza, a twenty-three-year-old Peruvian, was a returning student, wife, and mother of one who thought she was ready for SUNY Stony Brook right after high school. Her parents and boyfriend had all agreed that she should go to college, but they pressured her about getting married and having kids. She described it as being caught between fulfilling the expectation that she get married and become a mother and her desire to pursue a career.

> I wanted to go to college, but I also wanted the money and freedom to do something for myself. . . . But when I got pregnant, it was obvious what I had to do. . . . I figured I could go to school later on, especially if I got one of those jobs that helped pay for school. . . . I didn't expect that it would take so long to come back.

Several years later, after getting married and having a child, her employer helped Maritza return to school. She was determined to juggle her family responsibilities with taking twelve credits, but this balancing act would eventually jeopardize her college career.

Others took more circuitous routes to a second-chance educational opportunity. Eddie had graduated from high school ten years before and thought he could do fine as an artist without a college degree. Mari figured she would be a secretary in the office where her mother worked. By securing their own housing and jobs, both took acceptable and potentially upwardly mobile positions relative to their parents and peers. But both eventually realized that they needed more formal credentials and began second-chance journeys.

All the young people in these stories were at risk. They had issues with preparation, money, identity, and juggling expectations. Ray and Miguel needed extra preparation to pass their math requirements for graduation. Mari, Yvette, and Eddie were living on their own and had to work full-time to pay their rent. (Almost all the community college students in the survey had to work to survive.) Maritza did the same while caring for a child and nurturing a marriage. Luisa feared negative comments from faculty and staff who might not understand where she was coming from. Thirty-two-year-old Eddie felt the constraints of age and wanted to get on with his life. And others negotiated gender roles while pursuing their goals.

The community college could soften, but not entirely remove, the blows that made it hard for them to pursue an education at a four-year college. On a moment's notice, a busy spell at work, a sick child, or bad results in the inevitable math class could end a college career. The student-centered approach did provide courses and aesthetics that addressed the historical experiences and concerns of immigrants, their children, and other students of color and helped them navigate their precarious situations. But the more significant role it played was in channeling students in these precarious situations into practical opportunities.

Managing Ambition

The college employs a number of direct and indirect mechanisms to promote a vocational culture among its vulnerable students. Miguel and Ray, who were both about to drop out and take jobs they had gotten through the college's internship program, at first seemed to be unique cases. As time passed, however, it became clear that many others were following the same path, even those who could transfer to a four-year college:

> The December version of Juan's semiannual bash was smaller, but with similar stories. . . . Eddie says he has to delay graduation in order to fulfill more requirements, but he might consider taking more hours at the

gallery, or even moving to New Mexico to work at a gallery there. . . . Joey, twenty-three and Colombian, says he was thinking about running for student government again, but that his mom is pressuring him to get a job. When I ask about his prospects, he is silent first, then tells me about his internship placement with an insurance company in human resources. (field notes, December 21, 2000)

Mari and Yvette were excited—both had just completed their course work to transfer to a four-year school. But they tell me how hard it is to get classes. . . . Interestingly, neither seems too troubled. . . . When I ask why, they convey a similar outlook: "I'm in no hurry right now. I have a job and I know they like me," says Mari. Yvette, referring to her job at the bank, echoes, "Yeah, me too." (field notes, December 21, 2000)

According to La Guardia's institutional data, over 80 percent of its students enter with the goal of graduating and moving to a four-year college. One-third would like to go on to graduate school. Only 15 percent plan to terminate their studies at the associate level, and only a few actually register for a certificate program. Virtually all who spoke to me had been interested in transferring to a four-year campus when they started:

Yvette: I know I still want to get a degree from Baruch; I don't think I'd be going through this right now if I didn't. It's hard . . . but that was what I wanted in the first place. That's what you need in my profession [banking] to move up. . . .

Maritza: I see this as a starting point. . . . It's close to my job and my house, so I can get home to my family [her child] right away . . . and it's easy just to come here and try different classes . . . stuff like that. . . . Eventually I will go to Queens college . . . maybe Hunter . . . I still really want to do it [get a degree].

Ray: I don't think I'm the smartest person . . . but it would be cool to get my bachelor's degree. Nobody in my family has one. . . . Right now I'm taking EMT courses, but I have some other ideas about what I would like to major in. . . . Yeah, it would be nice to finish and be the first person in my family to get a B.A.

The unfortunate truth is that most do not make this transition. According to La Guardia's 1999 records, only one-quarter graduate within four years, a figure that rises to only one-third over ten years. In all likelihood, these numbers are lower for second-generation immigrants. These low rates reflect in part the difficulty that community college students have in completing curriculum requirements within a reasonable period. But the institution also provides mechanisms, whether direct or indirect, that, as Dougherty points out, "seduce" students in other directions.

In the context of limited resources to serve vulnerable students, community colleges evolved from two-year liberal arts institutions into places that teach students practical job skills related to local labor market demands. In fact, while La Guardia offers a variety of liberal arts programs and only a few students enroll in a vocational program, it makes many vocational opportunities available to its students. The most overt strategy is the required internship. According to school literature:

> Approximately 2,000 students each year are placed in both paid and unpaid internships with organizations like Citibank, Bear Sterns, the Port Authority, Bellevue Hospital and Bergdorf Goodman. Real experience is supplemented by an intensive curriculum that includes job-specific course work, career counseling and work preparedness training. This combination of approaches works. Fully 91 percent of co-op graduates continue their education or go on to work after graduation.

La Guardia takes this program quite seriously and emphasizes it as much as, if not more than, academic courses. According to one counselor: "Faculty members are required to spend a good portion of their time working with employers. . . . Students are graded and can be failed by employers."

The broader process of providing students who wish to graduate with alternative vocational opportunities has been referred to as "managing ambition." Steven Brint and Jerome Karabel (1989) argue in *The Diverted Dream* that, although community colleges offer the impression that they can give a further education to anyone who really wants it, most students terminate their education at that level. They further assert that the community college is a safety valve "in a society that generates far higher levels of aspiration for upward mobility than it could possibly satisfy" (Brint and Karabel 1989, 11). The community college allows students to regroup and guides them through a period in which they adjust their goals to be consistent with their life situation. In a sense, the college teaches students who they are by telling them what is (and is not) possible for them.

The curriculum bears evidence of vocationalization. La Guardia features courses that focus on the basic skills required by the local labor market, including secretarial skills and skills in hotel and restaurant operations—culinary and customer services—and other service-oriented fields related to travel and tourism. Within these majors, faculty members facilitate job placements by initiating and maintaining contact with the local business community.

College bulletin boards that frequently advertise job fairs and job placement services reinforce this bias. On one occasion, flyers advertised a job fair specifically in the airline industry for positions in customer service, baggage handling, and ticketing. (This was, of course, prior to the September 11, 2001, attack on the World Trade Center and the subsequent severe downturn of this sector of the local economy.) The flyer said nothing about being a flight attendant, joining management, or becoming a pilot. Community college students could reasonably attain most, if not all, of these positions. Such ads were posted near or even alongside the artifacts of immigrant and minority history described earlier in the chapter.

Strong links with local businesses that can employ terminal students facilitate the vocationalization of community colleges. In effect, the college has developed the unstated mission of providing the minimum skills necessary for placing students into jobs that require some skills but not a college degree. One top college official noted that the college was successful in placing students "because we are so committed to business."

Since the internship is required, many of the students I met were involved with the program. Miguel, for example, had an appointment at a Manhattan ad agency:

> Miguel: I was really into this internship, and I guess they liked me because they offered me a permanent job. It's cool, because I get to learn a lot about the business. Sometimes I talk to the graphic design people . . . they teach me things.
>
> Alex: Do they treat you well?
>
> Miguel: Yeah, usually . . . I mean, sometimes I have to do stuff I don't like . . . deliver packages, get lunch, or even take care of personal business like pick up gifts for the owner's family. Sometimes they ask me to pick up stuff for their wives [*he laughs*] . . . but I can't complain. If they send me to get lunch, that means I get to eat good food! I know people who have worse situations . . . besides, it won't be like that when I go full-time.

Judy, twenty-one and Dominican, also spoke favorably about her retail internship:

> I wouldn't say it's just another job. . . . I get to work with a lot of managers and stuff designing displays for all the stores. . . . It's more exciting than sitting in a classroom, and I know I can do this kind of work if I have to. I want to be my own designer, you know, but at least this teaches me something about the business . . . and I get mad discounts! [*she laughs*]

Yet, despite the positive outlook of some students and faculty about the program, and despite its success, the internship effectively lures vulnerable students out of the college trajectory. Miguel, for example, was obviously a bright, talented, young student working on many campus organizations. My role had been to listen passively, but many conversations with him made me feel like the younger, naive one. He had intended to transfer and get a graphic arts degree. After his struggles with the math requirements, he grew more comfortable with the idea of his position at the ad firm. Later in the evening of Juan's spring semester party, he told me:

> I'm droppin' out, man, I'm just not inspired anymore. I need to move on. Pretty soon I'll be old, and I need to get my career started. It's cool because I got the internship I wanted at a top design company and they want me to stay. . . . It's cool. . . . I don't need one [a degree] right now. I'll be back, though.

Miguel had built up a strong résumé through his extracurricular activities at the college, including several terms on a campus newspaper. When faced with his inability to pass the math class, he developed a rationale about needing to move on and used the internship as his ticket to do so. At this critical point the internship became a viable career opportunity. Rather than take another shot at math, he opted to take the opportunity, as he put it, to "get my career started." Mari and Yvette too had reasonable opportunities. Even without finishing at Baruch, they said, they would make enough to pay the rent, to eat, and to spend a moderate amount on social activities around the city. Miguel was right about the possibility that it could have been worse, and probably is for some.

It remains to be seen whether these jobs will lead to something even more meaningful or will prove to be dead ends. Some suggest that entry-level positions are only that. Priscilla told me at Juan's place that the internship she had started at a large finance company nine months earlier had a complicated outcome:

> I wanted to be an analyst at some point, maybe working with companies in Latin America. But every time I asked about it they told me to wait until such and such merger, or when I finished some other classes. I was even starting to take some of my classes at Baruch, but they were still very cold about it.

When my research ended, Priscilla had moved to a competitor across the street from her former employer. She made the move contingent upon her being trained as an analyst, but she found herself still doing what she called "administrative" work. It seemed that she was being retained as what she called a "glorified secretary." It was helpful to her office team that she knew about and understood financial analysis, but practically speaking, she was still "the secretary."

These experiences suggest that the community college enables students who have suffered earlier misfortunes to come and *try* to get the elusive college degree. Clearly, it helps them to gain practical skills and find a job. A few do move on to four-year colleges, though it remains to be seen whether they will graduate and get good jobs. This is more than they might otherwise have, and certainly more than most of their parents have.

At the same time, this success has limits that are more severe for some than for others. Those who enter the college dreaming of finishing a degree and moving on to a four-year program rarely do so. The fact that the college helps them manage the retrenchment of their ambitions is not a sign of success but rather of collusion in helping students continuously water down their goals. The college inundates them with the rhetoric of semiprofessional service occupations, keeping them informed of what is available and, at particularly vulnerable moments, coaching them in how to get such a job. When a pesky graduation requirement, an economic need, a familial demand, or just the feeling of being too old and needing to move on interferes with graduation, the institution stands ready with the perpetual plan C.

STUDENTS' DEFINITIONS OF THE SITUATION

On the one hand, community colleges express their focus on the needs and interests of the local population through a student-centered approach that is sensitive to their histories and experiences, which mainstream institutions often ignore. On the other hand, community colleges limit student opportunities by leading them into segments of the labor market that, while certainly not the bottom of the economic ladder, do not provide the upward mobility that students seek.

This presents an interesting situation for the theory of segmented assimilation, which assumes that the reality of leveled aspirations would demoralize students and lead to oppositional psychological responses. Undoubtedly, some students feel shafted and react by withdrawing. But many use ethnicity to rationalize their predicaments and sustain an empowered approach, even those, like Miguel, who clearly do not live up to their own expectations. In coping, students draw on the content to which they have been exposed at La Guardia.

Yvette's initial comment that Latinos have to "invent their way" was striking. She seemed to mean that Latinos have to be creative to accomplish things that come a lot easier to others. Several months later she used the term again:

> Yvette: It's harder for us [Latinos], you know, always inventing . . . I mean, we have all these extra things to deal with, and then we have to go to schools that are not so good. . . . Don't get me wrong, I like this place, and [I like] my friends, but . . . it's not like I'm getting the best education. . . .

Alex: What kinds of things do you mean?

Yvette: You know . . . strict parents that can't understand you; money for tuition; and worrying about getting home safely . . . and being a woman is like double the trouble. You have to know the system, you know?

Alex: Does it bother you, being Latina . . . with those kinds of challenges?

Yvette: Well . . . sometimes it bothers me because I feel like I have extra responsibility. But I'm glad that I have a better understanding of why it's like this. If I didn't know, it would be much harder.

For Yvette, "inventing" meant invoking a certain savvy that comes with being a child of Latino immigrants. Under her parents' supervision, she negotiated her outside American life, salvaging her college career while working.

Another example was Ray's reaction to having to drop out:

> I'll be okay. . . . I'm still doing better than my folks ever did, and, you know, it's not over . . . I think I could do better. The thing is, for Latinos there is a struggle, for all of us so you have to be strong. So many things can set you back like teachers who don't care. I know I messed up sometimes, I also know that people can make it if you pay attention to what's going on and you work together. Poco a poco (little by little).

The class conversations revealed that people from each Latino group—Colombians, Ecuadoreans, Peruvians, Dominicans, and even the few Puerto Ricans—could see their similarities both in life experiences and in the class material. Outside class one day, Norma, a twenty-four-year-old Colombian, told me the following story about housing in Latino communities:

> You know, sometimes this shit is so depressing. It's like, it's always so hard for immigrants to find jobs and have decent things. People act like everything is okay now just because we're not burning down buildings or having big protests. . . . It's like, people don't realize that some of these problems still exist. . . . But it's like that kid [from the class] was sayin', we have to be strong . . . just deal, cuz otherwise you'll be without anything.

Much of this discussion among the students did question Americanization and American problems, but it did not lead them to withdraw from wanting to be educated or to enjoy the benefits of upward mobility. Rather, they used their knowledge of their predicament as a source of empowerment. Norma could jump from a discussion of Puerto Ricans to her own situation.

The student essays from the Puerto Rican community class explored this.

Sandra, a nineteen-year-old Colombian and Peruvian woman, summed it up well:

> Nobody really knows why some Puerto Ricans are doing so poorly here in the United States. There are many reasons given, but most people believe there is not enough research on this situation. . . . What we do know is that despite the racism and other injustices that Puerto Ricans face, there are still many success stories. There are politicians, social activists, movie stars, and even Puerto Ricans who own large successful corporations. I believe that this will be true for other Latinos who are now living in El Barrio and other parts of the city that used to be Puerto Rican. We will continue to have our share of problems, and sometimes we will fail . . . but we will remind ourselves that we can succeed, even if it takes a little while. . . . We have to work as a group. Puerto Ricans, Dominicans, Colombians, Cubans, all of us.

CONCLUSIONS

La Guardia Community College is a place where immigrant children who faced earlier challenges sought to make progress in their educational aspirations. Their academic experience there produced a series of contradictory outcomes, including a reactive ethnicity in which students came to understand their predicaments in terms of being Latino. In the past, reactive ethnicity has been seen as a negative outcome associated with oppositional behaviors. Although it is apparent that these young people would be warranted in adopting some degree of rejection, this argument has a more general problem. Specifically, we have yet to fully understand how the formation of reactive ethnicity fits within the context of the changes wrought by the civil rights movement and forty years of immigration in American values and institutions and the historical continuum of ethnic groups (Kasinitz, Mollenkopf, and Waters 2002).

The La Guardia experience challenges the pessimistic notion of reactive ethnicity and suggests that the literature on the second generation needs to develop the notion of context. La Guardia students were diverted from their initial goals and were also aware that this had something to do with their status as children of immigrants and minorities. But they did not react by rejecting their initial educational aspirations, nor did they blame themselves for not being able to "make it." Even Miguel, who came close to this line of thinking, claimed that he would be back.

Instead, the Puerto Rican discourse at La Guardia helped students form a reactive ethnicity that drew on the Puerto Rican (and even the African American) experience. It afforded them an opportunity to understand some of the oppressive forces working against them. They also learned about the accomplishments and contributions of native minorities that mainstream institutions did not discuss. Puerto Ricans and African Americans have made many institutionalized advances in New York City that buffer the downwardly mobile children of immigrants against such challenges as not making it through school. Students saw the Puerto Ricans in themselves by understanding the institutional barriers facing Puerto Ricans and the ways in which Puerto Ricans have struggled to overcome them. This "in-between" perspective was matched by access to in-between occupations. While the college does have information on the incomes of nongraduates, the types of jobs they are taking seem likely to put their earnings between those of their parents and those of students who do graduate from four-year schools.

It could be that the children of immigrants are experiencing the other side of relative deprivation. Because they end up doing somewhat better than their parents or people with no college experience, it is not quite as much of a blow that they cannot reach their original aspirations. By learning about the civil rights era, they develop a reference point in past generations that had little or no opportunity. It may be problematic not to graduate, but the $25,000 job obtained through an internship is better than the jobs held by most of their parents.[7]

Since this is only a short-term outcome, we cannot reach any durable conclusion about what community college might mean for subsequent life trajectories. Graduation rates at La Guardia rise only slightly over ten years. Those who fail to graduate may drop out or end up somewhere else. Several years after my fieldwork was completed, seven of my fifteen key subjects are still in school, and only one has dropped out with no work prospects. What becomes of their outlooks and educational careers will tell us much about the trajectories of second-generation immigrants—and about the trajectory of America.

NOTES

1. In 1998 the City University board of trustees adopted a policy that requires students who are admitted to a senior college but fail one or more placement tests in reading, writing, and mathematics to take remedial courses at a community college or other university prior to enrolling. Previously, students could take such courses at the senior college in which they wished to enroll. Some community colleges offer such courses at the facilities of the senior colleges.
2. The term "student-centered" is used here in the broad sense and refers to a systematic group of courses or sequence of subjects that utilize student experiences, backgrounds, and interests.
3. Two were day courses, and two were in the evening. This exposed me to students who varied in age, employment status, majors, and interests.

Somewhere Between Wall Street and El Barrio 77

4. A youthful appearance helped me to blend in with the variety of students. It was also helpful to be Cuban and able to communicate in Spanish, which many students opted for. Over time some became interested in my work, while others who knew I was a teacher sought my help with course content or shared their frustrations with me.
5. While class discussions and activities did focus on specific geographic locations, the term "community" was used in a broader sense to refer to the entire Puerto Rican population in the New York metropolitan area.
6. This is an important qualification because the study ends and there is little possibility of knowing what happens down the road for the children of post-1964 immigrants until a later date.
7. According to La Guardia's institutional data, the average La Guardia graduate earned $29,211 in 2000. The figure is probably lower for those who do not officially graduate and/or transfer.

REFERENCES

Anyon, Jean. 1997. *Ghetto Schooling: A Political Economy of Urban Educational Reform.* New York: Teachers College Press.
Bailey, Thomas. 2003. "Community Colleges in the Twenty-first Century: Challenges and Opportunities." Brief 15. New York: Community College Research Center.
Bailey, Thomas, and Elliot Weininger. 2002. "Educating Immigrants and Native Minorities in CUNY Community Colleges." Brief 13. New York: Community College Research Center (December).
Brint, Steven, and Jerome Karabel. 1989. *The Diverted Dream: Community Colleges and the Promise of Educational Opportunity in America, 1900–1985.* New York: Oxford University Press.
Castro-Abad, Cecilia. 1995. *A Human Development Workshop on Cultural Identity for International Students.* Mid-Career Fellowship Program (ED 384 382). Princeton, N.J.: Princeton University.
Dougherty, Kevin J. 1994. *The Contradictory College: The Conflicting Origins, Impacts, and Futures of the Community College.* Albany: State University of New York Press.
Erkut, Sumru, and J. R. Mokros. 1984. "Professors as Role Models and Mentors for College Students." *American Educational Research Journal* 21(2): 399–417.
Kasinitz, Philip, John Mollenkopf, and Mary C. Waters. 2002. "Becoming American/Becoming New Yorkers: Immigrant Incorporation in a Majority Minority City." *International Migration Review* 36(14, winter): 1020–24.
Kasper, Henry T. 2002. "The Changing Role of Community College." *Occupational Outlook Quarterly* (March 15): 14–21.
Kirkpatrick, Laura. 2001. "Multicultural Strategies for Community Colleges: Expanding Faculty Diversity." Los Angeles: ERIC Clearinghouse for Community Colleges.

Massey, Douglas, and Nancy Denton. 1994. *American Apartheid: Segregation and the Making of the American Underclass.* Cambridge, Mass.: Harvard University Press.

Portes, Alejandro, and Rubén G. Rumbaut. 2001. *Legacies: The Story of the Immigrant Second Generation.* Berkeley: University of California Press.

Schmidt, Benno C., Herman Badillo, Jacqueline V. Brady, Heather MacDonald, Manfred Ohrenstein, Richard T. Roberts, and R. Schwartz. 1999. "The City University of New York: An Institution Adrift." Report of the Mayor's Task Force on the City University of New York (June 7).

Schneider, Barbara, and David Stevenson. 1999. *The Ambitious Generation: America's Teenagers Motivated but Directionless.* New Haven, Conn.: Yale University Press.

CHAPTER 4

"BEING PRACTICAL" OR "DOING WHAT I WANT": THE ROLE OF PARENTS IN THE ACADEMIC CHOICES OF CHINESE AMERICANS*

VIVIAN LOUIE

My mom and dad kind of want me and my brother to become doctors to carry on the family business. My brother and I would say that the only professions in my mother's eyes that were worthy were either a doctor or a lawyer.
    —*Victoria, eighteen-year-old Ivy League student and daughter of a doctor*

Growing up, parents keep on saying, "What are you going to do? Doctor, lawyer?" And when I was in high school, it was pharmacy school in particular. Everybody was going to pharmacy school—my cousins, it was pharmacy school. Parents push for something more practical, or applicable. And you can't get anything more practical than pharmacy and medical school or law school.
    —*Robert, twenty-one-year-old student at a public commuter university and son of a retired chef and nurse's aide supervisor*

DESPITE coming from nearly opposite socioeconomic ends of Chinese migration flows to New York, Victoria and Robert relayed a common experience of confronting parental pressure to follow a "practical" professional path. In this chapter, I explore how second-generation Chinese American college students understood the expectations of their Chinese immigrant parents as they were choosing what to study and pursue as a career. Across

*All names of individuals reported throughout the chapter are pseudonyms.

class and gender, my respondents heard the same message from parents: not only is education important—with the bachelor's degree seen as the minimum level of attainment (Louie 2001)—but the end goal of education is a stable, high-paying job, and the key to this is studying "practical" and "safe" fields.

Media and research accounts have depicted Asian Americans as overachievers in technical fields, and my respondents too understood this to be an ethnic phenomenon. As I show in this chapter, however, class matters in several key dimensions: in how students respond to their parents' views on the most appropriate fields of study for them to pursue; in how they make their decisions in very different institutions of higher learning; and, along with gender, in how parental pressures are often transmitted and experienced differently.

The very different life histories of Victoria and Robert reflect the great variety of socioeconomic trajectories among the 361,000 Chinese who make their home in New York City (according to the census of 2000), particularly those who arrived after 1965. Victoria's family, headed as it was by two highly educated and professionalized parents who made their home in the suburbs, belonged to what social scientists have called the "uptown Chinese." Victoria's father had left Taiwan in 1979 after graduating from the prestigious National Taiwan University to train as a doctor in the United States; her mother came to earn a master's degree in international relations. Instead of returning to Taiwan, the couple settled in a wealthy Long Island suburb and enrolled their children in its highly ranked public school system. Victoria in particular excelled academically. It came as no surprise to Victoria's parents, then, that she was admitted to an Ivy League school, Columbia College.

Robert's parents were part of a working-class immigrant stream of manual laborers who typically worked in restaurants and garment factories in an ethnic economic enclave described as the "downtown Chinese." Robert's parents left southern China in the 1960s and discovered that their limited education (his father had some high school, and his mother finished grade school) gave them few options in the United States aside from the ethnic economy. Robert's father waited on tables and cooked in Chinese-owned restaurants while his mother, a nurse's aide supervisor, worked mainly with Chinese clients. Eventually the couple moved to Bensonhurst, Brooklyn. In high school Robert could be found cutting classes and hanging out with friends more often than studying. After some run-ins with his parents, he straightened out, graduated from high school, and, much to his parents' relief, entered Hunter College, a public university.

Because of all these differences, it was unlikely that Victoria and Robert would come across one another, even though their families lived only twenty miles apart and they went to colleges in the same city. Nor were they likely to meet in an ethnic church. As Karen Chai Kim documents in this volume, ethnic churches increasingly draw second-generation Chinese Americans in New York City from diverse social class backgrounds, offering them a place to develop a frame of commonality that can sometimes bridge class differences. Victoria, however, participated in a campus Christian fellowship group that drew mainly Columbia students and was not ethnic-specific. And Robert had a much more ambivalent relationship to his parents' religious faiths: his mother was a devout Jehovah's Witness, and his father followed "superstitious Chinese" practices. Robert declined to adopt either faith, opting instead for a self-fashioned Buddhism acquired through martial arts training in Chinatown and reading on his own.

Even if their paths did cross by some chance, Victoria and Robert would have found that they had little in common, with one notable exception: their parents' aspirations for their schooling and careers. I met both Victoria and Robert during my year of fieldwork at Hunter and Columbia. My goal was to explore how the very different socioeconomic backgrounds of Chinese immigrant families had shaped the educational paths and aspirations of their young adult children (Louie 2004). Although the "model minority" stereotype portrays Asian Americans as high academic achievers, educational outcomes actually differ a good deal between and within groups.[1] The Immigrant Second Generation in Metropolitan New York Study found, for example, that first- and second-generation Chinese Americans both had diverse educational outcomes. As table 4.1 indicates, 11.7 percent of all second-generation respondents had only a high school diploma or GED, were still enrolled in high school, or had dropped out. Another 7.6 percent were enrolled in or had graduated from a two-year college, and 7.2 percent had some college but no degree.

Overall, however, a majority of Chinese survey respondents were going on to a four-year college. More than three out of five (61.4 percent), for example, were enrolled in or had graduated from a four-year college. But even so, they attended many different kinds of schools. Table 4.2 shows that 12.8 percent attended a two-year CUNY college and 32.1 percent attended a four-year CUNY school. At the other end of the spectrum, 36.2 percent attended a private college. Thus, while second-generation Chinese Americans were faring better than other groups in the Second Generation Study, sometimes even going to better schools than whites, their profile was certainly not homogeneous.

This chapter focuses on 1.5- and second-generation Chinese Americans attending Columbia, a national tier I private university, and Hunter College, a regional tier II campus of the public City University of New York (CUNY). I ask whether children's educational experiences vary with the class background of their immigrant families and what role gender plays in that rela-

TABLE 4.1   EDUCATIONAL ATTAINMENT OF CHINESE SECOND
            GENERATION

General Recoded Educational Status (Valid)	Frequency	Percentage	Valid Percentage	Cumulative Percentage
High school dropout	3	2.0%	2.0%	2.0%
Still in high school	7	5.0	5.0	7.0
High school graduate or GED	6	4.6	4.6	11.7
Enrolled in two-year college	9	6.6	6.6	18.3
Some college, no degree	9	7.2	7.2	25.5
Graduated from two-year college	1	1.0	1.0	26.4
Enrolled in four-year college	47	36.6	36.6	63.1
Graduated from four-year-college	32	24.8	24.8	87.9
Enrolled in graduate or professional school	7	5.2	5.2	93.1
Some graduate school, no degree	1	.9	.9	94.0
Postgraduate or professional degree	4	3.3	3.3	97.3
Other	4	2.7	2.7	100.0
Total	129	100.0	100.0	

Source: Data from the Immigrant Second Generation in Metropolitan New York Survey sample.

TABLE 4.2   TYPE OF UNDERGRADUATE SCHOOL ATTENDED BY
            SECOND-GENERATION CHINESE

Type of School (Valid)	Frequency	Percentage	Valid Percentage	Cumulative Percentage
CUNY two-year	14	10.5%	12.8%	12.8%
CUNY four-year	34	26.5	32.1	44.9
SUNY	13	10.1	12.3	57.2
Private NYC	27	20.7	25.2	82.4
Private non-NYC	12	9.1	11.0	93.4
Public non-NYC	7	5.2	6.3	99.7
Public NYC (non-CUNY)	0	.3	.3	100.0
Total	107	82.4	100.0	
Missing system	23	17.6		
Total	129	100.0		

Source: Data from the Immigrant Second Generation in Metropolitan New York Survey sample.

tionship. Specifically, I explore how Chinese immigrant parents develop and communicate aspirations for their children's academic choices and occupational paths and whether the children agree or disagree with those goals. Academic researchers and the media have said a lot about high achievement levels among Chinese Americans, their strong presence in technical fields, and the ways in which their families encourage these outcomes. My research suggests that we need to look through the lenses of immigration, class, community, and perceptions of the American racial structure when we examine how Chinese immigrant families affect their children's educational outcomes.

THE STUDY

From April 1998 to May 1999, I participated in classroom and informal settings at Columbia and Hunter three to five times a week and interviewed sixty-eight Chinese American students from both schools, seven of their immigrant parents, and two adult siblings. Much of the argument in this chapter is based on the student interviews, which explored the respondents' experiences from elementary school through college, career aspirations, views on racial and ethnic stratification, and perceptions of family attitudes toward education. Given the small number of family interviews, I rely on them more to give depth to the themes raised by the students themselves. The family interviews probed sibling experiences with education, discussed parents' attitudes toward their children's schooling and toward their own experiences with schooling, migration, and work, and traced their views on racial and ethnic stratification in the United States.

The two schools had varying entrance requirements for students and varying tuitions. About four thousand undergraduates enrolled at Columbia College during my year of fieldwork. As befits an Ivy League school, Columbia College[2] was highly selective: it accepted only 17 percent of more than eleven thousand applicants in 1997, and entering students had median SAT scores of 1346 out of a possible 1600. Columbia also resembles its Ivy League counterparts in its annual tuition and fees of about $30,000. A commuter school with fourteen thousand undergraduates, Hunter was founded to provide affordable higher education to the economically disadvantaged. Tuition and fees for a full-time resident of the city totaled $1,600 per semester, or $135 per credit for part-time students, in 1997. Academically speaking, Hunter was open in the late 1990s to high school graduates who had at least an 80 percent average, were in the top third of their class, or scored at least 1020 out of a possible 1600 on the SAT. According to its catalogs, applicants who had a GED score of at least three hundred were also eligible for admission.

I decided to conduct the study at these two sites to bring into view an understudied group, namely, Asian American students attending less selective universities and community and city colleges. In 1997, 41 percent of Asian Americans enrolled in college attended a public four-year institution, and 39 percent were at a public two-year institution (*Chronicle of Higher Education* 2000). Yet we know little about the experiences of Asian Americans in these institutions, particularly at community and city colleges, and how they complicate the model minority stereotype of Asian Americans.[3]

Another motivation for having a dual-site study was to tap into the dimension of social class background, which is often correlated with the type of postsecondary institution attended (Kwong 1987; Weinberg 1997). Thus, I expected that the Hunter students would tend to be downtown Chinese, and the Columbia respondents uptown Chinese. As table 4.3 shows, this was largely the case, although the class dimension turned out to be more complex.

More than half of the Hunter respondents grew up in or near Chinatown in Manhattan, Flushing in Queens, or Sunset Park in Brooklyn. Two-thirds of their parents were involved with the Chinese ethnic economy, mainly in the restaurant business (as cooks and waiters) or the garment industry (as seamstresses and pressers); a few were entrepreneurs who owned restaurants and other businesses and had middle-class status in the ethnic economy.[4] The remainder worked outside the ethnic economy as engineers, health care aides, and teachers but retained strong kinship and social ties to an ethnic enclave.

While a few Hunter students had started off at elite, private colleges (such as Cornell or Smith), their parents were not members of the uptown Chinese.

TABLE 4.3   HUNTER AND COLUMBIA CHINESE AMERICAN STUDENT CHARACTERISTCS

Student Characteristics	Hunter	Columbia
Percentage of Respondents	49	51
Grew up in intact family	73	77
Grew up in or adjacent to one of New York City's three Chinatowns[a]	52	14
Has at least one parent working in the ethnic economy	67	20
Parents own their home[b]	52	91

Source: Author's compilation.
Notes: N = 68 (74 percent female, 26 percent male). Sixty percent of the respondents were second-generation immigrants, and 40 percent were 1.5-generation. Sixty-nine percent had grown up in the New York City metropolitan area (the five boroughs, Westchester County, and Long Island).
[a] Manhattan's Chinatown, Sunset Park in Brooklyn, and Flushing, Queens.
[b] House, condominium, or coop.

Rather, their parents lived or worked in the ethnic economy, within which they had middle-class status and generally did not work in manual jobs.

Most of my Columbia respondents grew up in suburban, largely white neighborhoods with parents in professional occupations such as engineering, law, and medicine. As table 4.4 shows, more than half of the fathers had an advanced degree, and 45 percent of the mothers had a bachelor's degree, in contrast to the Hunter parents, most of whom had a high school education or less.

A minority of the Columbia parents, however, experienced downward mobility with migration—they had held positions of higher prestige and income in their home country and had fewer resources in the United States than their educational credentials might have suggested.[5] Some worked in the Chinese ethnic economy in New York City or elsewhere. But unlike most of the Hunter parents, these parents had obtained some college education either abroad or in the United States or owned property and operated their own businesses. Thus, they held a middle-class status in the ethnic economy.

TABLE 4.4   PARENTAL EDUCATIONAL ATTAINMENT

Parents' Education	Hunter	Columbia
Fathers		
Grade school	7	1
Junior high school	2	1
High school	17	3
Some college	3	3
Bachelor's degree	1	7
Advanced degree	1	19
Student does not know	2	1
Mothers		
Grade school	4	0
Junior high school	4	2
High school	17	4
Some college	5	6
Bachelor's degree	1	16
Advanced degree	0	7
Student does not know	2	0

Source: Author's compilation.
Notes: N = 33 (Hunter) and 35 (Columbia).

METHODS

Because of constraints of access, I could not draw a random and representative sample. However, I used a number of strategies to try to ensure that my respondents proved typical in their outlooks and experiences. Students were recruited through administrative, faculty, and student contacts and were briefly introduced to the project either by me personally or through e-mail at non-ethnic and ethnic organizations and in classes in various disciplines.[6] I emphasized my status as a second-generation Chinese American asking other second-generation Americans and 1.5ers to participate in a study about themselves. All but one of the interviews were conducted face to face, and all were tape-recorded. They lasted between ninety minutes and two hours. To gain perspective on the respondents' views of their parents and other family members, I interviewed seven parents and two adult siblings. The majority of these interviews took place in the family home, were also tape-recorded, and lasted between thirty and ninety minutes.[7]

Despite my attempts to have gender parity in the sample, women consistently volunteered to participate in greater numbers: nearly three-fourths of the respondents were women. To offset the gender imbalance, I probed more deeply into issues related to gender in the interview, asking about respondents' siblings and, more generally, about issues related to gender socialization, as they pertained to both men and women.

One theme expressed by both women and men of varying class backgrounds centered on the "Asian" fields of study, which they understood in the context of immigrant parents' expectations, and that is what I examine next.

THE "ASIAN" FIELDS OF STUDY

One day, in the second-floor sky café at Hunter, I was asking Jeff whether he thought Chinese Americans tended to major in some fields and not in others. He responded by volunteering to take me to Hunter's "Asian" wing. This area was home to the departments of physics, chemistry, and biology; here we would find, in Jeff's words, "research assistants and researchers and students, 70 to 80 percent of them Asian." Jeff was not alone in voicing this view. In the course of my interviews, it became clear that my respondents had varying takes on what it meant to be Asian American—who was included in the term and what it signified.[8] Yet they easily agreed that the technical fields were "Asian" fields and Chinese Americans were well represented in them.

Although this claim made by my respondents was mainly based on anecdotal evidence, there is much empirical data to support the idea that Asian Americans can be found in particular fields of study and occupations. In

1990, for example, Asian Americans represented 3 percent of the total U.S. population, but nearly 7 percent of the bachelor's degrees awarded in science in 1991, 7 percent of the nation's scientists and engineering workforce, and 9 percent of medical school faculty (Tang and Smith 1996; Elliot et al. 1996; Espiritu 1997). Several years later the trend continued as Asian Americans received 18.4 percent of all engineering doctorates awarded in 1998, 13.3 percent of the life sciences doctorates, and 12.9 percent of doctorates in the physical sciences. By contrast, only 3.2 percent received doctorates in education (*Chronicle of Higher Education* 2000).

These trends can be attributed, at least in part, to the brain drain that has drawn highly trained immigrants, particularly in the technical fields, to the United States. But these trends also seem salient among 1.5- and second-generation Asian Americans. Morrison Wong (1995a, 1995b) finds that Chinese Americans, particularly the foreign-born, overconcentrate in the sciences and math to maintain high grade point averages at the secondary and collegiate levels. Other studies suggest that Chinese parents perceive structural constraints to their children's future mobility and thus favor "safe" careers that rely less on face-to-face contact, subjective judgments, and language skills and more on objective data and licensing, such as law, engineering, math, medicine, and the physical and biological sciences (Lyman 1974; Kwong 1987). But as Dae Young Kim (this volume) demonstrates in his work with Koreans, and researchers studying other Asian ethnic groups have shown as well, this phenomenon is by no means limited to Chinese immigrant parents.

Although neither Hunter nor Columbia recorded the fields of study chosen by Chinese Americans as compared to other ethnic and racial groups, some data were available for Asian Americans. At Hunter, Asian and Pacific Islanders were underrepresented in the humanities and overrepresented in technical fields like the sciences and mathematics, trends similar to those found in national studies of Asian American educational performance (Jacobs 1996). At Columbia data were scarcer, but the university's 1999 statistical abstract on student enrollment readily revealed that Asian Americans made up 41 percent of the student body at the engineering school.

TYPICAL ADVICE FROM ASIAN PARENTS: "CHOOSE SOMETHING PRACTICAL"

In trying to explain why these fields had such a pronounced Asian presence, my respondents invariably brought up the role of parental pressure. In the words of one woman, "Asian families want their sons and daughters to be doctors and lawyers." In the view of my respondents, across class and gender, parents expressed this preference because they wanted their children to pursue occupations that held high promise for financial security and thus were "practical" and "safe." This was in keeping with the parents' generally utilitarian view of education. For instance, Deborah, the daughter of a waiter and garment worker, described her parents' cues about school: "The objective is to have a job at the end of the academic experience. It's just to strive for [academic] success to get a good job." Grace is another example. As a teenager, Grace, whose parents also worked in the ethnic economy, had an interest in fashion and thought about applying to the city's fashion high school, only to have her mother discourage her because "there's no money involved." Instead, she steered Grace toward Brooklyn Technical High School, and later she would come to have equally firm ideas about what her daughter should be studying in college. Grace observed:

> My mother will ask me which classes I'm taking each semester, and I will tell her. She's like, "What does that do?" She's like, "Why are you taking that?" Like once, I was taking an elective in film, and she was like, "What are you going to do with that?" I am like, I am just taking a class. I'll just take it for fun.

Most middle-class children were also socialized by their parents to have a utilitarian view of education. In the words of a young woman whose father was a lawyer and whose mother was a certified public accountant: "They're thinking of education as my way to a job, as opposed to education for education's sake."

The reasons for this orientation varied. Many students talked about their parents' traumatic experiences of everything from poverty to racial riots and precarious political and economic arrangements in their homelands. Some parents were born into economically disadvantaged families; others came from more privileged backgrounds only to undergo a precipitous decline in social status. Such dislocations were occasioned by the tumultuous events that befell East Asia from the late nineteenth century onward, in brief: civil war (1927 to 1937, 1946 to 1949) engulfed China, was interrupted by war with Japan, and finally culminated in the Communist Party's assumption of power; Japan colonized Taiwan (1895 to 1945), which was then taken over by Nationalist forces; and in nations like Vietnam, Malaysia, and Philippines, the costs of ethnic marginalization that came with being a Chinese minority often worsened the experience of political and social unrest within those countries.

The United States, while offering a refuge from such turmoil, presented its own share of challenges. According to my student respondents, the immigrant adjustment often proved to be difficult as their parents tried to recalibrate their sensibilities to a new language and culture. Some of the students also remembered their parents pointing to the racialized social structure as another challenge. For many parents, potential discrimination by whites in fields with a marginal Asian presence—or as one student respondent put it, the potential pitfalls of trying to make it in a "white man's world"—gave them further incentive to stress with their children a utilitarian view of education overall, and technical fields in particular.

Regardless of the provenance of these aspirations, the parents transmitted them to their children in very similar ways, as can be seen from the following accounts of five students from diverse socioeconomic backgrounds. Joan and Grace both grew up in Chinatown, though Joan's family had a more middle-class status in the ethnic economy.[9] Born and raised in Chinatown, Lois's parents now lived and worked outside the ethnic economy but still maintained strong ties to the community. In contrast, Milly and Laura both came from suburban, upper-middle-class households, and their parents were in law, medicine, and corporate finance.

These young women, however, proved similar in at least one dimension: they had decided to major in fields that were not sanctioned by their parents. Bear in mind that none of these students were thinking of pursuing law or medicine (in which case, their field of study would make little difference since they would end up following the prescribed career trajectory anyway). In their parents' eyes, they had only their majors to recommend them, and that was not enough. Lois, a Hunter psychology major said:

> They think it's a dead-end field. Because they feel that you can't really go anywhere in psych. It's like, "Where are you going to go? Are you going to work in a hospital?" Or the highest thing that you can basically do is to open your own office, you know, and to have your own clientele. But you know, I guess in a lot of ways my parents are the typical Asian-minded parents that are, you know, "you should be in the business field somehow." Computers and stuff like that. Sciences. Unless you become a doctor or something, you're not going to accomplish anything.

According to Laura, a Columbia anthropology major:

> They don't get it. You can do an anthro major, but you have to have a good job. And you can quote this: they always say, "You can't live in the dirt forever." My aunt actually said this to me this summer in Paris: "You can't dig in the dirt forever, you know." It's like, you have to take an econ class. So they don't understand the idea, but I think they trust my decision. Still, they worry about it. My dad is like, "Why don't you be a doctor?" because he's a doctor. My mom's like, "Why don't you go to law

school?" because she went to law school. And then my aunt, "Why don't you become like a trader?" Just like the things they do themselves. And they suggest fields that make money.

Joan, a Columbia archaeology major, put it this way:

> They're not happy about it exactly. Sometimes they try to guilt-trip me, by telling me how their friends feel so sorry for them. And then they start with money: "What happens if you get married and are dependent for an income. What else is there?" I'm not even sure they tell their friends I'm an archaeology major. They just say I'm interested in history.

According to Milly, a Columbia East Asian languages and civilizations major:

> Oh, they really dislike it. They really dislike it. They're like, "You, like, go to the States to, like, learn Chinese history, Japanese history. What are you doing?" I convinced them that, "Don't worry, look it, you know, like, my cousin's in psychology, and he comes out, he's employed, you know." I was like, "So don't worry, you know. It doesn't matter as long as I enjoy it." I mean, they're not, like, angry. They're just, like, "Why are you doing that?" What do they want me to do? Oh, that's easy— economics.

Grace, a Hunter geography major, said:

> When I told them about geography, they were really, what the hell are you going to do with that? And my grandfather found out. Every time I see him or talk to him on the phone, he's like, "How's geography going? What are you going to do?" And my aunts and uncles ask me, "What are you going to do? What are you going to do?" Geography is not like business or economics. Geography is not a discipline that you can do very much with.

This instrumental view of education bridged the many differences among these immigrant parents and was imparted to both daughters and sons. Even highly educated parents like Laura's and Milly's (who received their graduate degrees in the United States) did not perceive the practicality of fields like archaeology and East Asian languages and civilizations, with "practicality" understood to mean the potential to attract high-income jobs.

On one level, this finding seems counterintuitive. It would make sense for Chinese working-class parents to stress financial security because they probably rely on their children's financial contribution to the household (Kwong 1987; Hune 1998). In fact, several of the working-class students were either already contributing to the household through part-time work or anticipating having to contribute once they graduated and started working full-time. Studies on Chinese and Asian middle-class parents, on the other hand, have shown that they are more likely to define their children's education as a quest for knowledge than as preparation for a particular career, less likely to define education primarily in economic terms, and more likely to encourage their children to partake of the academic curriculum (Siu and Feldman 1995; Hune 1998). My interviews, by contrast, showed a remarkable convergence in parental aspirations, as they were conveyed to children, across class. Class did matter, however, as I demonstrate in the next section.

ETHNIC NETWORKS AND THE SECONDARY FIELDS

My respondents saw the "Asian fields" as a set of technical fields that their parents thought would bring their children stable and high-income professional lives, but even within these fields there were differences related to class. Although all the Chinese immigrant parents wanted their children to become doctors, lawyers, or engineers, not all of them believed that their children would actually *fulfill* their expectations. It was the children of suburban, middle-class families who reported that their parents actively encouraged them to pursue these professions. The children of working-class parents reported that their parents maintained the same ideals *in theory* but at the same time suggested a secondary tier of professions. These professions did not necessarily require years of graduate school and appeared to be more realistic aspirations for their children. Seen in this light, livelihoods like pharmacy, computer science, and accounting may have lacked the prestige of medicine, engineering, and the law, and they generally were not as lucrative, but they were stable occupations nonetheless that brought in a decent income.

When I asked my working-class respondents how their parents knew of occupations that were so far removed from their own frame of reference, my respondents pointed to their parents' use of ethnic networks. They gained information through family members (some of whom had been in the United States much longer), friends, and coworkers in restaurants and garment factories. Much as Min Zhou (1997) has argued, these ethnic networks serve as forms of social capital. My respondents' immigrant parents relied on the information relayed through these networks in particular to navigate the Byzantine bureaucracy of the New York City public school system and learn of magnet junior high schools outside of Chinatown and the city's specialized high schools (Mollenkopf et al. 1997). These networks also channeled information to downtown Chinese parents about which occupations were most viable for their children. This is evident from the following exchange between two Hunter female students whose mothers were both in the garment business, one as a seamstress and the other as an owner.

> Grace: One thing funny is that my mom, they always like to follow trends. Like, if one person's daughter is a pharmacist, that was the "in" thing this year. Being a pharmacist. She would always bring it up. Oh, you know, pharmacists make good money.

> Lily: What other people say, they listen. It's like, the whole workplace is saying, "My kids are into botany," or something, and they'll come home and say, "Why don't you go do botany?" It's always a trend.

What their children ended up pursuing was a further reflection of their parents' status within these ethnic networks, which had such an impact that my respondents did not report their parents feeling that their children were being locked out of the highest-tier professions (such as medicine and the law). Rather, the feeling was that, if the profession had been vetted by the ethnic networks, then it too was something for their children to aim for, and thus something that would give status to the entire family. Nor did my downtown respondents believe that they were being asked to pursue a secondary tier of professions. They understood the prestige attached to those professions for their parents.

To sum up, my second-generation Chinese American respondents—women and men from both uptown and downtown backgrounds—identified technical fields as being particularly Chinese or Asian and located immigrant parents at the heart of this phenomenon. At the same time, there were important class differences in how working-class parents suggested secondary-tier professions to their children that required fewer years of graduate study but nevertheless were seen as conferring prestige. According to my respondents, it was concern about their financial security that led to these parental expectations. In the following section, I turn to the subject of how students responded to these expectations—the majors they actually chose and why. As I demonstrate, while there was considerable common ground here as well, there were also key class differences.

How Children Respond

In the course of my interviews, I identified three groups of students—two groups chose the "Asian fields," for different reasons that at times overlapped, and the third selected non-Asian fields. I also found that social class background often intersected with the decisionmaking process.

The first category of students gravitated toward the "Asian fields" primarily because they wanted to follow the example of family members. For obvious reasons, this scenario occurred mainly in middle-class families in which the parents worked in the mainstream economy. Most working- and even middle-class respondents in the ethnic economy did not perceive their parents' jobs in the restaurant and garment industries as anything to aspire to; rather, they viewed education as a way to avoid such jobs. For middle-class, suburban children, it was a different matter. The experiences of family members provided a particular lens through which to view their own occupational choices. Monica's uncles were all engineers, so it was natural for her to consider engineering as well. Yet one of her uncles pointed to his own experience as a cautionary tale illustrating that basing one's choice on the familiar was not necessarily the best approach:

> He always says, "Just make sure you're happy with whatever you're doing." I think I agree with his views the most. He explained to me how he got into engineering because the family convinced him that, you know, that it was the best thing to do financially. He's still working as an engineer, but I think he's going through like a life change, you know, trying to find something that makes him happier.

The second group of students gravitated toward the "Asian fields" from the intersection of genuine interest and internalization of their parents' values— it was natural for them to think about which fields were secure and which were not. A young woman at Columbia described this process: "Asian parents kind of restrict the fields, like, you know, they probably wouldn't be happy if you majored in art or music, therefore you grow up with the pressure of limiting your own fields, eventually you take on those values." Margaret, a student at Columbia's School of Engineering, exemplified this type of reasoning. She came in thinking that she would pursue biomedical engineering but quickly realized after one class that her abilities did not lie there. In thinking through her options, Margaret never lost sight of the crucial issue: "What else would be a practical thing for me?" The answer in her case turned out to be operational research, a field that uses mathematical or computer models to improve an organization's operations and thus would allow her to pursue a high-paying business career.

Several of these students excelled in the humanities, receiving their best grades in fields that seemed to reflect their true interests. Nonetheless, they continued in engineering, a notoriously rigorous curriculum, or in computer science, another challenging field, or in economics, either because they had already invested so much time or because they thought those fields were more likely to lead to a high-paying job. Paul's story is illustrative. A junior at

Hunter, he was majoring in economics and accounting despite his absorption in philosophy and history, disciplines that he believed gave him a nuanced way of understanding human behavior. His reasoning was as follows:

> I don't really like economics, believe it or not. I mean, if I had my choice, I would major in philosophy and minor in history [*his voice brightens*]. *But* I don't see a future in being a philosophy major. I really don't, so I chose something more practical, a little more practical, so economics is what I chose.

As can be seen in Paul's comments, the idea of choice was more restricted in the lives of working-class respondents. Paul came from Chinatown, where he grew up with his parents and two brothers. The family of five had for many years shared a one-bedroom, tenement apartment; as often happens in tight spaces, studying or having the time to reflect was nearly impossible. If education was to be his ticket to a life outside of Chinatown, then education had to lead to a viable job and career. Seen in this context, economics makes perfect sense, and philosophy makes no sense at all. Such circumstances framed Paul's limited conceptions of choice. In his mind, he really had no choice. His family's financial situation had already made it for him.

A third group of students, both working-class and middle-class, in the ethnic economy and outside it, followed their interests in fields that lay outside the boundaries sanctioned by their parents. Asked what he liked about his major, Robert, a psychology and sociology major, replied, "None of the Asians are doing it." Yet Robert was very proud of being Chinese, and most of his close friends were Chinese American. Still, he was proud that his choice of a major ran counter to the expectations of Chinese immigrant parents— including his own, who wanted him to pursue a career in pharmacy: "You keep on pushing me, I go the other way." He was also cheered by his younger brother's fledgling stand of independence: "He's having doubts about [pharmacy], which is kind of good in the sense of, come on, it's about time you got out of Mom's wings and start to think for yourself. Mom says this, he'll do it. Maybe mumble a word or two."

In this group, Robert was an exception, however, because most of the other students spoke of wrestling with feelings of obligation and their own sense of trepidation at venturing into the unknown, a dilemma they often described in ethnic terms. Joan viewed her decision to major in archaeology as a deeply "American" one insofar as it was rooted in individual choice. Rather than factoring in her parents' wishes, she put faith in her own counsel. At the same time, she believed that she was taking a risk:

I'm thinking, this is my life, and I'm going to do what I want with it. I'm going to pick my major. I'm going to pick my job. Yeah, I've got to do what makes me happy, whereas I could have said, I'm going to be premed because it makes me and my parents happy. That's more of a Chinese decision. I feel guilty when I'm with more traditional Chinese Americans. Guilty because I'm not being practical. I'm not doing the sure thing.

For this group of students, mentors proved crucial. Robert specifically mentioned a generous national fellowship that allowed him to double-major in psychology and sociology and work on research projects with faculty members in both departments. Similarly, following her own interests in archaeology became easier for Joan once she was able to rely on mentors to show her how to make her way through the field. She met the mentors, all women, through classes she took at Columbia and other local colleges and institutions. These academic women introduced her to the world of archaeology, pointing her toward research opportunities and possible career paths. On one level the benefits were personal; as Joan observed: "I need the experience to be confident when I'm applying for a situation. I need to know that I actually do know what's going on, or what to do." But the benefits of mentorship also allowed her to make a stronger case for archaeology to her parents, who became persuaded of the seriousness of her intent: "My parents know they can't change my mind, and now they see that I've taken an actual effort to go to archaeology lab sessions, to go to digs, to talk to people. They're becoming more reconciled to it, as long as they can see I'm serious."

My respondents' accounts of how they chose their majors in the face of parental expectations, particularly the feelings of frustration, obligation, and guilt that many experienced, map onto the long-standing story told of the children of immigrants living between two worlds—that is, second-generation children trying to break free of parental aspirations. A missing element in my respondents' accounts, however, is the role of rebellion—none of them renounced their parents' expectations entirely. I do not mean to suggest that second-generation Chinese Americans do not rebel against their parents' wishes. Because my sample was neither random nor representative, it did not capture the experiences of those Chinese American college students who completely discount their parents' aspirations (and feel comfortable doing so). Even Robert, who saw himself as a rebel for not going into pharmacy, as his parents wanted him to do, was thinking of pursuing an advanced degree in the social sciences, which is still a high-prestige, if not high-paying, path.

In fact, what is interesting to note is the *limited* range of rebellion among my second-generation respondents—from an outsider's perspective. To many people, choosing to double-major in anthropology and economics, as Diana did at Columbia, to pursue a perfectly viable career in consulting for non-profit organizations might seem like a sensible decision. Diana, after all, was not thinking of pursuing a career as a novelist or film actor, notoriously diffi-cult fields to break into. To the students themselves, however, such decisions caused considerable soul-searching and anguish as they tried to negotiate their interests and their parents' very different aspirations for them. (Diana herself was deciding against a career in medicine, which her father wanted her to pursue.) Thus, in ways that were quite real to them, they did believe them-selves to be rebels of a sort, albeit very conflicted ones. What is also true is that along the lines suggested by Dennis Wrong (1976), even those students who completely fulfilled parental expectations by following the prescribed route still felt pressured, since they did not completely share their parents' world-view. This disjuncture was evident when these students spoke of the "Asian parent thing" in terms of the demands and frustration undergone by children and conflict between parents and children.

DIFFERENT SOCIAL WORLDS AND IDENTITY PROCESSES

The common thread in the responses of these students—their internalization of their parents' values about fields of study and careers and their feelings of guilt and obligation, especially when they charted their own paths—proved even more striking given their different educational settings and the varied so-cial identities they were developing in these settings. Just as family class back-ground shaped my respondents' paths to different universities, it figured prominently in how they saw themselves at these schools.

From educational mission to social space, the two colleges in this study were a study in contrasts. Although some of the Hunter students expressed discontent with the school's lack of a central campus area ("it's like high school" was a common refrain), a palpable sense of energy emanated from the four interlocking buildings, particularly during the changeover between classes as the students fanned out en masse into the hallways and onto the es-calators. As they ascended the Sixty-eighth Street subway stop (a reason cited by students for coming to Hunter rather than another CUNY school), stu-dents left behind their old neighborhoods and entered a physical space that embodies a contradiction. Situated in the midst of the Upper East Side, a neighborhood known for prime real estate and wealth, Hunter symbolizes a multi-ethnic, proletariat vision of access to higher education. Reflective of the city's immigrant, racial, and ethnic diversity, it is a place where minorities are the majority and where blacks, Latinos, Asians, whites, native-born and immigrants, twenty-eight-year-old reentry students and eighteen-year-old fresh-men, and young mothers with children all come together in search of an education.[10]

Yet as Alex Trillo (this volume) has documented at another site, my re-spondents expressed discontent at being shut out of the classes necessary for their graduation and, as a result, seeing their stay in school prolonged by sev-eral months to a year. Like the Latino students at La Guardia Community College, the Chinese students I spoke to and observed at Hunter were often perplexed by what they saw as complex and shifting rules governing the num-ber of credits needed to graduate and the work requirements for their classes. Some came to rely more on each other than on already overburdened admin-istrators and faculty.

On the other side of town, Columbia bespoke another kind of geographic inscription. Elite people from all over the nation and, indeed, the world con-gregated at Columbia's thirty-five-acre campus located in Morningside Heights, only blocks away from some of the city's poorest communities. At the time I was in the field, the ongoing construction of a new student center, coupled with the graceful walkways and imposing buildings, contrasted with the decaying housing stock and guarded stares of the pedestrians outside the school boundaries not more than a few blocks north and east.

None of this is to say that diversity was lacking there. Columbia is quite di-verse, especially for an elite institution: minorities made up at least one-third of the university's student population during my year of research.[11] At the same time, Columbia's institutional history of privilege is also evident.

In these two singular social spaces, my Chinese respondents were follow-ing two distinct assimilation patterns. For those respondents whose parents lived, worked, and/or had strong social ties to an ethnic economic enclave, being Chinese was a natural part of their world. They had grown up thinking of themselves as Chinese, an identity that had them speaking a mix of Chinese and English slang with friends (who were also 1.5- and second-generation Chinese American), keeping up with the latest Chinese films, ac-tors, and pop singers from Taiwan and Hong Kong, and attending Chinese pop concerts at nightclubs in Atlantic City, New Jersey. It was a particularly Chinese American world. In this regard, they differed from Sara Lee's work-ing-class Korean Americans, who strove to downplay their ethnicity and not mingle with co-ethnics as a way of avoiding negative comparisons with their "model minority" co-ethnics. The key difference was that Lee's working-class Korean Americans were a minority in a predominantly middle- to upper-middle-class ethnic group, whereas working-class Chinese have played a much more substantial role in the group's immigration patterns.

Thus, for my respondents who came from downtown Chinese backgrounds, their ethnicity was a daily given. It was *class* that they understood as differentiating them from their model minority co-ethnics. This became clear in their takes on the model minority stereotype, which most found alienating, grounded as it was on claims that Asian Americans are super-achievers and often come from wealth, neither of which claims corresponded to their experiences. Added pressures came not only from their parents' expectations for them to attend a four-year college—and ideally a prestigious, private four-year college—but also from the reality that some downtown Chinese children did go on to an elite four-year college like Columbia (as the parents were all too ready to remind their children).[12] In the face of such expectations, these students thought that they had failed in some way by attending Hunter, despite its reputation as one of the top CUNY schools. Hunter was where these students *ended up*. It was not where they wanted or had hoped to be.

And yet, by attending Hunter, a multi-ethnic institution populated by immigrant children of similar socioeconomic background, my working-class respondents found reaffirmation and extension of their ethnic identities. Ironically, this occurred in spite of the rich multi-ethnic dimensions at Hunter; for the most part, my respondents did not do much identity work at the institution itself, since they were busy negotiating school with jobs elsewhere in the city, commuting, and, sometimes, fulfilling family obligations. Additionally, the fact that Hunter was a commuter school allowed my respondents to quite literally go home to their parents and ethnic neighborhoods at night and thus to remain more closely tied to their ethnic identities as they had always known them.

In contrast, those respondents whose parents had settled in predominantly white, suburban communities and had few ties to an ethnic enclave grew up thinking they were little different from their white peers. Ethnicity among these uptown Chinese was largely confined to the home, to ethnic foods, and to the ethnic holidays they occasionally celebrated without knowing much about them (Espiritu 1994; Min and Kim 1999). In other words, it was a diluted form of ethnicity that they were experiencing, one that was tangential to their identities. For many of my uptown Chinese respondents, college was a time of ethnic awakening, either through student ethnic clubs, which provided a literal and symbolic space to engage in identity work, or simply through daily interactions with co-ethnics, often for the first time. At the same time, it was important to many of them, including Victoria, that they were not "abandoning" whites in favor of co-ethnics; rather, they actively sought a balance and blamed themselves if they were too ethnic.

In this process of becoming Chinese American, my uptown respondents at Columbia focused on the shared experiences of growing up as middle-class, second-generation Chinese Americans, but they understood this experience in particularly ethnic terms rather than class terms. This was evident in how these respondents related to the model minority stereotype. In many ways the stereotype of high academic achievement and economic privilege corresponded to their lives. Their parents were in fact doctors and lawyers, and they themselves were attending an elite college. While they were aware of the working-class stream of Chinese immigrants so present in New York City, most of my uptown respondents still believed that the majority of the Chinese were doing well. From this vantage point, my respondents felt that it was only natural that they were at Columbia.

Meanwhile, nearly all the respondents painted New York City as a unique urban environment, one that embraces all manner of racial and ethnic identities and welcomes a steady stream of immigrants, or what Sherri-Ann Butterfield and Alex Trillo have described as "cosmopolitanism." In New York City, my respondents said, being of Chinese descent is nothing out of the ordinary. By the same token, they were quite conscious that New York is a very particular case and that their experiences might be different elsewhere. Although the downtown Chinese recalled encountering hostility from other ethnic groups in the city, they believed that even worse forms of hostility existed *outside* New York City. Even Chinese who had grown up feeling part of their predominantly white communities were uncertain of their welcome in other places where people would not know them as well, and they too regarded New York City as an exception. Said one young man:

> Well, it helps that I'm in New York. There's so many different people here that I think people are a lot more understanding and accepting of differences. I think now because of the whole idea of "You're different, and I'm different. You're okay, I'm okay." Whereas in the past, it was maybe, "Oh, you're not white," like that. At least in New York, I think, I'm pretty much considered an American. I think if I was in maybe, like, Arkansas, maybe not. I'd get looked at differently.

In sum, the marked differences in my respondents' identity development, particularly in relation to the schools they were attending, only made their shared viewpoint on parental aspirations more striking. Thus far, I have focused on the role of social class background in parental aspirations and children's responses. In the next two sections, I address the impact of class and gender, taken together, on the parental message about careers, and I discuss the views of the second generation on their future.

How Class and Gender Matter

In addition to class, there was evidence of differences in parental expectations along the lines of gender, although the general pattern was for parents to have similar career aspirations for their sons and daughters.[13] Both Kim and Lee (this volume) discuss the mixed messages imparted by Korean immigrant parents to their daughters about their domestic and social roles. Like those two authors, I found evidence of some gender distinctions, mainly among Chinese working-class parents, who encouraged their daughters to pursue what one respondent described as "the traditional feminine fields." These families proved the exception rather than the norm, however, a surprising finding given that most working-class parents in my study strove to mold their daughters into "proper" women. The pervasive view among working-class parents was that daughters had to learn how to do women's work, which included but was not limited to chores such as washing the dishes, doing the laundry, sweeping, stocking up on groceries, and, of course, cooking. By grouping these tasks as specific to women, Chinese immigrant parents were attempting to socialize their daughters into traditional gender norms.

The message was clear: even if daughters did not end up performing these chores (and some refused to do them consistently, if at all), they *ought* to know how to perform them, and it was their duty as parents to ensure that those lessons were learned. It was not necessary for sons to learn these tasks because being a man meant something altogether different. Moreover, birth order and sex made little difference. Working-class women who had older brothers were just as likely as their counterparts with younger brothers to say they had to do more domestic chores. In working-class Chinese families, gender-specific conceptions were also expressed in the types of behavior that were considered appropriate for boys as opposed to girls and in the different sanctions they received for misbehaving. Boys were given greater latitude, whereas girls were expected to obey the dictates of their parents without question and faced greater punishment if they did not.

Perhaps not surprisingly, in those working-class families that did differentiate along the lines of gender in their occupational aspirations for their sons and daughters, the theme of "appropriateness" came up often. Benny, a Hunter student, spoke thoughtfully about such gender-based expectations. When he was growing up, his parents made it clear that the most Benny's sisters could hope for were jobs as clerical workers. Professional jobs were the province of men, not women. The longer they spent in the United States, however, the more their attitudes toward gender roles and work changed. What spurred the change was their understanding that things are done differently in America, a point that was made concrete when their daughter decided to join the police force (most definitely not a woman's job) over their vehement disapproval. Deborah, another Hunter student, remembered being steered into certain types of jobs by her mother and raised with the sensibility that girls could not do too much in the working world:

> My mom is very old-fashioned. She didn't think women were suited for certain jobs. [She thought] that women should only work in these lesser jobs. That was the impression I always got when I was growing up. I guess secretary, like, I don't remember specifically, but it was always, don't strive for too much because you're only a girl. That was the impression I got, that, you know, girls only do these things. But I didn't understand what those things were. But I remember having conversations with her where, you know, I would say, oh, I want to do this. But it's like, but you're a girl.

It is important to bear in mind that working-class daughters did not follow their parents' wishes in this area, nor did they experience much anxiety or guilt about not following their parents' wishes (as they did when they pursued fields of study that their parents disapproved of for *both* their daughters and sons).

Middle-class parents, on the other hand, expected both sons and daughters to have high career aspirations. Still, the effects of gender were not entirely absent. Some middle-class parents linked their daughters' education to their eventual roles as mothers. Since these parents largely understood child-rearing as the responsibility of women, their daughters had to have at least enough education to guide their children and serve as appropriate role models. In this vein, Mrs. Chang, Victoria's mother, said: "I think women's education is very important, very, very important, I think more important than men, because we raise the kids, right. Education is very important because we're molding our value in them."

Chinese middle-class parents were also all too aware of the burdens involved with balancing work and family. Since it was a burden that they saw as only affecting women, parents encouraged their daughters to have enough flexibility in their careers to be able to raise a family (Kim 1993). Sons did not receive this message. Mrs. Chang is one such example. She advised her daughter Victoria to pursue medicine in part because she saw it as a convenient way for her to have both a fulfilling career and motherhood. The key was that Victoria could work at the clinic that Dr. and Mrs. Chang had founded and built and she could set her own hours, a luxury she would not have otherwise:

> We think if she can be a doctor, right, she can just work with her dad. And we always say, "You can just work part-time." Because she said, "No.

American River College Library

I'm not going to be a doctor, because Dad has been working too much, too long hours." And I said, my husband also said, "But if you became a doctor, probably you won't have to work like twenty or thirty hours. You don't have to work as much because we started with nothing."

Victoria, however, had her own plans that were not necessarily consistent with her parents' ideas. She did not want to follow her father's path into medicine, nor did she want to be a stay-at-home mom like her mother:

> I think career will come first for me. At least at this point in my life, I see myself establishing a career before even thinking about getting married and having a family. Sometimes I wonder, my mom gave up a lot, she could have had somewhat of a career in journalism or maybe even one at the UN. She did give it up for us, which I'm very grateful for. But then I think sometimes, and I'm like, I wonder if I ever did that, would I regret it? I'm sure she doesn't. Because it worked out pretty well for her. But I think I couldn't be like her. At least at this point in my life. I see so much that I hopefully could be doing. I definitely see that I have a future, and I want to make the most of it before I settle and have family. I'm personally of the opinion that I'm not going to become a housewife, and I'm going to have a career equal of my husband, and I definitely want to have something before I have a family.

Some middle-class parents, both in and outside of the ethnic economy, believed that too much career drive would prove wearing for their daughters and put them in an awkward position. Anita, a Hunter student whose father was a computer teacher around the city and whose mother taught in a GED program in Chinatown, hoped to pursue a career in medicine but was mindful of her parents' advice about women, careers, and family:

> Ever since I was a little kid, I was aware that I would have a family one day. So choosing what I wanted for my education, and how far I wanted to go professionally, was difficult. My father had told me that it's very difficult if you wanted to have a career and a family at the same time as a woman. He always brought to my attention that it's difficult to have both if that's what you want. They told me, when you have a kid, the first couple of years, you want to be with them, you don't want to leave, you see them grow up really fast, and you want to be there for them for their own personal experience. You don't want to lose out on that.

CHILDREN'S VIEW OF THE FUTURE

Gender and class also influenced the second generation's aspirations for the future. When asked where they saw themselves in ten years, women respondents always brought up the issue of work. They clearly imagined themselves performing some kind of paid work outside the home. But there were differences in the kind of work they envisioned for themselves. Middle-class women thought in terms of careers—they would be doctors, engineers, lawyers, and real estate entrepreneurs. Take Monica, for example: "I'm still trying to decide between med school or staying in engineering or, you know, some other profession entirely. And if I choose medicine, then I'll still probably be in med school. But otherwise in a career doing something." A minority of the middle-class respondents put marriage and motherhood first and then career. These women could easily picture themselves being stay-at-home moms, just as their own mothers had been.

Working-class women, on the other hand, spoke of jobs in generic terms, not of specific careers. Grace said it best: "Working. I see myself working." This does not mean that working-class women saw themselves in traditional women's vocations, such as secretarial work. Rather, their comments spoke to the challenges they perceived with finding employment in whatever field they chose. They were mainly concerned with finishing school (which was never in doubt for middle-class women), obtaining a stable job, and achieving financial security. Few talked about choosing work over children; it was assumed that they would have to manage both (as their own mothers had done).

Men expressed a similar desire to have both a family and a career that also varied somewhat by class. Middle-class men thought in terms of careers, and working-class men expressed anxieties about getting a job. However, both working- and middle-class men hoped for marriage and children in their future. The difference was that all men viewed themselves primarily as the breadwinner. No mention was ever made of any potential conflict between family and work responsibilities. Nor did any of the men see themselves in the future staying at home to raise the children. In short, Chinese American men imagined a life uncomplicated by family.

Both working-class women and men, however, expected some kind of white-collar work. The point of acquiring higher education (in their minds as well as in their parents' minds) was to avoid not only the labor-intensive ethnic economy jobs of their parents (the restaurant, the garment factory) but also blue-collar jobs in general, even those in the mainstream economy. For them, the choice was between the ethnic economy and white-collar jobs. Many believed that they could not legitimately aspire to be like their model minority co-ethnics, but on the other hand, they knew of enough co-ethnics from more modest origins who were able to use their education to gain entrée to professional jobs, or at the very least, an office job. Thus, the lessons their parents had taught them about education and mobility were reinforced by the mobility they saw among co-ethnics whose backgrounds were in some measure similar to their own.

HISTORICAL AND CONTEMPORARY COMPARISONS TO OTHER GROUPS

In this chapter, I have tried to give depth to how second-generation Chinese Americans of diverse family social class backgrounds, who attended different colleges, understood the role of the family in their fields of study and their careers. Would I have found something similar in the occupational preferences of parents and their efforts to influence children among other immigrant or native-born groups? Historically, for example, we know that ethnicity has been associated with a group's occupational preferences in New York City, a phenomenon that Nathan Glazer and Daniel Patrick Moynihan (1970, xxxiii) aptly attributed to group members' "distinctive historical experiences, cultures and skills, the times of their arrival and the economic situation they met." Nor is this a New York City–specific phenomenon, as Stanley Lieberson and Mary Waters (1988) demonstrate, using census and other national-level data. If we were to look at the first wave of European immigration to the United States and their descendants, we would see that Jews, for example, have been concentrated in the garment industry, teaching, and other professions (Slater 1969; Glazer and Moynihan 1970; Steinberg 1981) and that Italians have taken jobs that rely on both skilled and unskilled labor (Glazer and Moynihan 1970).

Contemporary comparisons along these lines are scarce. However, a review of one-fourth of the in-depth interviews from the Second Generation Study reveals that across the different native-born and immigrant groups there were similarities between the Russian Jews and the Chinese in how they spoke of the parental pressure surrounding careers and the focus on professions. Like the Chinese in my study, the Russian Jews also spoke of their parents framing careers in terms of which were "stable" and "practical."

It is worth noting, however, the important differences in the samples that may affect choice of career. For example, among the Russian Jewish sample, even among the children of highly educated parents, the emphasis was on professional jobs that did not require several years of graduate study. Thus, across class, second-generation Russian Jews said that their parents suggested fields like computer science; in doing so, Russian Jewish parents used the same kind of rationale that only the parents of my working-class Chinese respondents did in endorsing a secondary tier of professions for their children to pursue, as opposed to medicine and the law. This preference was related not only to financial considerations but also to the fact that Russian Jews typically want to start their families by their mid to late twenties. Another important factor to keep in mind when comparing these two groups is that the arrival of these first-generation Russian Jews, even the highly educated segment, represents a more recent stream of migration. Thus, their children may have had less time to adjust to the educational system, and the family may have more pressing financial needs, compared to the uptown Chinese families in my study. This difference in immigration experience can certainly affect the kinds of occupational choices that parents favor for their children.[14]

CONCLUSIONS

In this study, second-generation Chinese American college students from diverse social class backgrounds reported that their parents expected them to pursue a narrow set of fields of study that the parents viewed as a route to financially secure careers. Words like "safe," "secure," and "practical" were routinely used to describe these fields and to contrast them with those that Chinese immigrant parents viewed as dangerous, and highly impractical. As my respondents told it, such parental aspirations crossed class and gender lines.

Class did matter, however. While Chinese working-class parents hoped that their children would pursue medicine, law, engineering, and the like, such outcomes seemed unlikely given the commitment of money and time involved. Drawing from ethnic networks, these parents championed a secondary tier of technical professions (pharmacy, computer science, accounting) for their children that involved fewer hurdles and were more likely to be within their financial reach. Nevertheless, these fields represented high prestige within the Chinese enclave.

Class also mattered in how 1.5- and second-generation children made sense of and responded to these parental aspirations. It was reasonable that middle-class children would follow their parents into professional occupations, while working-class children found themselves limited by economic constraints in their academic decisions. Yet both middle- and working-class children found themselves grappling with their internalization of their parents' messages about fields of study as they made their decisions. Their experiences were remarkably similar, even though they were developing different ethnic identities and making their way through such distinctive educational settings.

Gender and class also had a role in shaping the types of aspirations that immigrant parents had for their children and how children saw the future. Some working-class parents worried about which fields were "appropriate" for women to pursue, while middle-class parents were more likely to worry about how their daughters could combine high-octane careers with their eventual child-rearing responsibilities. Women from downtown backgrounds were more concerned about finding work and understood that they would be balancing work with family commitments. Their middle-class counterparts, on the other hand, never doubted that they would easily land professional jobs. Across class, men saw their future as uncomplicated by family, although working-class men expressed anxiety about finding white-collar work.

Choosing a field of study and, upon graduation, a career are only two steps, albeit key ones, in the transition from college to the workplace and the attempt to climb the mobility ladder. It remains to be seen where these second-generation Chinese Americans will end up. As far as class is concerned, the downtown Chinese seem likely to join the ranks of the middle-class mainstream, and the uptown Chinese will probably reproduce their parents' upper-class status. It is less clear where they will settle, if indeed they remain in the New York area. The uptown Chinese might be most comfortable living in largely white neighborhoods with perhaps a few co-ethnics; some downtown Chinese might settle in these areas but they seem more likely to live in neighborhoods that were once all-white but have a growing presence of middle-class co-ethnics. Future research should be done on whether second-generation Chinese American respondents like these attempt to socialize their own children with a utilitarian view of education and careers (and continue seeing it as an ethnic phenomenon) or whether they become less ethnically distinctive, and more like the mainstream, in their parenting strategies.

NOTES

1. Asian Indians, for example, have the highest attainment rates, and East Asians (Chinese, Japanese, and Koreans) also fare well, while Southeast Asians (Laotians, Hmong, and Cambodians) have the lowest levels of education (Espiritu 1997). Among Chinese, 29 percent of the nation's Chinese immigrants have less than a high school education, while 39 percent have a bachelor's degree or higher. Among native-born Chinese, about 33 percent have a college degree, but 24 percent have only a high school diploma or less (Weinberg 1997).

2. My research drew mainly on interview respondents from Columbia College but included three respondents from Barnard and four from the engineering school. Barnard and the engineering school maintain their own faculty, curriculum, administration, operating budget, and admissions. Both Barnard and engineering students, however, can take classes at Columbia College and participate in the same undergraduate organizations.

3. Sau-Fong Siu (1996) notes that since 1980 attention has increasingly been paid to Asian Americans who are at risk of school failure, particularly Southeast Asians. However, similar attention has not been given to students attending community and city colleges.

4. As Hsiang-shui Chen (1992) observes, the ethnic economic enclave comprises several different class categories: the capitalist class, who own large factories, companies, hotels, and restaurants; the small-business class, who own knitting factories, small shops, and restaurants; the new middle class, who are professionals, civil servants, and doctors; and the working class, the people who labor in the stores, garment factories, and restaurants.

5. Although I did not have data on family income, I used the parents' education and occupations as proxies.

6. I introduced the project to classes in economics, sociology, geography, Chinese language, and Asian American studies. At Columbia the dean of students was kind enough to write a letter introducing my project to all the Asian American sophomores, juniors, and seniors and provided my contact information to those who wished to participate.

7. I spoke with the adult sister of a respondent over the phone, and I communicated with the adult brother of another respondent by e-mail.

8. For further discussion of how Asian Americans, particularly the second generation, relate to pan-ethnicity in their daily lives, see Louie (2003), Kibria (2002), and Espiritu (1992).

9. Joan's father was a garment presser, but her mother, who had taken English-language classes, spoke English fluently and did accounting work for an uptown, white-owned firm.

10. According to figures released by the Office of Institutional Research at Hunter, the student population was 39.1 percent white, 20.1 percent black, 23.3 percent Hispanic, 17.3 percent Asian or Pacific Islander, and 0.2 percent Native American or Alaskan.

11. According to figures released by the Office of Planning and Institutional Research at Columbia, Asian Americans made up 17 percent of Columbia College's student population in the fall of 1998, blacks 9 percent, and Hispanics 7.2 percent; more than 10 percent of the students were categorized as being of unknown race.

12. Survey data from the Immigrant Second Generation in Metropolitan New York Study also suggest this significant upward mobility on the part of some downtown Chinese. Although children whose fathers worked in a restaurant were more likely to attend a regional II school like Hunter (43 percent), 19 percent attended a national I school like Columbia. This pattern remained consistent when looking at children whose mothers worked in the garment industry. The restaurant and garment industries are among the leading employers in the Chinese economic enclaves of New York City.

13. This may have to do with the expectation among Chinese immigrant parents that even if their daughters marry, they are likely to continue to work, just to maintain a higher standard of living. This expectation is also in keeping with the national trend toward dual-income families in the United States.

14. I wish to thank Jennifer Holdaway for these insights regarding the Russian Jewish sample in the Second Generation Study compared to the Chinese in my study.

References

Chen, Hsiang-shui. 1992. *Chinatown No More: Taiwan Immigrants in Contemporary New York*. Ithaca, N.Y.: Cornell University Press.

Chronicle of Higher Education. 2000. Almanac issue. Vol. 47, no. 1(September 1).

Elliot, Rogers, A. Christopher Strenta, Russell Adair, Michael Matier, and Jannah Scott. 1996. "The Role of Ethnicity in Choosing and Leaving Science in Highly Selective Institutions." *Research in Higher Education* 37(6): 681–709.

Espiritu, Yen Le. 1992. *Asian American Pan-ethnicity: Bridging Institutions and Identities*. Philadelphia: Temple University Press.

———. 1994. "The Intersection of Race, Ethnicity, and Class: The Multiple Identities of Second-Generation Filipinos." *Identities* 9(2–3): 249–73.

———. 1997. *Asian American Women and Men*. Thousand Oaks, Calif.: Sage Publications.

Glazer, Nathan, and Daniel Patrick Moynihan. 1970. *Beyond the Melting Pot: The Negroes, Puerto Ricans, Jews, Italians, and Irish of New York City*. 2nd ed. Cambridge, Mass.: MIT Press.

Hune, Shirley. 1998. "Asian Pacific American Women in Higher Education: Claiming Visibility and Voice." Washington: Association of American Colleges and Universities, Program on the Status and Education in Women.

Jacobs, Jerry A. 1996. "Gender, Race, and Ethnic Segregation Between and Within Colleges." Paper presented to the annual meeting of the American Sociological Association. New York, August 16–20.

Kibria, Nazli. 2002. *Becoming Asian American*. Baltimore: Johns Hopkins University Press.

Kim, Eun-Young. 1993. "Career Choice Among Second-Generation Korean Americans: Reflections of a Cultural Model of Success." *Anthropology and Education Quarterly* 24(3): 224–48.

Kwong, Peter. 1987. *The New Chinatown*. New York: Noonday Press.

Lee, Stacey. 1996. *Unraveling the "Model Minority" Stereotype: Listening to Asian American Youth*. New York: Teachers College Press.

Lieberson, Stanley, and Mary C. Waters. 1988. *From Many Strands: Ethnic and Racial Groups in Contemporary America*. New York: Russell Sage Foundation.

Louie, Vivian. 2001. "Parents' Aspirations and Investment: The Role of Social Class in the Educational Experiences of 1.5- and Second-Generation Chinese Americans." *Harvard Educational Review* (special issue on immigration and education) 71(3, Fall): 438–74.

———. 2003. "'Becoming' and 'Being' Chinese American in College: A Look at Ethnicity, Social Class, and Neighborhood in Identity Development." In *Immigrant Life in the U.S.: Multidisciplinary Perspectives*, edited by Donna Gabaccia and Colin Wayne Leach. New York: Routledge Press.

———. 2004. *Compelled to Excel: Immigration, Education, and Opportunity Among Chinese Americans*. Stanford, Calif.: Stanford University Press.

Lyman, Stanford. 1974. *Chinese Americans*. New York: Random House.

Min, Pyong Gap, and Rose Kim. 1999. *Struggle for Ethnic Identity: Narratives by Asian American Professionals.* Walnut Creek, Calif.: Altamira Press.

Mollenkopf, John, Philip Kasinitz, Mary Waters, Nancy López, and Dae Young Kim. 1997. "The School-to-Work Transition of Second-Generation Immigrants in Metropolitan New York: Some Preliminary Findings." Paper presented to the Levy Institute Conference on the Second Generation. Bard College, Annandale-on-Hudson, N.Y., October 25.

Siu, Sau-Fong. 1996. "Asian American Students at Risk: A Literature Review." Report 8. Baltimore and Washington: Johns Hopkins University and Howard University, Center for Research on the Education of Students Placed at Risk.

Siu, Sau-Fong, and Jay Feldman. 1995. "Success in School: The Journey of Two Chinese American Families." Report 31. Baltimore: Johns Hopkins University, Center on Families, Communities, Schools, and Children's Learning (October).

Slater, Miriam. 1969. "My Son the Doctor: Aspects of Mobility Among American Jews." *American Sociological Review* 34: 359–73.

Steinberg, Stephen. 1981. *The Ethnic Myth: Race, Ethnicity, and Class in America.* New York: Atheneum.

Tang, Joyce, and Earl Smith, eds. 1996. *Women and Minorities in American Professions.* Albany: State University of New York Press.

Weinberg, Meyer. 1997. *Asian-American Education: Historical Background and Current Realities.* Mahwah, N.J.: Lawrence Erlbaum Associates.

Wong, Morrison. 1995a. "Chinese Americans." In *Asian Americans: Contemporary Issues and Trends*, edited by Pyong Gap Min. Thousand Oaks, Calif.: Sage Publications.

———. 1995b. "The Education of White, Chinese, Filipino, and Japanese Students: A Look at `High School and Beyond.'" In *The Asian American Educational Experience: A Sourcebook for Teachers and Students*, edited by Don T. Nakanishi and Tina Yamano Nishida. New York: Routledge.

Wrong, Dennis. 1976. "The Oversocialized Conception of Man in Modern Sociology." In *Skeptical Sociology.* New York: Columbia University Press.

Zhou, Min. 1997. "Segmented Assimilation: Issues, Controversies, and Recent Research on the New Second Generation." *International Migration Review* 31(4): 975–1008.

PART II

WORK

No part of the contemporary immigrant experience has received more attention or stirred up more controversy than the impact of immigrants on the labor market (see, for examples, Portes 1995). Since most immigrants come to the United States to work, it is understandable that many Americans worry about the effect on their own jobs and wages of the prevalence of immigrant workers in the U.S. labor market. Questions about whether immigration hurts American workers and to what extent any negative effects are offset by the benefits it brings to Americans as consumers and taxpayers remain controversial, and attempts to answer them definitively rarely produce consensus, although they have kept a number of policy analysts, economists, and demographers gainfully employed and will probably continue to do so for some time to come.

Sociologists and other social scientists have looked at the actual conditions of immigrant workers in some detail, explored how immigrants use their social networks to concentrate in certain jobs and industries, and analyzed how the resulting "ethnic niches," "ethnic enclaves," or "ethnic economies" in turn affect their adaptation and that of their U.S.-born children (Wilson and Portes 1980; Waldinger 1996; Light and Gold 2000). Rich as this literature may be, it has had a hard time linking different levels of data. Numerous studies have looked at hiring conditions and workplace dynamics in specific industries for specific groups, yet they rarely add up to an overall picture of the labor market. On the other hand, quantitative studies seeking to paint a broad picture are limited to broad categories of groups, industries, and occupations and can only speculate about how general trends are linked to hiring or business practices within the firms that make up those broad sectors.

However difficult the problems are in studying immigrants in the labor force, they are multiplied when our study turns to their U.S.-born children. Only the Census Bureau's Current Population Survey (CPS) collects data on foreign parentage, and it is far from ideal for studying local labor markets and specific groups in any detail. Other data sources (like the census public use microdata samples [PUMS]) do not identify the second generation or use large pseudo-categories like "Hispanic" or "Asian," which obscure as much as they explain. Our study, along with parallel efforts in Miami, San Diego, and Los Angeles (see Portes and Rumbaut 2001), attempts to address this problem; all of these studies are limited to a given labor market.

If the data are limited, we have no shortage of speculation about the emerging labor market position of the second generation. Herbert Gans's (1992) "second-generation decline" thesis is based on how the second generation is presumed to react to a hypothesized economic exclusion, while Alejandro Portes and Min Zhou's (1993) model of segmented assimilation is based on assumptions about how parental and second-generation labor market position shape second-generation identity.

The two case studies in this section clearly do not answer the large questions about where the second generation will end up in the labor market compared to their native peers. Indeed, no ethnography or case study could do so. But they do address some of the key hypotheses raised in the studies speculating on how work life shapes the social identity of the second generation. There is more to work than economics, and labor plays too large a role in life to be left to the economists. Having a full-time job is one of the markers of adulthood for young people. For second-generation New Yorkers who grew up in segregated neighborhoods and schools, the workplace often provides their first encounter with large numbers of people who are ethnically different from themselves, including native whites.

The second-generation work experience also differentiates them strongly from their immigrant parents, who are highly concentrated in "ethnic niche" jobs. (The first-generation parents of our eighteen- to thirty-two-year-old respondents, being roughly thirty-five to sixty-five themselves, are even more "immigrant" in this respect than the foreign-born as a whole.) Almost half of the mothers of the Dominican and South American respondents and more than half of the Chinese mothers worked in manufacturing—mostly garment manufacturing. Forty-three percent of the Chinese fathers worked in restaurants, and 38 percent of the West Indian mothers were nurses or nurse's aides. In stark contrast to these patterns, the occupation distributions of our second-generation respondents were much more like those of all New Yorkers their age and gender.

This does not mean they worked *with* other New Yorkers—though they usually did. Only one-third of our Chinese respondents reported that most of their coworkers were Chinese, and only 27 percent said their supervisor was also Chinese. Working mostly with co-ethnics was reported by only one-fifth to one-quarter of the other second-generation groups, except for children of

South American immigrants, for whom the figure was under one in ten. No second-generation group was as likely to work with co-ethnics as were native African Americans.

The chapters in part 2 tell us something about what this means. Dae Young Kim examines the children of an economically successful and entrepreneurial immigrant group. Their parents were mostly self-employed professionals or small-business owners with considerable assets to pass on to the their children. Yet, counter to our stereotypes about entrepreneurial immigrants, few of these second-generation Koreans wanted to take over their parents' business, nor did the parents want them to. Kim reports that Korean parents viewed small-business ownership as a one-generation detour that would finance their children's education. They expected their children—indeed, often strongly pressured them—to regain upper-middle-class professional status in the *mainstream* American economy. As a result, children rarely went into the family business and were seen as failures if they did. (Kim's study used a "distinctive Korean name" sample to combine a telephone survey and in-depth interviews parallel to our main survey.)

Victoria Malkin presents an account of the daily lives of young retail workers, the most common job held by our second-generation respondents, and indeed by all New Yorkers their age. Along with fast-food jobs (Newman 1999), retail jobs are the most common "first jobs" held by Americans today. For the shop-floor workers studied by Malkin, the midtown housewares store that employed them was a step into the larger world. It took them out of working-class, ethnic neighborhoods and brought them into the heart of the nation's largest and most diverse city. In the store they worked and became friends with people from a wide variety of immigrant and native minority backgrounds, but served native whites, who were both customers and supervisors. Many were coming into frequent contact with large numbers of native whites for the first time through this job.

The promise of this new world was often illusory. Low wages and constantly changing "part-time" schedules made it impossible for them to support themselves, while "split shifts" and seasonal work schedules prevented them from taking an additional job or pursuing further education. Like Kim's respondents, these second-generation young people did not want to remain in the ethnically bounded world of their parents, although their "assimilation" took the form of more contact with each other than with natives. Unlike Kim's respondents, however, they could not achieve financial independence. They were poised on the edge of "mainstream" adulthood—and were expected to look and dress the part—but they survived on what would be considered a teenager's salary in other parts of the country. They sought solace through achieving a personal style of presentation that affirmed their multicultural selves. This style was rooted in the multiracial world of popular entertainment—the lingua franca of young adults—and allowed them to be independent in the one realm they saw all around themselves: consumption. These twentysomethings might not have been able to rent their own place, but living with their parents enabled them to buy fashionable sweaters. On the shop floor they learned far more about their roles and rights as consumers than as workers—or as citizens.

REFERENCES

Gans, Herbert. 1992. "Second Generation Decline: Scenarios for the Economic and Ethnic Futures of the Post-1965 American Immigrants." *Ethnic and Racial Studies* 15(2): 173–93.

Light, Ivan, and Steven J. Gold. 2000. *Ethnic Economies*. San Diego: Academic Press.

Newman, Katherine. 1999. *No Shame in My Game: The Working Poor in the Inner City*. New York: Alfred A. Knopf and Russell Sage Foundation.

Portes, Alejandro, ed. 1995. *The Economic Sociology of Immigration: Essays on networks, Ethnicity, and Entrepreneurship*. New York: Russell Sage Foundation.

Portes, Alejandro, and Rubén Rumbaut. 2001. *Legacies: The Story of the Second Generation*. New York and Berkeley: Russell Sage Foundation and University of California Press.

Portes, Alejandro, and Min Zhou. 1993. "The New Second Generation: Segmented Assimilation and Its Variants." *The Annals of the American Academy of Political and Social Science* 530: 74–97.

Waldinger, Roger. 1996. *Still the Promised City*. Berkeley: University of California Press.

Wilson, Kenneth L., and Alejandro Portes. 1980. "Immigrant Enclaves: An Analysis of the Labor Market Experiences of Cubans in Miami." *American Journal of Sociology* 86: 297.

CHAPTER 5

WHO'S BEHIND THE COUNTER? RETAIL WORKERS IN NEW YORK CITY

Victoria Malkin

A WALK DOWN Thirty-fourth Street in Manhattan's midtown becomes a corporate shopping oasis; music, clothes, cosmetics, and shoe stores compete for clientele from New York City and beyond. But anyone entering these stores will see that while customers cram the aisles, try on clothes, discard items, hunt for bargains, and return goods, a small army of employees, many of them indistinguishable from the shoppers, are wandering the floor, restocking shelves, responding to customers, and fighting with faulty cash registers. This labor force represents one cross-section of New York City's population—mobile, mostly young, and as diverse as the shops in which they work. The importance of retail as an employment sector for young adults in New York City is evident not only from anecdotal accounts of shopping in Manhattan's midtown mall but from the Immigrant Second Generation in Metropolitan New York Study's data, which show retail to be an employment sector in which all ethnic groups participate to some extent (see table 5.1).

In this chapter, I use the case study of one corporate retail chain to examine this workplace and its employees. Retail workers interact with a corporate power structure, experiencing and responding to managerial systems that exercise control in novel ways—from direct supervision to the technological and bureaucratic measures that are part of any contemporary workforce (Lamphere, Stepick, and Grenier 1994, 9)—while at the same time they are involved in complex social interactions with the customers whom they serve.

The focus on the workplace as a space that "restructures" diversity is nothing new (Lamphere, Stepick, and Grenier 1994). Nevertheless, this chapter departs from the focus on immigrant low-wage work sectors, immigrant en-

TABLE 5.1   EMPLOYMENT AMONG EIGHTEEN- TO THIRTY-FIVE-YEAR-OLDS, BY GROUP AND BY INDUSTRY

	Colombian, Ecuadorean, and Peruvian	Dominican	Puerto Rican	West Indian	Native Black	Chinese	Russian Jewish	Native White
Agriculture, fishing, forestry and mining		0.3		0.3				0.3
Construction	1.3	2.0	2.0	1.4	5.8	2.4	2.3	2.6
Manufacturing	7.4	6.5	4.3	5.2	3.1	8.5	4.6	11.3
Transportation, communications, and public utilities	9.7	8.5	7.3	10.1	9.6	6.1	3.2	9.4
Wholesale and retail trade	22.5	26.1	28.7	22.0	14.3	19.8	25.2	16.1
Finance, insurance, and real estate	14.8	7.8	7.7	10.1	6.8	16.2	11.0	12.9
Business repair and personal services	17.1	14.7	17.0	11.5	20.5	18.1	21.1	16.1
Professional services	22.8	30.0	28.0	32.5	30.7	25.9	31.2	25.5
Public administration	4.4	4.2	5.0	6.6	9.2	3.1	1.4	5.8
Total (numbers)	298	307	300	286	293	425	218	310

Source: Adapted from Zeltzer-Zubida (2003); data from the Immigrant Second Generation in Metropolitan New York Survey sample.

claves, and "immigrant entrepreneurs," all of which have contributed to the revitalization of New York's outer boroughs and inner-city neighborhoods. Instead, it focuses on the corporate retail sector—a sector that depends on as large a customer base as possible in a city famous for its consumer choices. It also needs "acculturated" employees who have the skills necessary to interact with a demanding and often confused public. Native minorities, white ethnics, and the children of immigrants are all assets to the corporate employer seeking a diverse labor force to match and serve its varied customer base (Goode 1994; Waldinger 1999; Waldinger and Lichter 2003, 132–78).

To date, research has been more focused on documenting how economic restructuring, labor demand, and immigrant or ethnic networks permit the emergence of ethnic niches, ethnic enclaves, and the sectoral concentration of different groups in specific labor markets (Goode 1994; Kim 1999; Logan and Alba 1999; Lopez and Feliciana 2000; Portes 1995; Rath and Kloosterman 2000; Waldinger 1996; Wilson 1999), all the while asking whether these social formations restrict or encourage economic and social mobility among different groups (see, for example, Logan and Alba 1999; Wilson 1999). An ecological model of assimilation and ethnic succession provides the backbone for a popular version of an American Dream: immigrants in ethnic enclaves or ethnic niches work hard and eventually move out to a suburban, symbolically white suburb. This literature highlights ethnicity's role as a catapult into the job market: ethnicity creates the "ties that bind," and the job market is organized by these social networks constructed through and within ethnic ideologies (Waldinger 1996, 1999). "Culture" here determines the job market through the primacy of ethnic ties over other ties and plays a main role in ensuring that immigrants stay ethnics. Meanwhile, the employees funneled through ethnic networks overwhelm other open or bureaucratic hiring practices, closing off these employment opportunities to other groups. Even without conscious intent on the part of managers, these networks can emerge to dominate a company, niche, or profession (Waldinger and Lichter 2003, 14). And with this fait accompli, managers then adhere to cultural explanations to understand certain (ethnic) workers as model employees, thus sealing the cycle and avoiding the structural realities that created the model (ethnic) worker in the first place (Waldinger and Lichter 2003, 172–76; Waters 1999). The power of this analysis is in its ability to unpack the role that social relations and ethnicity play in an "open" labor market: the focus is primarily on explaining how and why exclusion and difference remain in a job market in which a free market ideology posits human capital as the determinant of success. Furthermore, a labor market organized through ethnicity provides a sociological analysis to understand those groups that stubbornly refuse to follow the standardized model of assimilation that remains essential to the American Dream.

Such a model understands diversity in the low-wage workplace as a state of flux—the product of an ethnic succession in which one group is in the process of replacing or competing with another. In this model the workplace is represented as a social site that re-creates and reconfirms ethnic difference and tensions in spite of descriptions of friendship and cooperation taking place at individual levels (Newman 1999, 106–19; Goode and Schneider 1994, 151–60; Grenier et al. 1992). The labor market is primarily represented as a mechanism to preserve ethnicity and difference and as a site of conflict and competition among groups that aim to succeed each other and among whom ethnicity remains the most important defining feature. The limitations of this model are twofold: as it focuses on the level of the workplace, the individual remains a static concept over time. Social interactions in the workspace are not assumed to alter individuals and their concept of difference, or if they do, this is not assumed to change the nature of the competition and ultimately the niche itself. The relation between the individual actor and the niche thus remains undertheorized over time (Wilson 1999). Second, while restructuring and ethnic niches can encourage ethnic conflict and difference, the work space in the low-wage sector takes multiple forms. Methodologically it remains easier to find and investigate what is obvious and different—segmented labor markets occupied by specific ethnic and immigrant groups—especially when this contradicts a free market, ecological, and economic model of assimilation. Ethnic niches and enclaves and immigrant entrepreneurs are all visible "subjects" of and for research, even when many immigrants and ethnics are employed in diverse work sites that are not undergoing ethnic succession. The data from the Immigrant Second Generation in Metropolitan New York Survey sample suggest that large numbers of young adults in New York are employed in "multicultural" work sites (table 5.2). Very few are working in sites where their own ethnic group dominates, although in many cases race plays a more significant role and the workplace is more likely to be segregated according to race. Whites were the group most likely to state that they worked in "mostly" white work spaces.

The composition of many of these mixed work sites may be biased, unbalanced, and unfair in many ways, but they are not necessarily the product of ethnic competition. Large numbers of small businesses, companies, and organizations follow this model. In spite of tensions, these social milieus may provide the chance for new commonalties to form based on class, work, generation, or profession, challenging the cultural stereotypes that pervade a society where "cultural difference" is endlessly celebrated through a multicultural lens and other forms of identification and social action are negated as a peripheral concern (Hodson 1995). In this chapter, I examine one example of a work space that remains diverse through managerial and bureaucratic poli-

TABLE 5.2   RACIAL AND ETHNIC COMPOSITION OF WORK SITES
AMONG YOUNG ADULT NEW YORKERS

Group	Supervisor and Coworkers of Same Ethnicity as Respondent	Coworkers of Same Ethnicity as Respondent	Supervisor and Coworkers of Same Race as Respondent	Coworkers of Same Race as Respondent
Colombian, Ecuadorean, and Peruvian	2.1%	10.1%	13.4%	43.1%
Dominican	6.4	21.5	19	52.8
Puerto Rican	13.8	30	15.9	46.6
West Indian	6.7	23.8	24.7	56.8
Native black	23.9	41	27.6	60.5
Chinese	27.4	31.3	29.1	40
Russian Jewish	8.7[a]	22.5[b]	72.2	83.6
Native white	14.3	24.2	74.4	81.7

Source: Table from Zeltzer-Zubida (2003); data from the Immigrant Second Generation in Metropolitan New York Survey sample.
Note: Respondents were asked to self-report the race and ethnicity of "most" of their coworkers.
[a] An additional 9.2 percent work with Jewish supervisors and coworkers.
[b] An additional 10.9 percent work with Jewish coworkers.

cies (Lamphere, Stepick, and Grenier 1994; Waldinger and Lichter 2003). This provides a contrast with those studies that focus on the low-wage workplace as a story of ethnic succession and competition. I find that management hiring practices have not generated an "ethnic shop" floor, nor are employee networks structured exclusively or primarily through ethnicity. The diverse shop floor is more a reflection of New York City's demographics and the networks available to young adults than a conscious company policy, although it remains to a company's advantage to avoid a mono-ethnic workforce. I detail the company's labor practices and how these affect employees' social and economic mobility in very real ways, but perhaps more important, I examine how this social space engenders interactions that influence individuals' identity, their sense of themselves, and their place in the world in ways that are far more complex than the idea of a subject created through ethnicity alone (Hodson 1991, 1995). The microprocesses on the shop floor structure identity in different ways, emphasizing class, power, and race; they confirm a hierarchy of exclusion based on real experiences and allow identities to emerge, often guided by images from popular culture. Most important for the debates pertinent to the idea of an "immigrant second generation," I conclude that ethnicity remains a less salient category for these young adults in understanding their social position and identity than the material realities and constraints they face.

The chapter begins with a brief discussion of the retail sector and the study site. I then discuss how company policies influence the hiring process to create a diverse workforce that remains "flexible" enough to satisfy the retail cycle. I continue by looking at company practices instigated to centralize distribution and control store operations, and I consider how these policies, alongside other social interactions on the shop floor, play a role in structuring these young people's identity, either as workers or as other subjects in the city. Employees respond to management control by trying to create a meaningful social space where satisfaction is derived emotionally through their friendships and interactions with coworkers. Meanwhile, their wages allow them to enter into a consumer economy, fashioning a sense of self derived from images of consumption that each worker carefully cultivates. The chapter therefore speaks to a series of broader issues about how young workers, in particular those in the low-wage sector, manage in the face of the city's ongoing economic restructuring.

THE RETAIL SECTOR IN NEW YORK CITY

The retail sector is the nation's largest employer, with 15.2 million jobs in 2000 (Berman 2001).[1] Not only does this sector offer below-average hourly wages, but its average workweek in 2002 was twenty-nine hours (U.S. Department of Labor 2003).[2] New York City's retail sector has played a major role in the city's employment and opportunity structure. The city's economy is driven by the financial sector, but retail remains a crucial local job market whose workers are vulnerable to both the external economic changes that influence consumer demand and the changing nature of the retail sector itself.[3] Corporate retailers provide employment to both first-time job-seekers (Newman 1999) and other low-wage workers. This workplace is therefore an important rite of passage for many young people as they integrate into the city.

The retail sector is more than a labor market. Consumption is one of the cultural practices that forged the modern city, creating a new experience for residents who, as shoppers, could imagine a world outside of their personal borders (Leach 1993). While New York was once a city of department stores that were part of the modern imagination, it is increasingly dominated by corporate chain stores, which continually expand into the outer boroughs, economic development zones, and lower-income neighborhoods alongside the Korean and Dominican grocery stores, which recognized the spending power of the inner city long before Nike discovered Michael Jordan. Over the past decade the corporate retail sector has exploded to dominate New York's fashionable downtown shopping areas such as midtown and Soho. This sector reflects and contributes to many of the cultural and economic shifts experienced in the city: the upper and middle classes no longer claim exclusive rights to shopping as a leisure activity (Benson 1986; Leach 1993). Everyone is increasingly reminded of their *right* to consume, as witnessed in the Old Navy billboards that announced in 1999 to anyone who may have forgotten, "Shopping Is Fun Again." Contemporary retailers emphasize consumption as a lifestyle choice: products can accommodate each customer's individualized identity project. Advertisers now market products by constructing polyvocal images, appropriating symbols that suggest inclusiveness and diversity for all, while simultaneously seeking out the next new consumer—young, old, urban, elite, ghetto, Latino, African American, gay, or female, to name a few. Communities are imagined (such as the "Pepsi Generation" and the multicultural groups in the Benetton ad campaigns) through images of the postmodern consumer that negate earlier forms of identification based on concepts such as class, income, or profession—all markers that could risk excluding too many in today's multicultural arena—and encourage a postmodern identity instead.

Far from being peripheral to this project, employees play a major role in the operation of stores that aim to attract a diverse group while still assuring each consumer of his or her individual, unique identity. Employees work the aisles of stores like the Gap, Old Navy, the Wiz, and Pottery Barn promoting the latest fad. The physical spaces and social interactions within the stores are part of a corporate strategy to blur the line between workers and consumers. Advertisements for the Gap claim that a group of Gap employees are modeling Gap products. Music store employees could be on the covers of the CDs they sell.

Nevertheless, and in spite of this postmodern project, retailers' profit margins continue to rely on basic customer service. Outside of those retailers that opt for self-service, sales depend on shop-floor interactions. Companies may wish to control customers' decisions, but ultimately the customer has the final say. Successful service remains an intangible event: in the final moment, "service is produced and consumed simultaneously . . . [and] the consumer generally participates in its production" (Macdonald and Siriani 1996, 3). Employees in this "interactive service sector" are expected to respond in certain ways (Leidner 1996). Workers and customers have to be complicit for a sale to be successful. Either party can sabotage the company's final goal. Employees and customers operate in this power relationship, and retailers depend on complex social interactions that cannot be reduced to automated procedures monitored on production lines. Even temporary employees are asked to perform a significant amount of "emotional labor" that involves bringing aspects of their own personal identity and self-presentation into the job (Leidner 1996, 4).

This chapter considers these interactions through participant-observation at Crayton's, a housewares chain belonging to the parent company Crayton's Inc.[4] After corporate management denied me the access to research in the more fashionable retail chains I had initially targeted, such as the Gap and Express, a personal connection allowed me into Crayton's, where I chose to focus on two stores, both located in central Manhattan. With the management's permission, I worked (unpaid) alongside employees. The research took place over a seven-month period; after an initial concentration of time, I worked an average of three shifts a week. All managers and workers were aware of the nature of my research—"studying the retail sector and the labor market"—and my conversations with workers and store managers were not restricted in any way.[5] I would note down conversations and events as I was working, or shortly afterward. I interviewed individuals primarily while we were working or during lunch hours or breaks. Over time I was integrated into the daily patterns of the workday, and most individuals were extremely open with me. One of the major complaints on the job was boredom and routine: a new face and different conversations helped pass the time when it was quiet.

Crayton's Inc. is exemplary of many of the retail chains venturing into New York. Its 1999 company newsletter billed it as "a specialty housewares business, located primarily in mall, strip center and city locations, featuring new, trend-right merchandise from brand name manufacturers, as well as our own . . . private label merchandise." The company began in 1975 and by 1998 was the nation's largest housewares retailer, operating over six hundred stores in forty-two states through four different subsidiaries. In 1999 there were sixteen Crayton's stores in Manhattan and a few other outlets in Queens and Brooklyn. Store size varied; I chose two of the larger stores: one was in Manhattan's busy midtown shopping district on Thirty-fourth Street, where office workers, shoppers, and tourists mingle, and the other, which had the highest sales volume in the city, was in the wealthy Upper East Side neighborhood. Over the seven months the Thirty-fourth Street store employed about twenty individuals and the Upper East Side store had some thirty employees, although numbers varied radically depending on the season. Stores had anywhere from one worker (not ideal) to eight on the shop floor depending on the time of day and staff absences. Although these numbers may seem small, this floor arrangement is representative of a large number of retail establishments in the city (table 5.3).

TABLE 5.3   CHANGE IN NUMBERS OF RETAIL ESTABLISHMENTS IN
NEW YORK CITY, BY SIZE, 1993 TO 1999

Number of Employees	1999	Percentage	1993	Percentage	Change	Growth
Total	39,908	100%	38,208	100%	1,700	4%
0 to 4	23,965	60	24,256	63	−291	−1
5 to 9	7,711	19	6,930	18	781	11
10 to 49	6,861	17	6,003	16	858	14
50 to 99	993	2	690	2	303	44
100 to 499	410	1	303	1	107	35
500 or more	28	0	26	0	2	8

Source: Data supplied courtesy of New York State Department of Labor.

RETAIL STORES AS MULTICULTURAL WORK SITES

A homogeneous workforce is not an asset for retail chains marketing consumption through images of urban diversity and fluid identities. New immigrants may covet these low-wage jobs, but few corporate retailers would benefit if immigrant or other labor networks came to dominate their shop floor, in contrast to a more diverse labor force (Waldinger 1999). Retailers require a cross-section of employees who ideally can represent the diversity of their customer base. At the same time, they are challenged to recruit in a city where race, class, and networks frequently interact to racially or ethnically determine the labor force.[6] Crayton's exemplifies a business facing this challenge. It covets as large a customer base as possible, and its changing array of products promotes consumption as a lifestyle choice: plastic jugs with fish decorations in summer, rabbit mugs at Easter, millennium champagne glasses, all at accessible prices. Crayton's, however, lacks the brand identity that might attract large numbers of diverse young job-seekers. Discounts on housewares are less appealing than the discounts offered to employees at stores selling clothes, records, cosmetics, electronic goods, and sneakers. Nevertheless, in spite of the low wages (the starting salary was six dollars an hour), both stores maintained a relatively diverse workforce. No network, neighborhood, or ethnicity dominated the shop floor; the majority of the workforce was Latino and black, in particular Puerto Rican and African American. Workers were skewed toward a younger demographic age group. Nevertheless, both stores had a number of individuals with other characteristics: some were from other ethnic backgrounds, some were native-born, and some were immigrant or second-generation. Dominicans, Ecuadoreans, and West Indians were all represented, as were immigrant workers from El Salvador and Jamaica, not to mention one older white woman who had arrived at Crayton's some years before, a veteran retail worker from an older New York department store long closed—Alexander's (see appendix to this chapter).

The diverse employee profile was generated through a combination of mechanisms. Managers' main goal was creating a reliable yet flexible labor pool that could satisfy seasonal demand. Corporate policies had created a heterogeneous work site without the conscious actions of the managers. Managers at Crayton's were allocated a fluctuating number of weekly payroll hours according to their store's sales volume. Meanwhile, job-seekers dropped off applications throughout the year. Although management did express a preference for personal recommendations when looking for new employees, mostly because this reduced managers' own workload and provided some guarantee, at various times during the year, especially when seasonal demand peaked, managers delved into their applications to hire someone. In October 1999, Crayton's held its first open day to find workers for the busy Christmas season. The open day was advertised in the stores, where employees wore buttons that said, "Ask me about Oct. 15th," while other potential workers found in the managers' files were invited to attend. Open day was attended by 116 people, and the district recruiter, Fernando Macias, a Puerto Rican from Brooklyn who had worked his way up through the ranks at Crayton's Inc., estimated that about one in ten were hired to cover this particularly busy season leading up to the millennium celebrations.

In 1999 Crayton's centralized its hiring process so as not be caught off-guard by employees' departures. Officially this meant that all new hires had to be hired by the newly created district recruiter, Fernando Macias. In reality, managers chose employees and sent them to Fernando for the paperwork. Fernando ensured that all of the Manhattan stores (and later the Queens and Brooklyn stores) were staffed, hiring and occasionally moving employees around to the different stores. He also provided a basic introduction to new recruits. This two-day course focused on the basics of good service—how to greet and serve customers—and theft control. His main obstacle in terms of hiring, he stated, was applicants' presentation. Fernando bemoaned applicants who arrived in jeans, chewing gum. "I like people who try and make themselves successful," he said.

A large number of employees in both the Thirty-fourth Street and Upper East Side stores had obtained their job through open hiring—a case of being there at the right moment (Waldinger and Lichter 2003, 125). Sarah, a young, second-generation West Indian woman, had seen a for-hire sign in a small branch in Greenwich Village. She had no real job experience but had just finished a course at New York's Culinary Institute and needed to pay off her student loan. Her knowledge of baking convinced the manager that she would be an asset to the store. Lucia, a thirty-seven-year-old Puerto Rican woman with one daughter, had worked at Crayton's for seven years and was one of a core group of stable employees and a manager-in-training. She had begun her employment in the Crayton's Queens Plaza store, ten minutes from her house, after completing an application on a whim as she contemplated returning to work since her daughter had started school. The manager interviewed and hired her immediately, since he needed someone to fill the nine-to-five slot to compensate for the abundance of part-timers already employed at the store. Before she was married, Lucia had worked at a photography store that was run by two Jewish brothers ("good Jews") who had relocated to Florida. After her previous experience with applications, she decided to omit any mention of her time unemployed. References for the entry-level sales associate positions at Crayton's were rarely checked (to my knowledge), and as one sales associate who had spent some time in prison informed me, nothing would ever come up unless it was a major felony—although his cousin had recommended him for the job, so he had not been forced to put this logic to the test.

Open applications rely on timing and also on the possession of some feature that catches the employer's eye—be it previous experience, attitude, or a particular skill. Human capital matters for hiring, but not as a simple matter of education or experience. More important is the acquisition of the cultural capital that can give one the ability to present an image that the manager appreciates. Random applicants who possess the "right attitude" may find jobs. These walk-ins also allow for new blood—something management craves in the interest of customer service. Walk-in applicants may also become a self-selected group of workers—individuals who find their way into midtown and elsewhere to look for a job and who possess an amount of determination superior to that of some of their peers who lack the self-confidence to look for a job outside of their neighborhood.[7]

Others, especially those with less than standard résumés, find their employment through personal networks: first-time workers, single mothers who had difficult schedules, young men with shaky employment histories or even criminal records, all were present on the shop floor. Networks particularly benefited the last group, some of whom were working in the stockrooms—a primarily male domain where men unpacked and organized boxes delivered overnight. Juan, a Puerto Rican man in his thirties who had spent time unemployed and time in prison, obtained his job in the Christmas season through his cousin José. After Christmas he watched his weekly hours decrease from forty to sixteen and struggled to make up extra hours working at the Crayton's Staten Island branch. Juan's cousin José had finally been promoted to stockroom manager after two years. Getting this position guaranteed him forty hours a week at ten dollars an hour, plus benefits (which he celebrated by getting an elaborate tattoo on his arm that included the names of his four boys to accompany the name of his longtime on-again-off-again partner on his other arm). José also had a history of trouble until, in his words, "I just got tired of it." However, he would frequently discuss how to survive in prison with the store security guard, who herself was a retired corrections officer. José was also employed through networks, although he had not wanted to use the connection: "You know, I just wanted to be hired because [the manager] was looking at me." José turned out to be a reliable worker whose biggest problem on the job was his ongoing cell-phone arguments with his kids, who were starting to skip class.

Employees' networks also provided new workers for the store, but no one network dominated the work sites. Kinship and family were one route to employment, although company policy prohibited siblings from working in the same store (a policy that was not always enforced). Individuals belonged to multiple networks that were not structured through ethnicity alone. For example, Dolores, a young second-generation Ecuadorean (father from Ecuador and mother from Puerto Rico), lived at home in the Bronx. She found a job for both her sister, who was placed at the Forty-second Street store, and her high school friend Shakira, an African American woman who had recently had a baby and was trying to save up money to move out of her family home and in with her boyfriend. "Weak ties" (Granovetter 1995) were also instrumental for some individuals' job search. Sheree, a young African American single mother from Staten Island, found her job through her boyfriend: he worked for a private sanitation company and collected the trash outside of Crayton's, where he had fallen into casual conversations with the manager and, after enough persistence, found a job for Sheree. Such random encounters resulting in jobs were not isolated events. Notably, however, these networks and weak ties were rarely structured through ethnic ideologies but were more often the product of far more diverse interactions.

The central stores that I focused on guaranteed employees more weekly hours owing to their higher sales volume. Employees coveted these jobs, which guaranteed them more work hours than they could get at the smaller Crayton's stores and the ones in the outer boroughs. In these downtown stores no one ethnic group or race claimed privilege to the neighborhood or the labor market, unlike the fast-food stores in Harlem studied by Newman (1999). Newman found that African Americans claimed a local history in the Harlem neighborhoods and could interpret the employment of immigrant workers and others as a preference or racial bias against their neighborhood legacy. Crayton's employees, by contrast, arrived to work from all of New York's five boroughs. These downtown spaces were not present in the narratives that made up each employee's local history and sense of belonging. The overall profile of Crayton's employees could not be interpreted by workers, customers, or managers as an indication of (local) ethnic succession and neighborhood change. Nor could managers favor applicants from "outside" neighborhoods who they might think were less likely to attract trouble into the store, as Newman (1999, 234–45) found to be the case among managers of Harlem's fast-food chains. Few of the applicants were immediately "local" anyway; neighborhood residents rarely applied for these low-skilled, low-wage jobs, which provided little cachet for the young, middle-class residents of midtown and the Upper East Side. Recruitment in these downtown stores therefore bypassed the localist ideologies, rivalries, and stereotypes observed by Newman.

In the absence of a dominant network and with management's openness to variety, the hiring process did not perpetuate a racial or ethnic ideology. Managers did want hardworking, personable workers, but they had not, for all intents and purposes, constructed an image of a "better" or more desirable worker based on ethnic stereotypes (Kim 1999; Waters 1999; Waldinger and Lichter 2003, 172–78). Management was intent on filling these low-wage jobs as best they could. They hoped to find a few hard workers who would remain at the store for some time, but they assumed that most would leave when they had had enough. Nevertheless, through a combination of employment strategies—networks, weak ties, and open applications—they were able to obtain a continual pool of workers.

Diversity is also reflected in management at the store level. One store was managed by an older Jewish man who had been with the company for over fifteen years, and the other store was managed by Oscar, an African American and Puerto Rican native of the Bronx. Assistant managers were often internally promoted. Other managers in the area were mostly either Hispanic or black. The racial profile of store managers, assistant managers, and sales associates kept the company policy, discipline, and new initiatives from being interpreted as racial issues. This may not be the case in all retail chains. Sometimes race and ethnicity can increase an employee's racial positioning, as discussed by this young African American woman who had been at Crayton's for seven years and was an assistant manager:

> Today I spoke to Arleen in the manager's office. She finished a degree at Baruch College [CUNY] and managed to get a manager-in-training position at Crayton's [this option no longer exists]. I asked if she had worked in other places, and she said she had always worked in retail. Before Crayton's, she had worked in Banana Republic. I asked her if that was when it was still in its safari phase, and she said, a bit later. She worked in the flagship store on Fifth and Seventeenth. She applied while at Baruch. I asked

her what the difference was between Banana Republic and Crayton's, and she noted, if you want corporate, that was Banana Republic. They were much more organized and streamlined, she explained. I asked why she left, and she said she had had differences with the manager—they had put in a new one she didn't get on with. She said it had been interesting. Nearly all the men were gay, and she said she would hang out with them, she was the only black woman, and all they would do was comment on men. She said everyone had wanted to be in fashion, that she even saw her old manager on Channel 7 the other day. But at that time, she said, most of the people working there were also white. And the look was really important—they pushed you into a certain look. She said she got tired of always being pushed to help black people. I asked if they told her to do that, but she said that "it was like they made it obvious—when black people came in, you were expected to look after them. Or in the dressing room, then you were meant to see if they were shoplifting, and while there are some, not everyone is taking." This meant you had to follow them into the dressing room and listen for the click of them taking apart the security tags.[8] And she complained that some customers showed you too much anyway in the dressing rooms. It was like a Benetton ad, she said. There was her, maybe a few Latinos, and another black person who was hired because they were very black. But she told me that as a black person there she felt as if she were a mannequin, that you were hired because you were slim.[9] The Gap, she continued, was slightly more urban. Then she told me about a friend of hers in Jersey who also worked in a Banana Republic and who had told her that there all the kids who worked had all the money they needed, cars, clothes, and they lived at home, so they could ask for higher wages there because it didn't matter to them. After that she went to Staples, which she said she liked but which didn't have the job opportunities. (author's field notes, March 8, 2000)

Crayton's recruitment process generated a diverse workforce where small groups worked together during each shift. No specific racial or ethnic divisions were engendered through any institutionalized policies. Nor was one ethnic group being displaced from a local labor force and holding another group responsible. Furthermore, blacks and Hispanics were not being denied internal promotions in ways that could have been interpreted as racially motivated, although career advancement was hindered by other company policies (described later in the chapter). The company's home office is in New Jersey, too far away for most workers to entertain the possibility of working there. So a white corporate management structure remains physically distant and inaccessible to the workers, who, in any case, imagine their future elsewhere.

Workers did arrive with a subjective understanding and identification of their racial and ethnic selves, and they may have brought stereotypical notions of an "other" into the workplace as well, but company policy did not play on this. Parades, churches, schools, street festivals, even parking practices in New

York are by now all seen as reflecting cultural difference and a discourse about equal rights for all ethnicities, even when some "ethnicities," such as "Latino," are the construction of multicultural discourse and practices and have little basis in historical or cultural commonalities.[10] Race and ethnicity are not absent from the employees' lives—Dolores marveled at the smallness of the Ecuadorean parade in Jackson Heights when she went to visit her aunt there, comparing it to the huge Puerto Rican parade on Fifth Avenue. Leslie, a young second-generation woman whose parents were from St. Vincent, discussed the merits of West Indian cooking and food with other workers who shared their rice and beans. These youngsters have grown up in a society that promotes "cultural pluralism." Indeed, how could they not have an ethnic identity when schools, churches, and neighborhoods mark most public events with constant celebrations of ethnic identities? But these ethnic and racial understandings do not structure the employees' interactions with each other.

Conversations about race and ethnicity were also subject to endless joking and sharing with each other. Employees identified with the "ghetto" in different ways, but Crayton's was several stops away. For example, two Puerto Rican men took it upon themselves to spend time teaching Kelly, the one young white employee, who had transferred from a Crayton's in Oregon after she finished community college there and decided to move to New York, how to speak "ghetto" talk. "Whip is car," she told me, and as she listed new vocabulary words, everyone joined in. During another employee's birthday party at a reggae bar in the Greenwich Village, Kevin, a Puerto Rican employee, had arrived bringing in alcohol under his coat to avoid buying a drink. "That's so ghetto," laughed Leslie, the second-generation West Indian woman living in East New York, as she told me about it. José, the Puerto Rican recently out of jail, then told Sheree, the African American single mother living in Staten Island with her parents. "So ghetto," she agreed as the story was passed around the aisles all morning.

Stereotypes were brought up in casual conversations as individuals discussed the customers and the world around them. But they were also challenged in the daily interactions in which they participated (Goode and Schneider 1994, 135–68). These young people were interacting, sharing, and even arguing with a far more diverse group of people in their neighborhoods than were most of Manhattan's middle and upper class, who prize New York as the most cosmopolitan city in the world but whose experience of it may remain limited to student exchanges and annual parades. These young people in New York, many of whom live in the ghetto (their word, not mine), no longer see it simply as home to the African American experience. To them, remaining in the "ghetto" primarily suggests the inability to behave appropriately in different contexts.

For the most part, however, the interactions among employees were more creative than divisive and offered a more positive vision of the workplace in terms of race and ethnicity than has often been observed. This is not to paint a picture of wholesale harmony among all workers, nor between workers and management, but to stress that work spaces are not always detrimental to ethnic relations within the workforce and are indeed one of the sites of interactions that may lead to a new, more inclusive sense of self. In contrast, the more complicated interactions among workers, customers, and management remain infused with class and race and do influence many of these young adults and their understanding of their social position as they spend a portion of their coming of age behind the city's counters.

Ties Across the Counter: Service, Customers, and Respect

Employees complained about their salaries, the lack of benefits, the unpredictable and unsociable hours, and the working conditions. These complaints, however, were often overshadowed by their encounters with specific customers that they saw as infused with "disrespect." Corporate retailers are fighting intense competition. Their response has been to standardize and centralize their operations and distribution to avoid the accumulation of (unsold) inventory (Bailey and Bernhardt 1997; Hollander and Omura 1989). Technology now monitors all sales through cash registers. Computers then calculate the amount of stock in an individual store. Supply and delivery are predetermined according to sales, the previous performance of the item, and the store turnover. Thus, not only are managers unable to compensate for any unforeseen demand, but sales associates have no way of placing orders for disgruntled customers. Associates carry the burden of mediating between company policies and customers' discontent.

Many employees remember particular incidents in which they had to do battle with these policies. As I sat next to Kelly during her thirty-minute lunch break, I noticed a faded poster on the door leading onto the shop floor that proclaimed the company sales and service slogan, "**GO 4 IT**." Four simple ideals were laid out for sales associates:

Greeting every customer

Offering every customer a basket

Showing each customer the **I**tem of the month

Thanking every customer for visiting the store

This, it was hoped, would contribute to the company goal of increasing sales by 5 percent, as declared in the October 1999 issue of the Crayton's Inc. newsletter *Kitchen Talk* (which was rarely available for sales associates). The table where we sat was squeezed in between an overflowing stockroom and a doorway that led into the shiny white fluorescent-lit basement where bedroom and kitchen organizers, bathroom accessories, and an assortment of enamel plates were displayed. Kelly, a Puerto Rican single mother, had been a cashier at the store for two years. She described her worst encounter on the job.

Two older women were looking for a particular set of dishtowels. Kelly offered them a different set and then suggested that they return later in the week after the delivery truck came. Walking away, Kelly heard one woman mutter, "If you spend as much time helping as you do not helping, then you might have a nicer day." Kelly was indignant given that there was nothing she could do. "It's like they want me to produce [a dishtowel], and where am I going to do that?" The customer continued to complain about the youth of today, and when she announced that Kelly would never get anywhere, Kelly got "really aggravated." So she returned and reminded the two women that, first, she had gone to help them, and second, they were the ones worrying about $1.50, not her (in reference to the more expensive set of dishtowels they had left behind). She also told them that she was a woman, not a young girl (she was twenty-nine). Kelly was still furious over this lack of respect. As she explained to me, her father had always told her to respect everyone, young or old, "cuz if you give respect, you get respect." In the end the assistant manager got involved, telling Kelly to calm down and placating the two older women.

Another day, Kelly continued to discuss customers' attitudes with Valerie, an African American assistant manager who was studying at Monroe College, a private college where Kelly had also begun an accounting course. Both women had stories of individuals who would not put money directly in their hand. Kelly remembered one who threw the money down so hard that it fell on her side of the counter. She told us that now when they do this she makes sure that she puts their change on the counter. Valerie said that sometimes she thought it had to be a race thing, "like they don't want to touch you."

As management encourages customer service, associates are left to deal with customers upset by changing inventory, absent products, and standardized corporation protocols. Products are displayed on customized shelving of specific sizes, and items are organized according to a design plan (a "planogram") conceived at a central office for all stores. Promotions are decided at company headquarters, and every month the central office designates one product as the "item of the month." Associates have to promote this item to each customer regardless of the store location and its customer profile. Meanwhile, customers make their own demands on sales associates. They frequently ask for catalogs that do not exist. They want items to be gift-wrapped when there is no wrapping paper. They want rain checks on items that may take months to arrive, often after an employee has left. They ask for items that are no longer available, then ask why, but associates are usually not privy to that information. They ask for boxes to carry home items such as soap dishes when the boxes have been thrown away because they take up too much space. Workers are often wary when they see a series of special requests coming their way, since there is often little they can do apart from "customer service"—a new code term for placating a customer armed with words and smiles alone, which many associates may not have at their fingertips after eight hours on their feet with only a half-hour unpaid lunch break.

Associates take the brunt of customers' irritation and sometimes their insults as well. They also have to manage customers' fetishes—whether the drunks who urinate in the back aisle, the customers who sexually harass them, or the "pot lady," who would buy a pot every few weeks, burn it, and then come back for a refund. Associates usually politely conceal their irritation, but they do get tired—as one woman said, "They don't pay us enough to put up with some of these customers." Irritation often leads to blank refusal. One sales associate, an African American man who was stationed as the store greeter, refused one day to help a woman carry her baby carriage (which was also loaded with shopping bags) downstairs when the elevator was broken. Instead, he offered to look after the sleeping baby as the customer went downstairs to find what she needed. The woman threatened to sue. As Kelly recounted this story, she defended him: "If you were to break your back doing this, the company wouldn't pay, and carrying baby carriages was not in the job description anyway." Managers rush to placate customers in these conflicts and then often remain supportive of staff behind closed doors. Store managers can do little to solve the underlying working conditions—such as scheduling, pay, and benefits—that frustrate associates. Managers' support during these incidents with customers is often what creates a bond of respect between managers and their employees.

Although some interactions may cause amusement, in many cases associates feel that their main role is to serve and that customers see them in this light alone. Kathy, a twenty-four-year-old single mother with a seven-year-old son, was the daughter of a Russian mother and an African American father. She had worked at Crayton's for four months and had a history of working low-wage jobs, many in the service sector. She had begun at a CUNY community college several years before but had found it too difficult with her child and now could no longer afford it. "Back then it was crazy money," she commented, referring to the financial aid that used to be available. She wanted to leave retail: "It rubs off on you . . . the attitude rubs off on you." I asked for more specifics. "Well, it's like you get a lot of people here, like scholars and stuff, and they don't even take any account of you, they think that you amount for nothing cuz you work in retail." She added, "You just get kinda like 'fuck you' all the time underneath your breath."

Associates have different ways to manage their frustration. Many claimed their strategy was to be as nice as possible. As Arleen, the assistant manager, proclaimed, "I think, is that really all they have to worry about? That's the worst thing that happened in their day?" But race and class infuse these interactions. Kelly continued our lunchtime conversation discussing customers in general: "They come in and expect you to bend over and pick up everything when they say they want five of something. I take three and say I will meet them up front . . . and they have diamonds on their hands. I guess they are used to servants or something." It is of no small significance that many of the daily interactions experienced by these young and not so young adults are structured to confirm their more vulnerable social position. Meanwhile, the job gives them few resources to establish an alternative scenario within these daily interactions. Employees try, in small ways, to recoup a sense of respect and reassert their position, as described by Kelly. Others try to be as polite as possible. And some place the blame squarely on the company when customers complain to them, distancing themselves from their employer.

A wide range of people mingle in these downtown streets and stores. Associates interact with customers of all races, sizes, and age, any of whom could be difficult. Associates know that problem customers are everywhere; many have stories of difficult experiences and customers in their own neighborhoods (Newman 1999, 90–91). But interactions with customers are categorized and racialized in different ways depending on the spaces in which they occur. For many associates, their employment in the retail sector provides them with their first opportunity to come into regular contact with such a large number of white people. Young and not so young workers are reminded in different ways every day that they are a minority and that being a minority is not just a question of "equal but different." Customers would frequently turn to complain to me, even when an assistant manager was by my side, seeing my white skin color as a marker of seniority. Moreover, class differences are highlighted when customers rush in asking for items like fondues or crème brûlée burners, then become impatient when sales associates look blankly back at them. (As one associate asked me, "Why can't they melt cheese in a pot?") Retail stores become an important context within which they experience and re-create the lines of distinction that are part of a multicultural society. Power and race play out in much more obvious ways during these encounters than they do sitting next to someone on the subway. Within the context of these downtown stores, difficult customers were generically constructed by employees as white and wealthy. The reading of customers' (similarly difficult) behavior differed depending on these contexts: what was understood in local spaces and familiar neighborhoods as a loser's unpleasant behavior caused by individual problems (Newman 1999, 97–100) was transformed into racial stereotypes and resentments in this space that was shared with an "Other."

FLEXIBILITY AND AUTONOMY ON THE JOB

Retailers continue to value service as a key to their profits. Monitoring employees' service skills, however, is difficult. The "item of the month" initiative was one policy at Crayton's geared toward addressing this dilemma. It was advocated as a simple and quantifiable way to increase sales. In theory, it ensured that every associate tried to sell at least one item—without even having to think about it. Management had recently decided to further push this policy by instructing associates not only to carry the item (that month a knife and vegetable peeler) and show it to every customer they helped, but to then mark down every successful sale. These innovations annoyed employees, and the store manager was also not happy with them, knowing that the approach would not be appreciated by all customers. The company was stepping up control, however, and had threatened to send out undercover shoppers to check on compliance with the new instructions. Occasionally the central office did monitor employee behavior in this way. During one shift Sandra was told by an assistant manager that she had been reported for giving incorrect information to a customer about whether a particular hanger was stocked in wood as well as plastic. She was upset and told the assistant manager that she not only had tried to help the "customer" but had told that person that to her knowledge she had never seen the product. She complained to me, "If they wanted to make sure we know that much, they should have the information available and train the employees."

Standardization of store locations has not only stripped associates and managers of their autonomy and ability to innovate on the shop floor but also devalued their specific knowledge gained from experience. Mandates from the central office are seen not only as annoying but often as illogical. Tom, an older Native American man, Fred, a Jamaican immigrant who was a night manager, and myself were discussing loss prevention (against theft)—a company preoccupation and a large source of financial loss. The day before a woman had passed a flatware set (a favorite for shoplifters, who can resell it by the piece) to her friend, who exchanged it for store credit. Tom complained that there weren't enough people on the shop floor to cover the two women. He figured that if each item were stamped after a sale, this could not happen. Fred said that he had suggested this to management, but no one listened: "They prefer to have their man in a suit and with a pen in home office come up with ideas rather than listen to people on the ground who see things happening." Employees often said that they felt underappreciated by the company, both in terms of simple rewards and because their knowledge of the products and procedures, gained from their experience, was never taken into account. Employees were judged on their performance, but they were rarely consulted about company changes. Nor did they feel appreciated for their contributions to company success. (No bonus system existed, not even at Christmas.)

In spite of standardization, the retail sector offers workers particular possibilities for a degree of autonomy absent in other low-wage sectors. The complex interaction between management, employees, and customers necessary for "good customer service" allows associates to play these relationships off against each other and manage their own time at work. Associates have different daily tasks: unpacking boxes, cleaning, organizing and straightening shelves, pricing items, reorganizing the stockroom, and taking inventory, among other tasks. Workers gain some control by selectively pursuing different tasks. They also know that their service is seen as intrinsic to company success. Everyone is expected to provide service; managers can only encourage time spent with customers in the interest of sales. Associates can frustrate management when they fail to finish a task only to be found helping a customer at the back of the store. This is a strategy frequently used by the men who are asked to unload a never-ending pile of boxes that arrive after truck deliveries. As Juan commented to me early one evening after having hit, flattened, and folded countless boxes for recycling, "Whoever invented work must have done it to fuck us up—I mean, they might have liked it, but that doesn't mean we do."

Juan was one of the hardest workers, staying out of trouble and avoiding aggravation on the job because, as he told me, he knew he could lose his head otherwise. Juan and the other men frequently abandoned boxes in midaisle to attend to a customer's need, elaborately demonstrating a product's merits rather than rushing back to fold and stock boxes. Spanish-speaking customers gave some of these men a further excuse to engage in long conversations (especially with women) that management could only wonder about. In contrast, many women, tired of their designated customer service role, would disappear into a variety of other tasks to avoid ongoing customers' demands. One employee made it her business to try to decipher the company planograms, adapting them to the actual shelf space in the store as opposed to the company diagram. "No one bothers me when I am doing this," she said. Workers turn company demands back at managers, who are frequently seen running around the store trying to help customers, bag items, and tag products when employees have disappeared into other tasks and customers' feet are tapping.

Employees also respond to their unreliable timetable by prioritizing their own needs. Flexibility within the retail sector has become a mainstay of human resources.[11] Crayton's New York City recruiter estimated that 80 percent of the workforce was part-time. Part-time workers provide a flexible labor force—many of them need more hours and provide a pool of available labor that permits the company to meet its cyclical labor demands. Payroll costs are reduced as the company saves on benefits, holiday pay, and health insurance. A company handbook states that eligible employees receive benefits after a year; eligibility is limited, however, to those who have worked full-time (a forty-hour week) for a year. Since most employees were hired on a part-time basis and their hours were cut in slow seasons, they had to wait longer until they could argue their case. Neither management nor the workers imagined their employment as a long-term pact, even though many of the employees had stayed longer than the one year that the human resources manager told me was the standard time for most sales associates to remain. Both managers and associates constantly complained about "retail" as a job. Meanwhile, flexibility had been turned into a larger discourse: it was now seen not only to benefit the stores but to help the workers, who have "other commitments," as explained to me by Fernando Macias, the district manager. After a break from the field, I returned to see a large number of new faces in one store. Oscar, the store manager, commented after I expressed surprise at such a radical turnover, "It's good to have new blood in the store," and, "Keep everyone flexible."

The company advocates part-time hours as a way in which employees can continue their education and fulfill other responsibilities, even when this may not be the case. Employees are discussed as individuals who are looking for their future elsewhere. This expectation is even institutionalized in a company policy stating that employees who leave can be rehired, although they may lose their title and benefits on departure. This policy acknowledges that associates are looking for better opportunities or have life situations that make them quit, but it also suggests that the company would prefer hiring associates with prior knowledge.

Several employees had reappeared at the store after various periods of time away. Some had left for other retail jobs they imagined as a step up and returned when things did not work out. Antony, an African American employee originally from Florida, where he had finished college, had left Crayton's after three years, hoping to better his chances at Portico (another up-market home store retailer). He had previously tried to find employment at the Gap but suspected that his large size was a problem, since it would have been difficult for him to fit into their clothes. At Portico he was assigned to the clearance center, where he received a salary with no bonus while being held to sales quotas. He returned to Crayton's after several months of waiting for a transfer to a full-price store (these had no quota systems). At Crayton's they rehired him to help reorganize the window displays. After some months he was assigned to a new store in Chelsea, where he was unhappy. The store was small, and there were fewer workers to talk to, and fewer customers. But he had nowhere else to go.

The mantra of flexibility is appropriated by employees, who respond by setting their own schedules. One afternoon Kelly stopped the assistant manager to tell him that if the manager phoned, he should say she was not coming in the next day, in spite of the schedule. If she worked the next day, she said, she would have worked six days straight from 3:30 to 9:30 P.M. If she had worked four days straight from 1:00 to 9:30 P.M., that would have been fine, she told him, but as it was, she was too tired. "I might get mad I'm so tired," she said, suggesting that she could upset a customer, which would be worse than not coming into work as scheduled.

Managers are used to these absences, and one of their principal goals is to cultivate a small core of stable workers on whom they can rely, assuming that other workers will often call in sick. Managers and employees are aware of this game. On one very hot day, Oscar, the store manager, was looking over-worked as usual. He had planned to leave to check on the smaller store at Sixty-eighth Street that was also part of his responsibility, but the morning had been crazy—two employees had called out at the last moment. He was unsurprised, however, and, true to style, remained empathetic. "It's hot—who can blame them?" he commented as he stood behind the register ringing up sales.

Workers may also have erratic hours because they are moved to a different store to solve a staffing crisis or, as often happens, they receive a last-minute call asking them to work. If they can rearrange their classes, other jobs, child care arrangements, or appointments, many agree to work the few extra hours. Others refuse, much to the annoyance of assistant managers trying to fill in the gaps. "They all complain they don't get enough hours, and then you phone them to come in and no one can come," complained one. For many employees, however, it is no longer worthwhile to commute for an hour to ruin a day they had banked on as free, whatever their financial difficulties. As one young man said, "They call you and act like they are doing you a favor or something giving you hours. They never say please." Workers who have stayed on the job long enough have the luxury of creating their own schedule, but only through a certain amount of persistence.

RETAIL WORKERS: CONSUMERS IN THE MAKING

Once the daily routine of the job sets in, sales associates would do anything to help the day along.

Associates came and went during my research. Many began with an appreciation of the entertaining aspects of the job, as oddball customers, Japanese tourists, and harried husbands searched for the item of their choice. Each story sounded like old news to associates who had spent one too many Christmases listening to shoppers' cooking anxieties as they showed them the digital basting thermometer. After the initial learning curve, the major challenge on the job was to help time pass and keep busy. Some found specific tasks they made their own, such as Tom, the Native American, who made it his business to put beeper tags in items that could easily be stolen. In general a pattern on the shop floor emerged as associates congregated and dispersed with enough self-regulation so as not to draw attention to themselves. Gossip and conversation took place in the back aisles as workers stacked merchandise at their own pace and hid their coffee in the stockroom.

When there was a lull during the shift, especially late in the evening when there were often more staff than customers, the work went slowly. The company CD blared a compilation of songs but left everyone awaiting next month's repertoire. Magazines, food, and jokes were passed around. Catalogs were exchanged as employees discussed their favorite Victoria'a Secret item, the computers in *PC World*, the sexiest singer in *The Source*, and the best-looking model in *Latina*. In quiet moments the shop floor could be transformed into a space for entertainment—in contrast to factory floors, where workers are glued to assembly lines, or even offices, where employees' productivity can be surveyed more efficiently. These brief moments when the work space was transformed into a social space for workers to enjoy were also what kept many of them in the job. For many the resulting friendships also provided a strong incentive to stay where they were. After working for seven years in different retail establishments in the city, Diane, a twenty-seven-year-old second-generation Dominican woman, said, "I just got tired of traveling." She had remained at Crayton's for three years and also found employment there for her younger sister, Ana. Assistant managers had turned down promotions that would have involved moving to smaller stores. Two female assistant managers said that small stores offered less chance for innovation and that they had become used to the larger stores and their colleagues; small stores could have as few as two to three workers a shift.

Friendships within the stores were formed among employees with different titles. Generation and gender were stronger barriers to friendship than ethnicity. Assistant managers were given the difficult job of breaking up the chattering groups around the registers. But such problems were understood within the context of individual management style and not interpreted through racial characteristics. Management was aware of the dilemma of employees getting overly friendly with each other and being distracted from the job by cliques. Sometimes management counteracted this tendency by moving associates to different stores. One assistant manager was told in her annual review that her friendships made her less professional, and she was discouraged from bringing in lunch for the other employees—a common practice among the women, who often sampled each other's cooking. She was eventually transferred to an underperforming smaller store that the district manager hoped to improve.

Regardless of whether the workers took pride in their jobs or not, the bonds generated through these work patterns did not create a sense of collective purpose or engender an identity that could be interpreted as that of a "worker." Although work was an important site for social interaction, the heterogeneity of the workforce, its transience, and the mantra of "flexibility" did not permit associates to see themselves as long-term workers with a stake in the retail sector. The low starting wage was not enough for associates to maintain an autonomous household. Some employees even decided that raises and promotions were not worth the extra work. Kelly had been suggested as a possible internal key holder (being responsible for the cash register and its contents), but "for twenty-five cents an hour it's not worth it," she said. In the meantime she was trying to make her way through Monroe College, a small private business administration school in the Bronx, and imagining her future elsewhere, although at that point she was still in remedial classes.

Associates had no illusions about the possibility of economic mobility through their jobs at Crayton's. Even a promotion to assistant manager would get them only ten dollars an hour, although such a promotion would include benefits. Associates knew this compensation was much lower than the fifteen dollars an hour and more that an office worker could get. Valerie, a twenty-seven-year-old African American woman, had worked at the store for three years, after a career at Caldor's in the Bronx and other retail establishments. She was one of the few associates who lived alone in an independent household. Struggling to pay for her education at Monroe College, she used to dodge phone calls from debt collectors. "They can call all they want—I'm not paying," she said as another associate called her to the phone.

Valerie did finally finish her accounting course and found a bookkeeping job. She passed by the store sometimes to visit her friends. "She looked real cute in all her new clothes," Tom told Miriam, a twenty-eight-year-old woman from El Salvador who, after eight years, had been promoted to assistant manager two years before. She had been studying speech pathology at Lehman College (in the CUNY system) for the last seven years. Valerie and Miriam were close friends and lived in the Bronx. "Yeah, she said that what you get at Crayton's in management was a joke compared to what you get elsewhere," said Miriam, who worried that even if she did work as a teacher's assistant to deaf children, she would still be earning less than a living wage.

Few employees saw their future at the company, or even in retail, and associates constantly discussed other ideas to make money. Kevin—alias "K-Duce" to his friends who called—informed us of his moneymaking schemes. A large, bulky thirty-year-old of Puerto Rican origins, Kevin lived with his mother on Staten Island and had one young child who lived with the Jamaican mother. He had a variety of schemes, from selling pirated CDs to buying a bulk order of year 2000 woolen hats that he sold on New Year's Eve. Kevin's main dream, however, was to produce rap bands. His latest project was Bombsquad. "We'll have our own website soon too," he announced while showing me photos of the Wu Tang Clan (a rap group), whom he knew from the neighborhood, although as another employee pointed out "only minor members" of the clan. Kevin saw his future in rap: "What you have to do is get the kids off the street, give them a chance to produce, and then they will get signed up by a label, and get maybe seventy thousand, and then I get a cut." We had stopped believing this by the time he showed us a check for $52,000, which, as it was noted, if real, would have allowed him to stop working.

Among the young people, both in school and out, few seemed to consider their work within a larger career path. Those associates who continued to dream did so along different lines. Some were influenced by the images of money and power that popular culture sold them, and others had their imaginations stirred by the new economy and the possibilities offered by computers, which inspired them to try to enroll in the private business administration colleges they hoped would give them the computer skills they needed. Some were enrolled in CUNY community colleges, but many were on a break because they could no longer afford to continue or because they had been told they earned too much for financial aid.[12] Only one regular employee was enrolled in a four-year college course.

Although their shared work experience did not create a collective purpose, it allowed these young people to participate more fully in the world as consumers. Associates frequently came in and showed off their new purchases after payday. Jay lived in a public housing project with his Puerto Rican mother, his Dominican stepfather, and six siblings. He was on leave from

City Tech because of money problems. He constantly talked of getting his own place but always decided it would be too expensive; meanwhile, he was fast running up extra expenses. He showed me the G-shock watch he had bought the previous year: "It lasts for life." He assured me that it was still the same price at Macy's now as when he had bought it, and that meant, he explained, that it was not an item that was discounted. He had spent a good portion of his last check buying three shirts at Banana Republic because, he told me, "I just feel like I want to change my look." One day Jay realized he could now get a Macy's credit card, and he was telling everyone else in the store how they too could apply; Dolores told him that he was better off applying for a Discover card because the interest rate was much lower. Shakira, Dolores's friend from high school for whom Dolores had found a part-time cashier position at Crayton's, came over to her house one Saturday when I was visiting as well so that Dolores could show her how to apply for a Discover card online. They were using the computer that Dolores, her sister, and her mother had managed to buy pooling their income; it sat in the small alcove between the kitchen and living room in their apartment in a public housing project in Pelham Parkway. Shakira filled in the application (annual salary: $7,000) and received her card several weeks later.

At work the demarcations between who served and who shopped were clear, and they played out in ways that emphasized class, race, and power. Outside of the work space, however, associates took off their work uniforms and disappeared into the crowds of shoppers and pedestrians on the block, indistinguishable from the large and varied groups of young people mingling in Manhattan's commercial streets. Each associate had his or her own carefully conceived dress code that reflected an individualized identity. Edward, a nineteen-year-old Puerto Rican, myself, and Sandra, a young mother of two, also Puerto Rican, were all in the back arranging a new display of plates and other items. I had bought a new pair of Converse sneakers—the first item of clothing I had ever worn that aroused any interest from the other workers. Edward had on a new pair of Nikes, which he said had cost him $180.

"But I buy them because I like them—not to impress anyone." He then went through the rest of his wardrobe by price. I continued to ask why he wanted to spend so much of his money on clothes. Sandra asked me whether I didn't ever want to buy luxury goods.

"You feel good," she told me.

"I suppose so," I answered, acknowledging the other items of clothing I had paid for, but adding, "I just can't imagine spending that much on sneakers."

"Well, Edward, you see, he's on his own, he can afford to spend that much." With two young children, Sandra was more constrained in what she could spend. Edward lived with his mother. He was thinking of taking the GED exam so that he could become a paramedic, which he thought would be a good job. I said that most of my clothes tended to be cheaper and cited a list of brand names I was accustomed to buying.

"The Gap—they used to be good until they went high-class," Edward told me when that store came up. They went "high-class," he explained, when they started to sell things like pink shirts. "Who would want to wear pink shirts?" he wondered.

Banana Republic, it turned out, was even more counterfeit, according to Sandra. "Banana Republic—that's Working Girl in the Ghetto Look."

These young low-wage workers were educated consumers, having seen enough shoppers return items and complain bitterly about quality. They had learned from their work how to assess and project the consumer role, frequently discussing sales, return policies, where to get bargains on "hot" labels, and what to expect for their money. As soon as they began their working career they were simultaneously confirmed as consumers and knew their weekly salary could get them a credit card and a bank account. One morning when I arrived one associate told me that they were all waiting for a woman from Citibank to return. She had come in the day before and offered a "free" bank account to all the employees, along with a credit card.

Around February associates began to discuss what to do with their tax refunds. Some went to the discount malls in Jersey and Connecticut, and others paid off debts. Sandra, who worked part-time as a cashier, informed me that the tax refund was a major reason she continued in the job. "I use it to get something big—like a holiday or something." Associates even tried to sell bargains to each other. Kevin would try to sell his pirated CDs to his colleagues, and another assistant manager, Karen, tried to persuade us that Tupperware products, which she had begun to sell, surpassed the Rubbermaid products that filled the store's aisles.

CONCLUSIONS

This chapter examines the social space of two work sites. The workplace can be conceptualized as a site that integrates individuals into the city and whose effects depend on the workplace's structure, size, and the type of work being performed. In manufacturing companies, for example, workers usually have less time for social interaction, owing to the nature of the work. Racial and ethnic cliques may arise in large workforces, whereas the smaller shifts on retail shop floors require employees to cooperate and be in more intimate contact. The young adults who work in retail may be creating a far more inclusive culture than is usually envisioned in workplace ethnographies.[13] They are also finding ways to imagine themselves other than through ethnic stereotypes that attribute only problems to differences. The workplace is one of many sites that play a role in structuring identity and fashioning the life courses of these young adults, but it is an important one, and their workplace interactions play a major role in their lives. What is striking is that in this work space resentments based in race and ethnicity were suspended among employees as they all became part of an underpaid and flexible labor force. (In New York City this labor force is largely drawn from the black and Hispanic populations, who, as a result of their class position, are being priced out of the city and forced to travel over an hour to try to increase their odds of a forty-hour-a-week job in the retail sector.) Whether the open, creative exchanges of the diverse employees in these work spaces are taken back to the more segregated neighborhoods, schools, and churches is unclear. Nevertheless, if we are indeed made "in the practices of everyday life" (Goode and Schneider 1994), we can be sure that these experiences are played out elsewhere.

The dominant narrative on diversity in the low-wage sector most frequently understands it within a framework of ethnic niches and competition; at the high end the focus is on the integration of African American, Latino, or other ethnic groups into a white-dominated workplace with a glass ceiling. But as I show here, the low-wage sector may contain a large number of diverse workplaces that are invisible to the dominant culture. White workers are notably absent from the retail sector in New York City, which employs a multiethnic and -racial workforce. The interactions in the thousands of small retail establishments in the city may contribute to a new and more creative vision of racial and ethnic diversity among the lower-income residents of New York City who work their aisles, in particular when hiring practices do not rely on ethnic networks that generate income disparities. These interactions may have a part to play in the possibility that the new immigration will reorder our ideas of racial hierarchy and the black-white binary (Jaynes 2000). However, the interactions on retail shop floors also still work to confirm the class and minority status of many employees as they provide service with a smile. Indeed, these employees themselves frequently refer to their minority status. One assistant manager commented on my choice of cigarettes within the context of difference, noting, "We minorities, we always smoke Newport. I can't stand the taste of Marlboro" (my brand of choice). And after I had discussed my interest in writing about the retail sector and its workers, José asked me once how my book on "poor" people was going. For José and all the other Crayton's employees I got to know, their experiences on the shop floor confirmed that being white confirms social status and opportunity, although other racial lines may be blurring.

Although the shop floor breaks down some stereotypes, employment conditions do not encourage the creation of a worker identity. Classic conceptu-alizations of a worker identity revolve around the idea of resistance and or-ganization against management. This conceptualization constitutes part of a larger debate on workers' rights and social change in a world divided by class. Collective resistance continues to be a valuable tool in today's economy, but the workplace cannot be seen as a site that offers only two choices: resistance or oppression alongside control. Individuals may spend up to half their wak-ing day in this space, and the subjective experiences and emerging identities created here are richer than those contained within the resistance and oppres-sion dichotomy. Few associates had their sights set on the retail sector even if they did not expect their position at Crayton's to be their last store job. Nev-ertheless, they devised different ways to manage their space and time so as to find meaning and satisfy some of their needs (Hodson 1991). Although such an endeavor does not necessarily preclude the development of a worker iden-tity (Hodson 1991), no such development occurred at Crayton's. This study suggests that the image of the worker as either resisting or being oppressed may be an outdated concept when the images perpetrated by the new econ-omy and shifts in popular culture have blurred the lines between work, en-tertainment, and fashion and all but replaced the low-wage worker with a consumer who can take on any role he or she wishes. Nevertheless, consumers still have to work, and it is worth asking who continues to imagine himself or herself as a worker today, how this takes place, and what appeal this identity holds for many of the young retail workers around Manhattan, many of whom dream of continuing their education, acquiring computer skills, or fol-lowing some far-fetched scheme that will take them elsewhere.

At Crayton's, workers saw their employment as a way into consumption. And our economy needs consumers as much as it needs workers. The postin-dustrial economy faces the same crises and threat of overaccumulation as Fordism, but the solutions are now different as state-sponsored consumption recedes (Harvey 1989). As integral players in the industrial and postindustrial economy, young retail workers are part of a flexible workforce that can do lit-tle more than consume. Many of these adult workers spend their income in the very stores where they are employed. For many, their wages deny them the possibility of forming and maintaining an autonomous household, while cor-porate human resource policies make it even more unlikely that any type of collective organization will take place when flexibility rules. Naively, I asked two associates as we piled boxes whether they ever thought that they shouldn't buy Nike when their factories paid workers so little. I was told that "everyone is making a profit off someone." Nike posed less a case of false consciousness, it seems, than a more complex set of identity questions about how to create respect in a world where everyone gets one over one way or another. These jobs allow workers the power to consume and to engage in popular culture, re-creating and appropriating it as they desire, not the power to develop an identity that emerges out of their idea of workers' rights. Marginalization for these young adults is more extremely experienced when they are excluded from consumption rather than from other organized collective actions.

Some argue that these low-wage jobs are one way young adults can escape poverty, pursue an education, and avoid the "oppositional" culture that threatens to envelop inner-city youth. Newman (1999) describes young workers in fast-food restaurants who come to realize the value of a good job through their employment and resist peer pressure. But such an argument presupposes the idea of an underclass as a natural state of affairs that all youngsters need to resist. These jobs may provide some with the lift they need to move out of poverty, but large numbers of sales associates at Crayton's had been traveling the retail aisles around the city for several years. All of the associates knew the value of a job—they just did not always get the one they needed. Although the lucky few may possess both the individual and external resources they need to use these jobs for their own advancement, the company gains more through this flexible labor force then it gives back. Furthermore, the idea that these jobs teach the value of work may be turned on its head through an ethnographic analysis that also shows how the jobs promote the value of consumption and the power of the consumer over those who serve. Finally, the lack of union jobs and any real guarantee of economic security in the retail sector, past and present, is only exacerbated by the difficulties experienced by those trying to organize workers among whom a majority imagine their future to be elsewhere and internalize the rhetoric that everyone in retail is just passing through.

It is perhaps a fitting conclusion to note that Crayton's filed for bankruptcy about six months after my fieldwork was completed. At the time, an assistant manager at one store told me that the company had closed some of the smaller stores but her job was still safe. On October 12, 2001, all of Crayton's remaining stores were closed, however, and these young adults were tossed out to find work in yet another retail chain looking to expand its horizons.

Appendix

This is a brief descriptive list of the core employees in the two Crayton's stores studied during the fieldwork. Not included here are employees whose shifts did not coincide with the author's shifts and employees who came and went for very short periods.

THIRTY-FOURTH STREET STORE

Jay: Twenty-one years old, living in public housing on the Lower East Side with his Puerto Rican mother and Dominican stepfather. On leave from City Tech College, Jay was reenrolled by the end of the fieldwork.

Kevin: Puerto Rican in his early thirties from Staten Island, with one ex-wife from Jamaica and one child. He was living at home with his mother.

Dolores: Ecuadorean father and Puerto Rican mother. Working her way through Katharine Gibbs Business College, Dolores lived in the Bronx.

Shakira: Nineteen-year-old African American living in the Bronx with her parents. Shakira had just had a child and was hoping to go to the same college where Dolores was, as well as move in with her boyfriend.

Kelly: Twenty-five-year-old white woman, living in Queens. Kelly had moved from Oregon after finishing community college in film and TV. She had worked at Crayton's throughout her time in community college.

José: Puerto Rican in his early thirties. José had a criminal record, as well as five children living in Brooklyn.

Juan: José's cousin, also in his thirties. Juan had recently gotten out of jail and was living in Staten Island.

Sheree: African American single mother in her early twenties, living in Staten Island with her family. After one year at John Jay College, she was considering becoming a corrections officer, like others in her family.

Erika: Immigrant from El Salvador in her forties. Erika had two children born in the United States.

Lucia: Puerto Rican woman in her late thirties, married with one daughter, living in Queens.

Leslie: Second-generation immigrant from St. Vincent, living in Brooklyn. Leslie was trying to finish at Baruch College but had stopped owing to lack of money. She had finished a two-year community college in Brooklyn.

Sally: Second-generation Jamaican. Having just finished high school, Sally hoped to go to Katharine Gibbs Business College but was worried about the cost. She worked on weekends.

Neil: Manager in his fifties, Jewish, living on Long Island. Neil had spent many years with the company but never moved beyond being a store manager.

UPPER EAST SIDE STORE

Miriam: Twenty-eight-year-old immigrant from El Salvador, living in the Bronx. Miriam had worked for seven years at Crayton's and was trying to finish Lehman College.

Tom: Native American (Sioux) from the Southwest in his early fifties. Tom used to have a street stall.

Kathy: Living in Harlem with her mother, who was a Russian woman separated from Kathy's African American father. A single mother with a very patchy career history, Kathy had one year of college.

Diane and Ana: Two second-generation Dominican sisters. Ana had just finished high school and was postponing her plan to study "metaphysics" because she was pregnant. Diane was twenty-five and married to a Dominican. They all lived with Diane and Ana's mother in Washington Heights.

Fred: Jamaican immigrant in his early forties, living in the Bronx, working as the night manager.

Sarah: Second-generation West Indian living in Crown Heights, Brooklyn. Sandra had recently finished culinary school and left Crayton's to work at the Macy's cafeteria during the fieldwork.

Sandra: Puerto Rican in her late twenties, living in the Bronx with her two children. Sandra worked part-time for some extra money.

Edward: Nineteen-year-old Puerto Rican, trying to finish his GED, living in the Bronx.

Valerie: Twenty-nine-year-old African American woman, living on her own in the Bronx. After working at Crayton's for nine years, Valerie managed to finish an accounting course at Monroe College and leave Crayton's.

Kelly: Twenty-nine-year-old Puerto Rican single mother, living with her mother in the Bronx. Kelly hoped to get through Monroe College, where she had just begun by taking remedial classes.

Gregory: Thirty-two-year-old African American man living in Brooklyn, married with one young daughter. Gregory had been at Crayton's for three years.

Antony: African American in his late twenties. Antony had finished college in Florida.

Arleen: African American woman in her early thirties, living on the Upper West Side. Arleen had finished Baruch and had been at Crayton's as an assistant manager for seven years.

Karen: African American in her midthirties, living with her Puerto Rican husband and children in the Bronx. An assistant manager for seven years, Karen sold Tupperware and Amway products to staff.

Katherine: White woman in her sixties who worked the morning shift and had worked in retail all her life in New York department stores.

Gerry: Recently arrived eighteen-year-old immigrant from Jamaica, living in Brooklyn. Gerry got his job through Fred the night manager. He wanted to go to Brooklyn College but was told that his credentials would not be accepted; he was trying to get credits at high school.

Manni: Eighteen-year-old from the Congo, living on Kennedy Island. His parents were refugees in the United States.

Doreen: African American in her early twenties, at college in Virginia. Doreen worked at the store while she was at home in the Bronx for the summer.

Sara: Twenty-year-old half–Puerto Rican, half-Dominican. Sara was home from college in upstate New York.

Oscar: Puerto Rican and African American in his early thirties, married with one child, living in the Bronx. Employed as a manager, Oscar had worked previously at Model's sports stores.

Notes

1. In 1999 the Bureau of Labor Statistics (BLS) employment projections for 1998 to 2008 predicted that retail salespersons would provide the second-largest number of new jobs (563,000) after systems analysts (577,000), not including cashiers (another 556,000). In absolute numbers, there would be four times as many retail salespersons as systems analysts (the fastest-growing occupation). More recent revisions no longer predict retail as one of the fastest-growing occupations (U.S. Department of Labor 2001) but still cite it as the nation's major employer (Berman 2001).

2. U.S. Department of Labor (2003) statistics do not list the retail sector among the next decade's top ten salary providers. The average hourly wage of workers in the retail trade was $10.04 in 2002, compared to an average of $14.77 for all workers (U.S. Department of Labor 2003). The average weekly wage decreased from $244 in 1986 to $222 in 1995 (in 1995 dollars), during which time retail earnings decreased in all but nine metropolitan areas (Crispell 1997). In New York City in 1995 the average salary in the retail sector was $21,000, which was the lowest alongside the social services (New York State Comptroller's Office 1999). Retail wages have dropped as retailers' profit margins have shrunk in the face of intense competition and they have targeted payrolls to cut costs (Bailey and Bernhardt 1997).

3. As New York City came out of its recession in the early 1990s, the retail sector represented nearly one-third of all job growth in the city (39,000 jobs) but accounted for only 2.4 percent of real earnings growth (New York State Comptroller's Office 1999).

4. "Crayton's" is a pseudonym, as are all the names mentioned throughout the chapter.

5. I am indebted to the store managers as well as the regional manager who gave me this permission.

6. This was as much an issue in the past as it is today. Susan Benson (1986) shows that the development of the modern "palaces of consumption" (Leach 1993) required the development of a "respectable" workforce to welcome consumers. A lower-class workforce was thought to risk alienating consumers by highlighting the different class and race positions between the customer and the saleswoman, hindering the possibility of their bonding. Benson describes the measures taken by department stores to mold their workforces into respectable women. Stores operated training programs that educated working-class women about appropriate middle-class codes. The department stores mixed "good" young girls who worked to help their family with married women who were earning some extra household income. In all these cases, shared gender roles and ideals of womanhood were pushed on the shop floor. It was hoped that this would permit the emergence of a shared culture between workers and shoppers. That this strategy succeeded in creating such a shared culture—to the detriment of the managers—could be seen in the way customers' empathy (and complaints) were instrumental in the creation of welfare work programs at the turn of the century that supported sales associates in their quest for better working conditions. In the late 1930s and 1940s, sales associates further capitalized on this shared culture by gathering consumer support in their attempts to organize at specific department stores (Opler 2000).

7. While retail establishments in low-income neighborhoods may prefer employing residents from other neighborhoods, as shown by Katherine Newman (1999), it may also be the case that applicants who arrive from outside of the neighborhood already have some self-selected trait that enables them to make the journey in the first place. That is, among individuals with similar human capital, those who travel around the city looking for a job may be a self-selected group. Newman does not consider the issue of self-selection in her discussion of the overrepresentation of employees from other neighborhoods in Harlem stores, thus perhaps overemphasizing the bias of neighborhood employers.

8. This may be a standard practice among some retailers. In December 2000, the Massachusetts attorney general reached a settlement with a clothing store, the Children's Place, after employees complained that they were told to follow black customers around and not give them large shopping bags, in an effort to prevent theft (Goldberg 2000).

9. Abercrombie and Fitch, a young, hip clothing store, is being sued for dis-

crimination because of its policy of approaching attractive customers to offer them employment. It is a common practice in more upscale retail stores to look for "attractive" employees who represent the product you sell (Greenhouse 2003).

10. In New York City street cleaning and, more important, no-parking days are suspended for specific religious holidays. By now most religions have claimed holidays, much to the gratitude of the many residents who no longer need to look for a new parking space on days such as the Immaculate Conception (November 8), the Asian Lunar New Year (February 1), and Shemini Atzeret (October 18), to name a few.

11. Not only is the retail sector a source of a large number of low-wage jobs, but much of its job growth has taken place in the provision of part-time work. In 1985 one of every three retail workers was employed on a part-time basis, and 40 percent of job growth in this sector from 1973 to 1985 was in part-time work. The relative contribution of part-timers to total employment growth for non-agricultural industries during this time was one-fourth (Haugen 1986).

12. Many of the employees were following some form of higher education—which requires a flexibility that made them perfect for part-time work in retail—but many others were not. According to Newman (1999, 127–32), managers in a Harlem fast-food franchise had the stipulation in their franchise agreement that they had to encourage their employees who were studying. These Harlem managers monitored report cards, paid for books, sponsored tutoring programs for their workers, and cut workers' hours if their grades were falling (129). No such policy was in place at Crayton's; though managers were sympathetic, it was understood that school was not to interfere with work. There was no incentive to encourage individuals to study. In fact, after I helped one employee with her essay for remedial English during a quiet period, the assistant manager complained, accusing her of having an attitude when she protested. I overheard him reporting her supposed attitude problem the next day to the manager and remarking that she should do her homework on her own time (as he obviously felt he managed to do to continue his computer course).

13. For example, Guillermo Grenier and his colleagues (1992) show that in the construction industry the autonomy of the workers generates cross-ethnic ties, while a union facilitates the negotiation of complaints in ways that avoid misunderstandings along ethnic lines. In a comprehensive review of seventy-eight workplace ethnographies, Randy Hodson (1995) argues that what resonates beneath the surface is the possibility for new ties to form, although what these ethnographies often emphasize is the failure of these ties to materialize. He points out that even in studies that find ethnic shifts in employment patterns, individual friendships have been observed, as well as the sharing of ritualized events, such as birthdays, Christmas, and tragedies, regardless of workers' ethnicity. Newman (1999) finds that friendships form as workers try to avoid tripping over the obstacles that growing up in the ghetto puts in their way. She also

points out, however, that ethnic antagonism arises between new immigrants and African Americans in the workplace when Latino immigrants are hired to satisfy a growing Latino community in Upper Manhattan.

REFERENCES

Bailey, Thomas, and Annette Bernhardt. 1997. "In Search of the High Road in a Low-Wage Industry." *Politics and Society* 25(2): 179–202.

Benson, Susan Porter. 1986. *Counter Cultures: Saleswomen, Managers, and Customers in American Department Stores 1890–1940*. Urbana: University of Illinois Press.

Berman, Jay. 2001. "Industry Employment: Employment Output and Employment Projections to 2010." *Monthly Labor Review* (November): 39–56.

Crispell, Diane. 1997. "Retailing's Next Decade." *American Demographics* 19(5): 4–10.

Goldberg, Carey. 2000. "Retail Racial Profiling." *New York Times*, December 24.

Goode, Judith. 1994. "Encounters over the Counter: Bosses, Workers, and Customers on a Changing Shopping Strip." In *Newcomers in the Workplace: Immigrants and the Restructuring of the U.S. Economy*, edited by Louise Lamphere, Alex Stepick, and Guillermo Grenier. Philadelphia: Temple University Press.

Goode, Judith, and Jo Anne Schneider. 1994. *Reshaping Ethnic and Racial Relations in Philadelphia: Immigrants in a Divided City*. Philadelphia: Temple University Press.

Granovetter, Mark. 1995. "The Economic Sociology of Firms and Entrepreneurs." In *The Economic Sociology of Immigration: Essays on Networks, Ethnicity, and Entrepreneurship*, edited by Alejandro Portes. New York: Russell Sage Foundation.

Greenhouse, Steven. 2003. "Going for the Look, but Risking Discrimination." *New York Times*, July 8.

Grenier, Guillermo, Alex Stepick, Debbie Draznin, Aline La Borwit, and Steve Morris. 1992. "On Machines and Bureaucracy: Controlling Ethnic Interaction in Miami's Apparel and Construction Industries." In *Structuring Diversity: Ethnographic Perspectives on the New Immigration*, edited by Louise Lamphere. Chicago: University of Chicago Press.

Harvey, David. 1989. *The Condition of Postmodernity: An Inquiry into the Origins of Cultural Change*. Oxford: Blackwell.

Haugen, Steven. 1986. "The Employment in Retail Trade, 1973–1985 (Statistical Analysis)." *Monthly Labor Review* 109: 9–17.

Hodson, Randy. 1991. "The Active Worker: Compliance and Autonomy at the Workplace." *Journal of Contemporary Ethnography* 20(1): 47–78.

———. 1995. "Cohesion or Conflict? Race, Solidarity, and Resistance in the Workplace." In *Research in the Sociology of Work*, vol. 5. Greenwich, Conn.: JAI Press.

Hollander, Stanley, and Glenn Omura. 1989. "Chain Store Developments and Their Political, Strategic, and Social Interdependancies." *Journal of Retailing* 65(3): 299–325.

Jaynes, Gerald. 2000. "Immigration and the American Dream." In *Immigration and Race: New Challenges for American Democracy*, edited by Gerald Jaynes. New Haven, Conn.: Yale University Press.

Kim, Dae Young. 1999. "Beyond Co-ethnic Solidarity: Mexican and Ecuadorean Employment in Korean-Owned Businesses in New York City." *Ethnic and Racial Studies* 22(3): 581–601.

Lamphere, Louise, Alex Stepick, and Guillermo Grenier. 1994. "Introduction." In *Newcomers in the Workplace*, edited by Louise Lamphere, Alex Stepick, and Guillermo Grenier. Philadelphia: Temple University Press.

Leach, William. 1993. *Land of Desire: Merchants, Power, and the Rise of a New American Culture*. New York: Vintage Books.

Leidner, Robin. 1996. "Rethinking Question of Control: Lessons from McDonald's." In *Working in the Service Society*, edited by Cameron Lynne Macdonald and Carmen Sirianni. Philadelphia: Temple University Press.

Logan, John, and Richard Alba. 1999. "Minority Niches and Immigrant Enclaves in New York and Los Angeles: Trends and Impacts." In *Immigration and Opportunity: Race, Ethnicity, and Employment in the United States*, edited by Frank D. Bean and Stephanie Bell-Rose. New York: Russell Sage Foundation.

Lopez, David, and Cynthia Feliciana. 2000. "Who Does What? California's Emerging Plural Labor Force." In *Organizing Immigrants: The Challenge for Unions in Contemporary California*, edited by Ruth Milkman. Ithaca, N.Y.: Cornell University Press.

Macdonald, Cameron Lynne, and Carmen Sirianni. 1996. "The Service Society and the Changing Experience of Work." In *Working in the Service Society*, edited by Cameron Lynne Macdonald and Carmen Sirianni. Philadelphia: Temple University Press.

New York State Comptroller's Office. 1999. *Recent Trends in New York City Economy*. Albany, N.Y.: Office of the State Deputy Comptroller for the City of New York.

Newman, Katherine. 1999. *No Shame in My Game: The Working Poor in the Inner City*. New York: Russell Sage Foundation.

Opler, Dan. 2000. "Monkey Business: Consumption, Communism, and the Ohrbach's/Klein's Strikes of 1934–1935." Unpublished paper. New York University, Department of History, New York.

Portes, Alejandro, ed. 1995. *The Economic Sociology of Immigration: Essays on Networks, Ethnicity, and Immigration*. New York: Russell Sage Foundation.

Rath, Jan, and Robert Kloosterman. 2000. "A Critical Review of Research on Immigrant Entrepreneurs." *International Migration Review* 34(3): 657–81.

U.S. Department of Labor. Bureau of Labor Statistics. 1999. *Employment Projections 1999–2008*. Washington: U.S. Government Printing Office.

———. 2001. *Employment Projections 2000–2010*. Washington: U.S. Government Printing Office.

———. 2003. "Industry at a Glance: Wholesale and Retail Trade." Available at: http://www.bls.gov/iag/iag.wholeretailtrade.htm.

Waldinger, Roger. 1996. *Still the Promised City: African Americans and the New Immigration in Postindustrial New York*. Cambridge, Mass.: Harvard University Press.

———. 1999. "Networks, Bureaucracy, and Exclusion: Recruitment and Selection in an Immigrant Metropolis." In *Immigration and Opportunity: Race, Ethnicity, and Employment in the United States*, edited by Frank D. Bean and Stephanie Bell-Rose. New York: Russell Sage Foundation.

Waldinger, Roger, and Michael Lichter. 2003. *How the Other Half Works: Immigration and the Social Organization of Labor*. Berkeley: University of California Press.

Waters, Mary. 1999. "West Indians and African Americans at Work: Structural Differences and Cultural Stereotypes." In *Immigration and Opportunity: Race, Ethnicity, and Employment in the United States*, edited by Frank D. Bean and Stephanie Bell-Rose. New York: Russell Sage Foundation.

Wilson, Franklin. 1999. "Ethnic Concentrations and Labor-Market Opportunities." In *Immigration and Opportunity: Race, Ethnicity, and Employment in the United States*, edited by Frank D. Bean and Stephanie Bell-Rose. New York: Russell Sage Foundation.

Zeltzer-Zubida, Aviva. 2003. "Co-ethnic Employment and the Economic Trajectories of Second-Generation Immigrants in the Metropolitan New York Labor Market." Paper presented to the annual meeting of the Eastern Sociological Society. Philadelphia, (February).

Chapter 6

Leaving the Ethnic Economy: The Rapid Integration of Second-Generation Korean Americans in New York*

Dae Young Kim

At the time of the interview in 1998, Heesoo was a thirty-four-year-old woman born in Korea and raised in the suburbs of Maryland. She worked as a real estate developer for a major real estate acquisition and development company in New York. A graduate of a prestigious university in the midatlantic, she had also received an M.B.A. from an Ivy League university. Her parents were college-educated, but like many other Korean immigrants who had difficulty transferring their professions to the U.S context, they adapted economically by entering small business as grocers. During Heesoo's childhood her father struggled with the business. By the time her sisters were growing up, however, the grocery stores were thriving, and, as she recounted, the family had made numerous corollary residential changes, from a lower-middle-class neighborhood to upper-class neighborhoods. "When I grew up, we were very poor. When my younger sisters grew up, we were doing very well, so they are extremely spoiled. They have no values," Heesoo added. In fact, Heesoo recalled moving nine times. At the peak of their business success, her parents owned three homes, one with a swimming pool, and purchased a new car every year. When Heesoo started attending college, however, the business started faltering, finally ending up in bankruptcy.

Even during times of success her parents did not want Heesoo to continue in their line of work. For her own part, Heesoo was equally unwilling to inherit her parents' business or to become an entrepreneur. Despite all the sac-

* All names of individuals reported throughout the chapter are pseudonyms.

rifice and stress that her parents endured to run the business, Heesoo had no qualms about staying away from their line of work. She was more than satisfied with the pay, responsibility, work schedule, and benefits package of her job as a real estate developer. Not surprisingly, she was adamantly opposed to trading more work time for the leisure her job afforded her; having seen how little leisure time her parents had, she had no interest in the increased income that the grocery business might bring her. She had also seen how meteoric and ephemeral that success could be as business mistakes led her father to financial failure. She was relieved to see the business close, but her parents' financial difficulties created many obligations for her as she came to their aid. At the time of the interview Heesoo was most concerned with resolving her parents' financial problems.

Sharon was a thirty-three-year-old finance and strategy associate for a major financial firm when she was interviewed. She grew up in a suburb in northern California and attended a major state university in California. Her parents, although college-educated in Korea, turned to the motel business to earn a living in the United States. Growing up, Sharon, with her older brothers and sisters, worked in her parents' motel. She knew that helping out in a family business was rather uncommon among her peers in school. Her parents had become quite successful from the business and retired. Like other middle-class Korean parents who wished their children to avoid small business as their occupation, Sharon's parents pushed their children away from the motel business. Sharon recognized that her parents had had few occupational choices as immigrants and that the subsequent generation was in a better position to apply their educational credentials and language skills in securing professional jobs. Thus, Sharon had very little desire to become self-employed. Her concerns were marriage, family, and the question of how to balance work with family.

KOREAN IMMIGRANT ENTREPRENEURSHIP AND THE SECOND GENERATION

For many people, the idea of entrepreneurship evokes deeply idealized sentiments of mobility and financial independence. Natives and immigrants alike are drawn to the notion of striking out on their own to achieve financial success and freedom. Especially for immigrants, language difficulties, licensing requirements, and unfavorable labor markets may make entrepreneurship an alternative to secondary labor markets and, even more, the only means of combating unemployment (Light and Rosenstein 1995; Light and Gold 2000). In spite of the heavy costs that self-employment may entail, including long working hours, stress, and, at worst, business failure and financial troubles, immigrants have rushed to entrepreneurship. Known for their high self-employment rates, Korean immigrants have been no exception and have aggressively pursued entrepreneurship as a strategy for adapting to life in the United States (Kim 1981; Bonacich and Light 1988; Portes and Rumbaut 1990; Min 1996, 1998; Bates 1997; Yoon 1997). Indeed, Korean immigrant businesses, from greengrocers to dry cleaners, have become ubiquitous fixtures on the U.S. urban landscape.

Yet what enabled the first generation to regain their middle-class status in the United States has been strongly rejected by 1.5- and second-generation Korean Americans.[1] Despite the success of the strategies of mobility used by their immigrant parents, second-generation Korean Americans have shunned the small-business path. The view of Derek, a physical trainer at a gym, was reflective of the second generation's common rejection of immigrant entrepreneurship. "I am still not sure what I want to do, but I know what I don't want to do. . . . Not a deli. That's too hard. . . . [I'd rather do] something requiring minimal effort," Derek explained. Such sentiments prompt some critical questions: Why is the second generation snubbing the entrepreneurial route of first-generation Korean immigrants? Are they also rejecting the flourishing ethnic economy now visible in large metropolitan areas in the United States?[2] What does their concomitant embrace of mainstream strategies of mobility imply for the future of the Korean American ethnic economy as well as for the second generation's prospects for assimilation? This chapter addresses these issues by examining second-generation Korean Americans' rejection of immigrant entrepreneurship and the consequences of their swift departure from the ethnic economy of their immigrant parents.

METHODS

The primary data source for this study was the 1998 New York Second-Generation Korean American Survey (NYSGKA Survey), a closed-ended telephone survey conducted with two hundred second-generation Korean Americans, age twenty-three to thirty-five, in the metropolitan New York–New Jersey area.[3] The survey was conducted from June 1998 through November 1998, and the telephone interviews took an average of thirty minutes to complete. The sample was randomly drawn using a surname methodology,[4] taking advantage of the fact that Korean surnames are remarkably unique.[5] Research shows that a surname telephone sample generates a far more unbiased sample than other nonprobability methods of sampling, such as using alumni directories and organization membership lists. Surname research is more cost-effective, more up-to-date, and better for sampling a population that shows high residential mobility and geographic distribution than other methods. This method has been used with Hispanic-origin surnames and with Jewish surnames (Himmelfarb, Loar, and Mott 1983; Rosenwaike 1994). Korean surnames are even better suited for surname research than other groups because of the relative ethnic homogeneity of the Korean population (Shin and Yu 1984).

Although survey data provide valuable demographic and life history information, the closed-ended and polling nature of the data does not fully capture the specific reasons and circumstances for individuals' occupational choices. We therefore conducted, simultaneously with the telephone survey, forty follow-up, in-person, in-depth interviews with children of small-business owners and children of professionals in order to have a second data source. These open-ended, tape-recorded interviews lasted approximately one and a half hours. We asked about second-generation experiences with schooling, upbringing, labor market entry, and issues of identity and assimilation, social networks, parents' economic adaptation, language facility, and so forth. The qualitative data garnered through these interviews provide a rich and nuanced view of the dynamics of the second generation's transition from school to the labor market. The quantitative data provided by the survey and the qualitative data gleaned from the interviews together offer a more comprehensive look into the lives of second-generation Korean Americans than relying on either methodology alone would have afforded.

THE SELECTIVITY OF KOREAN IMMIGRATION AND EXIT FROM THE ETHNIC ECONOMY

The two vignettes that open this chapter register unanimous rejection of the small-business path by second-generation Korean Americans. What do the quantitative data on the self-employment rates of second-generation Korean Americans show? Using 1990 census data, Ivan Light and Elizabeth Roach (1996) find that only 11 percent of native-born Korean Americans in the greater Los Angeles area were self-employed, a rate significantly lower than the self-employment rate of Korean immigrants (around 35 percent based on Min's [1996] research and the 1990 public use microdata samples [PUMS]) and even that of native-born white Americans (13 percent). An article in the *Korea Times New York* reported that about 50 percent of second-generation Korean Americans were moving into professional occupations, in contrast to the self-employment route taken by the first generation. The data from my 1998 NYSGKA Survey (Kim 2001) corroborate such findings. As table 6.1 shows, self-employment rates had dropped markedly by the second generation: from 43 percent for fathers of the second generation to 11 percent for their children.

TABLE 6.1   THE SECOND GENERATION'S WORK STATUS, BY
             GENDER AND FATHER'S WORK STATUS

Work Status	Second Generation			Respondent's Father
	Men	Women	Total	
Self-employed	10%	11%	11%	43%
Family business (for pay or without pay)	8	3	5	9
Korean immigrant business employee	3	5	4	4
South Korea or South Korean subsidiary employee	3	5	4	4
Mainstream employee	75	76	76	40
Sample size	96	106	202	198

Source: Kim 2001.
Note: Work status refers to current or most recent job.

More than three-fourths (76 percent) of second-generation Korean Americans found employment in the mainstream economy, compared to 40 percent of their immigrant fathers.[6] Self-employment differences between second-generation men (10 percent) and women (11 percent) were also negligible, but owing to the size of the sample, these cross-tabulations must be considered with caution.

Although the substantial drop in self-employment from the first generation to the second generation indicates a rapid exit from the ethnic economy, the 40 percent rate of fathers of the second generation employed in the mainstream economy in table 6.1 demonstrates that roughly half of these fathers were uninvolved with the ethnic economy to begin with. Furthermore, when we look at the educational background of the fathers of the second generation (see table 6.2), the selectivity of Korean immigration can be readily discerned: 38 percent of the fathers had a college degree, and another 42 percent had graduate degrees. Thus, the fathers of the second generation, both professionals and entrepreneurs, were highly educated Korean immigrants.[7]

What this reveals, corroborating 1990 census data and other research on Korean immigration (Min 1984, 1996; Yoon 1997), is the urban and professional backgrounds of Korean immigrants to the United States, contrary to the typical media portrayal of Korean immigrants as proprietors of small businesses. Although there is a possibility of sampling error, the largely middle-class makeup of this sample is likely to be the result of the survey's emphasis on capturing the experience of the *adult* second generation (twenty-three- to thirty-five-year-olds). In other words, given the patterns of Korean immigrants who have entered the United States through the occupational

TABLE 6.2   EDUCATIONAL LEVELS OF SECOND-GENERATION KOREAN
AMERICANS, BY GENDER AND FATHER'S EDUCATION

Educational Level	Second Generation			Respondent's Father
	Men	Women	Total	
High school or less	2%	1%	2%	15%
Some college (A.A.)	15	6	10	4
College (B.A. or B.S.)	48	62	55	38
Some graduate school	8	7	7	1
Graduate degree or higher	27	25	26	42
Sample size	98	107	205	201

Source: Kim 2001.

preference system since the 1960s, earlier cohorts came from primarily middle-class backgrounds (Yoon 1997).[8]

Consequently, the mobility of the second generation is less remarkable than it is presumed to be since close to half of the second generation and their parents never set foot in the ethnic economy to begin with. The speedy exodus of the second generation from the ethnic economy into the mainstream was achieved in the context of professional advantage in the first generation. Moreover, as illustrated by the educational attainment of fathers of the second generation, the disproportionate self-employment rate of entrepreneurial fathers in table 6.1 is a notable example of the propensity of Korean immigrants, despite professional and urban backgrounds in Korea, to become entrepreneurs to offset the disadvantages of difficulties with English, strict licensing requirements, and discrimination in the U.S. labor market (Abelmann and Lie 1995; Min 1984, 1996; Yoon 1997). Therefore, the drive to abandon small-business entrepreneurship in droves for employment in the mainstream economy was hardly contemplated by the children of professionals, and similarly, the rejection of entrepreneurship by the children of entrepreneurs is expected given the middle-class background of their self-employed parents (discussed in the next section).

This can be further elaborated by comparing the self-employment rates of children of professionals and children of entrepreneurs.[9] We see in table 6.3 that children of entrepreneurs (11 percent) were equally rejecting the self-employment route of their fathers and seeking jobs in the mainstream (69 percent), even though this rate was slightly lower than the proportion of children of professionals (86 percent) seeking employment in the mainstream economy.

In light of this, it is no surprise that children of professionals were seeking careers in the mainstream economy. Similarly, children of entrepreneurs had

TABLE 6.3   THE SECOND GENERATION'S WORK STATUS, BY FATHER'S
WORK STATUS

Second Generation's	Father's Work Status		
Work Status	Professional	Entrepreneur	Total
Self-employed	9%	11%	10%
Family business	1	8	5
Korean immigrant business employee	1	7	4
South Korea or South Korean subsidiary employee	2	6	4
Mainstream employee	86	69	77
Sample size	86	102	188

Source: Kim 2001.
Note: Second generation's work status refers to current or most recent job.

broader employment options than their immigrant parents, who were bound
by language difficulties and licensing obstacles. As is characteristic in today's
postindustrial economy, such employment choices range from working for a
domestic firm or journeying abroad to tackle the South Korean labor market.
Additionally, multiculturalism and diversity initiatives in the United States
have expanded the role of ethnic mediators and brokers who might tap more
easily into minority and Korean community markets. Table 6.4 indicates that
two-thirds (67 percent) of second-generation Korean Americans participating in this study were securing jobs in a variety of professions (managerial and
professional specialty occupations). The 1990s financial boom in New York
triggered a huge demand for new hires to act as consultants, analysts, and investment bankers, and second-generation Korean Americans filled many of

TABLE 6.4   SECOND-GENERATION KOREAN AMERICANS' OCCUPATION,
BY GENDER AND FATHER'S OCCUPATION

Occupation	Second Generation			Respondent's Father
	Men	Women	Total	
Managerial and professional specialty	66%	68%	67%	51%
Technical, sales, and administrative support	26	27	27	44
Service	5	4	5	1
Precision production, craft, and repair	1	1	1	2
Operators, fabricators, and laborers	1		1	2
Sample size	95	103	198	193

Source: Kim 2001.
Note: Occupation refers to current or most recent job.

those positions. For second-generation Korean American women, in addition to the finance, insurance, and real estate industries, fashion design has been another route of entry into the primary sector.[10]

Paralegal work also served as an entry point into professional life. According to a respondent, although paralegal jobs required long hours and a college education, they paid relatively well as entry-level positions and could act as springboards to other corporate sectors like finance.

The next section examines the reasons for parents' emphasis on professional occupations instead of entrepreneurship and the prospects of self-employment for the second generation.

EXPLAINING CAREER TRAJECTORIES: CLASS, COMMUNITY, AND PARENTAL EXPECTATIONS ABOUT OCCUPATION

Korean parents placed heavy emphasis on high-status professional occupations (Abelmann and Lie 1995, 127; Kim 1993; Min 1998). Both Korean parents and the Korean community in general favor professional occupations, especially in medicine and law. The fact that close to half of the fathers of second-generation Korean Americans were professionals (see table 6.1) was a good predictor of professional careers for their children. Both the desire for social status and the pragmatism of first-generation parents were decisive factors (Abelmann and Lie 1995). That is, the first generation's difficulties entering the primary sectors led them to believe that professional occupations (in law, medicine, engineering, accounting, and the hard sciences) would better shield second-generation Korean Americans from discrimination and thus provide a solid entry into the middle class.

Furthermore, in the event that the second generation faces difficulty in the primary sector and is forced to seek alternatives, as did early Jewish professionals who were compelled by anti-Semitism to rely on an ethnic economy, professional skills are potentially valuable in the ethnic economy and elsewhere.

Peter, a twenty-eight-year-old research assistant at a hospital, confirmed that his parents had pressured him to become a doctor: "Ever since I was a little child, they ingrained in my brain I was going to be a doctor." Peter was born in the United States, and after graduating from a selective midwestern university, he spent a few years in Korea teaching English. Although he was in the medical field at the time of the interview, he had a particular interest in anthropology.

The same pressure to become a doctor was put on Paul, a thirty-two-year-old chief resident at a university hospital. Paul's educational credentials were remarkable: he graduated from a prominent boarding school, a highly selective liberal arts college, and then a top private medical school. Because his father was an anesthesiologist, Paul had grown up subscribing to the idea of also becoming a physician. He noted that "the kids get steered toward that direction." As the only child among his siblings to actually fulfill his parents' expectation, Paul felt he had readily internalized his parents' wishes. He was quick to point out that doing so was not that much of an obligation: "It's not only for them, because it's a good job. . . . It's not like suffering."

Some parents who found their children deviating from pursuing the profession they initially had envisioned for them advocated the next-status occupation in their perceived ladder of prestige. For example, when Heesoo's mother realized that her daughter was not following the premed route, she pushed her toward law. "Korean parents really know only three careers: law, medicine, and engineering. . . . She was astonished that there was work outside of that. And they have no idea what I do," Heesoo declared. Her father was happy in the end because she ultimately worked at a big firm, a position about which he could brag to his friends.

Others, like Eunjung's mother, stressed nursing or computer jobs and did not, to her surprise, expect her to become a lawyer or doctor. Eunjung conceded: "Maybe she wanted us to marry one." Even though most parents bore professional expectations for both their sons and daughters, many parents felt that getting their daughters married was their "ultimate" responsibility. Eunjung suspected that her father "wanted [them] to get married and be taken care of. I think he just wanted us to go to college, meet a nice man, get married." Eunjung was a twenty-eight-year-old assistant for a Korean chiropractor. Her mother was a nurse, and her father operated various businesses, including a deli and a jewelry store. She grew up on Long Island and attended a state university in upstate New York. One of the few who married a "Korean-Korean," Eunjung had met her husband while working for a South Korean multinational firm selling toddler clothes.[11] While most second-generation Korean Americans in this sample had no experience in the ethnic economy, Eunjung had yet to work in the mainstream economy.

As the statements of respondents reveal, many parents were not aware of the occupational diversity of the corporate world. This was not too surprising since many parents had little experience in the corporate world and thus lacked the relevant information. Some respondents mentioned that their parents, like other "typical" Korean parents, may have had professional careers in mind but refrained from pressuring them to pursue these occupations. Many of these were parents making a realistic assessment of the avenues available to children who were not academically oriented. These parents encouraged what they saw to be the next best option: bringing their children into their own business, arranging for their children to have businesses of their own if the means were available, or landing them suitable jobs through their social networks.

Chulsoo's parents, for example, agreed to allow their son to drop out of junior high school only when he promised that he would work in the family business. Chulsoo, one of the few fruit and vegetable store owners who had taken over the family business, believed he made the appropriate choice, since his friends who had graduated from high school and college were bouncing around from one job to another; one friend was delivering newspapers after graduating from college. He was thirty-three years old and one of the few respondents who was married with children. Chulsoo came to America at the age of twelve. He explained that his parents had emigrated with few assets and that small business had indeed played a big role in their economic mobility in their adopted country. Chulsoo often considered himself fortunate to have bypassed years of schooling to go directly into the labor market, where he quickly established himself while others his age were still struggling to do the same.

PARENTAL AND SECOND-GENERATION REJECTION OF SMALL BUSINESS

Self-employed parents, understanding that running a small business requires hard work and long hours for success, and familiar as well with the challenges posed by the interethnic and interracial conflicts that entrepreneurs encounter with minority customers in minority-clientele businesses, were reluctant to push their children to follow in their footsteps. Having established themselves in small business because their labor market options were limited, Korean merchants, as Pyong Gap Min's 1982 survey in Atlanta found, did not want their children to continue in small business and instead expected their children to obtain professional jobs (Min 1988; see also Waldinger 1989, 1996).[12] Nancy Abelmann and John Lie (1995, 129) explain:

> The decision to start a small business represents a calculated intergenerational mobility strategy—the strategic adaptation of the dreams of modernity and mobility. Like many petite bourgeoisie in contemporary capitalist societies, the stratum of small business people is transitional, not hereditary. Many Korean American shopkeepers balk at the prospect of their children's succeeding them in their businesses or opening small retail stores of their own; the first generation's desire for the second generation is for them to achieve prestigious and remunerative careers.

Sharon perceptively recognized that language barriers and limited employment opportunities were what pushed the first generation to start small businesses in the United States. Her parents' motel business "was a very hard, manual-labor job that they would not want for us, nor would we want it for ourselves. . . . There are certainly better ways of making money. They didn't have the opportunity unfortunately, but we do," stressed Sharon. Similarly, Heesoo's parents had instructed her to advance beyond the occupational limitations of the first generation: "We don't want you to follow in our footsteps. That's why we came here so you wouldn't have to do this."

Similarly, Joseph never considered taking over his parents' grocery store, and his parents were equally opposed to the idea, even though he was working for them at the store. "They thought I was just too smart to be doing something like that. They don't want me to do what they do," said Joseph. Thus, as Abelmann and Lie (1995, 137) state: "The whole rationale of the enterprise is for the second generation to achieve mainstream success and therefore upward mobility." U.S.-born or -raised children, products of an American upbringing and socialized in the mind-set of the host society, were less inclined to follow the low-status jobs of their immigrant parents (Zhou and Bankston 1998; Portes and Zhou 1993). Min (1988) noted that children of Korean immigrants were unlikely to tolerate the long hours necessary for survival in small business. Indeed, second-generation Korean Americans were unwilling to carry on with the labor-intensive "mom and pop" businesses of Korean immigrants.

Having witnessed her parents' struggles—the seven-day-a-week workload, the stress, and the financial volatility of business—Connie was unwilling to tolerate the emotional, physical, and financial strain and instability characteristic of small businesses. She was a twenty-four-year-old public relations representative for a fashion company. In spite of having attended a selective New York City public high school, a fondness for parties and "hanging out" had led her into academic trouble. Although she barely graduated from high school, Connie did manage to attend a private college in upstate New York. She attributed some of her teenage problems to financial and marital problems between her parents. While her mother's nail salon was profitable, her father's import-export business led to numerous periods of financial instability, causing family and marital strain. Similarly, Joonshik was disinclined to put himself or his family through the same uncertainties his father had inflicted on the family. "I've seen my father and our family suffer when things were bad," Joonshik noted.

A few respondents stated that they felt unfit for their parents' businesses and wanted to forge their own trails. "First of all, I don't think I am very well suited for running a store. This is fitting in. Most of your peers are working in businesses or starting their own companies, and to take over an established business, it kind of seems like a cop-out," Jonathan explained. He was a twenty-seven-year-old associate consultant for an accounting firm. Jonathan felt that his high school had made too many academic demands, which held him back and pushed him to go to a state university in New Jersey. Unlike his brothers, who had decided on private colleges, he chose a state school because of the financial burden on his parents. He regretted that decision by the time of the interview because he realized that a private education had more value in the labor market. Now that all of the children had finished college, Jonathan's parents were hinting that they would be pleased if one of their sons took over the family business. But realizing that they all had professional careers, Jonathan's parents accepted that their children were not going to make that move.

Junghoon lost interest in his parents' business when he concluded that there was no way a small retail business would enable him to reach his financial goal of having a net worth of $10 million. He was twenty-four years old and working for a Korean bank. Junghoon had come to America at the age of ten, and like others who came to America at an older age, he was more comfortable speaking in Korean. He graduated from a state university in upstate New York, and his parents owned a dry cleaners.

James, having had experience in managing cafés, understood how stressful running a business is, especially dealing with customers. He was a twenty-eight-year-old artist taking fine arts classes at a public university in New York City in pursuit of a master's degree. He grew up in Houston and graduated from a highly selective public university in California. While growing up, his parents owned a deli and a trading company. After his father passed away, his mother settled in Seattle, where she operated a dry cleaners. "I would like to avoid it [being in small business] because it's too much headache dealing with people," James explained.

Often parents attempted to assess who among their children was most fit to take over the family business. Connie's parents initially asked Connie to take over the business, but after they quickly concluded that she was uninterested, they did not push the idea further. Sarah's parents also perceptively chose not to pass on the dry cleaners to her, since they recognized that their daughter had a different goal. A graduate of an Ivy League university, Sarah was a twenty-six-year-old working in the HMO industry. Well aware that Sarah's younger brother was unsure about his career plans but was not headed toward a primary-sector occupation, Sarah's parents intervened and jump-started his career by arranging for him to have a small business.

SELF-EMPLOYMENT PROSPECTS

Although children of small-business owners, as their low self-employment rates attest, were reluctant to take over their parents' businesses, self-employment in the future was not completely out of the picture. Small businesses vary considerably in size and profitability. Although second-generation Korean Americans shunned labor-intensive retail businesses, they were not averse to taking over other lucrative businesses. A few of the respondents spoke about their difficulties in the mainstream labor markets and had plans to become self-employed in the near future. The appeal of financial independence was a big draw for these young adults.

The profitability of her parents' dry cleaners was extremely appealing for Martha. She was a twenty-nine-year-old high school teacher who had come to America at the age of ten and graduated from a state university in New Jersey. She was married, and her parents owned a dry cleaners. Martha would have taken over her parents' dry-cleaning business had it not been for her teaching job. Although her parents had never encouraged her to take over the business, she knew they were not totally opposed to the idea because of the considerable cash flow it generated. Had she been solely focused on the potential financial gains, she would have jumped into the business. Martha even considered hiring a manager to work the morning shifts while she worked the evening shifts. "I felt tempted. But I realized money is not everything, so I gave up that dream," Martha said. She strongly felt her older sister should have taken over the business. In fact, Martha attempted to convince her sister and her husband to run the business, arguing that entrepreneurship was the quickest way to achieve economic security, considering her brother-in-law's difficulties with English. "They didn't listen to me," Martha sighed. Martha plans to have her own business in the future, not in dry-cleaning but in the computer field.

Similarly, many of those who witnessed the rapid financial attainment of their parents through business in spite of language and cultural limitations were seriously considering running a small business themselves because of the appeal of financial independence. Joseph, who had made few significant inroads in the primary sector, was willing to consider any opportunity:

> Of course, they want me to do something better, but then it goes back to having opportunity. If a particular store is very profitable and where I could be my own boss, I would grab that. I don't have to be a white-collar worker. I would be a blue-collar, because I've tasted both of them. So I could do one or the other just as easily.

Joseph was a twenty-four-year-old who worked at the family grocery store. His father was an engineer in Korea but had turned to small business in the United States because of language barriers and limited opportunities. Joseph attributed his minimal educational success to his difficulties at a selective

New York City public high school, where peers, according to Joseph, had led him into too much socializing. Although Joseph attended a state university in upstate New York, he ended up transferring to a community college in New York City because of his low grades. He was now attempting to get back on track.

Others were willing to consider self-employment if and only if they could reduce the risks that plague businesses in general. Joonshik, who was planning to return to school for an M.B.A. degree, thought that what he would learn in business school would help him lower his business risks. He was a thirty-year-old financial analyst and one of two respondents who had secondary migration experience, having spent part of his childhood in Argentina. His family later moved to New Jersey, where he spent the rest of his childhood and teenage years. Joonshik graduated from a selective private college in the northeast and was moving to upstate New York, to pursue an M.B.A. at a private university there. His parents used to own a toy store as well as a shoe store. Joonshik presently had no plans to strike out on his own. Any thoughts about doing so were focused on areas he was already familiar with, such as a consulting or a brokerage firm. Yet, if he could form a partnership with someone in the high-tech area, he would be open to the idea. "A friend of mine is in information systems, so that might be a possibility," Joonshik speculated.

Some, like Sungsoo, held the idea that becoming their own boss was the best way to make it in the United States. Sungsoo was a twenty-three-year-old analyst for a major consulting firm. He had graduated from a selective New York City public high school and a highly selective public university in the midwest. His parents owned a dojang (a martial arts studio) and a candy store, but currently his father was in Korea working as a politician. Sungsoo claimed that his business aim was not simply to make money but to "make more of a difference." As the CEO of a company, he stressed, "you can have more say in the Korean community as well." Without doubt, many agreed that the ideology of being your own boss, being able to decide your own fate, is what the American Dream is all about. Many would have joined Jonathan in saying, "At some point I would want to start my own business," yet Sungsoo and others, in spite of their firm opinion about becoming their own boss, had no clear idea of how to determine which business model to use or where to get started in accomplishing that goal. At the time of the interviews most of them, like Junghoon, were garnering experience and meeting key people in their industries in the hopes of landing something lucrative in the future.

In sum, given their young age and limited experience in the mainstream labor market, it remains uncertain whether second-generation Korean Americans will turn to self-employment in the near future. Because the self-employment rate is a function of age (Min 1996, 1998) and many were in the early stages of their corporate careers, barriers in promotions or the glass ceiling might push the second generation to consider alternatives. During the tremendous explosion of high-tech, Internet-based venture firms (dot-coms), young people were lured by the possibility of striking gold in initial public offerings (IPOs). Others were attracted to independent contracting or consulting that provided professional services to corporations. With the burst of the dot-com bubble, followed by an economic recession and growing unemployment rates, self-employment and professional jobs in the ethnic economy may become attractive and, more important, function as a safety net. Yet the labor-intensive retail businesses that Korean immigrants have been known for seem to have been a one-generation phenomenon; second-generation Korean Americans are overwhelmingly opting for primary-sector jobs instead.

JOBS IN THE ETHNIC ECONOMY: AN ALTERNATIVE TO MAINSTREAM LABOR MARKETS?

The data discussed thus far have shown that second-generation Korean Americans reject self-employment and opt for professional occupations in the mainstream economy. Given the employment opportunities in South Korean multinational subsidiaries and ethnic enclave firms, why is the second generation eschewing employment there, as illustrated by their low rates of employment in these firms (4 percent)?[13] Despite discrimination in the mainstream and the relative ease of entry and cultural familiarity in South Korean multinational subsidiaries and ethnic enclave firms, second-generation Korean Americans unanimously preferred the primary sectors. Not only were benefits, pay, and promotions inferior in Korean firms, but especially for women sexual harassment and unequal treatment had left them with a "bad taste."

The few who chose to work in the ethnic economy, especially for South Korean firms (Samsung, Hyundai, and so forth), did so because of language ease, easier access, comfort level with the culture, and discrimination. In Jonathan's view, it was simply easier to obtain jobs in South Korean firms. Jonathan believed that Korean firms were less competitive when it came to hiring. He thought that these companies did not take into account high grade point averages (GPAs) or previous experience. "I don't want to malign them, but I don't think their standards are as high as American firms in terms of taking really good, qualified people," Jonathan elaborated. He added that Korean firms' employee turnover rates were exceptionally high.

For Junghoon, one of the few respondents who worked for a Korean firm (a South Korean bank), the main reason was language comfort. The cultural and language advantage (or preference) was especially relevant for 1.5ers who came to America when they were ten or older and who were more adept in speaking Korean than English. Conversely, language difficulty and cultural distance was what deterred highly assimilated second-generation Korean Americans from seeking employment in Korean firms. Howard was not interested in joining a Korean firm because he would be less effective in communicating in a Korean company than in an American firm. Howard believed that his promotion chances would thus be impaired.

As a consequence, despite ease of entry and language and cultural familiarity, many pointed out the inferior working conditions in Korean firms (salary, benefits, promotions, and so forth) and saw a bleak future in moving up the hierarchy or remaining in the firm (Kim 2000). For Junghoon, the disadvantage with Korean companies was their inferior pay and generally longer work hours. Kyunghee agreed with her parents that it was better to work for an American firm. She was a twenty-five-year-old assistant manager for a Korean immigrant fashion company. Her mother worked as a seamstress, and her father worked for a Korean newspaper. She came to America at the age of eleven and graduated from a public high school in Queens and a public university in New York City. "Everybody knows that it's better [health] insurance-wise," Kyunghee stated, because Korean firms underreported their taxes and underpaid payroll. "Korean people, it's all talk. You can't trust them," she added. In contrast, her brother-in-law, who worked at a major accounting firm, received all the major benefits. Kyunghee was willing to stay with her current company for a couple of years but was planning to leave thereafter.

Some raised objections to the hierarchical structure of Korean firms and their work customs. For example, Howard suggested that a competent employee who could finish a given task in three hours rather than six hours would effectively be penalized in a Korean firm because that employee would have to stay the same long hours regardless of being more efficient. Jonathan's objection was directed toward the lack of competitiveness and the awkward reward structure within Korean firms. Although jobs in these firms might be more stable, Jonathan suspected that the work was not as fulfilling and that there was less opportunity to learn. "A lot of Korean firms, they are not managed very well. It's good if you are an employee because they do not like to do layoffs, but they are not very competitive," he argued. This was a major reason why he thought there was so much turnover with Korean firms. "I've seen people go to Hanjin [parent company of Korean Air] and Daewoo. Some stay, but a lot of them, after two years, they are itching to get out and move on."

In addition, some respondents objected to the South Korean subsidiaries' policy of bringing in top managers from Korea. Martha had worked on a part-time basis for six months with a Korean company while she was at seminary pursuing a master's degree. Although the job paid for her tuition in addition to providing a competitive salary, she disliked it. Martha felt that the practice of passing over Korean Americans for higher-level managerial positions was discriminatory. "They would always have Korean people from Korea in higher positions. Local people, they are as . . . competent as anyone else, but they would get paid less, [have] less privileges. I didn't think that was fair," Martha explained. According to Jo Kim (2000), South Korean firms continue to engage in this practice, reproducing a Korean organizational structure and culture in the United States.

Moreover, for women, the gender inequality and sexual harassment they experienced in Korean firms were unacceptable. Kyunghee's sister, who was present during the interview, interjected that she caught her "boss looking at porno, and they think it's okay." She felt that this was not unusual in Korean companies because sexual harassment was not taken seriously and was hardly acknowledged. When Kyunghee's sister confronted her boss by explaining that talking about pornography over lunch constituted sexual harassment and that she would sue the company, her boss quickly dismissed the incident as a joke, telling her to lighten up. On top of this, Kyunghee felt that Korean men, but not Korean women, were able to get away with not doing office chores. For example, Kyunghee's sister noticed that men generally did less work than women and were seldom reprimanded. "They think women are not that important. Even simple things, they would ask me to do it," she fumed. Although Kyunghee's sister objected to the practice and told the men she was unwilling to do tasks beyond those required by her position, she was repeatedly asked to do so. She got especially tired of being asked, "Can you make some coffee?" She sighed: "No matter how many times you say it, it doesn't go through their head. I don't know if that's a Korean mentality, but I feel very uncomfortable." She pondered whether white women were asked to serve coffee.

Sarah recalled a similar incident with a friend who interviewed for a Korean company in New Jersey. Her friend had arrived an hour early for the interview, but the firm kept her waiting for an additional hour, and that "just left a bad taste in her mouth." Moreover, when her friend used the women's restroom, she found an assortment of dishes in the sink. Her friend was not sure whether the dishes were in the bathroom because the women had left them there after lunch or because they were expected to wash dishes as part of their work. All of these experiences show how ethnicity, gender, and generation intersect and compound in replicating the structures of male domination in the workplace (Kim 2000).

Not surprisingly, given their experiences, the overwhelming consensus among respondents was that primary-sector jobs were more desirable. Still, for some the ethnic economy served as a safety net while they made the transition into the mainstream economy. One explanation for the initial receptivity to ethnic economy jobs but in the end a rejection of them, as captured in the survey, could be that many of these South Korean firms held much promise and excitement. Asian economies were performing very well and expanding globally in the 1980s and early 1990s. During that time, according to one respondent, many second-generation Korean Americans were not only interested in working for Korean firms—as a way to experience Korean culture, learn the language, and visit Korea—but also saw that their Korean ethnicity helped them obtain jobs at a time when primary-sector jobs were very competitive. After a brief stint (either in summer internships or in full-time positions) in Korean firms, however, the second generation was disillusioned by their inferior pay and working conditions, and they quickly exited these firms. For second-generation Korean Americans who sought employment in South Korean firms, ease of entry and comfort levels determined whether they chose these firms over mainstream jobs. Whether a stint in these firms serves as a springboard to more lucrative positions elsewhere in the mainstream economy or instead becomes a mobility trap remains to be seen.

LITTLE DESIRE TO WORK IN THE KOREAN COMMUNITY

Unless they were fluent in the language and comfortable with Korean culture, highly assimilated second-generation Korean Americans felt uncomfortable in Korean community settings. In fact, they were much more at ease in an American environment. Joseph explained that his parents hardly emphasized working for a Korean firm or in the Korean community in part because his father had no special connections with the ethnic economy to begin with. The same was true for Sharon: because she grew up in a suburb, away from ethnic enclaves such as Koreatown in Los Angeles, she was never particularly attached to a Korean community. In fact, this issue never came up with her parents, since they were very detached from any such community and its networks. "I don't think we grew up in enough of a Korean community to feel that way. I don't think that ever came up. They don't even know any Korean people who could even. . . . it's not like they had a friend who had a job for us," Sharon pointed out.

Although the literature on immigrant incorporation underscores the benefits of ethnic solidarity, research also delineates the burdens or limits of ethnic solidarity (Gold 1994; Kim 1999). Joseph's apprehensiveness in dealing with other Koreans arose out of the obligations of ethnic solidarity. He preferred not to deal with other Koreans and if possible avoided working in the Korean community. He elaborated on this feeling, which was shared by many second-generation Korean Americans:

> I've had experiences where working with the Korean community is not profitable. Not profitable [and] it's more of a headache because [if] you're Korean, they expect you to give them a break here and [a] break there, give me special attention. And you can't do a business like that. So, no, I would try to stay away from them as well, unless it was a business which was strictly geared for Koreans. I don't know. If it arises, I would prefer not to work in the Korean community.

Sometimes the second generation's disinclination had less to do with their feelings about the Korean community and more to do with the experience of being chastised by first-generation Korean immigrants, or even by the 1.5ers, for not speaking Korean or adhering to Korean cultural practices. Sally was the most adamant about Korean firms discriminating against her. She was a thirty-three-year-old computer graphics freelancer. She grew up in Florida and graduated from a public university in Miami. Her father worked as an engineer, and her mother owned a health foods store. Sally lost her desire to associate with the Korean community or Korean firms after several encounters with Koreans expressing such views. "I would if they [the Korean community and Korean firm] didn't discriminate against me," Sally noted. "I guess what I mean is that sometimes the Koreans I've been around say very nasty things to me: 'You're an idiot if you're a Korean and you don't speak Korean.'" Sally wanted to be treated as a "professional instead of an idiot."

Consequently, highly assimilated second-generation Korean Americans were unlikely to look for work at a Korean firm simply because of their feelings of ethnic attachment. Her ethnicity would not draw Sharon to a Korean firm so much as the question of whether the available job fit her needs. "Sure, if the job was right. . . . It wouldn't be because it was Korean. It would be judged on the same basis as any other job," Sharon said. The same was true for Gina, who had been encouraged by her father to consider import-export businesses because of her Korean-Jewish connections. She was a twenty-five-year-old executive assistant for a major cable network. With outstanding educational credentials from an Ivy League university, she was one of the few biracial second-generation respondents. Her physician father was Jewish, and her mother was Korean. Gina grew up in the midwest. "Because I'm half-Korean and half-American, I have some kind of sensibility that maybe most people doing import-export with Asian communities don't have. So you would know the demand better than the average American," Gina explained. However, in the final analysis, choosing an industry or firm had to be based on whether the work corresponded with her needs and wants. "Sure. Why not? I'd consider anything. It would have to provide something that I needed and wanted. I wouldn't just do it because it was Korean," Gina observed.

Anecdotal evidence suggests that a growing number of 1.5- and second-generation Korean Americans are serving as professionals in the ethnic economy. Thus, I had expected to see a number of the 1.5ers working as professionals in the ethnic economy, playing broker roles between the community and the mainstream society in the survey, but I found that the reverse was true.[14] Most of the lawyers, doctors, and accountants in this sample were working in the mainstream economy. It appears likely that the second generation's knowledge of the Korean community, experience with other Korean Americans, cultural and linguistic competence, sense of identity, and opportunities in the mainstream economy determine whether they actively seek employment opportunities in the ethnic economy. Those who grew up in white suburban environments did not have ethnic attachments and identity strong enough to motivate them to seek employment in the ethnic economy. Professional employment in the ethnic economy seemed to involve those 1.5ers who were linguistically and culturally competent enough to act as go-betweens for the immigrant generation and mainstream society.

Yet a small number of highly educated professionals worked in the Korean community (and other Asian communities), acting as brokers between the community and the larger society and working primarily in nonprofit sectors (community-, city-, or state-based) that provide community services. Yen Le Espiritu's (1992) study of the operations of a pan-Asian ethnicity highlights this pattern among second-generation Asian Americans. In Los Angeles social power has slowly been transferred to 1.5ers and the second generation, in part because of the prominence of these groups after the Los Angeles riots (Min 1996). Mark was among the few who had been working in the community for a considerable length of time and continued to do so. He was a thirty-four-year-old teacher and manager of a hagwon.[15] He graduated from a selective New York City public high school and attended a highly selective private college in the northeast. Because his father was a minister serving the Korean community, for Mark involvement with that community came somewhat naturally and also as a duty. "I guess because my parents were working in the Korean community, they kind of always said to me to engage in what's going on with the Korean community," Mark explained.

OBSTACLES IN PRIMARY LABOR MARKETS: PROMOTIONS AND THE GLASS CEILING

The possibility of promotion and the impact of obstacles like the glass ceiling affect second-generation Korean Americans' views of their current labor market situation and will influence whether they seek alternatives to the mainstream economy in the future. Connie felt that promotions were "another huge problem." She knew a coworker who, even after four years in the firm, had not been promoted. Her coworkers told Connie that it took four to six years to be promoted in that firm, and that was an important reason why she was leaving the company. Had she stayed, she would probably have wanted to move up to a public relations manager position. Connie thought that doing so was possible. And even though Connie agreed that the glass ceiling was not imaginary, she also felt that being an Asian woman had its advantages in the fashion industry because women and Asian Americans were more visible in that context.

In contrast, Mark asked: "If someone gets promoted, gets a raise, and you were in line for promotion, you can't help [but] think, 'Oh, what's the difference? You know, I was here longer.'" Mark cited the case of his friend who worked as a federal agent and felt that promotions were not given fairly within the Federal Bureau of Investigation. Some of the agents over whom his friend had seniority had received promotions ahead of him despite his very good track record. For Mark, this was a clear example of the bias that still permeated the agency. He argued:

> All the Asian agents [in] the FBI, the Justice Department, anyone who was Asian seems to work on Asian crimes, but they don't get to deal with other cases. It's understandable that the Bureau might want to put Asian agents to work on Asian crimes, because they have that kind of perspective. But then I'm sure a lot of those agents can work on other things as well. So do you make all Italian agents work on Mafia crimes or Jewish agents work on [Jewish] crimes? Do you know what I'm saying?

The glass ceiling is a major corporate hurdle and a research issue that will have to be examined carefully as the second generation increasingly comes up for promotion. Defined as an invisible barrier that can be seen but not penetrated, experience with or beliefs in the glass ceiling will determine the second generation's enthusiasm for or disillusionment with corporate jobs (Fong 2002). Respondents' positions on the glass ceiling issue were divided. Some expressed a firm belief that it was possible to advance in the corporate sector and that individual ability (meritocracy) was the primary limit to fulfilling their goals. Many second-generation Korean Americans felt that their class attributes would overcome racial boundaries. Having had success thus far, those who were making inroads within the corporate hierarchy were very optimistic and confident in their abilities.

This was how Howard perceived the glass ceiling. A graduate of a state university in New Jersey, Howard was a thirty-four-year-old associate director for a pharmaceutical company. His parents had been very successful with a clothing store and owned several commercial buildings. Howard had similar success, having been promoted four times within a seven-year span, starting from a supervisory level, then moving up to the assistant directorship. His goal was none other than to become a corporate executive officer (CEO). When asked how far he could actually advance, Howard confidently replied: "Sky's the limit. If they like what you are doing, and you do your job and you are creative and young and talented, I would say the only stopping point is the final stop, cuz you got to the board of directors." Although he admitted that the corporate world was very hierarchical and had relatively few women or minorities in high positions, he was more than optimistic: "I say I will be the first."

Others, because they accepted the premise of meritocracy and saw their current position in terms of their own individual choice, were not convinced that the glass ceiling would hinder the mobility of minorities and women. Heesoo believed that she was unlikely to secure a top position in her firm because there was only one woman in its higher echelons, and she happened to be married to the boss. Yet Heesoo did not interpret this in terms of a glass ceiling but rather rationalized that she was simply uninterested in moving to a top position. Heesoo was content to stay at her current level, where she could competently meet her job responsibilities and expectations. In fact, in order not to perform a mediocre job, she preferred to have fewer responsibilities so as to be able to fulfill them capably. "If I want more responsibility, I can take it. I think it's definitely a meritocracy, but the higher up you go the more they expect from you," Heesoo contended. She was very attached to the idea of meritocracy and explained that it was out of her own volition that she chose to remain where she was. First, having seen her parents suffer through the stress of running a small business, sacrificing their lives for financial stability, Heesoo did not want to trade family and leisure time for monetary compensation. Second, her salary and work hours were more than comfortable, and the level of responsibility that her job demanded was ideal for Heesoo. In short, she wanted to maintain a reasonable balance between work and leisure, which she saw to be unlikely with the demands of a higher position.

Some argued that the profit goals of firms made the glass ceiling irrational.

As Jonathan asserted, firms would not pursue policies that hindered profits since that was their chief motive:

> If you are profitable and bring in business, it's really stupid of the firm not to hire you or to promote you. Because they know if you hit a ceiling then you are gonna leave and take all that money with [you]. America's goal is to make money. Maybe in some firms, where it is solid white or Jewish establishments, but in most cases I don't really worry about [there being a glass ceiling] as much as all these ethnic minorities and women say there is.

Others, aware that multiculturalism and diversity initiatives in the corporate world had expanded opportunities for minorities and women, were a lot more optimistic about their chances. Mark conceded that a glass ceiling existed but nonetheless felt that much progress had been made over the past twenty years. Sungsoo granted that, "in the past, you could see that it's all set, that everybody's Caucasian at the top level," but maintained: "Now the trend is, because everybody sees that, they know there is something wrong. Especially in Andersen [consulting firm], they changed their views on who should be hired, how many minorities should be hired, and diversity in the group. That's what they are concentrating on and opportunities will rise up." Mark pointed out that there were no African American CEOs in corporate America twenty years ago. "You see those now. Even though that's not big Fortune 500, you still see [them]. You notice a lot of women CEOs around the country, even in power seats. So that's surprising. We wouldn't have seen that twenty years ago. I think there's a lot of changes being made in a progressive sense. That's encouraging," Mark elaborated. When asked whether he would make it to the top, Sungsoo replied: "I don't really think about 'what if I don't get the position?' For me, that's my goal, and I will work hard no matter what position I am at. Even if they keep me as an analyst for the next ten years, I am going to work hard. I will probably leave [*laughing*]."

Thus, many of the second generation were optimistic and confident in their abilities to make inroads within the corporate hierarchy after having had initial success there. If the glass ceiling had been a problem in the past, they did not see it as an obstacle in the future as they pointed to the expanded opportunities resulting from diversity initiatives. Furthermore, many of the respondents were fairly young (their median age was twenty-seven in 1998) and had yet to face a glass ceiling in the corporate world. Whether second-generation Korean Americans will retain their current views ten or twenty years down the road, when the glass ceiling becomes more salient in their climb up the corporate ladder, is unclear. On the one hand, their presence and continued efforts to break the corporate glass ceiling may in fact reduce its impact. On the other hand, the present structure may retain some as tokens but frustrate the ambitions of many others as insiders maintain a vigilant guard against wholesale transformation (Waldinger 1996).

Those who were less sanguine about the mobility possibilities in the corporate world pointed to current institutional arrangements that remained fixed and static. Not only were the higher positions already occupied, but the persons in them were unlikely to relinquish them. Hyun felt that people at the top would not be bumped out and thus openings would not occur unless those at the top decided to leave.[16] She was a twenty-seven-year-old case administrator for an arbitration company who had graduated from a selective private college in the northeast. She had also lived in Korea for two years, working as an English instructor. Her father worked as a chemist and had moved to the suburbs for the children's education. Hyun had felt trapped in her suburban New Jersey high school, however, and struggled with questions of identity as a teenager. She contended that there would be discrimination in the corporate world owing to her gender and race. "I think that's relevant to a certain extent in any organization. The top person in our office is a white male," Hyun said. When she was working at a shelter (a nonprofit organization), the top person was also a white male. The lower-level supervisors were women and minorities. "When you look at the top, it's always a white male who's in charge," she added.

Peter could foresee a glass ceiling, although he had not yet experienced it himself. He was drawing on what his uncle had told him—that some chose to start their own business because they got stuck on the corporate ladder. As a consequence of being stuck, they had fretted that the glass ceiling would prevent them from rising into upper-management positions, and they usually cited the absence of Koreans in the upper tiers of the corporate world:

> Oh yeah, I think it's definitely real. Of course, it's probably very rare that an Asian person will get that high in an American company. There are some instances where an Asian American will get to a point where he may be president of the company or CEO, but it's unheard of. It's not going to be something that you hear often.

No matter how strong their credentials, Junghoon felt that there was a ceiling they would reach, and that was why he thought many qualified Korean Americans left American companies. "When you are a foreigner . . . if you go into an American company, [you face] that glass ceiling. . . . They give up. They face the reality," he said.

The glass ceiling was not the only obstacle Asian Americans faced (Fong 2002). Although affirmative action and diversity initiatives have opened up positions that were closed off for Asian Americans, in Mark's view, these tended to be lower-level positions that remained ghettoized, without much room for career mobility. As a result of corporate expansion into global and ethnic markets, the need for skilled ethnic mediators (those with cultural and linguistic expertise) provided increased job opportunities for Asian Americans in the corporate sector. Certainly, having expanded job opportunities in different sectors for previously excluded groups is to be commended. However, Mark noted, these positions have confined Asian Americans to the ethnic market, circumscribing their promotions. For instance, Mark observed that ethnicity played a role in the hiring of Korean stockbrokers by large firms: it was apparent that these employees were recruited to handle only Korean accounts. If they were not allowed to expand their customer base, Mark asked, how would they be promoted and climb up the career ladder?

Tammy felt that the "ethnicity card," especially as an Asian American woman, could work both ways. She was a twenty-seven-year-old sophomore dean at an Ivy League university. She grew up in Asia, where her father was a research agronomist for a development bank. Tammy attended an international high school there but came to America for college, graduating with a bachelor's degree as well as a master's in education from the same Ivy League university. On the one hand, she deduced that her initial hire as a sophomore dean had much to do with her ethnicity, which helped the school comply with affirmative action and diversity initiatives. On the other hand, she was not sure how far she could advance, considering that this diversity initiative represented mere tokenism:

> So that could work for me. But as far as how far they will let me get, I don't know. I really don't. So it could be a positive thing, depending on, I guess, if I'm docile . . . [or] not docile enough but [whether] I play along with the system enough to get me there. Then maybe they'll go for it.

Thus, Tammy was faced not only with tokenism and possibly a glass ceiling but also with the question of the extent to which conforming with persistent stereotypes of Asian American women as "docile" would work for her or against her. Especially in the corporate sector, Asian Americans are deemed capable as technical or research personnel, but at higher levels they are passed over for managerial positions because they are seen as less aggressive (Feagin and Feagin 1999; Fong 2002). Unlike the immigrant generation whose lack of fluency in English was used to deny them promotions, the second generation will not find language competence to be a major hurdle.[17]

CONCLUSIONS

The collected data indicate that second-generation Korean Americans are abandoning the small-business route of their parents in favor of primary-sector occupations. Employment in South Korean multinational subsidiaries, in ethnic enclave broker positions, and in Korean community settings is being firmly rejected by second-generation Korean Americans. In the process, the ethnic economy that served as the foundation for the first generation has become less important for the second generation. With the departure of second-generation Korean Americans from the self-employed venues of their parents into the mainstream economy, ethnic succession is in the not-too-distant future. Unless entrepreneurial parents (the parents of the second generation are approaching retirement age) find replacements among co-ethnics, they have no choice but to sell their businesses to other immigrant groups. This dilemma is very similar to the one that Jewish and Italian store owners faced as they were aging and as they and their children moved into the upper levels of manufacturing and of retail and wholesale distribution. This phenomenon is likely to break the pattern of intrabusiness exchanges, opening up niches for non-Korean immigrant groups in the future. Already, Arab, Vietnamese, and other non-Korean merchants are competing against Korean-owned small businesses (Louie 1996). These new immigrants may well drive some Koreans out of business, absorbing some of the Korean businesses along the way.

While ethnic collectivism served Korean immigrant entrepreneurs well as they established themselves economically, ethnic strategies of mobility have also kept them culturally and linguistically apart from mainstream society. That same success achieved through ethnic collectivism has accelerated the mainstream assimilation of the second generation, including the children of entrepreneurs. What had been paramount for the first generation is becoming less so for the second as many of the prior obstacles encountered by the immigrant generation are overcome in subsequent generations. Arriving at a period when the gains of the civil rights movement were gradually being felt, Korean immigrants were able to achieve residential assimilation as formal residential segregation was abolished. Through their rapid economic integration as professionals and small-business owners, middle-class Korean immigrants attained economic as well as residential assimilation. The American-born or -raised children of Korean immigrants arguably benefited from residential integration: they grew up in middle-class white neighborhoods and attended excellent suburban schools. Raised in the suburbs, second-generation Korean Americans absorbed the values, outlooks, customs, and tastes of middle-class whites. This class advantage facilitated the second generation's entry into prestigious colleges and subsequently their successful entry into primary-sector labor markets. With educational credentials that presented very few obstacles in the current labor market, second-generation Korean Americans entered the mainstream very rapidly.

In conjunction with the second generation's ease with language, superb educational credentials, and white middle-class speech, mannerisms, values, tastes, and so on, multiculturalism and diversity initiatives have opened formerly closed-off occupations to racial minorities, contributing to their rapid transition to corporate America. For instance, entry-level and technical jobs are now open to racial outsiders because established white ethnic groups feel less threatened by newcomers (Waldinger 1996). Furthermore, the unprecedented growth of the financial sector in New York in the 1990s expanded job opportunities beyond ethnicity when a shortage of qualified personnel developed (Waldinger 1996). In short, the second generation's success in the labor market has had as much to do with the opportunity structure of the financial sector in New York as their qualifications. Nevertheless, what is remarkable is how rapidly Korean Americans gained entry into the mainstream. What had taken several generations for European immigrants and two or three generations for Jews, middle-class Korean Americans were getting it done in one generation.

Regarding their prospects in the corporate world, thanks to their class advantage and current success there, second-generation Korean Americans were very optimistic. They believed that meritocracy was going to determine their upward mobility in the corporate world. Having had success, the second generation did not foresee much of a glass ceiling and were very confident that it would not be an obstacle to them. They believed that racial assignment would not be an impediment and instead were extremely confident that they would make it in the corporate world. This optimism, especially their favorable view of their chances in America, stemmed in part from the dual framework and idealism that their parents had passed on to them (Portes and Zhou 1993). In spite of their parents' initial labor market difficulties, which had turned highly educated first-generation Korean immigrants toward self-employment, Korean immigrants did not reject the American Dream and instead maintained a strong idealism. Their belief in the American Dream remained strong because they attributed their difficulties in the mainstream labor market to lack of English-language skills and untransferable credentials. More important, their success in running small businesses and their dual framework of mobility prospects reinforced their belief in the American Dream, which promises upward mobility to anyone with an individual work ethic. Thus, parents trusted that acquiring top American educational credentials and professions would help their children transcend the difficulties they had experienced themselves as immigrants, including any difficulties with racial boundaries (Abelmann and Lie 1995; Lee 1996). They also believed that professional occupations would help shield their children from racial discrimination. Undoubtedly, parents were also eager for their children to gain the status and monetary rewards of these occupations, thereby increasing their odds of attaining solid middle-class or upper-class lifestyles.

Additionally, the relative youth and limited experience of second-generation Korean Americans in mainstream firms explained their confidence about their possibilities in the corporate world. Their successful attainment of elite educational credentials and their initially promising transition into mainstream occupations had given them an optimism that made racial boundaries almost disappear or at least seem inconsequential—to the extent that they also denied the relevance of racial boundaries in the lives of poor immigrants and racial minorities. This paralleled the reaction by middle-class Asian American students at a public high school in Philadelphia studied by Stacey Lee (1996), who usually responded to racism with self-denial and shied away from confronting the perpetrators (see Lee 1996). Trumpeting their role as "model minorities" and hoping to earn the respect of whites by proving their merit, Asian-identified and Korean-identified students at Academic High minimized the racism that minorities faced and dismissed their experience as a random encounter (see also Abelmann and Lie 1995). In the same manner, second-generation Korean Americans were wary of minority denouncements of racism, for they had experienced racism less frequently. Not that they had not been reminded of difference or experienced discrimination. However, as respondents confirmed, they had not been victims of violent racism, and few recalled racist incidents. In short, there was a strong faith in individual ability as the primary determinant of achievement.

This unbridled optimism may become a self-fulfilling prophecy for some as their determination to not let racial boundaries obstruct their aspirations allows them to reach their career goals. But their faith in merit as the primary criterion for determining rewards and promotions may change when these fail to overcome the relevance of race. At higher corporate management levels, Roger Waldinger's (1996) insider-outsider niche protection may be operating much more forcefully than in entry-level and technical jobs. Denying that a glass ceiling exists because they have seemingly moved beyond such an obstacle could exact a psychological toll and provoke an identity crisis when second-generation Korean Americans confront these barriers in the future. Thus, what remains to be seen is whether the second generation, after a lengthy exposure to the corporate world, will come to realize that the glass ceiling is far more real in the upper corporate structure than they had anticipated and how they cope with this intransigent obstacle as racial and gender boundaries continue to sort individuals in the corporate hierarchy. The future impact of race and ethnicity will remain contingent on the level of racial assignment and discrimination, the ability of groups to assert their ethnic identities, and the economic resources they are able to command (Cornell and Hartmann 1998; Gans 1992; Portes and Rumbaut 2001).

As class and educational credentials have steered the mobility fortunes of second-generation Korean Americans, ethnicity has organized their lives very thinly and become increasingly symbolic (Cornell and Hartmann 1998). Nevertheless, because of the current celebration of ethnic and racial diversity, when such identities are far more prominent than they were thirty years ago, at least for some ethnicity may continue to play an influential role. Multiculturalism and ethnic pride are transforming the racial climate, prompting some to explore their ethnic identity. In addition, immigration has added a diversity that cannot be captured by a rigid white-black dichotomy (Fong 2002). New York City, the emblematic if not actual capital of diversity, embodies this particular cosmopolitanism. The New York City of the 1970s was not quite as diverse as that of the millennium. The Flushing of today is a major Korean enclave. In the 1970s these neighborhoods were still heavily white but undergoing rapid ethnic succession with the influx of new immigrants. With the explosive growth of Korean immigration in the 1980s, suburban enclaves have mushroomed throughout the metropolitan New York–New Jersey area. My respondents were growing up in this white milieu where rapid acculturation had taken place. However, for those second generation who grew up during periods of heavy immigration and ethnic succession, ethnicity was a lot more prominent. For second-generation teenagers who are growing up in an increasingly ethnic and multicultural environment, ethnicity is becoming a lot thicker, resulting in a different set of expectations, obligations, and identities. Finally, increasing transnationalization is keeping ethnic attachments alive and salient for the immigrant generation and perhaps for the second.

Yet it is one thing to identify ethnically and another to actively pursue ethnicity. Ethnic identities may remain salient in a multicultural world, but the trend seems toward a symbolic ethnicity (Gans 1979). Intermarriages among many different groups will destabilize the racial order and lessen the comprehensiveness of ethnicity across generations (Alba 1995; Cornell and Hartmann 1998). Furthermore, class disparities within the community complicate the intensity of ethnic attachments for second-generation Korean Americans. Children of middle-class Korean Americans are increasingly experiencing social acceptance, as indicated by their educational, occupational, and marital assimilation. The fact that second-generation Korean Americans are establishing themselves in mainstream America will result in greater economic power and influence and consequently ensure that their "honorary white" status and the advantages accruing thereto are not stripped away (Tuan 1998). Although conditions outside the group ("forever foreigners" or social acceptance) continue to dictate the level of ethnic assertion and racial assignment, the offspring of middle-class Asian Americans command class resources to contest and protect against racialized treatment.

The children of working-class Korean Americans, on the other hand, faced with racial and class disadvantages, may remain ethnic and continue to count on the ethnic economy to avert downward mobility. In this sample there were very few children of working-class Korean Americans. Instead, the rapid occupational assimilation of the second generation was a consequence of the selectivity of Korean immigration from the 1960s and 1970s, which produced a first generation made up of highly educated Korean professionals and entrepreneurs. The subsequent second generation, the teenagers who were ineligible for this study, will have more working-class parents, and their outcomes may be different from and less exceptional than those of the current second generation. This raises the question of whether the ethnic economy is able to extend its benefits to children of workers, as has been the case for children of entrepreneurs. What remains to be seen is whether second-generation children of working-class Korean immigrants will follow occupational trajectories similar to those of the current second generation. That will make evident the salient role that class, race, gender, and community continue to play in organizing and determining the occupational and identity trajectories of second-generation Korean Americans and those of other immigrant second generations.

I would like to acknowledge support from the following institutions: the 1997–1998 Social Science Research Council's International Migration Program Dissertation Fellowship; the 1998–1999 National Science Foundation's Grants to Improve Doctoral Dissertation Research, Program in Sociology, SBR-9811111; the 1998–1999 CUNY Graduate Center Dissertation Year Fellowship; and the 1999–2000 Center for Urban Research Predoctoral Fellowship. I would also like to thank the anonymous reviewers for their comments and the editorial assistance of Kandice Chuh. The views presented in this chapter do not reflect the views of the funding institutions but of the author.

Notes

1 The terms "1.5-generation" and "second-generation" are used here interchangeably. The second generation refers to those born in the United States with at least one parent who was born in Korea. The 1.5 generation comprises those born in Korea (or elsewhere) who came to America by age twelve or younger

with at least one Korean-born parent. I chose age twelve as a dividing marker because that age reflects a substantial upbringing in the United States. That choice also aligns this study with the comparable second-generation household survey by John Mollenkopf, Philip Kasinitz, and Mary Waters (1997), who operationalized the definition of the 1.5 generation using the same criteria. In this sample 70 percent of survey respondents were 1.5ers and 30 percent were truly second-generation.

2. According to Edna Bonacich and Ivan Light (1988, x), the ethnic economy is an economic formation that "incorporates the ethnic self-employed and unpaid family helpers, ethnic employers, and their co-ethnic employees." The ethnic economy is ethnic because business owners are ethnic and usually their employees are co-ethnics (xi). Ethnic economies incorporate both ethnic enclave economies and middleman minorities as the overarching theoretical formulation. For further elaboration on ethnic economies, see Light and Gold (2000).

3. More than half (52 percent) of the second generation were women, and 48 percent were men. The mean age of second-generation Korean Americans in 1998 was 27.49, and the median age in 1998 was 27.

4. A critical issue with surname research, as with other telephone-based interviews, is to verify telephone subscription rates, since the screening process relies on phone screens. As Eui-Hang Shin and Eui-Young Yu (1984) demonstrated, telephone coverage is not a major concern for Koreans because Koreans have high telephone subscription rates (approximately 98 percent). Unlisted phone numbers, nationally at 16 to 20 percent, were a problem; nonetheless, for Koreans, Shin and Yu estimated a 3 to 5 percent unlisted rate after a comparison of telephone directories with the Korean Association Directory and seven Korean church directories in Atlanta, Los Angeles, Chicago, and New York. Thus, unlisted telephone numbers did not pose a serious problem. Still, given the date of this research, telephone subscription and unlisted number rates may have changed. An additional challenge using a surname methodology is locating intermarried Korean women who adopted non-Korean surnames. One solution to address this potential exclusion is to include in the phone screens a question regarding children who live outside or away from their parents. Although it was unclear how effective this screening procedure was in tracking down intermarried Korean American women, this scheme did help locate some intermarried second-generation Korean women as well as some second-generation adults who were living outside the New York–New Jersey metropolitan area. Thus, 82 percent (166) of the second generation was directly located from the screened households, and 18 percent (36) were contacted through their parents who willingly gave out their children's contact numbers after the screening of households located eligible second-generation children living away from their parents.

5. Korean surnames were identified in published telephone directories in metropolitan New York boroughs and New Jersey counties. I selected the twenty

most prominent Korean surnames for this survey. The sampling frame covered a large percentage of the Korean American population, providing a fairly representative sample. For example, 22 percent of the Korean population bear the surname Kim (Shin and Yu 1984). As Ira Rosenwaike (1994) notes, ten Korean surnames account for fully 65 percent of the Korean American population. As a rough proxy for metropolitan New York–New Jersey, Korean surnames were drawn from the following area codes: New York—718, 212, 516, and 914; New Jersey—201, 908, and 973. A total of twenty-four thousand potential Korean households were identified, out of which thirty-five hundred households were randomly selected for screening, which subsequently produced the two hundred second-generation Korean American respondents at the center of this study.

6. Among the second-generation Korean American respondents, three-fourths (76 percent) were working and 24 percent were unemployed at the time of the interview.

7. Second-generation Korean Americans were attaining similar levels of education, although a smaller proportion (26 percent) were receiving graduate degrees compared to their fathers. This may change in the future, since second-generation Korean Americans are still young and may seek graduate degrees to further supplement their education.

8. When surveys focus on children of the later cohort of Korean immigrants—who, at age twenty-two and younger, were not old enough to be captured in this survey—more second generation from working-class backgrounds are likely to be found.

9. The differences should be interpreted with caution since the size of the sample is too small.

10. By primary sectors, I follow Torres's description of labor market segmentation based on a dual system of employers: large corporations and peripheral firms (1995, 13–14). Primary segments are characterized by job stability, high wages, good working conditions, and mobility opportunities. By contrast, secondary segments pay less and offer fewer benefits and protection than primary segments. See Torres (1995) for further discussion of labor market segmentation and pay and benefit disparities.

11. A "Korean-Korean" can be classified as a person who is linguistically and culturally very Korean, such as recent Korean immigrants, Korean foreign students, and Korean workers and managers who are dispatched to work in Korean multinational subsidiaries in the United States (or elsewhere) for a period of time, generally two to three years, before returning to Korea. Through marriage, work, and other means, it is not unusual for students and subsidiary workers to decide to reside permanently in the host country, becoming part of the immigrant community. In other instances, the subsidiary worker returns to Korea but the family remains in the host society, establishing transnational or split households.

12. According to Roger Waldinger (1996), ethnic succession among Jews occurred

because co-ethnics were retiring and the second and third generations were reluctant to take over the family businesses. Waldinger found similar responses from the Korean business owners he surveyed in New York.

13. Alejandro Portes and Robert Bach (1985, 203) define ethnic enclaves as the "spatial concentration of immigrants who organize a variety of enterprises to serve their own ethnic market and the general population."

14. Although the ethnic economy has become increasingly viable, contrary to anecdotal evidence, survey data revealed that highly assimilated second-generation Korean Americans were seeking employment in the mainstream economy.

15. A carryover from South Korea, hagwons have become a prominent institution within the Korean community in New York. These ethnic academic firms specialize in college entrance exam preparation, such as PSAT and SAT preparation courses. Hagwons also offer students after-school programs focusing on topics like English, math, computers, homework, and so on, to supplement their public school education.

16. See Waldinger's (1996) discussion of the protection of ethnic niches by insiders.

17. Pyong Gap Min and Rose Kim (1999) note that the primary difference between the first generation and the second is that the immigrant generation cites the glass ceiling and discrimination as major obstacles in the corporate world, while the second generation is primarily concerned with questions of identity and their place in America.

References

Abelmann, Nancy, and John Lie. 1995. *Blue Dreams: Korean Americans and the L.A. Riots.* Cambridge, Mass.: Harvard University Press.

Alba, Richard. 1995. "Assimilation's Quiet Tide." *The Public Interest* 119: 1–18.

Bates, Timothy. 1997. *Race, Self-employment, and Upward Mobility: An Illusive American Dream.* Baltimore: Johns Hopkins University Press.

Bonacich, Edna, and Ivan Light. 1988. *Immigrant Entrepreneurs: Koreans in Los Angeles, 1965–1982.* Berkeley: University of California Press.

Cornell, Stephen, and Douglas Hartmann. 1998. *Ethnicity and Race: Making Identities in a Changing World.* Thousand Oaks, Calif.: Pine Forge Press.

Espiritu, Yen Le. 1992. *Asian American Pan-ethnicity: Bridging Institutions and Identities.* Philadelphia: Temple University Press.

Feagin, Joe R., and Clairece Booher Feagin. 1999. *Racial and Ethnic Relations.* Upper Saddle River, N.J.: Prentice-Hall.

Fong, Timothy P. 2002. *The Contemporary Asian American Experience: Beyond the Model Minority.* Upper Saddle River, N.J.: Prentice-Hall.

Gans, Herbert. 1979. "Symbolic Ethnicity: The Future of Ethnic Groups and Cultures in America." *Ethnic and Racial Studies* 2: 1–20.

———. 1992. "Second-Generation Decline: Scenarios for the Economic and Ethnic Futures of the Post-1965 American Immigrants." *Ethnic and Racial Studies* 15(2): 173–93.

Gold, Steven J. 1994. "Patterns of Economic Cooperation Among Israeli Immigrants in Los Angeles." *International Migration Review* 28(105): 114–35.

Himmelfarb, Harold S., R. Michael Loar, and Susan H. Mott. 1983. "Sampling by Ethnic Surnames: The Case of American Jews." *Public Opinion Quarterly* 47: 247–60.

Kim, Dae Young. 1999. "Beyond Co-ethnic Solidarity: Mexican and Ecuadorean Employment in Korean-Owned Businesses in New York City." *Ethnic and Racial Studies* 22(3): 581–605.

———. 2001. "Immigrant Entrepreneurship and Intergenerational Mobility Among Second-Generation Korean Americans in New York." Ph.D. diss., City University of New York.

Kim, Eun-Young. 1993. "Career Choice Among Second-Generation Korean Americans: Reflections of a Cultural Model of Success." *Anthropology and Education Quarterly* 24(3): 224–48.

Kim, Ill Soo. 1981. *New Urban Immigrants: The Korean Community in New York*. Princeton, N.J.: Princeton University Press.

Kim, Jo. 2000. "Transnational Managers and Local Workers: A Study of South Korean Transnational Corporations in the United States." Paper presented to the American Sociological Association. Washington (August).

Lee, Stacey. 1996. *Unraveling the "Model Minority" Stereotype: Listening to Asian American Youth*. New York: Teachers College Press.

Light, Ivan, and Steven J. Gold. 2000. *Ethnic Economies*. San Diego: Academic Press.

Light, Ivan, and Elizabeth Roach. 1996. "Self-employment: Mobility Ladder or Economic Lifeboat?" In *Ethnic Los Angeles*, edited by Roger Waldinger and Mehdi Bozorgmehr. New York: Russell Sage Foundation.

Light, Ivan, and Carolyn Rosenstein. 1995. *Race, Ethnicity, and Entrepreneurship in Urban America*. New York: Aldine de Gruyter.

Louie, Elaine. 1996. "A Korean Family's Dream, a Community's Struggle." *New York Times*, March 13.

Min, Pyong Gap. 1984. "From White-Collar Occupations to Small Business: Korean Immigrants' Occupational Adjustment." *Sociological Quarterly* 25(1984): 333–52.

———. 1988. *Ethnic Business Enterprise: Korean Small Business in Atlanta*. New York: Center for Migration Studies.

———. 1996. *Caught in the Middle: Korean Communities in New York and Los Angeles*. Berkeley: University of California Press.

———. 1998. *Changes and Conflicts: Korean Immigrant Families in New York*. Needham Heights, Mass.: Allyn and Bacon.

Min, Pyong Gap, and Rose Kim. 1999. *Struggle for Ethnic Identity: Narratives by Asian American Professionals*. Walnut Creek, Calif.: AltaMira Press.

Mollenkopf, John, Philip Kasinitz, and Mary Waters. 1997. "The Immigrant Second Generation in Metropolitan New York." Proposal to the Russell Sage Foundation, New York.

Portes, Alejandro, and Robert Bach. 1985. *Latin Journey: Cuban and Mexican Immigrants in the United States*. Berkeley: University of California Press.

Portes, Alejandro, and Rubén Rumbaut. 1990. *Immigrant America: A Portrait.* Berkeley: University of California Press.

———. 2001. *Legacies: The Story of the Immigrant Second Generation.* Berkeley: University of California Press.

Portes, Alejandro, and Min Zhou. 1993. "The New Second Generation: Segmented Assimilation and Its Variants." *Annals of the American Academy of Political and Social Science* 530: 74–97.

Rosenwaike, Ira. 1994. "Surname Analysis as a Means of Estimating Minority Elderly: An Application Using Asian Surnames." *Research on Aging* 16(2): 212–27.

Shin, Eui-Hang, and Eui-Young Yu. 1984. "Use of Surnames in Ethnic Research: The Case of Kims in the Korean American Population." *Demography* 21(3): 347–59.

Torres, Andres. 1995. *Between Melting Pot and Mosaic: African Americans and Puerto Ricans in the New York Political Economy.* Philadelphia: Temple University Press.

Tuan, Mia. 1998. *Forever Foreigners or Honorary Whites? The Asian Ethnic Experience Today.* New Brunswick, N.J.: Rutgers University Press.

Waldinger, Roger. 1989. "Structural Opportunity or Ethnic Advantage? Immigrant Business Development in New York." *International Migration Review* 23(1): 48–72.

———. 1996. *Still the Promised City? African Americans and New Immigrants in Postindustrial New York.* Cambridge, Mass.: Harvard University Press.

Yoon, In-Jin. 1997. *On My Own: Korean Businesses and Race Relations in America.* Chicago: University of Chicago Press.

Zhou, Min, and Carl L. Bankston. 1998. *Growing Up American: How Vietnamese Children Adapt to Life in the United States.* New York: Russell Sage Foundation.

PART III

PARTICIPATION

EARLIER periods of migration to the United States inspired many rich studies of the social worlds of immigrants and their American children. This literature often focused on the political and institutional lives of these communities. Midtwentieth-century observers, including Nathan Glazer and Daniel Patrick Moynihan, often highlighted the crucial role that churches, political clubs, labor unions, and fraternal organizations played in helping the children of immigrants "become Americans." With only a few notable exceptions, however (see Cordero-Guzman 2002; Bozorgmehr, Kucukozer, and Bakalian 2004; Gerstle and Mollenkopf 2001; Warner and Wittner 1998; Jones-Correa 1998; Kwong 1996), contemporary observers have given much less attention to such organizations.

One reason may be that such organizations are simply a less important part of the lives of immigrants and their children—and indeed, of other Americans—than was true in past generations. In a nation that "bowls alone" (see Putnam 2001), social scientists may necessarily pay less attention to the organizational dimension of social life. We suspect, however, that this shift also reflects the changing tastes of the social scientists. Since the 1960s, sociologists and political scientists have been in the thrall of techniques based on random samples. Although survey research has its advantages, it also has the perhaps unintended effect of obscuring the institutional and organizational settings in which respondents live their lives. It allows us to study the people who are *in* organizations but rarely sheds much light on those organizations themselves. Of course, many in-depth interview studies do ask people about their organizational lives. Yet even this approach throws little light on the aspects of organizational life and culture that may shape respondents' lives but of which they are not fully aware. It has also become less fashionable to study community leaders, who, by definition, are atypical and thus nonrepresentative members of their group. As a result, contemporary social scientists rarely examine those aspects of community life that only leaders would know about or be able to articulate.

189

In an effort to bring social ties back into social science, much attention has recently been paid to "social capital" and the role of "social networks" in people's lives (for examples, see Coleman 1990; Lin 2001; Lin, Cook, and Burt 2001; Gabby and Leenders 2001). On the whole, this has been a positive development: researchers have paid more attention to the social contexts that envelope their subjects while still gathering the kind of systematic, quantifiable data that case studies or community studies generally do not. But these conceptual tools, however powerful, also have their limits. Social capital is an economistic concept that treats social connections as individual attributes rather than as social structures with a dynamic of their own. Although it is methodologically useful to reduce organizations to "nodes" in social networks, this approach clearly misses large parts of the story.

Ethnography can step into this breach by seeing people in their social contexts. It allows the researcher to watch what people actually *do*, rather than what they are able or willing to *say* to an interviewer. The three case studies presented in this section not only show how people are embedded in their particular social structures but enable us to study groups and organizations as entities in their own right. Ethnographers can uncover aspects of organizational history and culture that may have eluded individual members but that nevertheless affect their actions and vocabularies. Of course, as with all case studies, we must ask how representative the case studies in these chapters are, and whether the settings they study are comparable to other settings. Taken together with studies using more representative methods, we believe they offer unparalleled insights into the worlds inhabited by the children of immigrants as they come of age.

Amy Foerster presents the issues of ethnic and generational succession now facing a labor union that represents public-sector employees, mostly professionals. It is well understood that trade unions played a major role in the political lives of the previous second generation, the children of the migrants of 1880 to 1920, particularly in New York City. Yet students of immigration today are only just beginning to investigate how unions are now influencing the lives of first- and second-generation immigrants (see, for example, Waldinger et al. 1996). In this case, Foerster looks at the growing rift between an aging, largely native-born African American leadership elite whose defining life event was the civil rights movement and the largely West Indian rank-and-file members of the union. The leaders were trying to bridge divisions of ethnicity, generation, and gender—divisions they often did not completely understand—to convince younger members to care about the social mission of the union as the leaders defined it, a mission that the younger members in turn sought to redefine so that it made sense in their lives. The fact that all the union's members saw themselves as black—and were generally seen by others as black—made these divisions harder to articulate and added a special poignance to their efforts. The leaders saw themselves still as militant insurgents, as outsiders clinging to a small and hard-won piece of power. Yet many of the younger members saw them as the establishment. Such issues would not have come to light in a survey or in interviews with individual union members. The researcher had to be there to see it.

How typical is this story? Table P3.1 presents data from our survey of second-generation and native-born young people. It shows that native African Americans were the most likely to work at places with union representation, with West Indians and Puerto Ricans in second place, but the other second-generation groups (or indeed whites) were much less likely to work in unionized environments. This difference reflects the fact that the public and social service sectors, where these groups are more likely to work, are now the strongholds of union power as other unionized sectors, such as manufacturing, have been in steady decline and unionization has fallen in sectors, like retailing, where it had been stronger in the past. Given the similarities in the sectors in which African Americans and West Indians work, it is quite likely that the intrablack succession struggle and the explorations of pan-African cooperation described by Foerster are now happening in other unions as well. (Among Latinos, Puerto Ricans are the most likely to work in a unionized environment; this may account for why there is less tension in workplaces with many Puerto Ricans.) Few young people who are second-generation Korean, Chinese, or Russian or native white work in unionized settings. Leaving aside the declining membership of labor unions outside the public and social ser-

TABLE P3.1   JOB COVERED BY UNION, BY GROUP (FULL- AND PART-TIME WORKERS)

	Union at Job		
	No or Don't Know	Yes	Total
Colombian, Ecuadorean, and Peruvian	79.9%	20.1%	298
Dominican	77.6	22.4	286
Puerto Rican	73.8	26.2	279
West Indian	73.4	26.6	263
Native black	67.0	33.0	261
Chinese	89.8	10.2	374
Korean	92.0	8.0	199
Russian	90.2	9.8	205
Native white	86.5	13.5	319
Total	80.1	19.9	2,285

Source: Authors' compilation.

vice sectors, it seems clear that analogous "intraminority" succession struggles will unfold in neighborhoods, schools, and other institutions in which African Americans and Puerto Ricans were predominant in the past but which they now share with the children of black and Hispanic immigrants.

Nicole Marwell's chapter underlines how political organizations rooted in different types of neighborhoods respond to their changing composition. Washington Heights is New York's most Dominican neighborhood, and thus a Dominican nationalist impulse causes its political groups to focus on Dominican rather than Latino identity. Yet differences in ideology and cultural style have emerged between the older, first-generation political groups, which are often connected with Dominican political parties as well as New York's political establishment, and the younger, predominantly second-generation groups, which mix more militant rhetoric with greater comfort with "minority" politics. In North Brooklyn, by contrast, a surprisingly old-fashioned "political machine," seemingly almost completely devoid of ideology, is doing a good job of integrating 1.5- and second-generation Dominicans into politics (and delivering some patronage to them) under the banner of "Latino empowerment" and neighborhood service delivery. Indeed, this modern-day "clubhouse" spends much of its energy helping people navigate the social service bureaucracies that an earlier generation of political scientists thought had rendered political machines unnecessary.

In both neighborhoods the death of patronage-based "machine politics" has been exaggerated, although today's local politicians are more likely to dispense social service contracts than patronage jobs or Christmas turkeys. (If the stereotypical Tammany Hall club leader of the late nineteenth century was a saloon keeper and the typical midtwentieth-century clubhouse "pol" was a lawyer or real estate dealer, it is interesting to note that the leader of Marwell's North Brooklyn organization holds a master's degree in social work!) Access to political clout remains an influence on the life chances of second-generation groups, and politics remains, to a considerable degree, a matter of "bringing home the bacon."

Tables P3.2 and P3.3 provide information on electoral participation for the young people in our study. Like most Americans their age, these second- and 1.5-generation New Yorkers did not spend much time thinking about politics, and they didn't like politicians. Of the voting-age citizens in our survey sample, African Americans were again most likely to be registered and to vote, followed by native whites. Yet three-quarters of the West Indian and Latino second generation were also registered, a considerably higher share than among the economically better-off Koreans, Russian Jews, and Chinese. Democrats outnumbered Republicans in all groups—this was New York, after all. Even so, fewer than half of the Koreans, Chinese, and Russians de-

TABLE P3.2   REGISTERED VOTERS, BY GROUP (VOTING-AGE CITIZENS)

| | Registered | | |
	No, Don't Know, or No Answer	Yes	Total
Colombian, Ecuadorean, and Peruvian	26.2%	73.8%	332
Dominican	23.0	77.0	344
Puerto Rican	27.6	72.4	427
West Indian	25.0	75.0	312
Native black	13.7	86.3	422
Chinese	37.1	62.9	482
Korean	35.2	64.9	202
Russian	36.6	63.4	194
Native white	19.6	80.4	409
Total	25.7	74.3	2,922

Source: Authors' compilation.

clared themselves Democrats. These groups are clearly much more detached from the political system than the Latino groups, which in turn are not as politically engaged as West Indians and African Americans.

Studies of immigrant adaptation in the last century emphasized the importance of religion, another topic strikingly absent from the contemporary literature. This is clearly changing, however. The work of Karen Chai Kim, one of a growing number of young sociologists of religion interested in immigrant and second-generation communities, completes part 3. Our survey

TABLE P3.3   PARTY OF REGISTRATION, BY GROUP (REGISTERED VOTERS)

| | Party | | | | |
	Democrat	Republican	Independent	Other	Total
Colombian, Ecuadorean, and Peruvian	58.0%	16.3%	14.3%	11.4%	245
Dominican	69.4	9.1	9.8	11.7	265
Puerto Rican	64.6	12.3	11.7	11.4	308
West Indian	78.2	6.4	7.7	7.7	234
Native black	79.9	6.3	8.0	5.8	363
Chinese	42.1	21.4	18.8	17.8	304
Korean	49.59	26.02	18.70	5.69	123
Russian	37.9	33.9	13.7	14.5	124
Native white	49.7	23.5	19.2	7.6	328
Total	61.5	14.9	12.9	10.6	2,171

Source: Authors' compilation.

TABLE P3.4   MEMBERSHIP IN NEIGHBORHOOD, CIVIC, SPORTS, ETHNIC, AND OTHER ORGANIZATIONS, BY GROUP (ENTIRE SAMPLE)

| | Memberships | | | |
	None	One	Two or More	Total
Colombian, Ecuadorean, and Peruvian	52.0%	28.8%	19.3%	410
Dominican	50.2	26.2	23.6	424
Puerto Rican	47.3	28.9	23.8	429
West Indian	41.3	26.7	31.9	404
Native black	36.3	27.7	36.0	422
Korean	64.0	20.5	15.5	200
Chinese	45.5	29.2	25.2	606
Russian	48.5	29.4	22.0	309
Native white	42.8	31.8	25.4	409
Total	45.4	28.6	26.0	3,413

Source: Authors' compilation.

shows that Chinese second-generation young people are among the least likely to attend church regularly (interestingly, Koreans are the most likely; see table P3.5), but Kim demonstrates that, among those who do go to church, religion plays a pivotal role in creating their American identity. This is presented in table P3.4. In contrast to the experience of earlier groups, most of Kim's respondents were *more* religious than their parents. (Zeltzer-Zubida's chapter in part 4 shows that this was also true of a significant minority of the Russian Jews.)

The religion her respondents had taken up, evangelical Protestantism, is wholly American in origin and content. Indeed, many of their immigrant parents found their devotion unsettling. Yet this was not a simple case of "assimilation," however it might appear on a survey question. These young people often joined congregations that appealed specifically to second-generation Asian Americans. In the "downtown" church, this was an outgrowth of missionary appeals to convert immigrants, but the "uptown" church made no overtly "Asian" appeal. Its services were in English, and the liturgy was standard. Yet Kim notes an emerging style of worship and self-identity in these churches and among their congregants that is distinct from white or black American Protestantism or Chinese traditions. Indeed, this worship style brought uptown second-generation Chinese Americans together with second-generation Korean Americans (the group most likely to attend church regularly), with whom they shared race, a second-generation experience, and—perhaps most important—class position.

These studies show that organizational life and civic participation still count for a sizable minority of the second generation, even in a world that

TABLE P3.5   CHURCH ATTENDANCE IN THE PREVIOUS YEAR, BY GROUP (ENTIRE SAMPLE)

| | Church Attendance | | | |
	Never	Monthly or Less	More Than Monthly	Total
Colombian, Ecuadorean, and Peruvian	54.9%	17.6%	27.6%	410
Dominican	56.4	17.5	26.2	424
Puerto Rican	67.1	10.3	22.7	428
West Indian	61.4	9.7	29.0	404
Native black	62.3	12.6	25.1	422
Korean	40.58	10.87	48.55	138
Chinese	82.7	5.8	11.5	607
Russian	66.1	23.2	10.6	310
Native white	66.3	12.2	21.5	409
Total	65.6	12.9	21.5	3,414

Source: Authors' compilation.
Note: Of 202 second-generation respondents, 65, or 32.18 percent, did not have a religion. For those with a religion, I recorded according to the above categories.

"bowls alone." Through their participation in these groups, they are defining themselves and redefining many aspects of New York's civic life. By highlighting many subtle aspects of this process that would not be revealed in demographic tables or survey responses, including our own, these studies demonstrate the continuing value of ethnographic work.

REFERENCES

Bozorgmehr, Mehdi, Mehmet Kucukozer, and Anny Bakalian. 2004. "Ethnic Targeting and Organizational Response: The Role of Arab and Muslim American Organizations in the Post-9/11 Era." Paper presented to the Eastern Sociological Society. New York, February 19.

Coleman, James S. 1990. *Foundations of Social Theory.* Cambridge, Mass.: Harvard University Press.

Cordero-Guzman, Hector. 2002. "Immigrant Aid Societies and Organizations." In *The Encyclopedia of American Immigration,* edited by James Ciment. Armonk, N.Y.: M.E. Sharpe.

Gabby, Shaul M., and Roger R.A.J. Leenders, eds. 2001. *Social Capital of Organizations. Research in the Sociology of Organizations,* vol. 18. Oxford: Elsevier.

Gerstle, Gary, and John Mollenkopf, eds. 2001. *E Pluribus Unum? Contemporary and Historical Perspectives on Immigrant Political Incorporation.* New York: Russell Sage Foundation.

Jones-Correa, Michael. 1998. *Between Two Nations: The Political Predicament of Latinos in New York City.* Ithaca, N.Y.: Cornell University Press.

Kwong, Peter. 1996. *The New Chinatown.* New York: Hill and Wang.

Lin, Nan. 2001. *Social Capital: A Theory of Social Structure and Action.* New York: Cambridge University Press.

Lin, Nan, Karen Cook, and Ronald S. Burt, eds. 2001. *Social Capital: Theory and Research.* Hawthorne, N.Y.: Aldine de Gruyter.

Putnam, Robert. 2001. *Bowling Alone: The Collapse and Revival of American Community.* New York: Simon & Schuster.

Waldinger, Roger, Chris Erickson, Ruth Milkman, Daniel J. B. Mitchell, Abel Valenzuela, Kent Wong, and Maurice Zeitlin. 1996. "Helots No More: A Case Study of the Justice for Janitors Campaign in Los Angeles." Working paper 15. Los Angeles: University of Los Angeles, Lewis Center.

Warner, Stephen R., and Judith G. Wittner, eds. 1998. *Gatherings in Diaspora: Religious Communities and the New Immigration.* Philadelphia: Temple University Press.

CHAPTER 7

"ISN'T ANYBODY HERE FROM ALABAMA?": SOLIDARITY AND STRUGGLE IN A "MIGHTY, MIGHTY UNION"

AMY FOERSTER

On a sweltering summer night in New York City, hundreds of union members are gathered in the downtown headquarters of the American Federation of State, County, and Municipal Employees (AFSCME) to celebrate the Caribbean heritage of their members. Dressed in evening finery, Caribbean-style floral prints, and African caftans, the members dance and respond energetically to the evening's entertainer, a calypso performer who sings, "Who's here from Trinidad?" In response, Trinidadians jump even higher and dance even faster, while waving flags of their homeland. "Who's here from Jamaica?" she continues, before running through a long list of Caribbean islands. After whipping the crowd into a flag-waving frenzy, she retires from the stage, leaving the union's Alabama-born president clapping and thanking her. He then turns to the assembled crowd, shakes his head with mock consternation, and asks, "Isn't anybody here from Alabama?"

THE ETHNIC contrasts evident in this scene, which was played out in New York City's Social Service Employees Union (SSEU), are becoming increasingly common as America's churches, workplaces, educational institutions, and voluntary organizations are dramatically altered by immigration. In this case, the union, which was founded primarily by leftist Jewish and Italian caseworkers and African American civil rights veterans, has been significantly transformed as waves of Latin Americans, Africans, West Indians, and South Asians—and their second-generation children—have entered the city's social service workforce. The consequences for the union—and its members—have been dramatic: the union's structural practices and organizational identity have been altered, and concomitantly the members have struggled with what it means to be both "black" and a unionist in a new organizational setting. Some outcomes of these struggles have been inspiring as the union has served as an important agent of incorporation for its second-generation members and as a site in which pan-ethnic cooperation and alliances are formed; the union has also been a setting, however, that is fraught with ethnic tensions and generational disputes.

Both patterns are directly traceable to the union's history, its identity as a progressive "black" organization, and the particular role it has played in both civil rights and labor struggles. The union's identity—and indeed, its very existence—can be traced most directly to June 1965, when the young organization's leaders and members launched a historic strike against the city of New York. Although the four-week strike was technically illegal under the provisions of the Condon-Wadlin Act, and fifteen strike leaders were imprisoned as a result, the union members—primarily caseworkers in various city agencies—entered into a collective bargaining agreement with their employer. This agreement was the first of its kind in the nation: public welfare employees had never before negotiated a collective bargaining contract. As impressive—and historic—as this victory was, it came only after a powerful alliance was formed by leftist Jewish and Italian caseworkers, their predominantly African American clients, New York's established labor and civil rights leaders, and an emerging cohort of African American caseworkers fresh from the trenches of America's civil rights battles. By marching together on picket lines, sharing jail cells, and organizing fellow workers, the caseworkers and their supporters gave birth to a "mighty, mighty union" that continues to represent New York's social service employees in the twenty-first century.

What has happened since 1965 is, of course, a story that resonates in a number of American workplaces, houses of worship, educational institutions, and other organizations. The union has been dramatically transformed, not only by the city's shifting economic fortunes and political transitions but also by the large number of new immigrants—and the immigrant second generation—who have found employment in the city's social service sector. Once made up primarily of college-educated Jewish and Italian leftists and African American civil rights veterans, the union is now a colorful mélange of nationalities and races. First- and second-generation West Indians mix and mingle with Dominicans and Puerto Ricans at the union's various social events. The union's Jewish retirees share phone-banking duties with Jamaicans and Haitians. African American union veterans now attend Caribbean history celebrations sponsored by the union and ponder the meaning of being a "black" unionist in a shifting ethnic landscape. Perhaps most important, the union's newest members—the immigrant second generation—are introduced to the workplace, and other workers, through their participation in the union. As such, the union serves as an important space in which to examine issues of ethnic identity and assimilation and instances of cooperation and conflict between members of the immigrant second generation, their first-generation counterparts, and the "native" whites, blacks, and Latinos on whose shoulders the union is built. How does the immigrant second generation negotiate the contested terrain the union represents? What does the union do for them? How do longtime union members respond to their presence? What, if anything, will participation in union activities *mean* to members of the immigrant second generation?

LABOR UNIONS, EMPLOYMENT, AND IMMIGRANT INCORPORATION: AN OVERVIEW

These questions are all the more pressing when we consider that unions were important sites for the incorporation and assimilation of previous waves of immigrant workers and their second-generation children (Barrett 1992; Glenn 1990; Göbel 1988; Oestreicher 1986; Wilentz 1984). Then, as now, American workplaces were often divided by race, generation, language group, and national origin. Despite such divisions, the early Congress of Industrial Organizations (CIO) was able to form a culture of unity among disparate workers (Cohen 1990). Through the use of social and recreation programs and burgeoning forms of mass media, national and local unions forged new alliances and forms of solidarity that often transcended ethnic divisions and created new identities and affiliations, particularly among the immigrant second generation. Unlike their immigrant parents, who were sometimes reluctant to be marked as labor agitators, the immigrant second generation perceived union affiliation as a way to become American in part by rejecting the perceived passivity and ethnic inclusiveness practiced by their parents and fellow ethnics. Union membership apparently provided the second generation with a measure of dignity in a work life otherwise characterized by hostility, exclusion, and discrimination at the hands of native workers (Göbel 1988). Additionally, participation in union affairs set a whole new assimilation pattern for the immigrant second generation of the 1930s and 1940s. Because union membership entailed participation in trans-ethnic working-class lodges, the second generation had a great deal of interaction with members of other ethnic groups, an experience shared by neither their parents nor earlier waves of immigrant workers. In this sense, then, the immigrant second generation who participated in unions truly did "become American" (Göbel 1988).

Of course, today's immigrant second generation is very different from earlier waves, as is today's union movement. The contemporary labor movement struggles to maintain membership, and union members today are much more likely to be Mexican, Dominican, or Jamaican than Hungarian, German, or Italian. Although this may be the case, table 7.1 demonstrates that union membership is still fairly common for young New Yorkers between eighteen and thirty-two years of age, both native-born and second-generation.

Almost 19 percent of the total sample responded in the affirmative when asked if they were members of a union on their current job.[1] Native blacks were the most likely to be union members, followed closely by second-generation West Indians, second-generation Dominicans, and native Puerto Ricans. The high rate of unionization among these groups is attributable in part to the particular occupations and occupational sectors in which they were employed. As table 7.2 demonstrates, native blacks, second-generation West Indians, second-generation Dominicans, and Puerto Ricans were more likely than other groups to report that they were employed by government agencies. The Chinese, Russian Jews, and "other Hispanics," on the other hand, had some of the lowest rates of government employment; perhaps not coincidentally, these groups were also among the least likely to be union members.

These data demonstrate the important link between ethnicity, unionism, and government employment. This sector has proven a union stronghold over the past thirty years; indeed, while unionization in the private sector has declined precipitously since 1970, unionization in the public sector continues to climb (Bronfenbrenner and Juravich 1995; U.S. Department of Labor 2001).

TABLE 7.1   NEW YORKERS AGE EIGHTEEN TO THIRTY-TWO REPRESENTED BY A UNION ON CURRENT JOB

	Percentage	Number of Respondents
Total sample	18.6%	3,540
Chinese	9.1	536
Colombian, Ecuadorean, and Peruvian	18.9	476
Dominican	22.0	414
Native black	27.8	544
Native white	14.1	390
Puerto Rican	21.3	493
Russian Jew	8.7	275
West Indian	23.7	393
Other Hispanic	10.5	19

Source: Author's compliation.

TABLE 7.2   MOST RECENT OR CURRENT TYPE OF EMPLOYER FOR EIGHTEEN- TO THIRTY-TWO-YEAR-OLD NEW YORKERS

Ethnic Group	Government Agency	Not-for-Profit Organization	Private Company	University or School	Unpaid Internship	Other	Number of Respondents
Total	11.1%	5.8%	72.7%	7.5%	0.3%	2.6%	3,214
Chinese	6.3	5.3	76.4	9.5	1.0	1.4	505
Colombian, Ecuadorean, and Peruvian	8.9	3.0	80.2	4.8	0.0	3.2	440
Dominican	9.9	7.5	73.2	7.7	0.0	1.7	362
Native black	21.5	6.7	59.8	6.5	0.4	5.1	492
Native white	9.3	7.6	72.1	9.3	0.3	1.5	344
Puerto Rican	11.8	6.3	71.5	6.3	0.0	4.1	459
Russian Jew	5.2	4.3	79.3	9.9	0.0	1.3	232
West Indian	12.1	6.3	72.5	7.7	0.6	0.8	363
Other Hispanic	5.9	0.0	82.4	0.0	0.0	11.8	17

Source: Author's compilation.

The concentration of native blacks, Puerto Ricans, and West Indians in the public sector is perhaps not surprising when we consider that government employment—and particularly municipal employment—has long been considered a source of upward mobility for native minorities, because of the good salaries, strong benefits, job security, and relative status associated with the sector (Kerr and Mladenka 1994; Model 2001). Jobs in city government are attractive to this population because "discrimination exerts a less powerful influence on public sector employees" and because "the public sector seems to act as a ladder of mobility into the middle class for blacks more than whites" (Waldinger 1996, 206). Additionally, city jobs grew dramatically throughout the 1970s and 1980s, despite the fiscal crisis that rocked New York during that period (Mollenkopf 1992), and city employment continued to exhibit strong growth through the economic boom of the late 1990s. For these reasons, municipal employment has remained an attractive option for native-born blacks and Latinos and seems to be extending its appeal to the immigrant second generation of black and Latino heritage as well.

The public-sector unionized work space, then, provides a natural meeting ground for the immigrant second generation and native-born minority groups. It presents an integral location to examine the patterns of cross-ethnic cooperation and conflict that may emerge among groups of people who share the same skin color but come from very different cultural backgrounds and perspectives. Do young West Indians "become American" in this social setting? If so, what type of American do they become?

Service, Protection, and Socialization: The Culture of Solidarity in the "Mighty, Mighty Union"

I investigated these questions through a yearlong ethnographic examination of the 15,000-member Social Service Employees Union.[2] The SSEU proved to be an interesting site in which to examine these questions, not only because of its large membership base but also because of its tradition of interracial cooperation and struggle. Its roots are based in Welfare Employees Local 371 of New York's District Council 37, American Federation of State, County, and Municipal Employees, but it became a separate and autonomous organization in 1964 following a coup staged by left-wing Jews who felt that Local 371's leadership was inactive, corrupt, and weak (Bellush and Bellush 1984). These dissidents quickly found support from a number of idealistic younger Jews and African Americans who were entering the social service field as a result of the employment opportunities offered by the city's rapidly expanding welfare system (Walkowitz 1999). Together these groups sought to form a new, more radical organization that would not only represent social workers as employees but change the nature of the Department of Welfare altogether by treating clients with more respect and dignity.

Following the formation of the new organization, the members of SSEU launched the four-week strike that changed the history of municipal collective bargaining and solidified the organization's identity. During this period the new union established a firm culture of solidarity between Jews, Italians, African Americans, and civil rights organizations, which supported the strike because of its far-reaching impact on the lives of welfare clients, many of whom were African American. Following the successful resolution of the strike, the union endured several years of internal battles and strife before voting to merge, once again, with Local 371 of AFSCME. In the course of the merger, however, the SSEU was allowed to transfer its name and retain a fair level of autonomy (Bellush and Bellush 1984). It is now known as Local 371, SSEU.

Local 371 currently represents 15,000 members employed in 166 job titles throughout the city of New York's social service system. Many of these workers are caseworkers in the city's various social service agencies, while others are employed as addiction counselors, child protective specialists, fraud investigators, correctional counselors, and HIV counselors (American Federation of State, County, and Municipal Employees 1995). Most positions require a college degree and, depending on the agency in which one is hired, may also require successful completion of a civil service exam and an English-language proficiency exam. According to some union staff with whom I spoke, the manner in which job candidates are recruited for these positions leads to ethnic segmentation in the industry. Municipal social service positions are typically advertised on the city's website, through advertisements in newspapers, or through word of mouth, but some positions, according to one union official, are advertised extensively in *el diario*, New York's most far-reaching Spanish-language newspaper, while others are placed in the *Amsterdam News*, which is read primarily by the city's African American community. In addition, the same official asserted, the Administration for Children Services (ACS) often does not hire African immigrants, owing to recurring conflicts regarding definitions of what constitutes "abuse" of a child, and many whites and Spanish-speaking Latinos seeking employment in social service jobs are hired into fraud investigation divisions. This results in particular forms of ethnic segmentation: African American and West Indian workers often work side by side in children's services, while Latino workers are clustered in hospital agencies or fraud investigation and whites work in fraud investigation and other agencies (see table 7.3).[3]

The union is thus introduced to a workforce that is already divided along racial and ethnic lines at the time it becomes eligible for union membership.

TABLE 7.3   RACIAL PROFILE OF SOCIAL SERVICE WORKERS IN CITY AGENCIES, 1999

Agency	White	Black	Hispanic	Asian	Native American	Unknown	Number of Respondents
Administration for Children's Services	13.4%	71.2%	12.0%	3.1%	0.3%	0.0%	4,424
Department of Juvenile Justice	1.4	85.1	12.1	0.7	0.2	0.4	429
Department of Homeless Services	15.9	66.6	5.1	5.1	0.4	0.0	276
Human Resources Administration and Department of Social Services	10.9	65.5	18.4	3.6	0.2	0.0	6,876

Source: New York City Department of Citywide Administrative Services.
Note: Data are based on self-report questionnaires that follow EEOC guidelines.

One of the SSEU's primary organizational tasks, then, is to overcome these divisions and to form a new identity for its members, one that unites a disparate group of ethnically and racially diverse workers behind common goals. How does the organization attempt to achieve this? Primarily by offering the opportunity for extensive participation in the organization and by stressing the benefits of union membership. Such benefits include protection against capricious managers and an unyielding municipal bureaucracy, legal and representational services available only to union members, and political and civic socialization that broadens the scope of members' experiences. Although some of these benefits are surely more appealing than others, all of them serve to build loyalty to the organization and between members and, in some respects, provide a mode of incorporation for immigrant members and the immigrant second generation.

Social service workers are generally incorporated into Local 371—and introduced to one another—as part of the city's orientation sessions for new employees. In the course of this orientation the union's president and selected officers make a presentation regarding the benefits of the union and sign up new members. Because the union enjoys agency shop rights, virtually all of the city's social service workers are technically members of the union (and pay union dues) regardless of whether they choose to become active in the organization. Those who do wish to participate come together at least three times a year for the union's general membership meetings and are encouraged to contribute in a number of other ways. For example, members can run for "chapter chair" positions, which represent the specific work locations at which they are employed, or they may seek to join various committees that set policy and offer assistance to the union's members: currently members can seek positions on the legal assistance committee, the central election committee, and the executive committee, which carries out union policies and procedures on a day-to-day basis.

Additionally, each work location elects one or more union delegates and alternates, depending on the number of workers employed at the location. These delegates attend a two-day delegate training session and then are expected to attend monthly delegate assemblies at which they are briefed on grievance procedures, bargaining updates, changes to the union's benefit plan, and current controversies regarding work rules and conflicts with management and the city. They are then expected to return to their work sites to hold monthly location meetings in which they relay this information to other workers. The "business" of this union, then, as with many other labor organizations, is to assist workers in building the skills they need to represent themselves to—*and protect themselves from*—management. The union often offers the services of its paid staff to help with these protective functions. The staff, along with elected committees of worker-delegates, represent the employees during collective bargaining, for example, and also handle grievances and negotiate with management over issues as they arise.

These issues vary from day to day but typically revolve around worker safety and security, job autonomy, disagreements over pay scales and promotions, time and leave policies, and dress codes. At the time I was conducting my fieldwork, for example, workplace safety had become a major concern. Workers were sometimes assaulted on the job by clients and frequently expressed concern over lax security at their work locations. A series of workplace assaults in early 2000 resulted in hospital visits for two union members and produced a picket line at an office of the Division of AIDS Services. Concerns over rat infestations in city offices were also discussed—and sometimes protested—as were health concerns resulting from asbestos and fungal growth in city buildings. Local 371 was at the forefront of protesting these issues and also kept a watchful eye out for other violations of the union's contract. The union frequently processed member grievances about working "out of title," for example, and often pressed the city to pay the higher salaries associated with the out-of-title work that members were asked to perform.

The union is also sometimes called on to protect workers against unwarranted firings or overlooked promotions; interestingly, these situations are often inflected by race, ethnicity, and immigration status. This was evident in the case of a Latino worker once employed by the Administration for Children's Services who sought reinstatement after accepting a short-lived position in neighboring Westchester County. Despite the fact that the man had worked for ACS for eight years—and had never had a negative job evaluation during his time at the agency—he was asked to take an English-language proficiency exam as a condition of reinstatement. He did not pass this exam—which was initially implemented following complaints by family court judges who felt that caseworkers sometimes demonstrated inadequate written and oral English skills when interacting with the court—and was not rehired. Local 371 pushed the case all the way to the New York State Supreme Court and eventually won full reinstatement for the worker, with back pay. In her comments to the union's paper, Local 371's grievance representative argued in *The Unionist* (May 2000) that "the English proficiency exam is biased, and could serve to unfairly eliminate qualified workers from the [Administration for Children's Services]. This case clearly proves that point."

Such cases and allegations of bias are, unfortunately, not rare. In September 2001, *The Unionist* reported a similar story, this time involving a South Asian member who was passed over for promotion by a manager who accused him of poor work performance and called him a "little Indian" and a "foreigner" in front of his coworkers. The union encouraged the worker to file a complaint with the Equal Employment Opportunity Commission (EEOC), which resulted in a lawsuit and a $60,000 settlement for the worker. "I want people to know they don't have to tolerate abuse on location," he told *The Unionist*. "If they feel they are right, they don't have to compromise their principles."

Clearly, then, the union is well aware that its changing membership has diverse needs and often requires protection that may not have been necessary when the membership was primarily native-born. For the most part, however, the types of protective functions the union serves are the same for the majority of workers: keeping them safe at work, making sure the union contract is enforced, protecting them from unfair treatment, and responding to specific issues that emerge. In the course of the fieldwork, for example, former New York City mayor Rudolph Giuliani proposed tying employee raises to performance rather than to the cost of living, as had been done traditionally. This caused a great deal of consternation within the union and became a recurring theme at rallies and delegate assembly meetings. Changes to the city's prescription drug benefit plan were also passionately discussed and became a rallying point during subsequent contract negotiations with the city.

In addition to providing protection and representation, the union provides a wide variety of other services to its members. Members are offered legal representation, for example, and also are given access to union-led classes on financial planning, immigration policies, labor history, and domestic violence. The union also offers all-important information on the dates of upcoming civil service examinations and typically offers preparation courses for members hoping to "test up" within the city's civil service system.

Finally, and perhaps most importantly for our purposes, the union provides opportunities for social interaction between members and different forms of political and civic socialization that have far-reaching impacts. The union sponsors several interest-based committees, for example, that typically come together to plan large yearly celebrations or to sponsor events that educate the rest of the membership about particular issues. The women's committee, for example, has hosted several events focusing on gender and gender inequality. These included panel presentations on the state of women in the labor movement, a workshop on domestic violence, a march to raise funds for breast cancer research, and various fund-raising activities. There are also several ethnic committees. Presently Jewish, black, Caribbean, and Latino members can participate in a committee specific to their culture or ethnic group; interestingly, many members participate in several at the same time. One of the primary functions of these committees is to plan and host annual ethnic heritage events to which all members are invited. These celebrations typically offer dinners featuring ethnic foods, keynote speakers, music, dancing, and vendors selling ethnic wares.

The union sponsors a political action committee that introduces state and local candidates to the membership, makes endorsements, and mobilizes voters during federal, state, and local elections. All of these committees also hold fund-raising trips and events, which are often social in nature. The political action committee, for example, held a fund-raising Mardi Gras, while the women's committee has sponsored bus trips to Atlantic City and outings to Broadway shows. The black heritage committee has raised funds through a jazz dinner cruise and an expedition to an outlet mall in Connecticut. Given the large number of committees, chapters, and fund-raising events, a member could realistically expect to attend a different union meeting or function every night of the week, should she or he choose to do so.

A TENUOUS SOLIDARITY: LOCAL 371 AND THE IMMIGRANT SECOND GENERATION

Given the large number of opportunities to participate, it is perhaps not surprising that the union serves as a space in which members of various racial, ethnic, and immigrant groups come into contact with one another. It is clear, however, that members of the immigrant second generation are *not* the most active members of the organization. In fact, the percentage of active members who are under forty years of age is noticeably small, despite the fact that the social service profession has a fairly large concentration of workers under forty (Gibelman and Schervish 1997). This fact was recognized by both staff and leaders of the union, as well as by active members. Many staff were quite concerned about the problem. This first became evident at a women's history committee event at which a union officer addressed what she called her "pet peeve," saying that young women in the union were "very complacent" and that she could not get them to express concerns about workplace issues. She explained their reluctance to participate by saying to the audience: "Now, I know that we all said, 'I'll just work here a year and then leave.' I said the same thing, and now look at me, however many years later."[4] She then solicited suggestions from the audience and other panelists in hopes of increasing participation among younger members.[5]

One of the featured speakers—a young organizer from a health care union in Florida—suggested that the union sponsor a fact-finding mission to the South. After witnessing working conditions there, she thought young New York unionists might recognize the benefits of a unionized workplace. This might make them more appreciative of their union and more likely to participate. In response to this suggestion, an older member—and a veteran of the 1965 strike—objected, saying, "I came from the South. I know what it's like down there. We don't need to go to the South, because the South is right here!" Instead, she proposed a mentoring program pairing older members with younger ones and suggested calling it "Each One Teach One." The young organizer countered by suggesting that the union sponsor small demonstrations on issues important to younger members and not concentrate solely on economic or workplace issues. She suggested police brutality as an issue that might spark interest on the part of young members.

The same women's committee discussed this problem a number of times in its meetings and frequently tried to plan social events they hoped would attract younger people. One suggestion was to hold a fund-raising event in a local bowling alley frequented by New York University students. One staff member mentioned that she had bowled there and found the crowd to be "hip" and "fun." Once again, this suggestion met with significant resistance on the part of older members, one of whom mentioned that she did not like bowling and that it required too much skill. She suggested going to Atlantic City instead. Her motion was eventually passed, and the outing to the bowling alley was tabled.

Other members and staff were also cognizant of the lack of participation on the part of young members but attributed it solely to life stage and conflicting interests rather than immigration status, ethnicity, or any particular failing on the part of the union. One very active Jamaican member remarked that she was active in the union only because her child was now grown. "They are just too busy," she said of younger members. "Who has time to come to the union meeting when you are trying to get dinner on the table and raise a family?" A staff member concurred and remarked that the lack of participation on the part of young members—and second-generation members—was a nationwide problem and not one specific to the SSEU.[6] "You've seen our meetings," she said. "Why would young people want to come? They're busy doing other things, like going to discos [*laughs*] . . . or whatever it is young people do!"

The majority of union staff and members, then, attributed lack of participation among young members, and members of the immigrant second generation, to high turnover in the industry, life stage, conflicting interests, and, in a minority of cases, the lack of union activities that appealed specifically to the young. The president of the union, however, was not willing to let young members off the hook so easily. He often drew from his personal history in the civil rights movement in attempts to motivate and inspire members— young and old—to become more active. He gave the following address, for example, at a delegate assembly meeting:

What is a union movement? It's you, the members! It's the delegates, the alternates, all of us in this room. . . . The union movement is only as strong as the number of people willing to get involved in it! I tell you what, the other day I had this young worker say to me, "Why should I have to fight for all these things? That's what I elected you for." Now that's my pet peeve. I hate whiners, people who are dissatisfied but expect other people to do for them. Some of us, a lot of us, came up in the civil rights movement. . . . Do you think the little old ladies who wouldn't sit at the back of the bus wanted everyone else to do for them? No, they didn't. They fought hard, and they fought with a lot of other people who were willing to fight just as hard. . . . We've got some other struggles coming up now. The mayor, in his infinite wisdom, has challenged your pay raises and wants to base all of them on merit. He's serious about this now, and we're going to have to fight to keep our cost-of-living increases and our wage structure. . . . So that's what we're about here today. You are all delegates, and part of your job is to convince people that if we stick together, if we fight together, we can win this!

This statement seems specifically tailored to place the onus of participation squarely on the shoulders of young members, and it draws from a particular "mobilizing frame" in attempting to do so (Snow et al. 1986; Snow and Benford 1988, 1992). This frame pulls from memories of the civil rights movement and racial injustice and attempts to create parallels between the conditions experienced in the 1960s and those experienced today by New York City's multi-ethnic social service labor force. It is important to keep in mind that this address was targeted toward a primarily black audience. The president was assuming that the modern-day "fight," even though it was a fight clearly related to class and workplace issues, was deeply inflected by racial memories and meanings. By framing his appeal in this manner, he assumed that the assembled members would share this sense of history in struggle. For many of his listeners, this appeared to be true; other members clearly did not respond to his remarks. On one of many occasions on which the president alluded to his friendship with Angela Davis, for example, a young member was overheard exclaiming, "Angela! How many times is he gonna tell us about Angela already?" It is clear, then, that not all members appreciated the union's connection to the struggle for racial justice and civil rights. In this sense, the president may have been at risk of presenting a "frame repertoire" that did not resonate with the young second-generation members of his union (Kim 2000b; Snow et al. 1986; Snow and Benford 1988, 1992).

Perhaps understanding this, the president also clearly perceived the ethnic history celebrations as an alternative method through which to get more members—and particularly young members—involved. Many young members—particularly second-generation West Indians—did mention that

they initially became active in the union through participation on these committees. Many came out for the annual ethnic celebrations, for example, and
several participated in event planning and logistical arrangements for these
celebrations. One second-generation Jamaican, for example, commented that
he did not know much about the union but had come to help with decorations during the Caribbean celebration because an older coworker had solicited his assistance. On another occasion, a newly elected delegate approached the chair of the Caribbean committee and asked him when the
committee met. She explained that she wanted to become more involved in
the union but had felt "too intimidated" to join some of the other committees. She mentioned that she was Belizean and had initially attempted to join
the Latino committee. After discovering that many of their meetings were
conducted in Spanish, she stopped attending. The chair told her that she
would be more than welcome to attend the Caribbean meeting, to which she
responded, "Well, since I'm from Belize, I could go either way—to the Carib-
beans or the Latinos."

It did seem, then, that the ethnic heritage committees served as one clear
avenue of participation for young, second-generation members whose commitment to the union was tenuous at best. It is unclear, however, whether the
type of assistance they provided on these committees and the ways in which
they participated ever resulted in the more committed and engaged membership the union president was trying to promote. For the second-generation
Jamaican member just mentioned, for example, the transition from participation to activism did not seem clear; once he was finished inflating balloons
and hanging streamers, the young man left, commenting that he had other
engagements.

Solidarity Through Struggle: Building a "Black" Union

Although lack of participation in the union is certainly a pressing problem for
the union, the SSEU itself is generally a more participatory and democratic
union than many of its counterparts. Attendance at delegate assemblies and
general membership meetings usually numbers in the hundreds, and the
union has never failed to reach a quorum when discussing or voting on important issues. As such, this union provides an important glimpse at how
workers of different races, ethnicities, and immigrant generations come together to forge a sometimes tenuous solidarity, not only through their shared
experiences as workers but also as members of American minority groups.

The union's president was certainly responsible for many of the efforts to
forge a pan-ethnic culture of solidarity. Born and raised in Birmingham, Al-

abama, he was a civil rights veteran who came to New York City in the mid-1960s and quickly gained employment as a caseworker in the Department of Welfare. President of the union since 1982, he certainly recognized that the union he led had changed dramatically during his tenure, and he strongly believed that the increasing diversity of the union had to be recognized. He had taken a number of steps to ensure that goal, including hiring a number of different ethnic group members as full-time union staff. He had also encouraged many of them to run for union office.[7] Staff members frequently joked about his success, many commenting that the union's staff was now actually *more* diverse than the union membership. This was true to some extent. The president had recruited Nigerian, Guyanese, and Jamaican staff, even though the proportion of members represented by these individual ethnic groups was relatively small. One young Jamaican woman (herself a member of the 1.5 generation) explained how she was recruited by the president:

> I had been a caseworker and really liked working with the kids. I started coming to the meetings and getting more active and stuff. When [the union president] asked me to join the staff, I really didn't want to, because I didn't want to leave the kids behind. I told him I'd think about it, but he kept after me, and after a few months I agreed to take the position.

This seemed to be the general pattern in identifying and recruiting union leaders. The union president, other officers, and staff monitored which members were most active and respected by other workers and then attempted to recruit them onto the paid staff of the union. The president frequently alluded to the nationality of the staff during his remarks to the members, often commenting that he wanted to recognize the union's diversity by creating a staff that reflected the membership. For the most part, he seemed to have succeeded—and perhaps solidified his own position as a result. By recruiting a diverse staff, the union's president appeared responsive to the union's immigrant and second-generation membership; by handpicking this staff, he ensured that those recruited were amenable to his vision of the "mighty, mighty union." This vision was highly influenced by the legacy of the civil rights movement rather than the nationalist or identity movements that occurred in its wake.

Another diversity initiative sponsored by the president was the formation of the various ethnic committees within the union. Although the initial impetus came from the union's parent body (District Council 37, AFSCME), SSEU's president aggressively funded and supported the programs, primarily because of his belief that the committees brought diverse members together to learn about each other and offered a unique opportunity to introduce younger members—and members' children—to the value and history of the labor movement. He explained this belief in the course of a monthly delegate meeting:

> I've been criticized for spending so much of our members' dues money on these celebrations. I always tell people that the money is not wasted. Our events get people involved—people who might not normally be involved in the union. It gets them to look beyond selfish issues to political and economic issues. . . . We are celebrating our different selves all the time. We find strength in our diversity, in learning about each other.

The ethnic committees did seem to serve as spaces in which these goals were met. Although many members became active in the union by working only on the ethnic committee specific to their particular background, several eventually branched out, began attending other celebrations, and sometimes actually joined other committees. For example, José, a Puerto Rican caseworker employed in a city hospital, was active on the Latino heritage committee yet also devoted a great deal of time to planning and assisting with the union's Caribbean heritage event.[8] When questioned about this, he laughed and responded, "Yeah, and I'm on the Jewish committee too!" He then explained that he enjoyed meeting people from different faiths and cultures and particularly enjoyed the opportunity to hear different types of music and sample different types of food.

This focus on music and cultural forms of diversity was stressed by many members who were active on the ethnic committees. A number of West Indian members mentioned that they had known little about American-born Latinos before becoming active in the union but had learned to appreciate the similarities between themselves and their Latino compatriots through the heritage celebrations. Annie, a Jamaican caseworker, commented, "One thing I have to say about them [Latinos] is that when there is music playing, they don't sit down. They don't even have to have a partner! I didn't realize that about them before. Their outlook is very similar to ours in that way. Yes, life may be hard, but when there is music playing, you forget about it and dance."

The value of the ethnic heritage celebrations and committees was not uncontested, however. One staff member remarked that she worried that such attempts to recognize diversity might serve to divide the membership. The ethnic celebrations cost a tremendous amount of money and time and sometimes sparked disagreements over resources. Competition emerged over attendance and also over the fame and notoriety of the keynote speakers and musical entertainment that each committee was able to acquire. Additionally, as new groups entered the union, their push for inclusion sometimes strained the resources of the organization and created conflict with established groups. African newcomers to the union, for example, protested the fact that they did not have their own committee and felt that they should not be expected to join the established black or Caribbean committee. Some evidence of this tension was apparent. In the course of one of the Caribbean committee's planning meetings, the chair raised the issue of including African members on the celebration's program. "Bertrand [a Nigerian staff member] says that some of the Africans are complaining and think they ought to be listed on our program too. What do you think?" Several members responded loudly in the negative, to which he responded, "I agree, I mean, unless they are officially on our committee, which some of them are . . . but the problem is, they don't want to do a normal committee. They want to have all these little subgroups, like Liberia Week, Nigeria Week. . . ." This caused one woman in the audience to wave her hand in disgust while loudly proclaiming, "Bah! Forget it!"

Some staff also found fault with the fact that each group held its meetings separately, planned its own ethnic celebrations, and rarely discussed issues such as ethnic history within the union, ethnic contributions to the union, or the role of ethnicity in the labor movement more generally. These staff members felt that the ethnic committees and celebrations did not perform one essential function: drawing the members together as *unionists* in support of the union cause.

This concern with union culture—as opposed to ethnic culture—was frequently invoked when longtime members expressed discontent or concern over the behavior and participation of newcomers in the union. Some of the most visible conflicts in this regard were between native-born African Americans and the newcomers—both first- and second-generation—whom they disparagingly called "immigrant blacks." One longtime member, for example, when relating her experiences in the civil rights movement and in the union's 1965 strike, explained, "You know, there was a real sense then that we were all involved in the same thing . . . like we would help each other out, bring food to each other, sleep at the union headquarters. But you know, the union has really changed since those days, really it has." When asked what she meant, she said, "Well, you know, the union used to be mostly black. American black, I mean. Now it's a lot of immigrant blacks, and it just isn't the same." She then explained that "there was more of a collective feeling back in the old days." Now, however, "immigrant blacks" did not share that collective feeling and tended to become involved in the union only when "single-focus issues" came up, such as changes in the union's prescription drug plan. "That's just not a long-term focus," she concluded.

Other African American unionists clearly thought that "immigrant blacks," and West Indians in particular, believed they were superior to African Americans. In a forum sponsored by the women's history committee, for example, an African American member addressed the panelists by stating that she had a question she wanted to ask, "despite the fact that it is probably going to be controversial." She explained that she wanted to question the wisdom of attempting to organize immigrants, because "we all know that they are not so nice to African Americans. They learn the racism of their new country and begin to practice it against us as soon as they can." She concluded by remarking that she had experienced problems at her job with a West Indian woman who, believing she was superior to African Americans, became "backbiting" and "difficult." "This is a difficult, difficult thing," she said, "and I just wonder how you would suggest overcoming these kinds of difficulties?"

There was a brief moment of silence while the panel absorbed her comments. One panelist then responded, "Well, the only way I can tell you to overcome this is to practice. It doesn't come easy. A lot of times I tell my members to think about who is doing the oppressing." Another broke in and said, "Yes, and I'd also encourage you to think about it as 'What's in it for me to work this thing out?'" She then explained that people lose their prejudice only through life experiences and that the role of people of color and union members is to contribute to that education. A Latina organizer added, "Yes, and I think it's true that we have to focus on who is really hurting us." She then remarked that "we all need to learn about each other. Immigrants need to learn about labor struggles in this country. All I can say is that you have to be a very patient teacher, which is very hard." She added that it was helpful to realize that "we can also learn a lot from their experiences in their home countries." Finally, the second panelist—a university professor—broke in again and said that she was sympathetic to the issue raised by the questioner because she had faced the same issue in her class. She felt it was an issue because "some West Indians don't really have a good understanding of their own history" and thus make assumptions about their superiority that "are not appropriate." The issue had come up in her classes when West Indians created what she called a "fantasy history" about their own countries, such as "there's no discrimination in Jamaica." She encouraged the woman to keep trying, even though everyone on the panel acknowledged that it was difficult.

For the most part, incidents such as these were fairly infrequent and were generally overcome through appeals to a particular form of pan-ethnic union solidarity as well as through a focus on workplace-based issues on which all members could agree. Collective bargaining was one central rallying point; in the months in which I was conducting the fieldwork, the SSEU was preparing members for contract negotiations with the city. Although most economic issues were bargained by District Council 37, AFSCME, Local

371's parent union, the SSEU bargained individually on matters relating specifically to social service job titles, and the union's president and members all had individual votes when deciding whether to ratify the contract negotiated by District Council 37. They were therefore quite active in debating certain elements of the contract package, particularly issues of pay and justice. While discussing the contract negotiations, for example, the union's president warned members that a management representative had recommended offering 7 percent increases in pay to select caseworkers, a proposal that would have violated the union's existing contract. "We want them to give an across-the-board increase for everyone!" he explained. "I mean, how would my staff feel if I gave only my friends a 7 percent pay increase? Or how about if the mayor gave a 7 percent increase to cops who arrested the most black folks?"

Such an appeal was probably most salient to people who had experienced racial profiling and police abuse; again, it was an attempt by the union's president to stress the need for pan-ethnic—and pan-racial—cooperation in the union. The appeal for pan-ethnic cooperation emerged again during the 2000 political races. In the Democratic primary for Brooklyn's Eleventh Congressional District, a very sticky situation emerged when longtime congressman (and union ally) Major Owens was challenged by Una Clarke, a Jamaican city council member and former Owens protégé. The union had a long-standing relationship with Owens and had always endorsed him. Clarke, however, was a former member of Local 371 and was running on a platform that was at least partially inspired by a commitment to increasing Caribbean representation in the state legislature. During a meeting of the union's political action committee, a middle-aged woman loudly proclaimed that the union should endorse Owens because it was "time to push Una Clarke in the gutter!" The union president responded by commenting that Clarke "must be crazy" to challenge Owens and that he had told her so. "When we love people," he said, "we can tell them that they're wrong . . . and she's wrong!" He then remarked that "black people" should not play divisive games but instead should "lock arms together to win together." Another member, who seemed slightly more sympathetic to Clarke's position, responded by pleading with the union to keep the campaign on an even keel and not be dragged into a divisive situation. "This is not a situation of Caribbean versus non-Caribbean," he said, "but of one demagogue trying to capitalize on difference." He then concluded by reminding the audience that African Americans and West Indians had always worked together. "Look at Shirley Chisholm," he said. "She worked to improve the lives of all black people, and who knew she was from Barbados?" Following several minutes of continued discussion in which both Caribbean-born and African American members participated, several serious issues of concern were brought forward regarding the congressman's lack of visibility in the Caribbean community, as well as the personal nature of the battle between the two candidates. Ultimately, however, the committee voted to endorse Owens.

The discussion continued in the months leading up to the election. The candidates' records were evaluated during meetings of the political action committee, and the challenger was found to have "stood against us as an institution on a number of occasions," specifically by voting "the wrong way" on a number of issues facing municipal workers and by being "conspicuously absent from a number of important votes as well." During these meetings class- and work-based interests definitely took precedence over ethnic concerns, and there appeared to be little disagreement regarding the endorsement. Indeed, many Caribbean members with whom I spoke mentioned that they had not known Clarke's voting record when considering her candidacy; when provided with these materials, their choice, they said, was very clear.

In this vignette, the union member summoned the memory of Shirley Chisholm and made a specific appeal to improve the lives of all "black" people. This was a very common refrain in the union and probably emerged from the particular history stressed by the union's president and staff. The collective memory of this union centered on its history as an organization devoted to the struggle for civil rights and equal opportunity for black people. While we might wonder whether this sense of history served to exclude Latinos and "immigrant blacks," this did not seem to be the case. In discussing the layout of the Caribbean heritage program, for example, the committee chair reminded members that in previous years the committee had superimposed photos of Caribbean participants in the civil rights movement—such as Stokely Carmichael—on top of the program. This was clearly an attempt to claim part of the collective history so important to the union, but it was also a recognition of the fact that many important figures in "African American" struggles were in fact fully or partially Caribbean (James 1998).

The union's commitment to racial equality and equal opportunity for all members was very evident in the discourse that floated throughout the organization and was also reinforced in the nonworkplace-related activities in which the union chose to participate. The pages of the union's official newspaper, *The Unionist*, demonstrate this very starkly. Although its pages are stocked with stories of grievances filed, wrongful termination cases settled, and city policies that may harm social workers or their clients, it is also rife with discussions of the union's participation in other events emphasizing the struggle for racial equality in the United States. The November 1999 issue, for example, documents the union's participation in New York's annual African American Day Parade and its vigorous opposition to the Ku Klux

Klan's march outside city hall. The same issue also provides information on the case of Mumia Abu-Jamal, an African American journalist imprisoned on death row since 1982. Several other issues document long-term members' participation in conferences celebrating the achievements of the Congress of Racial Equality (CORE) and the Student Nonviolent Coordinating Committee (SNCC), as well as their participation in the twenty-fifth anniversary of the "Redeem the Dream" march in Washington, D.C.

There is also evidence of ethnically based participation in *The Unionist*'s pages, but interestingly, the coverage tends to focus on one issue: police brutality. This emphasis emerges very strongly in the March 2000 issue, in which a poem honoring Amadou Diallo is featured. The poem, entitled "Acquittal" and written by a union member, poignantly documents the despair felt by many in New York's black community following the police shooting of an unarmed African immigrant:

> *I look out my window*
> *In the dark*
> *And see another face*
> *In the night*
> *Is she too looking for Amadou?*
> *. . . With tears on her face*
> *She asks for prayers and grace*
> *And I can do no less*
> *To relieve the raging in my heart.*

The poem concludes with several lines in French. The same issue highlights the strong showing from Local 371 in a march protesting the incident in Washington, D.C., and also documents the arrest of the union's president and vice president on the steps of One Police Plaza shortly after Diallo's killing. One month later an advertisement written by the "Haitian Coalition for Justice" appeared in *The Unionist*'s pages, asking all New Yorkers to participate in a demonstration to end police brutality. Reminding readers that "[Mayor Giuliani] divides the city" and "criminalizes our children," the ad exhorts: "Let's all unite to fight to remove him from City Hall." Finally, the June 2000 issue documents a retreat sponsored by the Council of Jewish Organizations and attended by many of the union's longtime Jewish members and retirees. The Jewish population in the union is rapidly retiring, and thus one focus of the retreat—pension issues—is not surprising. The second highlight of the weekend retreat, however, is a bit more unexpected: a discussion of community relations with the New York City Police Department.

This emphasis on police brutality is one example of how the union promotes itself not only as a workplace organization but also as an organization more broadly concerned with promoting the interests and rights of people of color in the United States. In doing so, the union is continuing its long history of racial struggle while at the same time offering a salient movement "frame" in which Latino and West Indian members can comfortably fit. Such processes are not unprecedented. Claire Jean Kim (2000a, 2000b), for example, finds that Haitians, other West Indians, and African Americans formed an alliance based on a common experience of *racial* discrimination when engaging in a boycott of Korean-owned groceries in Brooklyn. Although this struggle was complicated significantly by the fact that Korean store owners responded with charges of racism, the boycott participants clearly perceived their behavior as a struggle against racial domination in U.S. society. In this sense, the participants emphasized a common experience of racial oppression rather than ethnic or national interests. This does not mean, of course, that the groups involved did not experience conflict; it merely suggests that they set their differences aside in to pursue a larger goal. One of the primary outcomes of the boycott, in fact, was that it "compelled Haitian immigrants to shift some of their attention from homeland politics to local affairs where race mattered more than national origin." As a result, the boycott "brought Haitian immigrants into the fold and encouraged them to see themselves as *black* people" (Kim 2000a, 94, emphasis added).

Rather than resisting this racialization, however, many Latino and black Caribbean members of the union participate in it actively. At the Caribbean heritage celebration described earlier, for example, the same Trinidadian performer who worked the largely Caribbean crowd into a frenzy introduced one of her numbers by commenting, "I consider us all part of one struggle. Maybe I am not part of the struggle in this union, because I am not a member. But we all know the struggle black people face, both here and worldwide, and we are all part of that together."

It is perhaps surprising that many Caribbean members of the union seemed willing to identify with a "black" identity rather than—or perhaps in addition to—a West Indian one. Previous research suggests, for example, that West Indians often wish to distinguish themselves from American blacks owing to their fear of being branded negatively by mainstream society (Foner 2000; Kasinitz 1992; Waters 1999). In the context of this union, however, being black does not connote the devaluation of learning or disrespect for authority that many have attributed to a specifically American "oppositional culture" (Fordham and Ogbu 1987; Ogbu 1978, 1990). Instead, being black is based on notions of collective struggle, racial pride, and dignity. To be oppositional in this sense means that one is willing to take on the fight—to stand up to managers and *for* fellow workers. West Indians—and Latinos as well—are eager to adopt such an identity. This was very strongly stated by a

Jamaican member who, when asked if any conflict between African Americans and West Indians existed in the union, forcefully responded:

> No! Why should it? African Americans embrace West Indians. It doesn't matter where you are born. The real matter is that this is a black union. There aren't many Caucasians left in it. The union holds them [African Americans] because it protects them; it can intervene on their behalf. We all join the union for that protection. I tell that all the time to the people who work here who complain about the union. I tell them, management won't listen to individuals, but together we can achieve something.

This, then, is the real promise the union holds for the workers it represents. As in decades past, unions offer these workers the possibility of protection against capricious managers, discriminatory policies, and unfair labor practices. These protections have historically been more important to minority workers because they have most often found themselves victimized by such practices and policies (Defreitas 1993; Hoyman and Stallworth 1987). Thus, it perhaps is not surprising to find that the diverse members of the SSEU are forming new forms of identity that are both class- and race-based. They understand that their collective struggle is based not only in class and ethnic interests but also in the continuing racial discrimination from which they all suffer.

Additionally, specific policies, practices, and beliefs implemented by the union, its president, and its executive officers have made the incorporation of new members—and immigrant members—much easier. In some respects, their willingness to recognize the industry's new diversity is somewhat surprising; previous research indicates, for example, that workplace organizations are more likely to do so when facing an organizational crisis, when a critical mass of immigrants enters the organization, or when the industry itself is not numerically dominated by a pool of native workers (Grenier and Nissen 2000; Nissen and Grenier 2000; Sherman and Voss 2000). None of these conditions exist in the SSEU; in fact, agency shop rights ensure the stability of the organization's membership base; the industry is still dominated largely by native black and Puerto Rican workers; and not enough immigrant and second-generation workers have entered the organization yet to outnumber native workers.

The key to understanding this organization's attempts to incorporate immigrants and the immigrant second generation rests in its particular history and conception of itself as a black-led, racially diverse, progressive organization. Formed in the zenith of the civil rights movement, the organization and its young members—who later became organizational leaders—placed a premium on building and maintaining a form of the "beloved community" so valorized in that movement. Because its organizational structure was built during this period, the union always valued inclusion and created ways in which its diverse membership—at the time primarily black, Italian, and Jewish—could participate equally. The ethnic heritage committees are certainly one example of an inclusive practice formed during this period; the emphasis on forming a diverse staff and encouraging participation in union offices is another. Immigrant members—and their second-generation counterparts—have thus found it relatively easy to integrate into the organization for this reason, even if their life stage or conflicting interests sometimes lead them down different paths.

It should also be noted that the particular leadership style of the union's president—and his history as a civil rights veteran—cannot be overlooked when examining the factors responsible for the relative ease with which diversity is handled in this organization. "Visionary" leadership is often credited in discussions of organizational transformation (Barnett and Carroll 1995: Kotter 1995), and this case is no exception. Although the union's president is undoubtedly interested in maintaining his own position in the organization—and hence grooms leaders who share his ideology and vision—this ideology is one that thus far has proven fairly successful at incorporating a diverse workforce while maintaining organizational identity and consistency. He is, in a sense, an example of what labor scholars have called a "class-conscious" leader, one who "recognizes that workers have multiple identities that are given meaning by their occupation, gender and race" and who promotes and nurtures these identities in such a way that activist strategies are created and democratic participation increased (Gapasin 1998, 14).

This setting, then, is ripe for more active participation from and incorporation of immigrant and second-generation workers. Early indications suggest that the immigrant second generation is not yet participating equally within the organization because of their relative youth, their stage in the life cycle, conflicting interests and responsibilities, and a low level of attachment to the social service profession rather than because they have an aversion to union activism per se. What remains to be seen, of course, is precisely what will happen as the second-generation West Indians, Dominicans, and South Asians currently employed in social service professions stay on the job. The union's president seems to be hopeful; in a monthly steward meeting he asked the assembled audience to think about the strike of 1965 and to remember that many of those galvanized then were young and inexperienced social workers who perceived their employment as a way station to a better position. "We all thought we were on our way somewhere else—graduate school, wherever," he commented. "And now look at all of us! We need to keep that spirit alive in this union!"

The ability of the SSEU, Local 371, to keep that spirit alive will rest, in no small part, on its ability to attract and retain the immigrant second generation currently present in its ranks. This chapter has argued that the union is well positioned to do so. It has created a structure and culture that places a premium on inclusion, and it is committed to a form of racial solidarity that, some argue, will prove highly attractive to immigrants and their American-born children, who face the daily struggle of negotiating both "interracial encounters in public settings" and "inter-class relations with the minority community" (Neckerman, Carter, and Lee 2000, 1). Nonwhite social service employees, of course, have extensive experience with both forms of interaction. By giving them the tools they need to negotiate these settings, Local 371 continues in its progressive tradition while at the same time promoting a "minority culture of mobility" (Neckerman, Carter, and Lee 2000)—two factors that should ensure its longevity and success among the workforce it represents.

This union, then, is not so different from its predecessors in the 1930s. Although it represents a very different group of workers than those found in early CIO unions—both phenotypically and occupationally—we find that many of the patterns of immigrant incorporation and acculturation are much the same. Workers in this union are indeed taught to "become American," but not through language classes, civics lessons, or citizenship ceremonies. Instead, new workers become American by "taking up the struggle"—by combating inequality where they see it, by participating in the union, and, most important, by sharing the legacy of racial struggle and lessons learned during the strike of 1965.

NOTES

1. This figure, which is a bit higher than comparable national figures, reflects New York City's relatively high rate of union density and its large concentration of public-sector employees who are unionized.
2. This research is based on an ethnographic examination of the union, its staff, and its members. I gathered data through participant-observation, examination of archival materials, and several informal interviews with union staff and active members. As a participant-observer, I attended monthly delegate assembly meetings, quarterly membership meetings, monthly committee and location meetings, as well as numerous social events, rallies and demonstrations, and ethnic history celebrations. I also collected and examined archival information, including copies of the union's monthly newspaper, *The Unionist*, as well as the *Public Employee Press* (the monthly newspaper of Local 371's parent union, District Council 37, AFSCME) and the *Chief* (a citywide newspaper covering issues of interest to the city's municipal employees). I culled additional information on

the union from local newspapers as well as from flyers and leaflets produced by the union itself.

3. Although it is difficult to assess the claim that specific ethnic or immigrant groups are clustered in particular occupations, data gathered from a Freedom of Information Act request to the city's Department of Citywide Administrative Services do reveal some patterns in city hiring. Table 7.3, for example, demonstrates that "black" employees make up the greatest majority of the city's social service workforce, followed by Hispanics and whites. Although the particular way in which the data are collected masks ethnic differences, it is quite clear that some racial groups are clustered in particular agencies. Whites make up almost 16 percent of all social service workers in the Department of Homeless Services, yet only 1.4 percent of the social service workforce in the Department of Juvenile Justice. Hispanics are most heavily clustered in the Human Resource Administration, which does in fact include many fraud investigator positions.

4. Union staff and members often cited high turnover in—and lack of commitment to—the industry as factors contributing to the lack of participation among young members and second-generation members. In general, this concern seems to be borne out by data. Michàl Mor Barak, Jan Nissly, and Amy Levin (2001) estimate turnover in the social service industry to range between 30 and 60 percent per year, and they point to burnout, job dissatisfaction, stress, lack of social support, availability of other employment options, and low commitment to the profession as the likely culprits.

5. All quoted material is transcribed from notes taken in the field in 2000.

6. For the most part, this assertion is correct. Young workers generally, particularly those under twenty-five, are much less likely to be members of unions than are other workers, owing to the fact that many of them are clustered in industries and occupations that are not heavily unionized (Payne 1989). Literature addressing union *participation* among workers who are actually members, however, is much less developed and generally does not focus on age as a predictor of union commitment or participation.

7. Elections for chapter chair positions, executive committee officers, local trustees, and membership on the legal assistance committee are held either yearly or during the spring of every third year. In general, the majority of such elections are uncontested, and most candidates run on the union president's slate. There have been notable exceptions: in 1991 a Dominican member went to the press with complaints that the union and its leaders had sabotaged his campaign to win a chapter chair position at his work location. After losing the election by only four votes, the member contended that he and many of his coworkers had never received ballots in the mail, as is required by the union's constitution. He appealed the election to the union's parent body, but the appeal was denied. Additionally, in recent years the president's slate has been challenged during several elections by one specific individual. This individual's challenges do not seem to be motivated by racial or ethnic concerns, however, and he has been soundly defeated on

every occasion on which he has run. His most recent campaign for the union's presidency resulted in 310 votes for him and 2,070 for the incumbent.

8. All names have been changed to respect the privacy of union members.

References

American Federation of State, County, and Municipal Employees. 1995. *1995–2000 Social Services and Related Titles Agreement.* New York: District Council 37, AFSCME, and Local 371, AFSCME.

Barnett, William P., and Glenn R. Carroll. 1995. "Modeling Internal Organizational Change." *Annual Review of Sociology* 21: 217–37.

Barrett, James R. 1992. "Americanization from the Bottom Up: Immigration and the Remaking of the Working Class in the United States, 1880–1930." *Journal of American History* (December): 996–1020.

Bellush, Jewel, and Bernard Bellush. 1984. *Union Power and New York: Victor Gotbaum and District Council 37.* New York: Praeger.

Bronfenbrenner, Kate, and Tom Juravich. 1995. *Union Organizing in the Public Sector: An Analysis of State and Local Elections.* Ithaca, N.Y.: ILR Press.

Cohen, Lizabeth. 1990. *Making a New Deal: Industrial Workers in Chicago, 1919–1939.* New York: Cambridge University Press.

Defreitas, Gregory. 1993. "Unionization Among Racial and Ethnic Minorities." *Industrial and Labor Relations Review* 46(2): 284–301.

Foner, Nancy. 2000. *From Ellis Island to JFK: New York's Two Great Waves of Immigration.* New York: Russell Sage Foundation.

Fordham, Signithia, and John Ogbu. 1987. "Black Students' School Success: Coping with the Burden of Acting White." *Urban Review* 18: 176–206.

Gapasin, Fernando E. 1998. "Local Union Transformation: Analyzing Issues of Race, Gender, Class and Democracy." *Social Justice* 25(3): 13–31.

Gibelman, Margaret, and Philip H. Schervish. 1997. *Who We Are: A Second Look.* Washington, D.C.: National Association of Social Workers Press.

Glenn, Susan A. 1990. *Daughters of the Shtetl: Life and Labor in the Immigrant Generation.* Ithaca, N.Y.: Cornell University Press.

Göbel, Thomas. 1988. "Becoming American: Ethnic Workers and the Rise of the CIO." *Labor History* 29(2): 173–98.

Grenier, Guillermo, and Bruce Nissen. 2000. "Comparative Union Responses to Mass Immigration: Evidence from an Immigrant City." *Critical Sociology* 26(1–2): 82–105.

Hoyman, Michele M., and Lamont Stallworth. 1987. "Participation in Local Unions: A Comparison of Black and White Members." *Industrial and Labor Relations Review* 40(3): 323–46.

James, Winston. 1998. *Holding Aloft the Banner of Ethiopia: Caribbean Radicalism in Early-Twentieth-Century America.* New York: Verso.

Kasinitz, Philip. 1992. *Caribbean New York: Black Immigrants and the Politics of Race.* Ithaca, N.Y.: Cornell University Press.

Kerr, Brinck, and Kenneth R. Mladenka. 1994. "Does Politics Matter? A Time-Series Analysis of Minority Employment Patterns." *American Journal of Political Science* 38(4): 918–43.

Kim, Claire Jean. 2000a. "The Politics of Black-Korean Conflict: Black Power Protest and the Mobilization of Racial Communities in New York City." In *Immigration and Race: New Challenges for American Democracy*, edited by Gerald D. Jaynes. New Haven, Conn.: Yale University Press.

———. 2000b. *Bitter Fruit: The Politics of Black-Korean Conflict in New York City*. New Haven, Conn.: Yale University Press.

Kotter, John. 1995. "Leading Change: Why Transformation Efforts Fail." *Harvard Business Review* 73(2): 59–67.

Model, Suzanne. 2001. "Where New York's West Indians Work." In *Islands in the City: West Indian Migration to New York*, edited by Nancy Foner. Berkeley, Calif.: University of California Press.

Mollenkopf, John Hull. 1992. *A Phoenix in the Ashes: The Rise and Fall of the Koch Coalition in New York City Politics*. Princeton, N.J.: Princeton University Press.

Mor Barak, Michàl E., Jan A. Nissly, and Amy Levin. 2001. "Antecedents to Retention and Turnover Among Child Welfare, Social Work, and Other Human Service Employees: What Can We Learn from Past Research? A Review and Meta-analysis." *Social Service Review* (December): 626–61.

Neckerman, Kathryn M., Prudence Carter, and Jennifer Lee. 2000. "Segmented Assimilation and Minority Cultures of Mobility." *Ethnic and Racial Studies* 22(6): 945–65.

Nissen, Bruce, and Guillermo Grenier. 2000. "Local Union Relations with Immigrants: The Case of South Florida." *Labor Studies Journal* (Spring): 76–97.

Oestreicher, Richard Jules. 1986. *Solidarity and Fragmentation: Working People and Class Consciousness in Detroit, 1875–1900*. Urbana: University of Illinois Press.

Ogbu, John. 1978. *Minority Education and Caste: The American System in Cross-National Perspective*. New York: Academic Press.

———. 1990. "Minority Status and Literacy in Comparative Perspective." *Daedalus* 119(2): 141–68.

Payne, Joan. 1989. "Trade Union Membership and Activism Among Young People in Great Britain." *British Journal of Industrial Relations* 27(1): 111–32.

Sherman, Rachel, and Kim Voss. 2000. "Organize or Die: Labor's New Tactics and Immigrant Workers." In *Organizing Immigrants: The Challenge for Unions in Contemporary California*, edited by Ruth Milkman. Ithaca, N.Y.: Cornell University Press.

Snow, David A., et al. 1986. "Frame Alignment Processes, Micromobilization, and Movement Participation." *American Sociological Review* 45: 787–801.

Snow, David A., and Robert D. Benford. 1988. "Ideology, Frame Resonance, and Participant Mobilization." *International Social Movement Research* 1: 197–217.

———. 1992. "Master Frames and Cycles of Protest." In *Frontiers of Social Movement Theory*, edited by Sheldon D. Morris and Carol McClurg Mueller. New Haven, Conn.: Yale University Press.

U.S. Department of Labor. Bureau of Labor Statistics. 2001. *Union Members Summary.* News release. Available at: http://www.bls.gov/news.release/union2.nr0.htm.

Waldinger, Roger. 1996. *Still the Promised City? African Americans and New Immigrants in Postindustrial New York.* Cambridge, Mass.: Harvard University Press.

Walkowitz, Daniel J. 1999. *Working with Class: Social Workers and the Politics of Middle-Class Identity.* Chapel Hill: University of North Carolina Press.

Waters, Mary C. 1999. *Black Identities: West Indian Immigrant Dreams and American Realities.* New York: Russell Sage Foundation.

Wilentz, Sean. 1984. *Chants Democratic: New York City and the Rise of the American Working Class, 1788–1850.* New York: Oxford University Press.

CHAPTER 8

ETHNIC AND POSTETHNIC POLITICS IN NEW YORK CITY: THE DOMINICAN SECOND GENERATION*

NICOLE P. MARWELL

STUDIES of the political incorporation of immigrants often have employed the concept of "generation" to understand how newcomer groups establish a voice in American politics. Such works include studies of the political behavior of "old" immigrants (Treudly 1949; Wirth 1941; Wolfinger 1965), African Americans (Browning, Marshall, and Tabb 1984; Keiser 1997; Pinderhughes 1997), and "new" immigrants (Filipcevic 2000; Kasinitz 1992; Pessar and Graham 2002; Warren 1997). The general thrust of all these studies is that second and later generations of immigrants (or, in the case of African Americans, the descendants of southern migrants to the North) will be more familiar with political institutions, more interested in politics, and more likely to express their political inclinations through activism and voting. This process, it is then argued, eventually gives rise to the classic indicators of political incorporation (Browning, Marshall, and Tabb 1984): attainment of elective office, greater representation in public agencies, a role in the governing coalition, and increased attention to group needs.

This chapter argues for a more nuanced understanding of how the "new second generation" is experiencing political incorporation. Even for immigrants of the same national origin, there is no uniform process by which the new second generation achieves political incorporation. Instead, while past patterns of ethnic politics contribute to the ways in which immigrant groups, or parts of groups, travel toward political involvement, other important factors shape modes of immigrant political participation as well. These variable

* All names of individuals and organizations reported throughout the chapter are pseudonyms, except as noted. In the case of quotations, pseudonyms are listed in brackets.

factors also may produce uneven outcomes within and across groups. In particular, local demographics and the neighborhood political context have strong mediating influences on the political behavior and prospects of new immigrant groups, whether migrants or their U.S.-born children.[1] The concept of immigrant generation per se appears far less salient in explaining the experiences of the new second generation than factors such as these, a finding echoed in a number of other chapters in this volume (for example, Butterfield, Malkin, and Trillo). This conclusion is underscored in an examination of the contrasting modes of political behavior found in two New York City neighborhoods with high concentrations of Dominicans, both first- and second-generation.

BACKGROUND

Ira Katznelson's (1981) classic study of urban politics argues that political participation in the United States has been shaped by the growing spatial separation between home and work. People concentrate their political activities on issues arising where they live—not where they work—because political representation has a residential territorial base. Katznelson maintains that this separation leads to the predominance of community politics—a narrower politics of identity—over workplace politics—a broader politics of class. Individuals participate in politics largely to make immediate changes in the places where they live: for instance, improving the local park, stopping construction of a nearby homeless shelter, or getting better response times from the police. As a result, he argues, political activity in the United States has failed to create a significant, progressive movement that could achieve broadbased economic and social change.

To the extent that immigrants both old and new are residentially concentrated, Katznelson's "city trenches" increasingly are identified not only as particular places within a city's geography but also as tied to specific racial or national-origin groups. An immigrant group gains classical political incorporation—especially the first key step of elective office—when its members come to constitute a sizable plurality or majority of voters in a specific geographic area. In the theory of ethnic politics (see, for example, Wolfinger 1965), the first principle seems to be that members of any ethnic group prefer to elect "one of our own." The 1965 Voting Rights Act's emphasis on demarcating "protected groups" has reinforced this ethnic essentialism. Under the act's requirement that districts be drawn so that minority voters have an equal chance to "elect the candidate of their choice," "majority-minority" districts have been created to institutionalize the (perhaps correct) "one of our own" assumption.[2]

But political mobilization in any given neighborhood depends significantly not only on its mix of ethnic groups but also on its local history of political organization. We can distinguish two broad possibilities along each dimension. First, a neighborhood may or may not be dominated by one ethnic group. Second, the neighborhood may or may not have a strong, preexisting approach to political organization that would seek to channel political involvement. The importance of these two dimensions is apparent in the contrasting nature of second-generation Dominican political activity in two neighborhoods in New York City. The Washington Heights–Inwood (WH-I) section of northern Manhattan is overwhelmingly Dominican (about 70 percent).[3] Some 25 percent of all Dominicans in New York City live in this single neighborhood. Within this context, second-generation Dominicans have formed their own political organization to promote a "Dominican agenda." Their ability to organize independently of existing local political groups has been fostered by the relatively open political traditions of the WH-I City Council district and State Assembly district, which were drawn after the 1990 census specifically to provide a majority-Latino district likely to elect a Dominican.

North Brooklyn offers a contrasting setting. The adjacent neighborhoods of Bushwick and Williamsburg (B-W) also have a majority of Latino residents (just under 60 percent), but the population is far more diverse, with no one national-origin group constituting a majority of the Latino population.[4] Puerto Ricans are the largest Latino national-origin group in B-W, about twice the size of the next largest group, Dominicans; together, Puerto Ricans and Dominicans constitute 70 percent of the B-W Latino population. There are smaller concentrations of Ecuadoreans, Mexicans, and Central Americans, with these latter two groups growing quickly. B-W also has significant white and African American populations, at 20 and 15 percent, respectively. Equally important, the local assembly district is home to a strong "regular Democratic" political club,[5] led by Assemblyman Tony Rodriguez.

DATA AND METHODS

The study is based on participant-observation in nonprofit community-based organizations and neighborhood political settings in the two study areas. The B-W research was conducted between May 1997 and September 2000 and includes data from an earlier study (Marwell 2000). The research in WH-I took place between September 1999 and September 2000. In both study areas data gathered from participant-observation were supplemented with formal interviews with knowledgeable informants from within and outside the study neighborhoods.

The two main research settings in WH-I included Young Dominicans and a youth program of the Dominicanos Juntos para el Futuro (Dominicans Together for the Future, hereafter DJF). At the time of the fieldwork, Young Dominicans was an open, informal organization of young, mostly 1.5- and second-generation Dominicans. It conducted its activities in WH-I and at the City College of New York—in neighboring Harlem—and had a leadership group of about ten people. By the end of the fieldwork, Young Dominicans had incorporated as a nonprofit 501(c)3 organization. DJF is a large, community-based service organization that runs health, education, housing, and youth programs, including a youth program at a junior high school in WH-I, the site of most of my DJF participant-observation.

The participant-observation settings in B-W included the Housing Division of the Bushwick Center for Service (hereafter Bushwick Center), the Neighborhood Democratic Club (hereafter Neighborhood Democrats), and Moviendo Juntos (Moving Together). Bushwick Center's Housing Division develops subsidized housing for low-income families and the elderly. The Neighborhood Democrats are run by Tony Rodriguez, the New York state assemblyman who represents the area. Moviendo Juntos is a federation of approximately 350 members from nonprofit organizations, block associations, low-income housing cooperatives, and other similar groups in B-W.

My initial entry into all these settings, except Young Dominicans, was through volunteering to undertake whatever tasks each organization asked me to do. These included housing organizing, planning events, doing clerical tasks, and working in a summer youth program. At Young Dominicans I simply attended open meetings organized by the group; I also accompanied Young Dominicans members to other settings when I was invited. In all settings I made it clear that I was there as a researcher. Most participants identified me as a non-Latina white female, but my ability to speak fluent Caribbean Spanish sometimes complicated their evaluations of me. Data from the study were recorded in field notes throughout the research.

Privileging Ethnicity: Dominican-ness in Washington Heights–Inwood

New York City is the focal point of the Dominican community in the United States. It contains the largest Dominican population outside of the Dominican Republic, and remittances from New Yorkers supply 25 percent of that country's GNP (Gutierrez 2000). Within New York City, Washington Heights–Inwood is the undisputed center of Dominican life. Prior to 1960, the neighborhood was primarily Irish and Jewish. By 1980, after nearly twenty years of continuous migration, Dominicans had established themselves as the dominant presence in the area. By 2000 about 70 percent of its residents were Dominican.

As a result of this massive, rapid shift, WH-I has become known throughout New York City as *the* Dominican neighborhood. Ongoing public demonstrations of Dominican ethnicity in the area have raised this profile further. A walk along the commercial arteries of Broadway, St. Nicholas Avenue (both running north-south), and West 181st Street (running east-west) shows that the vast majority of stores are either owned by or targeted toward Dominicans (see Duany 1994). The Dominican owners and their relatives spend long hours tending to travel agencies, restaurants, bodegas (corner grocery stores), taxi services, and beauty salons. Clothing stores, supermarkets, music stores, and jewelers also stock products preferred by Dominican customers. Although non-Dominicans own some of these larger enterprises, they nearly always employ Dominican workers, some of whom are Spanish-monolingual.

Nearly all of the important Dominican festivals and public events also take place in WH-I, including the annual Dominican Day Parade, begun some twenty years ago. Although an official Dominican Day Parade also now takes place along Fifth Avenue in midtown Manhattan—the site of other important ethnic moments like the St. Patrick's Day Parade and the Puerto Rican Day Parade—WH-I continues to host its traditional parade as well. Now combined with a two-day festival, the event represents the neighborhood's claim to being the most authentic Dominican place in the city.

City government officially recognized this status when, on July 23, 2000, it held a celebration of the renaming of St. Nicholas Avenue between West 162nd Street and West 193rd Street in honor of Juan Pablo Duarte, the founder of the Dominican Republic. (Over one-third of the laws passed by the New York City Council in the last ten years consisted of naming various city streets, parks, plazas, piers, squares, triangles, corners, and ball fields after local heroes.)[6] The blocks in question form the heart of WH-I, and the renaming was a signal event for the Dominicans of the neighborhood. I recorded in my field notes the heated debate that took place at a meeting of the WH-I Community Board where the issue was discussed:[7]

> There appears to be some kind of major debate about what street exactly should be named after Duarte. One faction seems to want St. Nicholas Avenue [between West 162nd and 193rd Streets]. Another faction seems to want West 181st Street. About ten different people speak to the Board about their views, including a very official-looking man in his late fifties from something called the Juan Pablo Duarte Institute U.S.A. He is wearing a very formal suit adorned with a colored sash with the organization's name printed on it, and is accompanied by four or five other

people similarly attired. He supports the 181ˢᵗ Street position, stating passionately that it is unworthy of such a great hero as Duarte to have only a *portion* of a street named after him, which is why they need to use 181st Street—all of it—and not merely a part of St. Nicholas Avenue. He says Duarte deserves the same recognition as George Washington and John F. Kennedy. [This is a reference to two boulevards in Santo Domingo that are named after these two U.S. presidents.] Another speaker agrees with the first part of that sentiment, but argues instead that Duarte should therefore get *all* of St. Nicholas Avenue. (field notes, October 26, 1999)

The argument over which New York City street to name for a nineteenth-century hero from a small island-nation may seem insignificant. To Duarte's advocates, however, the contestation was about gaining New York's proper respect for Dominicans. One speaker equated the renaming of this U.S. street for the Dominican Republic's first hero of independence with the naming of a Dominican street for the first hero of U.S. independence. This relationship could be adequately continued, he argued, only if Duarte received the same treatment as Washington: having a *whole* street, not a *partial* one, named after him. Anything less, the speaker implied, would be a terrible slight.

Enrolling in Power: Dominicans in Bushwick-Williamsburg

The population mix of the Bushwick-Williamsburg section of Brooklyn more closely approximates the composition of other Latino neighborhoods in New York City and the city's overall Latino population. No single national-origin group dominates the area's ethnic makeup as Dominicans do in WH-I. While B-W is approximately 60 percent Latino, this population comprises two large groups—Puerto Ricans and Dominicans—and also contains smaller and growing numbers of Ecuadoreans, Mexicans, and Central Americans. Significant groups of African Americans and non-Latino whites (many of them Hasidic Jews) also live in the area.

Because B-W's Latino population comes from so many different places, no single group puts its ethnic stamp on the area. When the New York media cover Williamsburg, they often identify the area as an "artist," "hipster," or perhaps Hasidic Jewish neighborhood.[8] When they do describe Williamsburg as a Latino neighborhood, they use the composite term and do not single out any one national-origin group. As one of the poorest neighborhoods in New York City, and indeed the United States, Bushwick has even less public presence. Most New Yorkers have no idea where it is, much less who lives there or how to get there. (Unlike Williamsburg, which is located just across the East

River from Manhattan and has been undergoing gentrification for over fifteen years, Bushwick only now is beginning to see the earliest signs of gentrification.)

The politics produced within the mixed population of B-W's local assembly district cannot be conceptualized as "ethnic" in the sense of that term that prevails in WH-I. Rather, the politics and claim-making arising from B-W's city trenches are organized around the *low income* of its residents. Indeed, the focus on low income emanates not only from Latinos and African Americans but from the area's Satmar Hasidim as well (Sexton 1997a, 1997b, 1997c, 1997d). When politicians do make ethnic claims, they are on behalf of the composite "Latinos" or a cross-minority group of Latinos and African Americans. Local elected officials rarely single out a national-origin group—be they Puerto Ricans, Dominicans, or African Americans—in their political discourse.

Subordinating ethnic politics to geographically defined low-income interests is particularly pronounced in the political outlook and strategies of the area's powerful assemblyman, Tony Rodriguez. He frequently protested that he paid no attention to the ethnicity of his constituents and thought that focusing on ethnic differences only diluted the district's power in the larger political system. In one conversation, recorded in my field notes, he described the ethnic dynamics of his political club, the Neighborhood Democrats, in response to my question about whether there were many Dominicans involved in the club:

> [Tony] tells me that right now, his organization is about half Latino, about 15 percent black, and maybe 30 percent white. I ask who's in the Latino group. [Tony] says most of them are Puerto Rican, but that overall, about 10 percent of the club is Dominican now, and that number is growing very quickly. He says it's good to have new people join the club, but that people's focus on "oh, he's Puerto Rican, oh, she's Dominican" is really not helpful, that everybody needs to put those divisions aside and work together to bring resources into the neighborhood. (field notes, December 17, 1999)

This group-neutral stance was typical of Rodriguez's statements on the subject. According to him, because his foremost concern was building and maintaining political power *for his district*, he was willing to work with anyone who could mobilize voters and put long hours into clubhouse politics. As discussed later in the chapter, Rodriguez's claim that he ignored ethnicity was at times disingenuous, as he proved to be a skillful manipulator of ethnic loyalties when that helped him in the larger struggle for political power. But his occasional use of ethnicity as an organizing principle differed greatly from the way ethnic politics operated in WH-I. B-W politics revolved instead around building broader alliances across a variety of groups; ethnic mobilization was only one small piece of a larger strategy of accumulating power.

HOW THE SECOND GENERATION LEARNS POLITICS

New immigrants and their descendants achieve political incorporation by learning how political business gets done in their host society and then playing that game. Understanding this political learning process in New York City requires an appreciation for how the mechanisms of political activity differ across the city's neighborhoods. Different neighborhoods present different models for political incorporation. The two neighborhoods under discussion provide Dominican first- and second-generation newcomers with contrasting "political opportunity spaces." In WH-I, second-generation Dominicans continue to draw on ethnic politics because this approach has enabled their neighborhood to make its presence felt in New York City politics over the last fifteen years. In contrast, to get ahead in B-W, second-generation Dominicans must participate in a style of coalition building that minimizes ethnic differences, plays up ideological divisions, and incorporates a politics of class.

The Dominican character of electoral politics in WH-I is manifested in the area's elected officials, the first Dominicans ever elected to office in the United States. Guillermo Linares[9] was born in the Dominican Republic and emigrated to the United States in his late teens. In the wake of an enlargement and redistricting of the New York City Council in 1991, he was elected to represent the Tenth City Council District. He held office continuously until 2001, when he was forced out by term limits, to be succeeded by another Dominican, Miguel Martinez.[10] Linares's election was enabled in significant measure by the 1991 redistricting, which created an open district specifically designed to favor the election of a Dominican. Linares won the seat after many years of community activism, including serving on the local school board (district 6), cofounding an important community-based organization and being active in Dominican and Latino student groups at City College.

Linares has always stressed his status as the first Dominican American elected official in the United States, appealing both to his co-ethnics and to outsiders as *the* Dominican political representative. Within the context of the powerful ethnic pride and authenticity that are touchstones of WH-I, Linares draws strongly on his Dominican identity. In Linares's last reelection bid (1997), however, one of his challengers, Roberto Lizardo,[11] sought to belittle Linares's "Dominican-ness." Lizardo's campaign referred to him as "the real Dominican," implying that Linares was somehow *not* real. The genesis of this criticism lay in Lizardo's opposition to the construction of a huge Pathmark supermarket in a part of East Harlem where some Dominicans owned and operated smaller supermarket chains. In a highly controversial last-minute move, Linares had changed his position to provide the deciding vote that enabled the construction of the Pathmark. Lizardo stressed this issue in the 1997 election, asserting that Linares was not an authentic Dominican because he sided with the non-Dominican Pathmark owners.

At about the same time Linares's position as the preeminent Dominican elected official faced another challenge. In 1996 Adriano Espaillat,[12] who was born in the Dominican Republic and migrated to New York at age eleven, won the Seventy-second District seat in the New York State Assembly, representing WH-I. Like Linares, Espaillat had spent fifteen years as a local community activist, most recently holding the Democratic district leader position for the Seventy-second Assembly District. As with Linares's election, redistricting was key to Espaillat's victory. In 1992 the Seventy-second Assembly District was redrawn to increase the odds that it would send a Latino candidate to Albany. The newly drawn district was approximately 80 percent Hispanic—about two-thirds of whom were Dominican—as opposed to only 50 percent Hispanic in the old district. In 1996, with the help of over 2,500 newly registered voters, Espaillat beat sixteen-year incumbent John Brian Murtaugh[13] in the Democratic primary by less than 200 votes. Given the heavily Democratic registration in the district, Espaillat coasted to an easy victory in November's general election.

Espaillat and Linares are intense political rivals. Their conflict stems partly from Linares's victory over Espaillat for the newly created Tenth City Council District in 1991. But the fight is also over who can claim to be the premiere *Dominican* political representative—in WH-I, New York City, and the United States. Espaillat's victory confirmed that Dominicans had finally displaced the Irish and Jewish residents of the neighborhood. But now *two* Dominicans claim primacy in the nation's most visible Dominican neighborhood; the result has been a competition over whose voice will speak loudest. Although Linares had a slight edge over Espaillat during the study period, more powerful officeholders have hedged their bets. Term limits now have forced Linares out of office, and his designated successor, Victor Morisete, lost badly in the 2001 City Council elections to Martinez, an Espaillat protégé. With Espaillat not facing term limits in the State Assembly, WH-I politics seem set to cohere in his favor.

Within the flux of politics in northern Manhattan, the participation of 1.5- and second-generation young adults takes on critical importance. They are likely to be U.S. citizens either by birthright or because of their length of residence (DeSipio 1996).[14] Citizenship is incredibly important because so many Dominican residents of Washington Heights, including legal residents, do not have citizenship and cannot vote.[15] As such, second-generation Dominicans are an increasingly important part of a WH-I political base. However, important disconnects separate the second generation from the local political establishment. Most people involved in WH-I politics are first-generation immigrants, like Linares, Morisete, and Martinez, with a few from the 1.5 generation, like Espaillat. Few second-generation Dominicans work with either Linares or Espaillat. One reason for this surely is age: younger people are less likely to engage in civic participation than older people (Verba and Nie 1987; Verba, Schlozman, and Brady 1995). Other explanations for the lack of second-generation involvement in local politics include age effects, such as competition from other life activities like school, work, and family (see, for example, Plutzer 2002; Verba, Schlozman, and Brady 1995) and period effects, such as minimal feelings of political efficacy and a lack of outreach by the political establishment (see, for example, Abramson and Aldrich 1982).

The exceptions to this rule are the young 1.5- and second-generation Dominicans who have formed Young Dominicans. Young Dominicans appears to be the only organized group of second-generation Dominicans in the neighborhood. Although the organization does not have a *specifically* political agenda, its broad notion of "community involvement" makes it a likely site from which second-generation political activity might emerge (Jones-Correa 2001). During the study period Young Dominicans was an open-membership group composed of people in their late teens and twenties, with a core leadership group of about ten individuals in their midtwenties to early thirties. This leadership group came together in 1997 to plan a vision for Dominicans in the United States. In the words of the official history of Young Dominicans:

> Ultimately, the objective of this grassroots leadership [the initial planning group] was, and remains, to involve Dominicans living and working in all sectors and cities throughout the U.S. in the development of a national agenda, a movement that will work to provide a new direction to community [that is, Dominican] empowerment. (Young Dominicans 2000)

Two members of the seven-person group that began meeting in 1997 still lead Young Dominicans today: Jorge Guerrero and Migdalia Santos. Guerrero, who emigrated from the Dominican Republic at age seventeen, comes from a leftist, activist family. Before leaving for the United States, he co-founded an organization called Jóvenes Dominicanos en Adelante (Young Dominicans in Action, hereafter JDA). Seeking to continue the JDA's work in New York, Guerrero established a youth education and support program for WH-I teenagers based at City College (in neighboring Harlem). Guerrero also is employed as a teacher at a transitional New York City public high school designed to help immigrant teenagers acclimate to New York, learn English, and participate in positive activities. A modest, kind, and dedicated man, Guerrero clearly is beloved by the young people with whom he works. On the final day of a major conference organized by Young Dominicans in February 2000, short speeches were given by Nancy Rivera (a Young Dominicans leadership group member), Thomas Morales (vice president of City College's Office of Student Affairs), Lorraine Cortez-Vasquez (president of the Hispanic Federation), Johnny Ventura (mayor of Santo Domingo and a major international recording artist), Councilman Linares, and Guerrero. I then recorded the following in my field notes:

> Hillary Rodham Clinton comes to the podium for her address. She starts out by thanking [Young Dominicans] for their commitment to "translating words into action" by organizing the conference. There is applause. She then goes on to say, "[Jorge], you really have a future!!" At this, the applause from the crowd is enormous, a standing ovation. [Jorge] smiles, nods at Mrs. Clinton, and waves at the crowd. As Mrs. Clinton starts to speak again, she is drowned out by a chant from the mass of young people crowded near the front of the auditorium: "[JOR-GE! JOR-GE!]" [Jorge] smiles and waves again, which only makes them louder. The strength of their support for him is remarkable. (field notes, February 27, 2000)

Guerrero is the acknowledged head of the Young Dominicans leadership group, with the title of general coordinator. He has achieved this position because of his age (he is about eight years older than most of the other Young Dominicans members), personal charisma, history of activism, and dedicated work with young people at his high school and in the JDA.

Migdalia Santos, the other original member of the Young Dominicans leadership group, is more representative of Young Dominicans' other current leaders, who are 1.5- and second-generation Dominicans in their midtwenties with impressive educational and employment records. Unlike Guerrero, whose professional employment intersects administratively and programmatically with the work of Young Dominicans, the other leaders work at private-sector jobs but devote long hours to Young Dominicans. Santos, age twenty-five,[16] emigrated from the Dominican Republic at age seven, received a bachelor's degree from Harvard University, a master's degree from Cambridge University, and a law degree from Columbia Law School. Another leader, Nancy Rivera, age twenty-six, was born in New York City and raised in the

Dominican Republic as well as the United States. She has a bachelor's degree from Bucknell University and a master's degree from New York University, and she works as a senior associate at a major Wall Street investment firm. Twenty-five-year-old Luis Guerrero (Jorge's younger brother) came to the United States at the age of ten, earned a bachelor's degree from Dowling College and a master's degree from Hunter College, and works as a policy associate for an immigrant advocacy organization.

These energetic and impressive young adults are seeking to create what they describe as a more inclusive political and community voice for the Dominicans of WH-I, particularly its young people. As Rivera put it in an interview I recorded in my field notes:

> [Young Dominicans] wants to hear people talk about all aspects of Dominican life and the "Dominican reality." The group is interested in a wide range of issues, around which they've formed committees, including inter-ethnic relations, political empowerment, education, arts and culture, religion, and the media. . . . She says that [Young Dominicans] wants to create change, to empower people, and to establish a cycle of leadership so that when the current leadership group moves on to other things, there will be another group of young leaders ready to take over. The idea is to do something "comprehensive," to be an "organizational resource for other Dominicans," and to "create a dialogue with the public." (field notes, November 20, 1999)

Young Dominicans attempts to be "more inclusive" by working outside the status quo structures of politics and organizations in WH-I. The group also seeks to transcend the limits of the local political activity undertaken by Linares and Espaillat, primarily by conceptualizing itself as a "national" organization. This point was emphasized repeatedly in the planning meetings and public events sponsored by Young Dominicans, as in Jorge Guerrero's speech at the group's conference in February 2000. Speaking in Spanish, Guerrero said that everyone at the conference was there

> to build "our *national*, I repeat, *national*, *NATIONAL* agenda" [for Dominicans in the United States]. Three years ago, he says, a small group of young people got together to "discuss a beautiful dream." The dream would be pursued "without patronage or compromise," without the elected officials, without the politicians or the political institutions. [Young Dominicans] had no money, yet they pressed on. . . . [Young Dominicans'] task is not just to analyze problems, as everyone did [in conference workshops] yesterday, but *to commit to implementing solutions to those problems.* (field notes, February 27, 2000, emphasis in original)

Even in casting this wider net, however, Young Dominicans continues to emphasize Dominican ethnicity as its main political organizing principle. It is using the same tool that has worked so well for Linares, Espaillat, and others who achieved a political voice in WH-I. The entrenched position of this ethnic approach can be seen in Young Dominicans' main activity during the study period: planning and holding a large, national conference that brought Dominicans from all over the United States and from other parts of the Dominican diaspora to northern Manhattan.

In the months leading up to the conference, the Young Dominicans leadership group members stressed the importance of shaping a specifically *Dominican* organization and political voice. Interestingly, when the leaders met with other, less-involved participants to plan the conference, some questioned this approach. The following excerpt from my field notes illustrates this tension:

> A man who identifies himself as Colombian says that the conference shouldn't exclude other Latinos. A young Dominican woman who says it's her first time at a [Young Dominicans] meeting says that even the name of the group—[Young *Dominicans*]—sounds too exclusive of non-Dominicans. One of the leadership group members replies that the conference is inclusive of all who want to participate, but it is specifically *marketed* at Dominicans. There is some additional discussion of this point, and then [Jorge Guerrero] stands up and says it's important to understand that "uno no puede limpiar la casa de su vecino si no limpia la suya" ("you can't tend to your neighbor's business until you get your own house in order"). He says that the focus of [Young Dominicans] and the conference is on Dominicans, but of course it's important to look at relations with other Latinos and other ethnic groups. Another leadership group member adds that it's O.K. to include other groups, but since this is an organization called [Young *Dominicans*], they need to encourage Dominican pride, concentrate on cleaning up the public image of Dominicans, and so on. [Young Dominicans] can get close to other Latinos, he says, but it should be closer to the Dominicans. He says that [Young Dominicans] should learn from African Americans, or Cuban Americans, who stick together and help each other out. (field notes, November 7, 1999)

In the face of this and similar challenges to a specifically Dominican focus, Young Dominicans leadership group members argued in its favor strongly and continuously. About a month after this discussion, the Young Dominicans leaders held another planning meeting at the home of two members, Ana Roldán and Joel Guzmán. In the following discussion, recorded in my field notes, they debated how to conduct the conference's opening session and who the keynote speaker would be:

[Nancy Rivera] says that they need to set the right tone for the conference right from the beginning, and that doesn't necessarily mean having Hillary Rodham Clinton or Al Gore as the opening speaker. [Luis Guerrero] agrees, says that to set the right tone for the conference, they want someone to "make people feel comfortable," like maybe Oscar de la Renta [the Dominican fashion designer]. . . . [Delfa Alvarez] says that [Young Dominicans] shouldn't tailor the conference around the [high-profile] speakers [like Rodham Clinton and Gore] but rather should choose the speakers to further the [Young Dominicans] agenda and purpose. [Hector] says that the conference should start with a "*Dominican person with the Dominican values of* [*Young Dominicans*]." [Delfa] says [Young Dominicans] members should open the session, present the conference project, and then introduce a keynote speaker, someone who supports and is close to [Young Dominicans]. At this point, someone calls for a vote on this subject, and the group votes to accept [Delfa's] opening plan, and to have a Dominican as the keynote speaker. (field notes, December 6, 1999, emphasis added)

This exchange indicates that the Young Dominicans leadership continued to focus on Dominican ethnicity—even after an earlier meeting in which some other Young Dominicans participants had questioned this approach. The final conference program contained the following organizational mission statement:

Our mission is to act as a voice of the Dominican community in the United States and abroad. We aim to encourage and fully develop Dominican initiatives to their highest potential and simultaneously magnify Latino and minority initiatives in the United States. (Young Dominicans 2000)

The emphasis on Dominican ethnicity is clear, although it recognizes that Dominicans are located within a larger Latino and minority population in New York City and the United States. Indeed, the Young Dominicans leadership group evinced a genuine interest in wider, non-Dominican issues, such as police brutality and the Mumia Abu-Jamal death penalty protest campaign. But when it came to organizing, they chose to emphasize ethnicity. As this excerpt from my field notes shows, the leadership group even couched its criticism of WH-I's elected officials in ethnic terms:

When I ask [Nancy Rivera] directly about Linares and Espaillat, she says that they are both too entrenched in the political system and have lost their connection to the [Dominican] community. Indeed, their political ambitions are such that they are both "already running" for the new Congressional seat that is expected to be apportioned in WH-I after the

2000 Census.[17] She says that they are "a really sad couple" who don't collaborate at all, and "that's just because of blind politics." When I ask what they should be doing, [Nancy] says that they only talk about things that will get them media attention, things that are easy: the Louima incident,[18] the blackout last summer,[19] and so on. They don't lead on any issues that are important *to Dominicans*; they "just jump on bandwagons." (field notes, November 20, 1999, emphasis added)

While demonstrating the ethnic politics stance of Young Dominicans, this critique also begins to show us Young Dominicans' engagement with the WH-I political establishment. All of the local elected officials clearly were taking note of Young Dominicans' conference: Linares and Espaillat sat on one of the event's panels, publicly noting the importance of the large numbers of young people who attended; local congressman Charles Rangel gave one of the conference's opening speeches; and then-candidate—now Senator— Hillary Rodham Clinton also was a featured speaker. For its part, Young Dominicans took pains to publicly distance itself from the WH-I politicians, especially by refusing Linares and Espaillat seats on the dais during the opening and closing ceremonies. At the same time, however, Young Dominicans received an enormous amount of assistance in conference planning and fundraising from a well-connected Democratic political consultant brought to them by Linares.[20] If Linares was trying to co-opt Young Dominicans, however, the attempt proved unsuccessful—in the 2001 Democratic City Council primary elections, Young Dominicans' leader, Jorge Guerrero, ran his own campaign for the Tenth District seat rather than support Linares's candidate, Victor Morisete. Guerrero came in third, Morisete fourth.

Young Dominicans is the main vehicle through which second-generation Dominicans are working on political issues in WH-I. Their model of political action echoes that of the first-generation Dominicans who gained initial entry into New York politics. This continuity is explained by the dominance of Dominicans within the neighborhood and by a "path-dependence" in the ways in which second-generation young people have been exposed to "doing politics" in WH-I. This highly ethnic form of politics contrasts strongly with what second-generation Dominicans are doing in north Brooklyn.

The multi-racial, multi-ethnic population of Bushwick-Williamsburg does not necessarily prevent ethnic politics from emerging. But second-generation Dominicans in these neighborhoods are exposed to a model of "doing politics" very different from the model that prevails in WH-I. Within B-W, the politically aggressive Hasidic Jewish community defines one side of the area's political struggle. Other ethnic groups are hardpressed to compete with Hasidic political organization.[21] B-W's Dominicans, who make up about 15 percent of the neighborhood's total population, instead must look for other ways *besides* a Dominican ethnic politics to have an impact.

The most successful political projects in B-W are based on the simple philosophy that if a particular constituency consistently provides large numbers of votes, it will be rewarded with political influence.[22] B-W's Satmar Hasidim have long claimed political influence significantly beyond their population size on this basis (Price 1979). The group practices "bloc voting"—turning out in large numbers in every election, both to vote for candidates who can deliver something back to them and to demonstrate their political strength. Given the low overall turnout, the four thousand or so votes cast by the Hasidic community can regularly provide the margin of victory in local voting. Although the Hasidim are not concentrated in Assemblyman Rodriguez's district but in an adjoining one, the various overlapping political districts of the area give players in the wider political environment reason to be concerned not only about specific assembly district elections but about more general voting behavior in the area.

Potential ethnic competitors with the Satmar Hasidim include several Latino ethnicities, African Americans, and some non-Hasidic whites. But politics in B-W challenges the notion that ethnic affinities are the primary way to hold a political constituency together. A "political influence" formulation offers a better explanation. Two forces contend to represent the non-Hasidim of B-W. The less successful strategy is that of Representative Nydia Velasquez,[23] who holds the local congressional district and was the first Puerto Rican woman to be elected to the U.S. House of Representatives. She draws her supporters primarily from the area's Puerto Rican population, which preceded the arrival of the Dominican population by about twenty years. Velasquez, who previously represented the government of Puerto Rico in New York, continues to promote a specifically Puerto Rican ethnic politics.

The area's strongest non-Hasidic political constituency is affiliated with Assemblyman Rodriguez, whose district covers most of Bushwick and large sections of Williamsburg. Prior to becoming an assemblyman, Rodriguez was a city social worker at a community center in Bushwick. In 1976 he founded a nonprofit community-based organization, the Bushwick Center for Service. Rodriguez built a strong following through his work at Bushwick Center, and he ran for and won a special election for the local assembly district when the seat became vacant in the middle of a term. He has held the seat continuously since 1984. Over the years Rodriguez has gained power in the State Assembly, currently chairing an important assembly committee. He focuses on building and maintaining a strong constituency in B-W that can deliver key votes during local elections. This allows him to strike deals with other elected officials—such as the governor of New York, the mayor of New York City, and New York's U.S. senators—who will exchange resources for these votes (Marwell 2004).

Rodriguez consistently argues against an ethnically based politics, insisting that his organization be open to all who accept his political method and will do the grunt work that is the heart and soul of "regular" politics. While he has political reasons for downplaying ethnic politics, Rodriguez's position is almost necessary because, despite his Spanish surname, he is mostly of Italian extraction and would be counted as white by most people.[24] Nevertheless, Rodriguez has strongly associated himself with Latino groups and Latino causes.

One of Rodriguez's most important constituency-building mechanisms is Moviendo Juntos, a coalition of 350 neighborhood "leaders," including members of tenant associations, block groups, low-income cooperatives, parent-teacher associations, nonprofit organizations, and other community organizations. Moviendo Juntos operates under the nonprofit umbrella of Bushwick Center but is run out of Assemblyman Rodriguez's district office. Alina Villardo, his former chief of staff—and significantly for this discussion, a second-generation Dominican—was in charge of its activities during the study period. In 2001 Villardo succeeded a termed-out incumbent in the local City Council district.

Moviendo Juntos bills itself as "the largest group of Latino leaders in New York City." This foregrounding of ethnicity—albeit a composite one—does not mesh with Assemblyman Rodriguez's stated ethnicity-neutral stance. But this public image must be understood within the larger political context of the city and state, in which ethnic politics is practiced as a shorthand method of coalition-building. Mayoral, gubernatorial, and even presidential candidates do not rely on the minutiae of clubhouse politics but seek ways to appeal to broad constituencies, particularly those who vote in general elections. Relying on ethnic cues is a well-proven way to do so. Assemblyman Rodriguez understands this well, so he has publicly positioned Moviendo Juntos as an organized constituency of Latino leaders, despite the fact that some members of Moviendo Juntos are not Latino and—many would argue—neither is Assemblyman Rodriguez.

It is a testament both to Assemblyman Rodriguez's political clout and the idea of an organized Latino constituency that Moviendo Juntos can draw high-ranking elected officials to its monthly meetings. During the fieldwork period an impressive list of guest speakers took the long trip to Bushwick to speak to Moviendo Juntos. The annual highlight for Moviendo Juntos is a three-day retreat held at a nonprofit conference center in upstate New York. The formal goal of the retreat is to allow Moviendo Juntos leaders to build relationships with the policymakers and agency officials who administer public programs in B-W, thereby contributing to neighborhood organizations' abilities to get more funding for their programs. The latent purpose is to help Assemblyman Rodriguez to strengthen and show off his constituency, thereby shoring up his ability to command political influence at higher levels of government.

During the Saturday and Sunday of the retreat, Moviendo Juntos members attend workshops on such topics as affordable housing, welfare reform, and domestic violence. Each features a panel of four to six speakers who give short presentations and then answer questions. A mix of high-ranking public agency officials and representatives of Bushwick and Williamsburg community-based organizations make up the panels. These sessions deal with themes related to the work of Moviendo Juntos members, but the retreat's leisure activities cement participants' loyalty to Assemblyman Rodriguez. There are four parties during the retreat: one each on the bus trips to and from the conference center, one on Friday night, and one on Saturday night. On the bus trips Moviendo Juntos members share food they have made and mix drinks from an impromptu bar set up in the bus aisle. The Friday and Saturday parties feature a disc jockey from Brooklyn, flashing lights (also from Brooklyn), drinks, and lots of dancing.

Besides the workshops and parties, Assemblyman Rodriguez regularly holds an informal Friday evening chat session with a select group of high-ranking B-W community leaders. When I stumbled upon this gathering at my first conference, Rodriguez took the opportunity to give me a lesson in how politics work in New York, which I recorded in my field notes:

> [Tony] says to me that as a graduate student, there's something I should know about politics. "The most important factor in politics is loyalty. The second most important is respect." [Jennifer Pertutti] and [Ann Watson, Rodriguez's two top deputies at Bushwick Center] nod their heads. [Tony] continues, saying that the way to get things done in politics is to make sure you have all your supporters together; that way you can make deals and bring things into the district. Says some people don't think that's the way to do it, that they can just take help from someone, then "shit all over you" when they feel like it. [This is surely a thinly veiled reference to some people in Williamsburg who are not ideologically aligned with Rodriguez.] Some people don't agree with how he operates, and that's fine, but they can't expect him to keep helping them, and keep putting up with their attacking him. Says people like [Susana Vasquez] and [Marla Lowen, both Williamsburg housing organizers who have argued with [Rodriguez's] way of working] say they're entitled to say what they think, oppose him when they think he's wrong, and "that's fine, they're entitled." But, at the same time, they come to him and ask for help. They think they can say, "[Tony's] no good," and that he'll keep on helping them. Well, if they have the "right" to attack him, he too has

the right to challenge them, and if they lose their reputation—and a lot of people, especially in city and state government, where the money comes from, will listen to a [nonprofit organization's] local political representative—then they're going to be in a lot of trouble. (field notes, January 9, 1998)

Here Rodriguez made his political philosophy clear. A constituency's political power is synonymous with its ability to command votes in an elected official's district. If the constituency's leader cannot count on them to flex their political muscle on cue, then he or she has no clout to exercise within the larger political system.

Later in the fieldwork period Rodriguez demonstrated the veracity of his ideas about accumulating political power. On November 2, 1999, Bob Reltona, a candidate supported by Rodriguez, won a hotly contested election in the local judicial district. Reltona's race had been marked from the beginning as a contest between Rodriguez's organization and that of Williamsburg's Hasidim.[25] After an intensive, nine-month, grassroots campaign coordinated out of Rodriguez's political club, Reltona pulled 6,364 votes to his challenger's 4,313. At a meeting of Moviendo Juntos two days after the election, Rodriguez drove home the importance of this win:

[Tony] says that [election day] was a "very, very successful day" for the organization. The Hasidim lost, and they lost badly. He says that they [Moviendo Juntos] put together a great coalition of black, white, and Latino voters, and they won. . . . He says that the victory is only the beginning of a larger struggle, in which they have to find out who their friends are. Candidates have to choose sides, and if they want the support of one of the more impressive Democratic organizations in the city [Moviendo Juntos], they [the candidates] are going to have to play with [Rodriguez and his organization]. . . . He says that you can't expect things to move your way without understanding the politics of what's going on. A political favor means that when there are two hundred requests for public money, and only two get funded, the people who are owed a favor get one of those two. At work today, he had three high-level people from the Mayor's office call to talk to him about what Bushwick needs. He says he's not sure if he wants to take that step [of getting so close to the Republican mayor, Rudolph Giuliani], since it's a little scary, but this is the kind of recognition the organization is getting now. (field notes, November 4, 1999)

The New York press also noted the importance of Rodriguez's victory. One veteran political reporter agreed that Rodriguez's win had gained him and his organization some highly significant political clout:

[On a largely quiet election day, w]hat blood was left on the floor was oozing mostly from three top elected officials who backed a bid by [Leonard Smithson], a lawyer . . . who ran on the Independence and Conservative lines, to block [Reltona's] Democratic Party election. . . . If [those three officials] were the losers, *Democratic Assemblyman [Tony Rodriguez] was the big winner* after his soldiers in the [Neighborhood] Democrats . . . went door to door to pull out as many as 2,000 voters for the party's Civil Court candidate. [Reltona] credited [Rodriguez's] troops with carrying him to victory, and [Rodriguez] was quick to accept the credit. (Liff 1999, emphasis added)

Rodriguez's focus on constituency-building and the minutiae of clubhouse politics makes him one of the best practitioners of machine politics in New York City (Marwell 2004). His success has attracted many supporters, including some second-generation Dominicans, who fill out the younger ranks of his organization. A trademark of the urban political machine is that it recognizes and eventually adapts to ethnic succession. What remains, however, is its approach to building and exercising political power. In both its latter- and present-day forms, machine politics operates along the lines espoused by Rodriguez. In B-W, then, Lopez's organization is incorporating first- and second-generation Dominicans along traditional lines.

B-W's growing Dominican population has been accompanied by a concomitant increase in the number of Dominicans who belong to Moviendo Juntos and Rodriguez's political club. As their number grows, Rodriguez has brought some into the front ranks of his political operation. During the study period at least half of his six-person district office staff were second-generation Dominicans, including his protégé, Alina Villardo, who was born and raised in Williamsburg and currently lives in a Bushwick house built by the Housing Office at Bushwick Center. Villardo and Rodriguez's other second-generation staff members have very different biographies from the members of Young Dominicans. They attended local public and Catholic schools in north Brooklyn, and some earned college degrees at CUNY campuses. They got jobs with Rodriguez because their families were involved in local community-based organizations or supported Rodriguez's political activities. These relatively modest—and very local—backgrounds help the district office staffers do the daily work of responding to constituent requests for help.

Over and above employing Dominican staff members, Rodriguez took a major step toward bringing Dominicans into the leadership ranks of Brooklyn Democratic politics in 2000. In another political showdown with his long-standing rival, Congresswoman Velasquez, Rodriguez supported Villardo for the Democratic district leader position in his assembly district. Though the office is relatively minor, it positioned Villardo for her 2001 City

Council victory. Villardo ran against Yvette Rosa, a Puerto Rican woman supported by Velasquez who had been active in the Williamsburg Latino community for many years. With only about 5,000 votes cast, Villardo won decisively, pulling 3,000 votes to Rosa's 2,200. At Rodriguez's political club on election night, Villardo gave an emotional acceptance speech, which I recorded in my field notes:

> [Alina] finally arrives at the club at about 9:30 P.M. She greets people with hugs and kisses as we wait for [Tony] to come out of the back room to say how the votes look. . . . When he finally announces [Alina's] victory, a big cheer goes up. He asks [Alina] to say a few words, and she stands in front of the crowd with her parents, her two sisters, her grandmother, and [Tony]. She is clearly exhausted, but, as always, pulls together for the speech. She first thanks all of her family, looking at them teary-eyed and giving each of them a hug. Then she thanks everyone who worked long hours on the campaign. She says it has been a long struggle, but now it's all worth it. Finally, she says the biggest thanks go to [Tony], who has been her undying supporter and taught her so much about serving people *and doing politics.* Everyone claps and cheers. (field notes, September 12, 2000, emphasis added)

Villardo kept her remarks focused on the campaign and seemed genuinely overwhelmed by the warm response from her supporters. A few weeks later, in an article about her victory in a community newspaper run by Bushwick Center, she obliquely addressed the importance of working with people from all ethnic backgrounds to build political power. Although Rodriguez's feud with Velasquez is often couched in ethnic terms—Velasquez argues that Puerto Ricans, like herself, should represent B-W—Villardo told readers of the October 2000 edition of a community newspaper, "I am proud that I ran a very positive campaign. I am saddened by the personal attacks *and ethnic slurs* by some of the supporters of my opponent."[26] The "ethnic slurs" to which Villardo refers were alleged anti-Dominican sentiments directed at her.[27] Although Villardo had not mentioned these comments in the relative privacy of the clubhouse victory party, she made sure to include a Rodriguez-style minimization of ethnicity in her public comments. For her, a political focus on ethnicity was negative and hurtful rather than a productive way of organizing a campaign.

Villardo had expressed similar sentiments a year earlier when I asked her to comment on Young Dominicans. Given that she is a young, politically active Dominican, she would seem to be a prime member of Young Dominicans' target audience. I recorded her unequivocal response to my question in my field notes:

I ask [Alina] what she thinks about [Young Dominicans]. She says she's heard a little about them, but hasn't liked what she heard. I ask why not. She says she doesn't understand why they're just focusing on being Dominican, that she thinks it's counterproductive to do that. She says she's proud of being Dominican, that her parents and family are Dominican, and she'd never deny it or anything. She says that it's fine if they [Young Dominicans] want to do that [organize around being Dominican], but that's not the way she wants to work in the community. I ask if she's interested in going to the conference in February, and she makes a face, says she won't, that she considers it "a waste of time." (field notes, October 18, 1999)

Villardo consistently demonstrated her adherence to Rodriguez's philosophy of downplaying ethnic politics. Although the Dominican–Puerto Rican ethnic conflict may have been flowing beneath the surface of her election, the most important thing was that the Rodriguez organization made a significant show of political strength. This flexing of political muscle, which embarrassed one of his rivals, made Rodriguez a little giddy, as the following excerpt from my field notes shows:

When [Tony's] turn to speak [at Alina's victory party] comes, it's clear that he's really happy about the win. He also seems a bit vengeful, though, saying that [Alina's] winning was so important for showing [his political] club's strength in the Williamsburg part of his district. Says it's been clear for a while that he has Bushwick under control, but now people see they also have Williamsburg. He says that in a little while he's going to go and do something that he's never done before, and that people should join him, whoever's feeling up to it. He says again that he's never done it before, but he's going to get together people in their cars and drive over to Williamsburg in a caravan,[28] honking the horns and making a ruckus, so that "all those people [the opponent's supporters] can stick it up their asses!" (field notes, September 12, 2000)

This was the first time in three years of observing Rodriguez that I saw him try to humiliate a political opponent. There are two principal reasons for this. In the 1999 judicial race Rodriguez demonstrated to citywide politicians that although the Hasidim were strong, he was stronger. Although Rodriguez knew that his win certainly would not freeze the Hasidim out of political influence, it was an important victory nonetheless. With the district leader race, however, Rodriguez defeated another elected official seeking to represent the non-Hasidic constituencies in B–W. He sensed that beating Velasquez's candidate would give him the edge in speaking for the minority constituencies of the area. It was critical to Rodriguez that he establish himself—not Velasquez—as the more powerful representative of this group.

As the population of B-W becomes more Dominican, Rodriguez's organization is likely to incorporate more Dominicans, particularly members of the second generation, who hold Rodriguez's all-important resource: the right to vote. Villardo's election to the City Council in 2001 made her the first U.S.-born Dominican to hold elective office in New York State. With Rodriguez's track record of working with anyone who commits himself or herself to clubhouse politics, it seems likely that his organization will foster the careers of other second-generation Dominicans.

CONCLUSIONS

How do we understand the idea of political incorporation? If a newly naturalized immigrant or second-generation native votes in every presidential election, does that constitute incorporation? Or does it require multiple, deep, and active connections to governing, as discussed by Rufus Browning, Dale Rogers Marshall, and David Tabb (1984)? Examining the latter formulation more critically requires that we explore how individuals achieve meaningful participation in the "governing coalition." This is not a uniform process. Rather, it begins at the neighborhood level, where new immigrants and their second-generation descendants engage with the people doing politics around them, learn how political institutions function, and begin to influence them. In effect, they become the latest generation of soldiers in the "trenches" (Katznelson 1981) of the battle for city resources.

Since urban political incorporation is built on these neighborhood-level processes, it is governed primarily *not* by generational status or ethnicity but rather by local contexts and local forms of political practice. My research describes two very different models of such practice. Each has emerged in response to specific neighborhood demographic and political contexts. In Washington Heights–Inwood, second-generation Dominicans have learned that engaging in ethnic politics is the most effective way for them to advance politically. In Bushwick-Williamsburg, however, they have learned to work within a multi-racial, multi-ethnic power grouping that downplays ethnicity in favor of an old-fashioned, geographically based model of trading political cohesion for greater resources from the wider governing structure.

Both of these models have important limitations. Young Dominicans' second-generation ethnic politics approach in WH-I may have no place else to go. It is unlikely that any neighborhood in New York City, to say nothing of the rest of the United States, will ever reach a Dominican population concentration so great that it will sustain political organizing mainly on the basis of being Dominican. Given a district-based system of representation, the exclusive focus on ethnicity will be useful in promoting initial steps toward incorporation only where immigrant ethnic concentrations are unusually high—the zones of first immigrant settlement. For their part, the second-generation Dominicans of B-W are subject to the continued hegemony of "regular" politics. As new members of a political organization that survives by minimizing political participation from potential challengers, these young people are unlikely to develop a progressive challenge to the political establishment. As they learn from Assemblyman Rodriguez how to gain power, they also are learning how to manipulate the political process and exclude competing voices.

Urban politics played as "city trenches" largely is about securing benefits for the places where voters live. Power is instantiated in geography. While ethnic politics dominates in WH-I, in B-W it is employed as part of a wider political strategy that seeks to build a dominant position within district boundaries. In this sense, geography trumps ethnicity. Comparing the two areas, we see that the ethnic politics scenario found in WH-I is likely to be the exception rather than the rule for Dominican second-generation political incorporation. Most of New York's Dominicans live *outside* the main Dominican enclave in WH-I, in neighborhoods more like B-W. Most second-generation Dominicans thus will have to participate in ethnically heterogeneous neighborhood organizations and political entities that are addressing local issues. Indeed, in B-W this multi-racial, multi-ethnic character can be found both in the "regular" organization that dominates politics in the neighborhood and among its political opponents. Across political factions in B-W, the focus is on the mechanics of generating neighborhood-based political influence and tangible benefits. Thus, the B-W case is in fact more typical of how the Dominican second generation will progress toward political incorporation in New York City.

The second-generation Dominican comparison also is instructive for understanding immigrant political incorporation more broadly. Since most immigrant groups are less residentially concentrated than Dominicans in WH-I, if we assume a district-based system of representation,[29] the B-W scenario is the more probable path to political incorporation for other immigrant groups as well.[30] Rarely does any national-origin group reach the level of concentration achieved by Dominicans in WH-I; even among Dominicans this concentration decreases significantly for the second generation as it disperses from the original area of settlement. The newer urban and suburban zones into which Dominicans and other immigrant groups are settling generally do not provide them with the possibility of dominating the electorate. Thus, while WH-I has provided a springboard from which Dominicans could establish a place on the political map of New York, continuing a strategy of focusing only on Dominican identity would not seem to offer the

Dominican second generation much potential for future influence. Instead, if new second-generation immigrants become involved in politics at all, the varieties of coalition-building practiced in B-W are much more likely to shape their political activity. These lessons apply not only to the benefits-focused version of coalition-building that is the bread and butter of regular politics but also to more ideological coalition work—whether progressive or conservative.

In addition to support from the Immigrant Second Generation in Metropolitan New York Study, this research was supported by the National Community Development Policy Analysis Network, the Nonprofit Sector Research Fund of the Aspen Institute (grant 96-2-NSRF-07), and the U.S. Department of Housing and Urban Development (agreement H-21140SG).

NOTES

1. This argument in some ways parallels the work of Alejandro Portes and his colleagues (Portes 1996; Portes and Bach 1985; Portes and Rumbaut 1996), which ties the success of immigrant incorporation to the institutional context into which different immigrant national-origin groups are received in the United States.

2. Racialization theorists (for example, Omi and Winant 1986) would argue that voters' usual preferences for candidates of their own racial or ethnic background are a function of broader processes of racial formation, which produce enacted social divisions based on constructed categories like "race."

3. Demographics for Washington Heights–Inwood are drawn from New York City subarea analyses of 2000 census data presented online by Infoshare. For WH-I, I use figures from Infoshare's administrative designation "Manhattan Community District 12 (Washington Heights–Inwood)." (For further information on Infoshare's administrative designations, see www.infoshare.org). Infoshare figures show that WH-I is 54 percent Dominican, and 75 percent Latino overall. However, the 54 percent Dominican proportion reflects neither the large population of undocumented Dominicans in WH-I nor the large number of un-enumerated residences in the neighborhood. The U.S. Immigration and Naturalization Service (INS) estimates that 91,000 undocumented Dominicans live in the United States (U.S. Immigration and Naturalization Service 2003). Audrey Singer and Greta Gilbertson (2000) estimate that 80 percent of all Dominicans in the United States live in New York City. Infoshare data show that 25 percent of all New York City Dominicans live in WH-I. This makes for an estimate of about 18,200 undocumented Dominicans living in WH-I and raises the Dominican proportion of WH-I to 62 percent of the to-

tal population. Given the facts that INS figures on the undocumented are generally conservative estimates and that numerous un-enumerated households exist in New York City and in WH-I, I estimate the total Dominican population of WH-I to be closer to 70 percent.

4. Demographics for Bushwick-Williamsburg (B-W) are drawn from New York City subarea analyses of 2000 census data presented online by Infoshare. To compile figures for B-W, I use two different Infoshare administrative designations, which together offer the best approximation of the boundaries of the study area: "Brooklyn Community District 4 (Bushwick)" and "NYC neighborhood Williamsburg."

5. The term "party regulars" dates from the days of the nineteenth-century political machine (see, for example, Riordan 1948; see also Wilson 1962) and refers to individuals who are members of neighborhood-based political party organizations, usually called "political clubs." These clubs engage in the various activities that have formed the basis for controlling many political outcomes at the local level, such as maintaining district voter lists, carrying nominating petitions for candidates, door-to-door organizing, encouraging election-day turnout, phone banking, and so on. In the heyday of the political machine the activities of local clubs were aggregated through centralized control to produce city- and state-level victories and contribute to national electoral efforts. Party regulars may be of either the Democratic or the Republican Party.

6. From January 1, 1990, to June 1, 2000, the New York City Council passed 873 local laws, 36 percent of which (315) were name changes.

7. Throughout this chapter I use excerpts from my field notes to present the participant-observation data on which the analysis is based. For methodological reasons, I specifically do not convert my field notes into narrative. This is an issue of degrees of fidelity to the actual social processes observed and reported during participant-observation. Field notes are already two degrees removed from the actual experience: once as observed through the eyes of the researcher, twice as recorded by the researcher from memory of the experience. I hope to prevent a third remove by resisting the urge to paraphrase the field notes in the chapter's narrative.

8. The Northside of Williamsburg has become home to a concentration of artists and young professionals who have been pushed out of Manhattan over the last fifteen years by sharply rising real estate prices. Hasidic Jews of the Satmar sect make up a dominant proportion of Williamsburg's white population, but it is their distinctive visibility more than their numbers (some 15 percent of the area's total population at most) that sometimes inspires the characterization of the neighborhood as "Hasidic."

9. Not a pseudonym. Because all information on the elected officials in WH-I was collected from the public record, rather than through participant observation, I use real names for these individuals.

10. Not a pseudonym.

11. Not a pseudonym.

12. Not a pseudonym.

13. Not a pseudonym.

14. Michael Jones-Correa (1998) reports the median age of naturalization among Latino immigrants in New York City to be somewhere in the midthirties.

15. It is important to note here that the political organization of the Dominican population of WH-I began with a focus on school board elections and educational issues in the neighborhood. Significantly, U.S. citizenship is *not* a requirement to vote in school board elections: while all regularly registered voters in a district may vote in New York City school board elections, so too may any parent or guardian of a child enrolled in a district school. Linares and other Dominicans won seats on the district 6 school board by organizing mostly first-generation Dominicans, many of whom were not U.S. citizens but had children in the local schools. In elections for traditional offices like a seat on the City Council or in the State Assembly, however, U.S. citizenship is a requirement.

16. Ages are those of the named individuals at the time of the research.

17. Despite these hopes, the seat did not materialize. New York State in fact *lost* two congressional seats, and statewide redistricting left the New York City districts more or less intact.

18. On August 9, 1997, Abner Louima, a Haitian immigrant, was brutally attacked and tortured by several New York City police officers after he was taken to a Brooklyn police station following a fight outside a local nightclub. Four of his attackers were eventually convicted of the assault, which included an infamous incident in which one of the officers, Justin Volpe, sodomized Louima with a broken broom handle.

19. On the night of July 6, 1999, WH-I suffered a nineteen-hour blackout as a result of faulty equipment in the electrical power grid operated by Con Edison. WH-I was the only area of the city affected by the blackout.

20. The consultant was Luis Miranda, special adviser for Hispanic affairs to former mayor Ed Koch and now principal of the political consulting firm Miranda y Más.

21. In recent years, as the Satmar community has grown and expanded beyond its Williamsburg settlement into an independent town in upstate New York, a division based on religious leadership has developed between the two settlements. Within Williamsburg itself, however, there are only tiny pockets of dissenters.

22. In New York City elections, particularly elections for city and state positions, "large numbers" of votes is an exceedingly relative concept. Because of extremely low voter turnout rates for most local elections, the absolute number of votes needed to win is usually very small. In a viciously fought 1999 election for Civil Court judge in north Brooklyn, for example, the winning candidate received a mere six thousand votes in a district of some sixty thousand registered voters.

23. Not a pseudonym.

24. Rodriguez is recognized by all his close associates as an Italian American. His

last name comes from one of his grandfathers, who was from Spain. This grandfather traveled to Italy, where he married an Italian woman. The couple then emigrated to New York, and the family's descendants became part of the Italian American community. Despite this background, and despite the fact that he speaks no Spanish, Rodriguez usually replies, when asked directly if he is "Latino," that he is. Rodriguez also is a member of the New York State Assembly's Black and Puerto Rican Legislative Caucus. His ambiguous ethnic identity allows him to safely encourage his constituents to minimize ethnic divisions without running the risk of being accused of betraying his own ethnic group.

25. Many political reporters and observers would argue that this election was primarily about a long-running political feud between Rodriguez and Congresswoman Nydia Velasquez. While that battle played some role in the election, and Rodriguez was quoted several times in the press making some comments about Velasquez, I would argue that at this moment the more important battle for Rodriguez was with his prime competitors for political influence in the area, the Hasidim. Nearly all of Rodriguez's continuous comments about the election—at his office, at his political club, at Brooklyn Unidos meetings—were directed toward the Hasidim, not Velasquez.

26. *The Bushwick Observer.* 2000. "Diana Reyna: Victorious." *The Bushwick Observer.* p. 1.

27. Although I myself never heard anti-Dominican remarks from Puerto Ricans during the campaign, my association with the Rodriguez organization made it difficult for me to participate in depth with the Velasquez camp. This may have precluded my hearing such comments, if they in fact were made.

28. The political caravan is a traditional Latin American and Caribbean method of campaigning (Jones-Correa 1998). In WH-I, the caravan is used heavily during both the U.S. and Dominican Republic campaign seasons. Before the night of Villardo's victory, however, I had never observed an electoral caravan in B-W.

29. As opposed to an at-large system in which political representation is not geographically based.

30. But see Massey and Denton (1993, 153–60) for a discussion of the political incorporation difficulties that may face immigrants of African descent if they are subject to levels of housing discrimination and segregation similar to those faced by African Americans.

References

Abramson, Paul R., and John H. Aldrich. 1982. "The Decline of Electoral Political Participation in America." *American Political Science Review* 76: 502–21.

Browning, Rufus P., Dale Rogers Marshall, and David H. Tabb. 1984. *Protest Is Not Enough: The Struggle of Blacks and Hispanics for Equality in Urban Politics.* Berkeley: University of California Press.

DeSipio, Louis. 1996. *Counting on the Latino Vote: Latinos as a New Electorate.* Charlottesville: University Press of Virginia.

Duany, Jorge. 1994. *Quisqueya on the Hudson: The Transnational Identity of Dominicans in Washington Heights*. New York: CUNY Dominican Studies Institute.

Filipcevic, Vojislava. 2000. "Reclaiming Urban Trenches: The Processes of Dominican Sociopolitical Incorporation in Washington Heights, New York." Paper delivered to the annual meeting of the American Political Science Association. Washington, D.C., August 30.

Gutierrez, John A. 2000. "Dominican Elections Heat up the Heights." *Manhattan Times*, May 4.

Jones-Correa, Michael. 1998. *Between Two Nations: The Political Predicament of Latinos in New York City*. Ithaca, N.Y.: Cornell University Press.

———. 2001. "Political Participation: Does Religion Matter?" *Political Research Quarterly* 54: 751–70.

Kasinitz, Philip. 1992. *Caribbean New York: Black Immigrants and the Politics of Race*. Ithaca, N.Y.: Cornell University Press.

Katznelson, Ira. 1981. *City Trenches: Urban Politics and the Patterning of Class in the United States*. New York: Pantheon.

Keiser, Richard A. 1997. "After the First Black Mayor: Fault Lines in Philadelphia's Biracial Coalition." In *Racial Politics in American Cities*, 2nd ed., edited by David H. Tabb. New York: Longman.

Liff, Bob. 1999. "Voters Nix New Charter, Dem Bigs' Man." *New York Daily News*, November 4.

Marwell, Nicole P. 2000. "Social Networks and Social Capital as Resources for Neighborhood Revitalization." Ph.D. diss., University of Chicago.

———. 2004. "Privatizing the Welfare State: Nonprofit Community-Based Organizations as Political Actors." *American Sociological Review* 69: 265–91.

Massey, Douglas S., and Nancy A. Denton. 1993. *American Apartheid: Segregation and the Making of the Underclass*. Cambridge, Mass.: Harvard University Press.

Omi, Michael, and Howard Winant. 1986. *Racial Formation in the United States: From the 1960s to the 1990s*. New York: Routledge.

Pessar, Patricia R., and Pamela M. Graham. 2002. "Dominicans: Transnational Identities and Local Politics." In *New Immigrants in New York*, edited by Nancy Foner. New York: Russell Sage Foundation.

Pinderhughes, Dianne M. 1997. "An Examination of Chicago Politics for Evidence of Political Incorporation and Representation." In *Racial Politics in American Cities*, 2nd ed., edited by David H. Tabb. New York: Longman.

Plutzer, Eric. 2002. "Becoming a Habitual Voter: Inertia, Resources, and Growth in Young Adulthood." *American Political Science Review* 96: 41–56.

Portes, Alejandro. 1996. *The New Second Generation*. New York: Russell Sage Foundation.

Portes, Alejandro, and Robert L. Bach. 1985. *Latin Journey: Cuban and Mexican Immigrants in the United States*. Berkeley: University of California Press.

Portes, Alejandro, and Rubén G. Rumbaut. 1996. *Immigrant America: A Portrait*. Berkeley: University of California Press.

Price, Stephen Charles. 1979. "The Effect of Federal Antipoverty Programs and Policies on the Hasidic and Puerto Rican Communities of Williamsburg." Ph.D. diss., Brandeis University.

Riordan, William L. 1948. *Plunkitt of Tammany Hall: A Series of Very Plain Talks on Very Practical Politics*. New York: Alfred A. Knopf.

Sexton, Joe. 1997a. "In a Pocket of Brooklyn Sewn by Welfare, an Unraveling." *New York Times*, March 10.

————. 1997b. "No Room to Grow: Day Care Center Fills as Working and Welfare Parents Compete." *New York Times*, March 24.

————. 1997c. "When Work Is Not Enough: Religion and Welfare Shape Economics for the Hasidim." *New York Times*, April 21.

————. 1997d. "Going on Sixty, and Going to Work for Their Welfare: Older Recipients Often Ill and Ill Prepared." *New York Times*, July 1.

Singer, Audrey, and Greta Gilbertson. 2000. "Naturalization in the Wake of Anti-immigrant Legislation: Dominicans in New York City." Working paper 10. New York: Carnegie Endowment for International Peace, International Migration Policy Program.

Treudly, Mary Bosworth. 1949. "Formal Organization and the Americanization Process, with Special Reference to the Greeks of Boston." *American Sociological Review* 14: 44–53.

U.S. Immigration and Naturalization Service. Office of Policy and Planning. 2003. *Estimates of the Unauthorized Immigration Population Residing in the United States: 1990–2000*. Washington: U.S. Government Printing Office (January).

Verba, Sidney, and Norman H. Nie. 1987. *Participation in America: Political Democracy and Social Equality*. Chicago: University of Chicago Press.

Verba, Sidney, Kay Lehman Schlozman, and Henry E. Brady. 1995. *Voice and Equality: Civic Voluntarism in American Politics*. Cambridge, Mass.: Harvard University Press.

Warren, Christopher L. 1997. "Hispanic Incorporation and Structural Reform in Miami." In *Racial Politics in American Cities*, 2nd ed., edited by David H. Tabb. New York: Longman.

Wilson, James Q. 1962. *The Amateur Democrat: Club Politics in Three Cities*. Chicago: University of Chicago Press.

Wirth, Louis. 1941. "Morale and Minority Groups." *American Journal of Sociology* 47: 415–33.

Wolfinger, Raymond E. 1965. "The Development and Persistence of Ethnic Voting." *American Political Science Review* 59: 896–908.

Young Dominicans. 2000. Personal correspondence. January 22, 2000.

CHAPTER 9

CHINATOWN OR UPTOWN? SECOND-GENERATION CHINESE AMERICAN PROTESTANTS IN NEW YORK CITY

KAREN CHAI KIM

IT IS seven o'clock on Friday night. A group of Chinese and Korean American evangelical Protestants gathers together in the midtown Manhattan apartment of a Chinese American investment banker for the regular meeting of their church-sponsored home fellowship. Seated in a circle on the living room floor, they begin the evening by distributing copies of the *Cornell University Korean Christian Fellowship Songbook* and singing several contemporary praise songs, accompanied by acoustic guitar. After the songs they take turns answering the icebreaker question of the week: "What is the most unpleasant experience you have had while living in New York City?" At the same time, a group of evangelical Chinese Americans sits in a sixth-floor classroom of a large church in Chinatown for its regular Friday night Bible study and fellowship. They also begin with a selection of praise songs, led by a few members, with lyrics projected onto a classroom wall by an overhead projector. A third group of evangelical Protestant Chinese Americans has gathered in their midtown church office location for a time of Bible study and fellowship. Each of these groups is sponsored by an evangelical Protestant church in Manhattan. Each of the churches has large numbers of second-generation Chinese Americans. However, the members of the first gathering attend a multiracial church, the members of the second group attend a Chinese church in Chinatown, and members of the third group attend an Upper West Side church for second-generation Chinese Americans.

Introduction

Religion has long been one of the most important institutions for immigrants in the United States. Ethnic churches have been characterized as a "microcosm" of the society that immigrants left behind, serving as a place to meet new people and maintain cultural traditions, as well as to seek spiritual comfort and meaning (Hurh and Kim 1990). In addition to these functions for the first generation, immigrants often believed that ethnic church attendance would help their children form friendships with co-ethnic peers and retain their cultural heritage.

The fact is that the majority of Chinese Americans—of any generation—are *not* active in organized religion. However, just as the Chinese population has rapidly increased in the United States, the number of Chinese churches has grown steadily. Whereas there were only 65 Chinese Christian churches in the United States and Hawaii in 1952 (Cayton and Lively 1955), there are now over 750 Chinese ethnic Christian churches in the United States (Yang 1999; Ambassadors for Christ 2002). Although immigrants of Chinese descent have a lower participation rate in religious institutions than other groups, such as Korean immigrants, the Christian church stands as the most important social institution for Chinese Americans today (Yang 1999). Ironically, while Korean immigrants lament the fact that their children are leaving the ethnic churches, some non-Christian Chinese immigrants are surprised to discover that their children are active in evangelical Protestant ministries.

Linguistic and cultural barriers may limit immigrants to membership in ethnic churches and temples, but their American-born and American-educated children experience no such limitations. Unlike many of their parents, second-generation Americans are fluent in English and have been educated in American schools. They therefore are better equipped to establish racially and ethnically diverse social networks. Whereas religious immigrants may deliberately seek out ethnic congregations, second-generation Chinese Americans who are interested in religion can potentially feel comfortable in many different types of churches.

According to the results of the telephone survey portion of the Immigrant Second Generation in Metropolitan New York Study, 55 percent of the second-generation Chinese Americans said that they had no religion. However, 15 percent of second-generation Chinese Americans identified themselves as Protestant, 5 percent as Catholic, and 18 percent as Buddhist. Of those who claimed a religious affiliation, 37 percent attended church or other religious services. Of those who attended church, however, 70 percent attended churches that were mostly or all Chinese. This last statistic indicates that despite having grown up in the United States, second-generation Chinese Americans who attend religious services make a point to attend those that are predominantly Chinese.

This chapter focuses on three groups of second-generation Chinese Americans in New York City. They attend one of three evangelical Protestant churches in Manhattan: "Chinatown Church"—an ethnic Chinese church located in Chinatown; "ABC Church"—an Upper West Side church of second-generation Chinese Americans; and "Multiracial Church" (MRC)—a large, multiracial church offering services on both the Upper East and Upper West Sides.[1]

Although these churches are in different locations and are of different sizes, they all hold English-language worship services and Bible studies. These three churches share similar evangelical Protestant doctrines and have large numbers of second-generation Chinese American attendees. They are very well known in the Chinese American community and have active and growing ministries. Despite their similarities, however, these churches present contrasting environments for the nurturing of second-generation Chinese American religiosity.

This chapter begins with a brief description of each church and proceeds to address three questions:

1. What types of second-generation Chinese Americans are attending these different churches?

2. What type of second-generation Chinese American identity do these churches foster?

3. How are Chinese American Christians affecting their churches and their communities?

CHINATOWN CHURCH

Chinatown Church is a church for Chinese Christians to meet overseas, for the purpose of proclaiming the gospel of God.
—Chinatown Church, mission statement

Fighting through the Sunday crowds on the sidewalks of Chinatown in order to reach Chinatown Church, one might look forward to a quiet, meditative haven upon entering the church building. Instead, the frenetic activity carried out in the Chinatown shops just outside the church is echoed as members of all ages scurry about the lobby, sanctuary, stairwells, and classrooms of this building. The stairwell gets so crowded, in fact, that signs stating, "Keep to your right," must be posted prominently on every floor, in both Chinese and English. Located in a bustling section of Manhattan's Chinatown, Chinatown

Church is the oldest of the three churches in my study and is currently the largest Chinese church on the East Coast, with 1,400 attendees. My study involved members of Chinatown Church's English Ministry, attended by a total of 600 attendees each week.

Chinatown Church was founded in 1961 as an outgrowth of a Bible study group for Chinese students. Members originally borrowed meeting space from a non-Chinese church, but the group consistently outgrew its facilities until it moved to its current location. The church is now located in a ten-story building in a section of Chinatown that in years past was known as Little Italy. The building originally served as a Catholic school for Italian American children. Like the majority of large ethnic Chinese churches in the United States, Chinatown Church is nondenominational. It is affiliated, however, with the National Association of Evangelical Churches and borrows from the Presbyterian and Baptist traditions.

With a fourteen-member pastoral staff, the church sponsors numerous activities for its diverse Chinese ethnic membership. For example, the church runs a senior citizens' service center as well as an after-school program for children on weekdays. On Friday nights each of the different age groups within the church sponsors a fellowship meeting. On Sundays the church holds four worship services attended by a total of 1,600 people each week: a Chinese worship service from 8:30 to 10 A.M.; an English worship service from 10:00 to 11:30 A.M.; a Chinese worship service from 11:30 A.M. to 1 P.M.; and another English worship service at 1:45 P.M. The Chinese services are usually conducted in Mandarin, with translation into Cantonese. If the speaker uses Cantonese, then it is translated into Mandarin. The largest service of the day is the afternoon Chinese worship service, which requires overflow seating with closed-circuit television. The morning English worship service draws about 400 people, most of them second-generation Chinese American college students and professionals. The afternoon English worship service draws 200 high school students as well as college students and professionals. While these four services are being held, there are simultaneous Sunday school programs for children and for adults in Cantonese, Mandarin, and English.

As is typical in large ethnic Chinese churches, members and staff must work hard to accommodate the large degree of internal diversity (Yang 1998). Among the Chinese-speaking members, about 20 percent are Mandarin speakers from Taiwan, but the majority are Cantonese speakers from Hong Kong. There are also many ethnic Chinese members from mainland China, the Philippines, and Vietnam. Within the Chinese-speaking congregations, about 25 percent are professionals; this group is primarily responsible for financially supporting the activities of the church. Not only does the church incorporate at least three different language groups, but it has learned to accommodate the needs of ethnic Chinese from different countries, with different political orientations, different socioeconomic statuses, and different religious histories.

Although most of the staff members are ethnic Chinese, they reflect the diversity of the membership as well as of the Chinese diaspora, hailing from areas such as the Philippines, South America, Hong Kong, and Taiwan. There are also two second-generation Chinese American pastors who head the English ministry. The one non-Chinese staff member is the white youth director for the junior high and high school groups.

No other Chinese church in New York City has a larger ministry to second-generation Chinese Americans. Until recently, Chinatown Church was unrivaled in its area, its nearest ethnic Chinese "competitor" being the Rutgers Community Christian Church in New Jersey. The English ministry at Chinatown Church has separate fellowship groups for members according to their age and family status: a college group, a singles group for people up to their late twenties, a "career" singles group for older singles age twenty-seven and older, a young married couples group, and an older married couples group (usually with children). Each group meets in its own classroom at the church on Friday nights. After their respective Bible study or fellowship activities, the groups adjourn to a late dinner at one of the many Chinese restaurants in the neighborhood. These group outings occur so regularly at certain favorite restaurants that restaurant workers know to brace themselves around 9:00 P.M. each Friday for the large influx of diners from Chinatown Church.

ABC CHURCH

To build a culturally sensitive and spiritually dynamic urban church that would impact our community and city culturally, socially, economically and spiritually with the Gospel of Jesus.
—ABC Church, mission statement

ABC Church is the first English-only daughter church of Chinatown Church. Four years ago the head pastor of Chinatown Church's English ministry, Joseph Chau, requested permission from the church board to plant a new church that would cater exclusively to the second generation. Although the church services would initially be held at Chinatown Church, the goal was to gradually build financial autonomy and eventually move the congregation out of Chinatown. Pastor Joseph believed that by moving the ministry out of the ethnic enclave, he could reach a larger number of "unchurched" Chinese Americans who might otherwise not bother to travel to Chinatown each week. As one staff member told me, "A lot of second-generation Chinese Americans who don't live in Chinatown would not want to go to church in Chinatown, especially one that is called Chinatown Church!"

The initial planting of ABC Church was a difficult and even traumatic experience for the leaders and members of the two churches. First, Chinatown Church's English ministry lost its head pastor. Second, the English ministry members were required to choose between staying at Chinatown Church and following Pastor Joseph's vision and helping to plant ABC Church. Although ABC Church would still meet at the Chinatown Church building, members were asked to make a full commitment to either ministry, with no option of attending both churches. Those who chose to help plant ABC Church left with the blessing of Chinatown Church members, but the sudden loss of key leaders and members was particularly traumatic for those who remained at Chinatown Church. In the words of one Chinatown Church leader, "ABC Church took the best and the brightest of Chinatown Church. It was really hard for a while. Our praise band was really bad for a long time with the loss of talent. It has just begun to recover."

In February 1998, ABC Church finally moved out of Chinatown Church to a location on the Upper West Side of Manhattan. Although meeting space for new churches is notoriously difficult to locate in Manhattan, ABC Church successfully negotiated a landlord-tenant arrangement with the leaders of a historic center for spirituality. Because of its prime location and elegant facilities, a countless number of groups had approached the board of this spiritual center. One of ABC's leaders confided that he had been very pleasantly surprised that the center's board approved the rental of their building to an evangelical Christian group. He believes that the fact that ABC members were Asian Americans made the board perceive the church as a cultural group more than as one of the many evangelical Christian churches that had approached the board in the past.

Since moving to its new location, the church has grown steadily: only a fraction of its current members were part of the founding group from Chinatown Church. ABC Church has grown so much, in fact, that it has now developed into the main competitor with Chinatown Church for second-generation Chinese Americans in the area. Whereas Chinatown Church is still a strong presence in the local ethnic community, ABC Church is now known as "the church to go to" for Chinese Americans new to New York. About two hundred people meet on the Upper West Side location each week. After each Sunday 4:00 P.M. service, a large group of ABC attendees eat dinner together at one of the local Upper West Side restaurants. "One disadvantage of moving uptown," says a founding member, "is that we have such a hard time finding good restaurants to accommodate a large group, and we have to spend so much more money eating out in this neighborhood." Although the new location is convenient in some ways, members do spend much more time and money once they leave the ethnic economy of Chinatown. Every Sunday after the service the large dinner group must walk to different restaurants, in search of a place that can accommodate their size and taste buds. Sometimes the group travels from restaurant to restaurant in search of one that is suitably large and empty. At other times the group is forced to split into two, since more restaurants are able to accommodate a smaller crowd.

ABC Church is Chinatown Church's attempt to incorporate previously unreached people, going where they would feel comfortable—into their residential neighborhood, away from ethnic exclusivity, and offering a more contemporary worship style. ABC Church has now grown into its own, preserving the evangelical elements of Chinatown Church but leaving behind the "messy" elements of Chinatown—the crowds, the immigrants, the functional-but-unaesthetic church building. The church consciously tries to distance itself from a Chinatown association or an ethnic enclave atmosphere that may turn off more assimilated Asian Americans. Nevertheless, ABC Church remains unmistakably Chinese American.

MULTIRACIAL CHURCH

> *Multiracial Church is a center-city community of changed people who are committed to serving and renewing New York City through a movement of the Gospel of Jesus Christ.*
> *—Multiracial Church, mission statement*

The roots of Multiracial Church (MRC) reach back to the winter of 1989 when a fifteen-member prayer group began meeting in an Upper East Side apartment. The group met regularly to pray about planting a church in Manhattan for professionals in the city. By the spring the group held its first worship service in the evening in a borrowed church building. Its first morning worship service was held in September 1989. This modest group has grown exponentially over the years to become one of the largest churches in New York City. Every week three thousand New Yorkers attend its three Sunday services: 10:30 A.M. and 6:00 P.M. on the Upper East Side, and 5:00 P.M. on the Upper West Side. Although MRC started out as a predominantly white church reaching out to "meet the spiritual and intellectual needs of Manhattan's educated elite," the "educated elite" who attend this church now are heavily Asian American. According to my survey of the congregation, 43 percent of those who attended every week were of Asian descent: 17 percent were

Chinese, and 27 percent were Korean.[2] MRC's ethnic and racial diversity now makes it stand out from other churches in its conservative Protestant 95 percent white denomination.

In many ways, MRC is a full-service mega-church, offering numerous specialized fellowship groups, including a divorced and separated ministry, moms' groups, a racial unity study group, a sports network, singles fellowship events, a college ministry, and a single parents' ministry. In addition, the church sponsors long-term and short-term missionaries around the world.

Most MRC members are students and professionals in their twenties and early thirties. Although there are 150 children from kindergarten to the sixth grade, only eight students are enrolled in the high school youth group. Although most churches struggle to keep teenagers involved, at MRC Church the drop-off in this age group's attendance also reflects the fact that by the time many of these children reach junior high school their families have moved out of the city—in search of more affordable housing, lower taxes, and better-quality public education. MRC members are mostly middle- to upper-middle-class and have at least a college education.

Although MRC's forty-member staff is predominantly white, it does include four full-time Asian Americans in ministry or counseling as well as two African Americans. Of the lay leadership, several Chinese Americans serve as deacons, heads of leadership teams, and heads of community outreach programs. There are also five predominantly Asian American Bible study groups sponsored by the church, each led by Asian American members. As one second-generation Chinese American put it, "MRC has an interesting suck/magnetic effect on many Chinese Americans."

WHAT TYPES OF SECOND-GENERATION CHINESE AMERICANS ATTEND THESE CHURCHES?

One of the most difficult aspects of my study was determining how many of MRC's attendees were in fact Chinese American. I knew that I could easily get a sense of the Chinese Americans at the Chinese ethnic churches, but I could not identify them at MRC. I could tell that a large number of Asian Americans were in attendance, but I did not know whether they were Korean, Chinese, Japanese, or of another ethnicity. When I asked the church staff for some background information on the members and attendees of MRC, I was told that they knew even less than I did. Because the majority of MRC attendees were not registered members, even the church staff had no information on their backgrounds. In fact, the staff had no solid understanding of how they chose to attend and what they really wanted from the ministry.

Sensing an opportunity for mutual benefit, an MRC leader encouraged me to create a written survey for distribution to attendees of the church. Because there was no roster of weekly attendees, I could not mail surveys or seek a truly random sample of the population. Although this sampling method is flawed, my only choice was to distribute a survey to the attendees at the three services held by MRC on one given Sunday.

In order to be able to compare the MRC population with those at Chinatown Church and ABC Church, I also obtained permission to distribute a similar survey to attendees of those two churches. What follows are some of the results of the written survey, distributed to the attendees of the worship services held by the three churches on one Sunday in April (MRC) and one Sunday in May 2000 (Chinatown and ABC). Although this study is primarily an ethnography, these survey results have been extremely helpful in giving me a sense of overall differences in the populations of the three churches.

At Chinatown Church there was an approximate response rate of 40 percent. Despite the fact that this was a Chinese ethnic church, 8 percent were non-Asian. Forty-five percent of the attendees were born in the United States, 13 percent were born in mainland China, and 23 percent were born in Hong Kong. Four percent were born in Taiwan. Most Chinatown Church respondents were children of immigrants from mainland China or Hong Kong.

Chinatown Church members were heavily New York–based and had strong ties to the New York Chinese community. Most of the Chinatown Church respondents (60 percent) lived with their parents. Over half were attending a four-year college or had at least a bachelor's degree. Sixty-five percent were either professional or technical workers.

Thirteen percent lived in Manhattan's Chinatown, 11 percent elsewhere in Manhattan, and 45 percent in Brooklyn or Queens. Over 72 percent grew up in one of the five boroughs of New York City. A full 30 percent of the respondents grew up in Manhattan's Chinatown.

Among Chinatown Church respondents, over 83 percent considered themselves members, and over 44 percent of the respondents had been attending Chinatown Church for at least seven years. Although 44 percent were raised in the Protestant Christian tradition, over 24 percent of the respondents grew up with no religious tradition. Over 18 percent were raised in the Buddhist tradition, and about 7 percent were raised as Catholics. Thirty percent said that religion was not important in their families growing up.[3]

Like Chinatown Church, ABC Church drew second-generation Chinese Americans whose parents had immigrated mainly from Hong Kong and mainland China. There were a higher number of children of immigrants from Taiwan, however, than there were at Chinatown Church. There was an approximately 60 percent response rate at ABC Church. ABC Church had very few families with children, largely for the same reason that MRC had relatively few established families—families with children tend to move to the suburbs and prefer to worship in suburban churches on the weekends.

ABC Church attendees were a highly educated group. Forty-three percent held a bachelor's degree, but an additional 45 percent had at least some graduate training. Although Chinatown Church members were also a relatively educated group, more attendees of ABC Church were graduates of elite colleges and universities. As Vivian Louie discusses in her chapter in this volume, there are significant differences between students and graduates of elite private colleges and those of public colleges.

Fifty-three percent had lived in the New York metropolitan area for ten years or more. Forty-eight percent grew up in New York City, and the rest grew up all over the country. The largest percentages grew up in Manhattan's Chinatown (16 percent) and in the Northeast (16 percent). Thirty-nine percent lived with their parents. Although ABC attendees also had strong ties to the New York area, they were less New York– and Chinatown-based than members of Chinatown Church.

ABC Church is a new church, so no one had been a member for over three years. Roughly half of the respondents reported that they were members of Chinatown Church before coming to ABC Church. There were almost as many newcomers (31 percent) as there were founding members (39 percent).

Compared to Chinatown Church attendees, more ABC attendees said that they were raised with no religious tradition (33 percent). However, 46 percent of ABC attendees were raised in the Protestant tradition. Seven percent were raised as Catholics, and 10 percent were raised as Buddhists. Thirty-eight percent said that religion was not important in their families growing up.[4]

At MRC my survey had a response rate of about 50 percent. There were a total of 1,491 respondents from the three Sunday services. Confirming what I had been told by MRC staff members, fewer than 25 percent of the respondents were registered members of the church. Seventy-five percent, however, said that Multiracial Church was the only church they attended in the New York metropolitan area. Eleven percent attended other churches in the New York area regularly, and 8 percent reported that they were trying to decide between MRC and another New York City church.

Sixty-five percent of the respondents were churchgoers before coming to Multiracial Church. Thirty percent, however, were not churchgoers. By far the most important reason given for attending the church was the preaching. The pastor, a former seminary professor, was known to give intellectually satisfying yet spiritually challenging sermons. The high quality of the preaching at MRC was talked about constantly among MRC attendees and was well known in the New York area.

Chinese Americans at MRC had an even lower rate of registration as members of the church—only 20 percent of the Chinese Americans were members. This group of Chinese Americans was the most educated of those at the three churches: over 90 percent of the Chinese had at least a bachelor's degree and 8 percent had a doctorate. A higher percentage of MRC Chinese Americans were the children of immigrants from Taiwan.

In contrast to those at the other two churches, only 6 percent of the Chinese at MRC lived in Manhattan's Chinatown. Fifty-seven percent lived elsewhere in Manhattan, and 14 percent lived in Queens. MRC's Chinese grew up all over the country, with only 7 percent having grown up in Manhattan's Chinatown. An additional 22 percent grew up elsewhere in New York City. A significant number grew up in the Northeast (20 percent) and the West (12 percent).[5]

The results of my survey confirmed many of my observations about the three churches in my study. First, there seemed to be a degree of sorting according to class background. Those who attended Chinatown Church had stronger roots in either Chinatown or the New York metropolitan area. Although they themselves were now professionals, many of their parents were employed in garment factories or restaurants. Chinatown Church attendees had college degrees, but their degrees were not necessarily from elite schools. The members of this church more closely resembled the Hunter College students in Louie's study. Those who did graduate from elite universities tended to have roots in the Chinatown community.

Because of the strong tie with Chinatown Church, attendees of ABC Church also had roots in Chinatown and the New York area. However, those who chose to leave Chinatown Church to help plant ABC Church generally had more elite backgrounds than those who remained at Chinatown Church. Furthermore, the deliberately chosen Upper West Side location helped draw more elite Chinese American members who resided in the area to the church. ABC Church was, in a sense, an upwardly mobile version of Chinatown Church. Although it had roots in Chinatown, it aimed for a more cosmopolitan image and membership. It was ethnically Chinese, yet any potentially negative associations with Chinese-ness were deliberately left out. As a result, many of the newer members were from elite backgrounds and had high-status careers. This made ABC Church an excellent base for Chinese Americans of all class backgrounds to meet one another and to network. Although cliques did form, evangelical Christianity at this church worked to maintain a sense of unity and promote interaction among all members.

MRC's Chinese Americans seemed to have the highest socioeconomic status of the Chinese American members of all three churches. Because the church was known to be one of the urban elite, the Chinese Americans at

MRC had usually heard about the church through elite school and friendship networks. Because the Chinese Americans with no ties to Chinatown were likely to hear about MRC through their school friends first, MRC was often the first church stop for a well-educated Chinese American Christian who was new to New York City. The multiracial atmosphere there and the intellectual sermons were reminiscent of college Christian fellowship groups and offered an easy transition to the city. The size and initially impersonal atmosphere at MRC had its drawbacks, but the biggest benefit to the upwardly mobile, career-driven Chinese American was that it required little commitment or time. Although there were many committed and very active members, MRC's low official membership rate points to the fact that it had a large number of free riders (Finke and Stark 1992; Iannaccone 1994) who attended services on Sundays but did little else at the church. Chinese Americans at this church were less active than those at Chinatown Church or ABC Church, despite the fact that many of the Chinese American attendees of MRC had been leaders in ethnic churches or fellowship groups in the past. Although their more passive presence at MRC might have indicated a sense of marginality in this large church, taking a passive role was often a welcome relief for many who had spent countless hours in the past on church activities and now wanted to focus on establishing their careers.

Social Class and Church Participation

Because of the tremendous diversity of the Chinese American population, immigrants of different classes do not generally interact with one another socially (Chen 1992; Louie, this volume). Churches are often founded to serve the needs of one class of Chinese immigrants. As a large regional church, Chinatown Church is somewhat exceptional, as it brings together a wider diversity of immigrants. English-language ministries, however, are much more effective in bringing together children of immigrants from many classes. In fact, church attendance can be a way of unifying the second generation on the basis of race-ethnicity and religion, despite differences in family class background. It can even serve as a vehicle for upward mobility.

For example, people from working-class backgrounds may be interested in broadening their social circle and meeting people of higher status. They can easily do so by attending churches like MRC. Joe, a Chinese American in his early twenties, grew up in Brooklyn and attended another church in Chinatown. This church is much smaller than Chinatown Church, and it is known to be a church of working-class Chinese, many of whom are undocumented and work in factories and restaurants. He had started attending MRC a year before and was now in a fellowship group with people from more privileged backgrounds. The other members of the home fellowship group were from different parts of the country, and most of them had attended elite colleges. They held prestigious jobs and had high aspirations. This fellowship group enabled Joe to meet other Chinese Americans from more privileged backgrounds and more elite social networks. Outside the context of the church, it would have been very difficult for someone of Joe's background to have such close contact on a regular basis with more elite co-ethnic peers. Ultimately, this fellowship group could serve as a means of upward mobility for Joe.

Although there were subtle class differences between the three churches, one constant across all three was striking: regardless of family background, second-generation Chinese Americans were expected to be college-educated professionals. Despite the fact that many of the second-generation Chinese Americans in the churches came from working-class families in Chinatown, they were all expected to attend college and enter a professional career. College and even graduate degrees were the norm among members of all three churches, regardless of their family class background. The more subtle differences between the churches can be seen in the fact that Chinatown Church members tended to hold degrees from local public universities, whereas those at ABC Church and MRC tended to hold degrees from more elite private institutions.

It is difficult to determine whether church membership actually encourages educational and professional achievement, or whether those who attend church are a self-selected subgroup of reasonably "successful" Chinese Americans. For example, churches in Chinatown often sponsor after-school programs for local youth. One interviewee, Tim, who had grown up attending such a program, joked that "Chinese parents see church as a free babysitter." Although his parents were not Christians, they sent their son to church programs while they worked. By engaging in group activities and gaining exposure to co-ethnic role models, Tim had developed a deep commitment to Christianity that provided him with much positive support. In fact, he was currently attending a Christian college suggested to him by a Christian mentor.

The cases of Joe and Tim illustrate the role that churches can play in encouraging upward mobility and achievement. Nevertheless, it is likely that another factor has contributed to the high rates of educational and professional achievement among the second-generation Chinese Americans attending these churches. Because professional status is clearly expected in the cultures of all three churches in the study, it is unlikely that someone who does not fit this mold would be comfortable participating in church activities for an extended period of time. Thus, those who attend these churches are a self-selected sample of those in the Chinese American community who are relatively accomplished.

FLUID BOUNDARIES AND CONSUMER CULTURE

Although I had expected different types of Chinese Americans to attend the three different churches in my study, I found that the boundaries were remarkably fluid. Each church had a tight-knit group of very committed members at the center, but they were surrounded by a vast number of uncommitted attendees at the periphery. There are an endless number of reasons why a person chooses to attend a particular church, but I believe that the fluidity of boundaries is indicative of a consumer culture perpetuated by the churches.

With the much-touted growth of evangelical Christian churches such as Willow Creek Church in Illinois and Saddleback Community Church in California, a whole new concept of marketing has entered the evangelical Christian community. There are now numerous networks of churches whose leaders gather regularly to share new ideas about how to reach the "unchurched" people in their communities. Although different leaders have taken different approaches, the underlying principle in this new way of thinking is to eliminate any elements of church life that make people feel uncomfortable and replace them with user-friendly programs and services. According to Kimon Howland Sargeant (2000, 7), "The 'tradition' that seeker church pastors want to throw out is not the belief in the authority of the Bible or the divinity of Christ, but the form of the church in which they were raised." Although the demands of membership at these types of churches may eventually become high, initially a visitor finds nothing but openness and low demands. These types of churches offer many programs and services that are useful on a practical level, appealing to the consumer in everyone (Sargeant 2000).

This consumer-oriented culture could be observed at the three churches in New York as church leaders strove to identify what it was that attendees "wanted" and the second-generation Chinese American attendees tried out different churches in search of a good fit. In fact, it was their desire to understand better their target population that led the leaders of all three churches to allow me to distribute my written survey to attendees. Because of its large size and high number of uncommitted "free riders," MRC is the best example of this consumer culture.

MRC serves as a well-known port of entry for many young adults new to the New York area. College and church alumni networks spread news of this church through word of mouth. Its intellectual sermons and organized programming are a welcome relief for many second-generation Asian Americans who have been burned out by the high demands of serving at ethnic churches. The church also provides a comfortable anonymity to a Chinese American who is not a Christian but is interested in learning more—a "seeker," in evangelical Christian language.

To some extent, there is a trend for Asian Americans who have attended an ethnic church elsewhere in the country to start attending MRC when they move to New York City. Doing so could be interpreted as a step toward assimilation, and MRC attendance for some Asian Americans has in fact led to interracial friendships and marriages. However, MRC seems unique in that Asian Americans feel comfortable attending MRC but tend to return to an ethnic church if and when they leave. In other words, a second-generation Chinese American's decision to join MRC does not necessarily mean that he or she has permanently moved away from the ethnic church.

Marilyn, a second-generation woman, grew up in Chinese churches all of her life. In college she also attended a Chinese church. When she came to New York City, however, she decided that she wanted to try something different. She was now very active in an MRC home fellowship group made up of Asian American women. She liked the fact that she was away from the ethnic church, yet in her experience MRC was essentially like an ethnic church with access to a lot more resources. She said that this stage of her church life, however, was temporary. One reason she chose MRC was that she wanted to learn from the church and then "take it back to the Chinese church." She ultimately planned to use what she gained from MRC to build up Chinese American churches.

As a large multiracial church, MRC also helps the second generation resolve the ever-present internal conflict: "I am Chinese, and I like to be with people like myself. However, as a Christian, I want to be open to non-Chinese. I also feel stifled by the imposing norms of the Chinese community." As a multiracial church with a significant number of Asian Americans, MRC allows its second-generation attendees to reach a happy medium of stepping away from ethnic exclusivity but still maintaining primary ties with fellow Chinese Americans.

Thus, MRC is many churches to many people. To some, it is a large church with a lot of resources to offer attendees and a place to meet new people from diverse and possibly more elite backgrounds. It has the added benefit of offering Asian Americans ethnic fellowship while being a non-ethnically based prominent church. On the one hand, a Chinese American leaving an ethnic church and attending MRC may seem to be taking a step toward assimilation into white, mainstream Christianity. On the other hand, because MRC draws a critical mass of Chinese and Asian Americans, it offers the experience of a de facto ethnic church that draws resources from a larger church.

EVANGELICAL CHRISTIANITY AND A NEW FAMILY MODEL

Although liberal mainline Protestant Christianity has had a historic association with Chinese Americans, evangelical Christianity now dominates Chinese Christianity in North America (Tseng 2002). Because evangelical Christianity is a very important influence on the worldviews and lifestyles of second-generation Chinese Americans in New York, boundaries between churches can become more fluid. Although the consumer culture facilitates this movement, movement occurs almost exclusively between evangelical Protestant ministries.

For example, many of the Chinese Americans who start out at MRC end up joining an ethnic church later on. Others who grew up attending an ethnic church in Chinatown end up at MRC or at Chinatown Church. Some even attended ethnic Korean churches as college students, recruited by their Korean American friends. What makes this large degree of movement possible is that all of the churches are evangelical Protestant. In some ways, the doctrine and worship style of a church is considered more important than its ethnic makeup. As a result, evangelical Protestant Christianity is an important dimension of its adherents' identities, shaping the way in which they relate to others, just as their Chinese ethnicity shapes their interactions.

One thing that I found both in the interviews (from the larger project) and in my own ethnography was that second-generation Chinese Americans did not communicate well with their parents. There were language barriers as well as generational barriers. Rather than bringing them closer to their families, however, their Christian identity took them further away. They adopted a worldview and family model that was quite different from those of their parents, and they began to see their parents and other relatives as people who needed to be "saved." They were introduced to a new family model that was different from those that they had observed growing up.

Although there has been a long history of Christianity among the Chinese in North America, most churchgoing Chinese Americans with whom I spoke did not come from Christian families. In fact, praying for the salvation of their relatives was a frequent prayer request in small group prayer sessions. The families of some individuals were not even aware that they were attending church. For example, one woman had been attending ABC Church for one year and had become a Christian without the knowledge of her parents, with whom she lived.

One week the topic of MRC's home fellowship group was the persecution of Christians. One female member shared with the group that she believed she had been persecuted for her Christian beliefs by her extended family. She recounted a trip to Taiwan with her family during which her uncle constantly mocked her for praying before her meals. He also jokingly asked her to make seemingly frivolous requests in her prayers, such as him winning the lottery or being able to stop smoking. This example illustrated just how much her Christian identity separated her from her family. Such separation, of course, is not limited to Chinese Americans and can be seen in the lives of many evangelical Christians.

Evangelical Christianity also changes the second generation's perceptions of their own families and co-ethnics. Instead of regarding Chinese cultural practices as a natural part of retaining their Chinese heritage, some see them as "un-Christian" acts of idolatry. Furthermore, their co-ethnics become the primary targets of their efforts at evangelism. For example, evangelism at Chinatown Church and ABC Church was a stated purpose and goal, but it tended to be thought of in terms of evangelizing to other ethnic Chinese—because most Chinese are not Christian and there are a whole lot of them.

Not surprisingly, most of the short-term mission projects that Chinatown Church and ABC Church support by making financial contributions or sending church members focus on converting the Chinese, whether in China or in other parts of the world. For example, the ABC Church pastor and a lay leader went on a one-week mission trip to Eastern Europe in March 2000 as part of a team (in conjunction with another Chinese church) to evangelize to the Chinese workers in that area of the world.

HOW HAVE CHINESE AMERICANS AFFECTED THEIR COMMUNITIES?

Evangelical Christianity often creates more distance between the second generation and their parents and extended families. However, it brings the second generation into close contact with each other, enabling them to develop networks within the Chinese American community and therefore have a closer connection to their ethnic heritage. This facilitates marriage with co-ethnics in a way that has been similarly described in the case of Korean Americans (Chai 1998).

At places like ABC Church and MRC, there is evidence that a pan-ethnic Asian identity is emerging based on a common identity as evangelical Christians. For example, the home fellowship group that I attended through MRC was about 90 percent Chinese and 10 percent Korean. There is also a fellowship for pastors of second-generation Korean and Chinese American ministries in New York City. In each case, a new identity is forged, based on both a common Asian identity and a Christian one.

While Chinese American members are changed by their church participation, formerly white churches are also changed by the presence of the Chinese and other Asian Americans in their congregations. First, MRC church leaders had learned that they had to grant Asian Americans the space to create an environment within MRC that felt comfortable to them. The most obvious example was the sanctioning of home fellowship groups that were exclusively Asian American. These served essentially as mini–Asian American churches that drew from the resources of MRC. MRC served as an "umbrella" church in the sense that it was many different types of churches to different people. Although some Chinese Americans got involved in the MRC programs and did have the multiracial church experience, others associated only with fellow Chinese or Asian Americans and essentially re-created an ethnic church environment while drawing from the resources offered by a larger church.

Another example is the monthly "Praise Night" event at MRC. One of the most common complaints that I heard from Asian Americans at MRC had to do with the music style. MRC usually recruited professional musicians to play classic hymns as well as jazzy contemporary arrangements. However, the Asian Americans were more used to contemporary praise choruses produced by groups such as Vineyard Christian Fellowship and Hosanna Integrity Music. A group of Asian Americans within the church decided to start a praise band within MRC that would play the type of music typically preferred by the majority of Asian Americans. Their inaugural Saturday night praise concert was attended by hundreds of people, most of whom were Asian American. Thus, the Asian American members of MRC, with the support of church leaders, created a space within the larger church in which they could enjoy more familiar styles of worship and also take on a more proactive role.

Most important, MRC leaders realized that they needed to hire an Asian American pastor. According to one lay leader, hiring an Asian American pastor was something the church leadership had not really considered until he had insisted that they interview Asian American pastoral candidates. Furthermore, MRC leaders have begun building formal ties to the Asian American Christian community. For example, MRC leaders have been meeting with ABC Church leaders in formulating a strategy to reach out and minister to second-generation Asian Americans. Both groups are following another evangelical Christian trend and realizing that Asian Americans are a large population with a lot of potential. Rudy Busto (1996) discusses the implications of this relatively recent development, noting that the Christian Asian American stereotype is comparable to the stereotype of Asian Americans doing well in school. Busto refers to Asian American Christians as potentially being considered "God's whiz kids."

A NASCENT PAN-ASIAN IDENTITY BASED ON EVANGELICAL CHRISTIANITY?

Although most of the Asian Americans I met at all three churches were quite proud of their ethnic heritage, there was an emerging sense of Asian American pan-ethnicity based on Christianity. Although this was occurring at all levels, it was most pronounced at the pastoral and congregational levels. At the individual level, there was a sense of symbolic unity, but ethnic divisions and allegiances still persisted.

At the pastoral level there is a network of evangelical Asian American pastors who are connected through seminary affiliation and common organizational membership. They meet regularly, pray, and share concerns. Although this religious solidarity is not necessarily limited to Asian Americans, there is a shared sense of purpose in ministering to the second generation of all ethnicities.

At the congregational level ABC Church has formed a sister church relationship with another Manhattan church, "Korean Church." Although Korean Church tries to be considered "multi-ethnic" or "multi-racial," it is basically a very conservative second-generation Korean American church. It is different from ABC Church in that it is very charismatic. (For example, practicing glossolalia, or speaking in tongues, during weekly fellowship meetings.) ABC Church's pastor, Joseph Chau, and the Korean Church's pastor got to know each other through a fellowship group for pastors in New York City. When they saw that they had similar goals for their churches, they established an informal relationship. The Korean Church pastor is occasionally called upon to fill in for Pastor Joseph in the pulpit and vice versa. In the summer of 1998, when Pastor Joseph went on sabbatical, the Korean Church pastor served as interim pastor at ABC Church. The two churches also exchange song leaders and worship bands on occasion, and they host joint activities. Although I did not observe much personal interaction between the members of the two churches, both churches seemed pleased with their relationship with another Asian American church.

At the individual level many second-generation Chinese Americans have attended a Korean church at one point, usually during college. Because there are more Korean churches than Chinese, college students often find that a local Korean church is more convenient for them to attend than a Chinese one. At any given Korean church, there are always a handful of Chinese Americans in the English ministry. Another reason Chinese Americans attend Korean churches is that they have Korean American friends whom they follow to church. Some of these Chinese Americans are already Christian; others have been converted through their Korean friends.

For example, Jane, a member of ABC Church (and former member of Chinatown Church) attended a Korean church while she was a college student at one of the SUNY campuses. All of her roommates were Korean, most of her friends were Korean, and she loved Korean food. She knew many short Korean phrases and once told me that she had regretted not learning more Korean from her friends. She never studied it but had hoped to pick it up through living with them. When I was driving her and two other people to the retreat in October 1999, she blurted out, "I just love Koreans and Korean food . . . I feel like I was born into the wrong race!" She added that she was very proud of her Chinese heritage and that she was glad to be Chinese. When one of the other passengers pointed out the contradiction, she continued to insist that she was proud to be Chinese. While I am sure that she would be open to dating Koreans, it is significant that she returned to an ethnic Chinese church after college (she had grown up attending a Chinese church as well). Perhaps she felt a symbolic or spiritual solidarity with Koreans; but when it comes down to it, the Korean church was more of a phase for her and the other Chinese Americans I met.

Another Chinese American who went through the phase of attending a Korean church in college was Lee, a medical student. I had known him quite well in Boston, because he had attended my Korean church all through college (with his Korean roommate). He was now engaged to a fellow Chinese American and did a lot of work at Chinatown Church. He had been a great resource for my research, especially since everyone seemed to open up to me a bit more when they saw that I knew him well. As expected, I saw less of the pan-Asian identity or desire at Chinatown Church. Not only was the church located in a thoroughly Chinese environment, but the stated mission of the church was to serve the ethnic Chinese. The food they ate together was always Chinese, many of them lived in Chinatown, and they were always coming into contact with first-generation Chinese immigrants, so they could not forget their roots. ABC Church members, on the other hand, were more distant from the Chinatown community as a church because of their Upper West Side location.

Conclusions

Although there were general differences among the second-generation Chinese Americans in my study, I found that there was also a great deal of fluidity in church boundaries. Members of one church would often visit others.

Sometimes people switched churches because of personal conflicts. Others went elsewhere in order to meet new people. All of this movement between churches was made easier by the fact that Manhattan is a relatively small area, with a high density of people and churches. Transportation to any of the three churches was relatively easy. Depending on their stage in life, their aspirations, and their current needs, the three different churches offered different benefits to attendees.

For second-generation Chinese Americans seeking a familylike atmosphere and a connection to the larger Chinese community, Chinatown Church had the most to offer. With its prime location in Chinatown and its historic role in the community, it offers deep roots to Chinatown and to generations of Chinese Americans. For those wanting to meet fellow second-generation Chinese Americans without the hassles of Chinatown, a social group can easily be found at ABC Church. MRC Church is ideal for Chinese Americans who seek ethnic fellowship but feel uneasy with ethnic exclusivity and the usually high demands of ethnic churches.

Although each of the three churches in my study had a core of dedicated members, they also had a group of more consumer-minded members who chose to attend certain churches at certain times for certain purposes. To be more palatable to the masses, evangelical Christianity has adopted a market-oriented strategy targeted at certain types of people. Thus, not only are individuals generally more consumer-minded today as they look for churches that suit their purposes at particular times, but evangelical churches treat them as consumers, offering spiritual products and opportunities with the hopes of eliciting a greater commitment to the Christian cause.

There were some general differences among the churches in my study. However, it was not necessarily true that certain people went to certain kinds of churches forever. They might have been more likely to prefer one type of church over another, but they also were likely to choose different types of churches at different times in their lives. Regardless of the type of church they attend, second-generation Chinese Americans continue to seek out other Chinese Americans or even other Asian Americans for fellowship.

NOTES

1. The names of the churches and individuals have been changed.
2. A discussion of my written survey appears in the following section.
3. More results from the Chinatown Church survey: Although there were slightly more women than men at Chinatown Church's two English worship services, the ratio was roughly fifty-fifty. An overwhelming 81 percent had lived in the New York City metropolitan area for ten or more years. Only 6 percent had

moved to the area in the past year. Sixty-eight percent were single. Of those who were married or had been married in the past, nearly all of their spouses were of Chinese ethnicity. Chinatown Church was a family-oriented church, and there were a number of people from various age groups. They ranged in age from under seventeen (17 percent) to over fifty-three (3 percent). The largest group (25 percent) was between the ages of twenty-three and twenty-seven. Nearly 18 percent were in their late twenties to early thirties, and 10 percent were in their mid to late thirties. Chinatown Church was the only church that 83 percent of the respondents attended in the New York City metropolitan area. For over 70 percent of the respondents, Chinatown Church was the first church they had ever attended regularly.

As for friendships, over 88 percent said that their closest friends were also Chinese. Eighty percent reported that between one and five of their closest friends (outside of their family) attended Chinatown Church. This is not surprising given that over half of them reported that a very important reason for attending the church was that their friends attended. Thus, most people chose Chinatown Church in part because of the ties they already had with members. Once there, they formed close friendships with other members of the church as well.

4. More results from the ABC Church survey: As at Chinatown Church, ABC's congregation was about half male and half female. ABC Church had less internal diversity, since it was largely a church of those in their twenties—47 percent were between the ages of twenty-three and twenty-seven. An additional 23 percent were between twenty-eight and thirty-two. It follows that about 29 percent were thinking of becoming a member of the church but did not currently consider themselves members. Seventy-six percent said that ABC Church was their main church, while 8 percent said that they were trying to decide which church to attend.

This group's friendships were slightly more diverse than those of Chinatown Church's members. Seventy-seven percent reported that most of their closest friends were Chinese. However, 31 percent said that none of their closest friends attended ABC Church.

5. More results of the MRC survey: There were slightly more Chinese American women than men at MRC, but the ratio was roughly half and half. Most of the Chinese Americans at MRC were in their midtwenties to late thirties. Seventy-four percent of the Chinese were single.

Seventy-six percent of the Chinese said that Multiracial Church was the only church they attended in New York. Four percent said that although Multiracial Church was their main church, they attended another New York church regularly. Six percent said that although they attended Multiracial Church regularly, they considered another New York church to be their main church. An additional 8 percent were trying to decide between churches. Of those who attended other New York churches, 82 percent were going to Chinese churches.

Of the Chinese who attended MRC, almost all had at least one of their five closest friends attending the church as well. Seventy percent said that most of their friends were Chinese. Twenty-six percent were raised with no religious tradition, 53 percent were raised as Protestants, 6 percent were raised as Catholics, and 9 percent were raised as Buddhists. Over 40 percent said that religion was not important in their families growing up. Only 13 percent lived with their parents. Forty-one percent had lived in the New York City metropolitan area for over ten years. Eighteen percent, however, had lived in the area only one year or less.

REFERENCES

Ambassadors for Christ. 2002. *Directory of Chinese Churches, Bible Study Groups, and Christian Organizations in North America.* Paradise, Pa.: Ambassadors for Christ.

Busto, Rudy. 1996. "The Gospel According to the Model Minority: Hazarding an Interpretation of Asian American Evangelical College Students." *Amerasia Journal* 22(1): 133–48.

Cayton, Horace R., and Anne O. Lively. 1955. *The Chinese in the United States and the Chinese Christian Churches.* New York: Bureau of Research and Survey, National Council of Churches of Christ in the U.S.A.

Chai, Karen. 1998. "Competing for the Second Generation: English-Language Ministry at a Korean Protestant Church." In *Gatherings in Diaspora: Religious Communities and the New Immigration,* edited by R. Stephen Warner and Judith G. Wittner. Philadelphia: Temple University Press.

Chen, Hsiang-Shui. 1992. *Chinatown No More: Taiwan Immigrants in Contemporary New York.* Ithaca, N.Y.: Cornell University Press.

Finke, Roger, and Rodney Stark. 1992. *The Churching of America 1776–1990: Winners and Losers in Our Religious Economy.* New Brunswick, N.J.: Rutgers University Press.

Hurh, Won Moo, and Kwang Chung Kim. 1990. "Religious Participation of Korean Immigrants in the United States." *Journal for the Scientific Study of Religion* 29(March): 19–34.

Iannaccone, Laurence R. 1994. "Why Strict Churches Are Strong." *American Journal of Sociology* 99(5): 1180–1211.

Sargeant, Kimon Howland. 2000. *Seeker Churches: Promoting Traditional Religion in a Nontraditional Way.* New Brunswick, N.J.: Rutgers University Press.

Tseng, Timothy. 2002. "Second-Generation Chinese Evangelical Use of the Bible in Identity Discourse in North America." Semeia (Society of Biblical Literature), edited by Tat-siong Benny Liew (90–91): 251–67. Available at Tseng's home page: http://hometown.aol.com/TSTseng/index.html (accessed June 23, 2004).

Yang, Fenggang. 1998. "Tenacious Unity in a Contentious Community: Cultural and Religious Dynamics in a Chinese Christian Church." In *Gatherings in Diaspora: Religious Communities and the New Immigration.* Philadelphia: Temple University Press.

———. 1999. *Chinese Christians in America: Conversion, Assimilation, and Adhesive Identities.* University Park: Pennsylvania State University Press.

Part IV

Identity

THE ISSUE of how race will affect the future of the new second generation has been a major cause of worry. Since the vast majority of immigrants arriving since 1965 have been nonwhite, many scholars have suggested that the persistence of racial discrimination in the United States may hurt their life chances if whites see them less as immigrants and more as nonwhite (Gans 1992; Waldinger and Perlmann 1998). Indeed, the theory of segmented assimilation explicitly argues that racial discrimination will lead young nonwhite immigrants to a reactive ethnic identification with native minorities and a rejection of mainstream American values (Portes and Zhou 1993; Zhou 1997; Portes and Rumbaut 2001). Concern about these questions has led many scholars to ask whether the children of nonwhite immigrants are in danger of becoming a new, permanent, excluded underclass, worse off than their immigrant parents, who at least find some solace and dignity in the racial and ethnic hierarchies of their homelands.

This worry accompanies a growing recognition that immigration has forever changed the racial landscape in the United States. Nearly one-third of all Americans told the census that they were black, Asian, or Latino in 2000 (Bean and Stevens 2003, 230). In 1970 blacks made up two-thirds of all nonwhites in the United States. By 2000 that figure had fallen to 40 percent. A center of immigration, New York has been even more transformed than the nation as a whole. In 2000 the city was only 35.7 percent non-Hispanic white, 25.9 percent non-Hispanic black, 27.2 percent Hispanic, and 10.2 percent Asian. Moreover, according to the Current Population Survey—which, unlike the census, asks about parents' place of birth—a majority of the city's residents are first- and second-generation immigrants. Only half of all whites are native-born people with two native-born parents, while 41 percent of all blacks, the most native-born group in the city, are immigrants or the child of an immigrant. With this demographic transformation of New York, not only are native whites with native parents no longer the majority of the city, but they are a small minority (19 percent) within a highly complex multicultural world. This new reality provides a fluid environment in which young people grow up to create an identity—an environment in which individual identity remains quite important but the old racial and ethnic categories have been breaking down. Indeed, even as social scientists recognized that this demographic revolution had made our racial categories outdated, they expected that the new immigrants and their children would place themselves within these outmoded categories.

The city is far more diverse than the second-generation groups we surveyed—West Indians, Colombians, Ecuadoreans and Peruvians, Chinese, Dominicans, Russians, and native whites, blacks, and Puerto Ricans—even though these include the main racial and ethnic groups in the city.[1] Although a high level of residential segregation between blacks and whites continues to frame who lives near whom in New York City, these groups, or at least combinations of these groups, have high levels of interaction with each other. And as these chapters show, young people in New York define themselves through their interaction with each other.

While our survey asked about ethnic and racial identity, language use, and ethnic practices and found widespread unwillingness to be confined to the simple racial dichotomy of white and black, the rich and informative ethnographic material presented here adds a great deal to our understanding of subjective identities. As table P4.1 shows, the vast majority of all three Latino groups and the Chinese refused to be categorized as either white or black. Instead, these groups mainly chose to be racially identified with their national origin—such as Chinese or Puerto Rican—although many of those from Spanish-speaking groups were willing to say they were "Hispanic," "Spanish," or "Latino." (Only a few Chinese labeled themselves "Asian.") And even among blacks and West Indians and among native whites and Russians, who were all certain that they were black or white, some laid claim to additional racial identities, including not only the other race but "West Indian" and "Native American."

Part 4 presents studies of two of our groups, Russians and West Indians, and two other important groups in the city, Korean Americans and Indo-Caribbeans. These four chapters examine how young people are identifying themselves in terms of their race, ethnicity, class, gender, and nationality. As all the authors make clear, the identities of these young people cannot be understood apart from the situations in which the groups find themselves. The diverse, vibrant, hybrid culture of New York creates a rich environment for developing youthful identities. Although these young people all decided "who they were" with some reference to the black-white divide, it was very much in the background. These young people found identity an endlessly fascinating and important aspect of their everyday lives. The same cannot be said for social scientists attempting to conceptualize the role of race. By and large, our young people experienced race as a fluid, situational category that was important to their lives at some times but irrelevant at others. To them, distinctions of class, gender, color, ethnicity, religion, cultural con-

TABLE P4.1 WILLINGNESS TO IDENTIFY AS WHITE AND/OR BLACK, BY GROUP

	Neither Black nor White	Any White	Any Black	Both Black and White	Total
Colombian, Ecuadorean, and Peruvian	73.7%	22.0%	4.4%	0.0%	410
Dominican	74.8	12.3	13.2	0.2	425
Puerto Rican	68.7	18.9	12.4	0.2	428
West Indian	0.0	1.2	100.0	—	404
Native black	0.0	0.2	100.0	—	422
Chinese	97.2	2.8	0.0	0.0	606
Russian	0.0	100.0	0.0	—	309
Native white	0.0	97.5	2.5	—	408

Source: Authors' compilation.

sumption, and lifestyle were equally important. While people talked a lot about boundaries and distinctions, they also talked about creative combinations and multiple and situational ties. Most recognized that they thought about race and ethnicity in ways that were far different from the ways of their immigrant parents. Yet they were often at odds with traditional American notions of race as well. They sometimes had a hard time defining exactly who they were in racial terms—the vocabulary in which they usually discuss such things simply fails to capture the complexity of their situations.

Sherri-Ann Butterfield and Natasha Warikoo examine two sides of English-speaking Caribbean immigration to New York. The situation of the "black" West Indian second generation studied by Butterfield is better known. These young people must cope with a society that often overlooks their ethnic identity as West Indian because of their black skin color (Kasinitz 1992, 2001; Foner 2001; Vickerman 1998; Waters 1999). Yet Guyana and Trinidad, two important sources of migration to New York, have also sent many immigrants of Indian descent to New York. (About 10 percent of all New Yorkers who were born in the West Indies or Guyana say they are partly or wholly of Indian ancestry.) Often confused with immigrants who have come directly from India and Pakistan, these Indo-Caribbean people are descended from indentured servants who arrived in the Caribbean in the midnineteenth century. They are racially Asian Indian, ethnically West Indian, and religiously Hindu, Muslim, Christian, or Sikh—traditions they mix and blend in ways that residents of the Indian subcontinent would find unrecognizable and even shocking.

Natasha Warikoo's study of second-generation Indo-Caribbeans shows just how out-of-date conventional American racial categories can be. Although these young people were generations removed from the South Asians brought to work on sugar plantations in Trinidad and Guyana, they identified as "Indians" but quickly faced questions of authenticity about their "Indian-ness" from Indian immigrants and others. To complicate matters further, they lived in some of the most diverse neighborhoods in Queens, the most diverse borough in the city and perhaps the most diverse county in the nation (Sanjek 1998). In this environment, it is both expected and celebrated that everyone will have an ethnic identity, but no ethno-racial group is dominant, and the boundaries between them are open to contestation and negotiation. Warikoo examines not only how these young people described their identities but what they liked, what they consumed, and who was included in their social networks. For example, the music they listened to expressed hybridity and dynamism by borrowing from many different traditions, both from the multiethnic societies of the Caribbean in which their parents grew up and from the Indian, African American, and Caribbean influences operating in New York. The ease with which they described their complex social environment is striking. One boy said that his friends were "Puerto Rican, Dominican, Jamaican, Indian, Arabic, Chinese, Vietnamese, and European." Another girl with a Muslim mother who had children by three different men—a Christian, a Hindu, and a Sikh—described her background in these words: "I go to Catholic school. . . . My father is Hindu, half my family is Muslim, I've been to Hindu temples, I've been to Sikh gurdwaras, I've been to the mosque. . . . I fasted during Ramadan, I fasted during the Hindu holy month, I fasted the Christian month. I'm faced with so many different religions and races. It's cool . . . I like it like that."

Butterfield studies second-generation West Indians of African descent. Although they shared some ethnic characteristics and ties with the Indo-Caribbeans studied by Warikoo, race was a more central aspect of their identities. As one of Butterfield's respondents put it: "I knew that my parents weren't American because they were not from here, but I was born here and still feel like I didn't belong." One key way in which the experience of the Afro-Caribbeans differs from that of the Indo-Caribbeans is the high degree of residential segregation for blacks. Butterfield reports that her respondents deeply valued the multicultural diversity of New York City that they experienced in the subway, the workplace, and the parks and gathering places of the city. Yet in their own neighborhoods they lived mainly with other West Indians and some African Americans. They thus lived in an Afro–West Indian world. Butterfield also finds that West Indian men felt racial exclusion more strongly than did West Indian women and thus tended to identify more strongly with African Americans.

Even within the strong confines of American racial divisions, Butterfield finds that Afro-Caribbean racial and ethnic identities are highly flexible and situational. Although Afro-Caribbeans sometimes distanced themselves from African Americans, as other researchers have found, she also finds much distancing based on class rather than ethnicity. Middle-class West Indians did not want to be identified with poor and working-class West Indians or African Americans. They struggled to maintain a middle-class identity in the face of persistent negative stereotyping of blacks by other New Yorkers. Thus, Butterfield turns our attention to the importance of class and gender in shaping how ethnicity and race are experienced and embraced in the second generation.

Although ongoing racial discrimination causes many to worry about the fate of the second generation, Sara Lee explores the negative effects of a different kind of stereotype—the "model minority" view of second-generation Asians. Like Butterfield, Karen Chai Kim, and Louie, Lee contrasts the experiences of middle- and working-class members of the second generation.[2] Nearly twenty years ago, Robert Bach (1986) called for greater attention to class in the study of immigration. With so much attention given to ethnicity, few have heeded his plea, and class remains surprisingly understudied. Most previous writing on Korean Americans has focused on the better-off members of the community: their middle-class origins, the entrepreneurial successes of the first generation, and the remarkable educational and occupational achievements of the second generation (see, for example, Kim 1981; Bonacich and Light 1988; Min 1996; Min and Kim 2002; Dae Young Kim, this volume). Both scholars and the Korean Americans themselves maintain a popular image of the group as highly successful. Lee introduces a new dimension by describing how this definition leaves less successful Koreans with little room to express their ethnicity. If economic success is part of being Korean American, then how can those who are less successful be authentically ethnic? In Lee's study, working-class Koreans downplayed their ethnicity as much as possible, refrained from co-ethnic interaction, and often rejected ethnic identity altogether. In a remarkable inversion of a straight-line assimilation story, Lee describes a respondent whose family decided to go to an American rather than a Korean church because they were embarrassed that their child did not get into an Ivy League college!

Aviva Zeltzer-Zubida examines another highly successful group: children of Russian Jews. These respondents have the advantage of being "white" and would thus seem to face few impediments to acceptance into American society and have many reasons to assimilate quickly. They did indeed report a great deal of acceptance and assimilation. Yet, as Zeltzer-Zubida reports, they also experienced a good deal of ambivalence about their ethnic and religious identity. Although her respondents ultimately did not feel that being a Russian Jew was at odds with becoming American, they reported confusion and ambivalence about being Russian and Jewish and about what kind of American they were becoming. Their parents had been officially labeled as Jews in the former Soviet Union and faced persecution as a result. In Russian society, "Jewish" was perceived as a racial or "national" identity as much as a religious one. Many of their parents were strongly identified as Jewish while not being at all religious. As one of Zeltzer-Zubida's respondents put it, "We knew we were different because we *looked* different" (emphasis added). In the United States, by contrast, these young people were not perceived as looking different from the white majority, and being "Jewish" was an optional identity defined in large part by the practice of religion.

Zeltzer-Zubida's respondents in some ways resemble the Indo-Caribbean youth described by Warikoo. They moved easily among friends of many different backgrounds and enjoyed the diversity of New York, which defined America for them. As one respondent put it, "I would definitely identify myself as an American New Yorker. . . . I can have incredible Ethiopian food for lunch and then have a wonderful Korean dinner. And that's what being an American is: [having] all the liberties to express how you feel about that, as you wish." Yet they also faced the question, as did the Indo-Caribbeans and working-class Koreans in our study, of whether their identity was authentic. When Russian Jews claimed a Jewish identity even though they had only a tenuous knowledge of and connection to the religion, or when they claimed a Russian identity even though their families had been persecuted in the former Soviet Union for being Jewish and not "really" Russian, they too stood on uncertain ground.[3]

Taken together, these chapters suggest that young people are coming of age in a community where diversity is truly celebrated, where individuals have a great deal of latitude in creating their own identities, and where being ethnic can be taken for granted as part of being an American New Yorker.

Notes

1. As noted earlier, Dae Young Kim surveyed Koreans using a similar instrument but a different sampling technique (see Dae Young Kim, this volume).

2. For another look at class differences among second-generation Asian Americans, see Lew (2003; forthcoming).

3. For a marvelous fictional account of how some of these identity dilemmas play out in the life of one 1.5-generation Russian-Jewish New Yorker, see Shteyngart (2002).

References

Bach, Robert L. 1986. "Immigration: Issues of Ethnicity, Class, and Public Policy in the United States." *Annals, AAPSS* 485(May): 139–52.

Bean, Frank, and Gillian Stevens. 2003. *America's Newcomers and the Dynamics of Diversity*. New York: Russell Sage Foundation.

Bonacich, Edna, and Ivan Light. 1988. *Immigrant Entrepreneurs: Koreans in Los Angeles: 1965–1982*. Berkeley: University of California Press.

Foner, Nancy, ed. 2001. *Islands in the City: West Indian Migration to New York*. Berkeley: University of California Press.

Gans, Herbert. 1992. "Second-Generation Decline: Scenarios for the Economic and Ethnic Futures of the Post-1965 American Immigrants." *Ethnic and Racial Studies* 15(2): 173–93.

Kasinitz, Philip. 1992. *Caribbean New York: Black Immigrants and the Politics of Race*. Ithaca, N.Y.: Cornell University Press.

———. 2001. "Invisible No More? West Indian Americans in the Social Scientific Imagination." In *Islands in the City: West Indian Migration to New York*, edited by Nancy Foner. Berkeley: University of California Press.

Kim, Illsoo. 1981. *The New Urban Immigrants*. Princeton, N.J.: Princeton University Press.

Lew, Jamie. 2003. "Korean American High School Dropouts: A Case Study of Their Experiences and Negotiations of Schooling, Family, and Communities." In *Invisible Children in the Society and Its Schools*, 2nd ed., edited by Sue Books. Mahwah, N.J.: Lawrence Erlbaum.

———. Forthcoming. *Achievement Gap Among Asian American Youths: Significance of Social Class, Social Capital, and School Context—A Case of Korean Americans in Urban Schools*. New York: Teachers College Press.

Min, Pyong Gap. 1996. *Caught in the Middle: Korean Merchants in America's Multiethnic Cities*. Berkeley: University of California Press.

Min, Pyong Gap, and Rose Kim. 2002. "Formation of Ethnic and Racial Identities: Narratives by an Asian American Professional." In *Second Generation: Ethnic Identity Among Asian Americans*, edited by Pyong Gap Min. Walnut Creek, Calif.: Altamira.

Portes, Alejandro, and Rubén Rumbaut. 2001. *Legacies: The Story of the New Second Generation*. Berkeley: University of California Press.

Portes, Alejandro, and Min Zhou. 1993. "The New Second Generation: Segmented Assimilation and Its Variants." *Annals of the American Academy of Political and Social Science* 530: 74–97.

Sanjek, Roger. 1998. *The Future of Us All: Race and Neighborhood Politics in New York City*. Ithaca, N.Y.: Cornell University Press.

Shteyngart, Gary. 2002. *The Russian Debutante's Handbook*. New York: Riverhead.

Vickerman, Milton. 1998. *Cross Currents: West Indians, Immigrants, and Race*. New York: Oxford University Press.

Waldinger, Roger, and Joel Perlmann. 1998. "Second Generations: Past, Present, Future." *Journal of Ethnic and Migration Studies* 24(1): 5–24.

Waters, Mary C. 1999. *Black Identities: West Indian Dreams and American Realities*. New York: Russell Sage Foundation.

Zhou, Min. 1997. "Growing Up American: The Challenge Confronting Immigrant Children and Children of Immigrants." *Annual Review of Sociology* 23: 69–95.

CHAPTER 10

"WE'RE JUST BLACK": THE RACIAL AND ETHNIC IDENTITIES OF SECOND-GENERATION WEST INDIANS IN NEW YORK*

SHERRI-ANN P. BUTTERFIELD

People talk to each other about "home" in thick island dialects. Grocery stores line the block advertising products such as coconuts, plantains, mangoes, and hot pepper sauce, and retail stores are filled with brightly colored flags and bundles of island newspapers. Cars slowly meander down the street blasting the latest reggae, calypso, or soca music, with the driver making frequent stops to talk with family and friends who are on foot. All the while, smells of curry spices, jerk seasoning, and beef patties from restaurants and bakeries permeate the air. This is not a Caribbean island. This is central Brooklyn.

NEW YORK has been transformed by West Indian immigration. This scene in Caribbean Brooklyn also typifies West Indian neighborhoods throughout metropolitan New York. The rising predominance of West Indian communities in New York is a direct result of the rapid increase of black Caribbean immigrants over the last few decades. The 1999 Current Population Survey puts their numbers at roughly 600,000, which constitutes almost one-third of New York's black population. West Indian immigrants and their children now outnumber African Americans in New York—54 percent of the blacks in the city in the year 2000 were West Indian. In fact, many residents of these neighborhoods argue that in many ways New York City is more Caribbean than the Caribbean itself.

*All names of individuals reported throughout the chapter are pseudonyms.

Other chapters in this volume wonderfully demonstrate the ways in which various immigrant groups and their children have been transforming New York as they settle in the city and form communities there. This chapter explores how West Indians are also changing—and being changed by—the system of race and ethnic relations in New York City specifically, and in the United States more generally.

The women and men discussed in this chapter are the children of West Indian immigrants and have been raised (almost) entirely in the boroughs of New York City. Although they have significantly diverse personal experiences, they all share similar stories about growing up as second-generation West Indians and demonstrate that these experiences were (and continue to be) crucial to their identity development. This chapter argues that for these second-generation immigrants, having a racial *and* an ethnic identity is a salient part of their lives. It is not an either-or proposition; being black and being West Indian are identities that coexist and greatly inform how the adult second generation conceive of race and ethnicity for themselves and for other racial and ethnic groups in American society.

The main objective of this research is to examine the intricate nature for West Indians of having a racial *and* an ethnic identity.[1] I uncover the mechanisms that shape ethnic identity formation for second-generation West Indians while emphasizing the complexity of these identities and the contexts and circumstances that produce them. In this chapter, I ask: Do the existing categories of identity in extant literature fully capture the experience of second-generation West Indian immigrants in New York City? Or is ethnic identity construction unique and more complex, especially where boundaries are both flexible and open for contestation? The former model assumes that second-generation individuals adopt a primary identity that reflects either their parents' culture or the ethnic enclave, on the one hand, or a hyphenated American one that resembles an assimilated identity, on the other. In contrast, the latter model assumes that identity is more fluid in nature and that structures of identity choice are themselves changing, especially in a place like New York City.

Significantly affected by the shifting demographics of New York City's immigrant communities, residential segregation and integration, and the presence of a large African American population, second-generation West Indians find their identity in constant flux. However, their identity choices are grounded in a race and ethnic continuum rather than a dichotomy. In this vein, second-generation West Indians are expanding previous conceptions of "blackness" to include multiple ethnic groups, and New York City, I argue, provides a context in which racial and ethnic constructions are problematized on a daily, lived basis. For example, in a space where it is as common to hear reggae and Latin music as it is to hear rap and pop music, can we continue to assert that there is one "black" culture? The second-generation West Indians in this research not only illuminate the process of identity construction in particular contexts but demonstrate the critical role of the urban landscape.

To provide the context for this research, the chapter begins with a brief overview of previous work on second-generation West Indian immigrants. The discussion then turns to the importance of New York City as a site of identity development and the contribution of the physical landscape to both racial and ethnic segregation and integration. The chapter then identifies the ways in which educational institutions, class, and gender shape the contexts in which second-generation West Indians emphasize their ethnicity. I conclude with some tentative predictions about the future of racial and ethnic categories and their significance.

RESEARCH FRAMEWORK

Early researchers of the West Indian experience theorized that second-generation West Indians would adopt an African American identity, thereby rejecting their parents' ethnicity. This strong racial identification was predicted to be a result of the interaction between West Indian children and African American children in school and in different neighborhoods (Laguerre 1984; Stafford 1987; Vickerman 1994, 1999; Woldemikael 1985, 1989).

Mary Waters (1994, 1996, 1999) further explores this question in her study of second-generation West Indian youths in New York. She finds that the identity choices of second-generation West Indians are significantly affected by their race, gender, and class status. Waters outlines three paths of identity development for West Indians: identifying as African Americans, identifying as ethnic (or hyphenated) Americans, and adopting or keeping an immigrant identity. West Indians who identify as African American tend to be from disadvantaged economic backgrounds, while middle-class youths are more likely to identify as West Indian Americans. Interestingly, those who identify ethnically use their ethnicity as a mechanism for distancing themselves from the negative stereotypes of, and discriminatory practices toward, blacks in American society. Waters also finds that gender differences affect the meanings that boys and girls place on their racial and ethnic identities, with boys feeling more racial solidarity with African Americans and girls feeling less independent than their male counterparts, owing to parental control.

What is missing from this research is an explicit discussion of the importance of context in identity development.[2] Since the majority of second-generation West Indians reside in areas where there is a critical mass of West

Indian immigrants (both first- and second-generation), do three categories of racial-ethnic identity still hold for this population? In a context where adult second-generation West Indians are just as likely to interact with other West Indians as they are with African Americans, what does this mean for their identity construction along racial and ethnic lines? Additionally, previous research has presumed that the impact on identity would be unidirectional, with African Americans influencing West Indians. However, given the changing demographics and culture of New York City, can it not be argued that identity development is bidirectional, simultaneously affecting West Indians and African Americans?

DESIGN AND METHOD OF THE STUDY

This chapter is based on an analysis of semistructured, open-ended interviews with sixty-five second-generation West Indians between the ages of twenty and thirty-two. I chose the upper limit of age thirty-two because this was as old as children born of post-1965 immigrants could be in 1998. I chose the lower age limit in order to tap the experience of adults who had some work experience.[3] The men and women in this age bracket had come into full adulthood and were experiencing socioeconomic advantages and disadvantages, since they were now primarily responsible for their own lives. In addition, this is the age when young people form their own families. I defined "West Indian" to include all people not of Asian ancestry descended from those born in the Anglophone Caribbean: those from the thirteen CARICOM member nations, the mainland countries of Guyana and Belize, and the Caribbean British colonies, and English-speaking Panamanians.[4] I defined "second-generation West Indians" as those for whom at least one parent was born in the West Indies.[5]

I used the snowball technique to recruit the sample. In selecting respondents for interviewing, however, I was guided by theoretical sampling (Strauss 1987): I selected respondents based on some basic demographics—age, gender, education level, socioeconomic status—with my sampling strategy shifting as I tried to ensure that no relevant categories were missed.[6]

The interview schedule included questions about racial identification and self-identification; the composition and structure of social networks; and the incorporation of ethnicity into household life and the negotiation of ethnic boundaries. The interviews averaged two hours and fifteen minutes in length: the longest interview lasted five hours and the shortest was one hour.

In addition to the in-depth interviews, I also conducted ethnographies at two different sites from December 1998 until May 1999. After observing the goings-on in several neighborhoods in Brooklyn and Queens, I selected two service industry stores as my sites of study: a farmers' market in central Brooklyn and a unisex hair salon in southeast Queens.[7] In both cases I used a small business in the neighborhood as a way of meeting and talking to people. In addition, these locations were home to the majority of the West Indian community in New York City (Foner 1979, 1985, 1987, 2001; Kasinitz 1992; Vickerman 1994, 1999; Waters 1994, 1999). By spending approximately three days a week at each site, I was able to become familiar not only with the people frequenting the businesses at both sites but also with the people who simply hung out in both neighborhoods.

The Brooklyn store, Plantain Market, is located on the corner of two major streets.[8] It is patronized primarily by West Indians; during the course of my research, I did not observe any non-West Indian patrons, even though the store is owned by Korean grocers.[9] The store lies next to a West Indian bakery, so many people shopped at the store while they were waiting for their orders from the bakery.[10] Plantain Market is a rather large corner store and carries specialty foods from the Caribbean that are used in traditional dishes, as well as fruits and vegetables that can be found at regular supermarkets. Plantain Market was often full of customers, regardless of the time of day or week.

The Queens store, Hairstyling, is located on a major street, situated between a drugstore and a dine-in/take-out restaurant. Although it is a unisex hair salon, the majority of the clients are women. Hairstyling is relatively small, by salon standards, but has a rather large clientele.[11] Most clients have a standing appointment and frequent the salon every week to two weeks. Many people have formed and sustained friendships based on seeing each other every week for several hours at a time. As with Plantain Market, Hairstyling's clientele is predominantly West Indian.[12] However, the clientele often interacts with the ethnically mixed clientele from the drugstore and the restaurant.[13]

Although both sites cater to a predominantly West Indian clientele, the neighborhoods differ in various ways; the Brooklyn neighborhood has a predominance of West Indians living in the area, and the Queens area is home to a more ethnically diverse population.[14] The working-class Brooklyn neighborhood contains many small storefronts and high-rise apartment complexes next to each other, with a major subway station located nearby. The working-to middle-class Queens area is almost the direct opposite of the Brooklyn location: a few stores are located on the main streets, but the area mainly consists of private homes, and only a bus line runs down the main street.

New York City: Identity and the Concrete Jungle

The city of New York presents a unique context for second-generation West Indians compared to other major immigrant cities such as Miami and Los

Angeles. New York draws not only a disproportionately large share of all recently arrived immigrants but also a large percentage of the nation's West Indian immigrants as well. For example, among all West Indians arriving as long ago as the 1980s, 45 percent of all Jamaican immigrants lived in New York, as did 49 percent of all Trinidadians, 61 percent of all Barbadians, and 70 percent of all Guyanese (Salvo and Ortiz 1992). The physical proximity of racial and ethnic groups in the five boroughs of New York City lends itself to a commingling of individuals from a variety of backgrounds. Many of the West Indians with whom I spoke mentioned the physical structure of New York City as being conducive to their contact with co-ethnics and with other groups, and that contact, in turn, affected the way they saw themselves in the larger New York City social world (see also Butterfield and Trillo 1999; Butterfield 2001). The second generation often cited the easy access provided by the city's twenty-four-hour transportation system (trains and buses) to cultural activities, including parades, parks, concerts, dance clubs, restaurants, and neighborhoods in general. For example, Shauna stated that after living in New York for thirty years, she decided to take advantage of some of its annual events:

> Last summer I went to every major ethnic parade. I didn't care that I didn't belong to most of the groups that were represented, but the fact was that I could go and be some other ethnicity for a day. And why not? The trains and buses will take you anywhere you want to go. Let me see . . . I did the Puerto Rican Day Parade on Fifth . . . I went to the St. Patty's one too on Fifth, the Dominican parade in the Heights, some Asian celebration in Flushing . . . I sorta accidentally came across that one . . . the African American festival in Harlem, a Russian something—not sure what—in Brighton Beach, and of course the West Indian Day Parade on Eastern Parkway. Where else are you going to be able to do all that but in New York?

Echoing a similar sentiment, patrons at both Plantain Market and Hairstyling often said that they could not envision themselves living anywhere except in New York.[15] Immigrants appreciated New York not only because of the ease of access to a variety of activities but also because they could interact with those they deemed "like-minded" individuals. No one was able to articulate what "like-minded" meant, but most seemed to assume that the majority of West Indians were "like-minded."

When the conversations became borough-specific, there were notable differences in the way respondents and patrons spoke of their experiences and identities. For the West Indians who resided in Brooklyn, the main influence on their identity development was the presence of other West Indians in the neighborhood. Stacy, a twenty-seven-year-old Barbadian high school teacher, asked:

> What am I? . . . West Indian of course . . . Trinidadian to be exact. Isn't everyone who lives around here [Flatbush] from the Caribbean? I mean, every island is here . . . big or small. I met some guy at the train station the other day from Anguilla. He said that his block was filled with people from there. Now, I have heard of Anguilla . . . couldn't tell you exactly where in the Caribbean it is . . . but I know that it's small as hell. So how do we have a whole block of people from there? Only in Brooklyn. Hell, I think that we've even managed to run the African Americans out of here, cuz you rarely see them around here these days . . . unless we've converted them [*laughs*].

Nadine, a thirty-one-year-old Guyanese computer programmer, had this to say:

> Look 'ere, missus, I am Guyanese and will be to the day I die. Even though me grow up in America, I know what I am. New York has too many Guyanese people for me to try to be anything else, my family would kill me. You know how many of dem live right here on this block? My God, you can't get away from them . . . unless you leave Brooklyn.

Brooklyn also presents an interesting case in that it is such an insular community that West Indians could function entirely in a West Indian world (and some do)—working with other West Indians, shopping at West Indians stores, frequenting West Indian social events. Living in the high-rise apartment complexes that typify central Brooklyn facilitates a larger understanding of the West Indies in general. Although many West Indians in Brooklyn socialize with their fellow countrymen, the majority of them are at least exposed to the cultural dialects, traditions, and foods of different West Indian countries. Pearl, a thirty-three-year-old Jamaican nurse, observed that

> for years my parents would talk about why they didn't like Trinidadians, but they never said why. Now our neighbors are Trinis, and they make my mother try to remember why she did not like them in the first place. And of course she can't remember, so now they just argue back and forth about why the Federation of West Indian Countries never happened back in the sixties. . . . They are cool with each other, sorta. But I hang out with the neighbors' children all the time. We don't give a damn about the federation cuz we weren't alive then, and we couldn't care less anyway. . . . We like the food and music.

The second generation from Queens strongly identified with their ethnic identity; however, because the neighborhood composition in Queens is more ethnically diverse, respondents there often had social networks that extended beyond the West Indian community. Denise, a twenty-two-year-old Jamaican college student, said

> Me and my friends are like a tiny United Nations up in here . . . well, without the white people anyway. I think every major Caribbean country is represented, and I mean all parts, English-speaking, Spanish, and French. Everybody thinks their country is better than everybody else's, but it's all love. We teach each other about where we're from, and then we're brand-new. I know some Spanish, and they know some patois. Queens is good for that.

Interestingly, several of the Queens respondents and patrons from Hairstyling mentioned a specific store in Queens that they felt best reflected the diversity of ethnicities in Queens. Key Foods is a New York supermarket chain. However, the Key Foods on Jamaica Avenue in Queens Village has a unique feature: it displays flags from various Caribbean, Central American, and South American countries on top of the building.[16] Donovan, a twenty-five-year-old Jamaican disc jockey, commented: "That shows you the different kinds of people that live around here, if everybody got their own flag. In fact, they got a bunch of flags from white countries too."

Overall, for those who resided in concentrated West Indian neighborhoods, the similarity in background among the second generation's neighborhood peer group fostered an intense West Indian identity, while residence in more ethnically heterogeneous areas seemed to lead to a pan-Caribbean identity.

In addition to the neighborhood contexts and interactions, second-generation West Indians' conceptions of self were also significantly affected by their experiences in school. As evidenced in the next section, the second generation, who came from homes where education was heavily stressed, found themselves subject to the pressures of being "ethnic" children (and adults) in an extremely racialized social environment.

Being "Raced" in School

Varied experiences in the New York City educational institutions they attended greatly influenced the process of identity development for second-generation West Indians. The respondents thought that their varied experiences in school contributed to their shifting identities throughout their childhood. School became a source of great stress and emotional upheaval for the second generation in that it was school where they first learned what their "blackness" meant. Steve, a twenty-nine-year-old Trinidadian, recalled

> being in the first grade and the teacher not calling on me for the answer even though I was the only one with my hand up. I know that she saw me. . . . I mean, how could she have missed me, there weren't that many other black kids in the class. So after a while I stopped trying to answer any of the teacher's questions. . . . That would have been all right, but she had the nerve to tell my parents that I didn't participate in class at a parents-teachers meeting. I was so mad!

Even in the first grade, it was apparent to Steve that his teacher was treating him differently for some reason that had nothing to do with his abilities. Not alone in his experiences with school personnel with questionable behaviors, many other respondents spoke of their mistreatment at the hands of school staff.[17] In fact, as happens with Spanish-speaking immigrant children, teachers often held students back a grade because they felt they were uneducated, owing to their West Indian accents.

When the second-generation children complained about their experiences to their parents, they were often met with disbelief that the school and school personnel would not act in the best interest of the child. The immigrant parents assumed that the school knew what measures were most appropriate to take with their child. Whereas well-educated immigrant parents were likely to communicate with the school about their displeasure, many of the skilled yet undereducated immigrants were self-conscious about not having enough training to know that their children were being deprived of an equal education. A heated discussion at Hairstyling between Diana and Dina, a first- and second-generation West Indian mother and daughter, clearly outlined the heart of the problem:

> Oprah is on the television talking about the importance of parents being involved in their children's education. Dina and her friend Carolyn are at opposite ends of the shop and begin complaining that their parents weren't involved enough. Their conversation turns to how racist schools were when they were growing up and how their parents did not believe them for some inexplicable reason. Dina's mother, Diana, starts shouting from the sink (as she is getting her hair washed), why would they think that teachers would be racist? She states that the parents had raised them to be good kids and figured the only way that they would not be getting good grades or being mistreated would be due to their own behavioral patterns. Diana gets agreement from other first-generationers who argue racism is the last thing they expected. Dina accuses her mother and the other first-generation women of not being willing to even consider

racism as a possibility because they assumed that teachers would know that West Indians were not like those "other" blacks. Dina asserts that she doesn't blame them anymore because she now realizes that due to their immigration status, the first generation were "learning" race right along with their children . . . which often created its own set of issues. (field notes, January 16, 1999)

Classmates also had an impact on much of this "race and ethnicity learning" that the second generation underwent. Elementary school was the place where many of the respondents realized that they "spoke and dressed funny." One respondent, Donna, a thirty-year-old Guyanese banker, stated: "I was teased so badly about my accent that I remember trying to lose it just so I could fit in with the African American kids. I can still hear them calling me 'the little boat girl.'"

The transition from elementary school to high school proved to be a particularly trying time for the second generation. The process of choosing a high school often reflected their parents' fears about the increasing violence and lower educational standards in their neighborhood schools.[18] Through the utilization of West Indian ethnic networks, which included a significant number of teachers, many parents of my respondents (who were disproportionately middle-class) became knowledgeable about the "better" schools that their children could attend rather than the neighborhood schools that were turning into dangerous environments. The majority of the respondents I spoke with were sent to Catholic schools in their neighborhoods; the specialized high schools, such as Stuyvesant High School, Bronx High School of Science, and Brooklyn Technical High School; magnet schools; or "good" neighborhood schools.[19]

The high schools, like the elementary schools, forced the second-generation West Indians to situate their "racial and ethnic" selves within the broader context of school personnel and their peer groups. For the most part, the Catholic schools had predominantly white student bodies, and the specialized and magnet high schools were much more racially integrated, with a high percentage of Asian students. The local neighborhood schools tended to be filled with black students. However, regardless of school, respondents reported that the transition from elementary school to junior high and then high school was the most traumatic to their sense of self. Winston, a thirty-two-year-old Jamaican truck driver and part-time college student, recollected:

Well, when I was younger, I don't really . . . remember thinking about my parents being from Jamaica. We sort of just lived it. There were things that me and my brother could not do, and neither could any of the other West Indian kids in the neighborhood. All of us had strict parents, and that's the way it was. . . . It was not until I went to high school that I realized that I was different. The African American kids thought that I knew about grits, and the teachers thought that . . . I knew all about black history, so I should be able to tell the white kids about it. . . . I hated [it] . . . I wanted to go around with a sign saying, "I'm Jamaican, I'm not from this country," even though I was born here and had been here my entire life. I was just different.

Another respondent, Marie, talked of a time in high school when she was asked to talk about her family's migration from the South to the North for Black History Month in her high school AP history class. There were only three black students in the class, a Jamaican, one Haitian, and one Panamanian, and the teacher could not believe that none of them were familiar with what she called "the black experience."

What the hell is the "black experience"? I am thirty years old, and I still don't know what that is, so why was I supposed to know when I was fifteen? I remember that day in class so clearly because I was pissed. Here this teacher had her doctorate . . . I guess I should have wondered why someone with a Ph.D. would work in a high school, but who cared at the time . . . anyway, and she's wanting me to say what? Even if there had been an African American in the class, I wonder what they would have said. . . . But this teacher was so clearly annoyed with me that I couldn't tell the story she wanted . . . whatever that was.

Problems with being understood by teachers and classmates pressured many West Indians to want to conform to what they thought of as being a "black American." However, many of them met with stark resistance from their parents. First-generation West Indians could not understand why their children would want to deny their ethnicity. They tried to explain to their children the importance of being "different from the Americans" and being proud of where they came from.[20] The second generation's efforts to convince their parents that they were not actually better than their peers were often met with frustration and anger. Many of the first generation classified African Americans as lazy, unwilling to work, and not placing enough importance on education. Many respondents reported that they often did not respond to their parents' comments because their parents would not listen, and at some level they just believed their parents. However, they still wanted to fit in with the people at school, so they just kept quiet. The struggle to negotiate their identities at home and at school often became an unbearable burden to the second generation. One respondent stated that she spent high school "being black by day and being West Indian by night." In fact, many second-generation West Indians engaged in code switching: they utilized their accents with their parents and spoke American English with their peers.

As a result of these experiences, including their treatment by school personnel, many second-generationers began differentiating between being black and being African American when they were in high school. Jeffrey, a twenty-two-year-old Barbadian college student and a salesperson at a major retail store, said:

> In high school me and my friends were all black. . . . We were treated like crap by the teachers together, followed around the corner store together, and chased by the cops a few times together. Even if we didn't think we were black, those things told us we were. But we still wasn't all the same . . . some guys were from down South, some from places where they speak Spanish, and the rest of us was from the West Indies. So we may all have been black, but everybody had their own thing . . . culture . . . you know? It was all good, though.

For those students who attended predominantly black elementary and high schools, their ethnic identity was not as pressing an issue as it was for those who attended predominantly white schools, yet it brought about a different kind of struggle. John, a thirty-one-year-old Jamaican employed as a financial aid advisor at a CUNY school, explained:

> With all the black kids at my high school, our fights weren't about why all the black people were sitting together during lunch. Instead, our fights were about which ethnic group was better. Everybody hung out with their own people . . . the Jamaicans together, the Trinis, the Haitians, and the African Americans. Those were the major groups, and if you didn't fit into one of those, then you had to choose. It was crazy, everybody would make fun of everybody else, and to this day I can't tell you why or what we thought we were doing. People would dis each other's clothes, how they spoke, how they dressed, etc. Basically what all high school kids do, only we did it based on what part of the West Indies or America you was from. The only thing that would get all the groups together was if someone was fighting a Haitian. . . . No one liked the Haitians.[21]

It is clear that the identity struggles that second-generation West Indians experienced during their teenage years largely depended on what school they attended and on their peer group. The presence of other West Indians who identified as such moved the situation away from one of race toward one of ethnicity.

In dramatic ways, college functioned as a catalyst for identity formation

and transformation among the second generation. For those who attended
college, it brought second-generation West Indians into contact with other
second-generationers who represented countries from all over the world.
These interactions not only created a better understanding of various ethnicities but validated the second generation's feeling of living between two
worlds—the culture of their parents' home country and U.S. culture. Many
noted that the City University of New York (CUNY) educational system was
largely responsible for the commingling of cultures. Garnett, a twenty-four-
year-old Trinidadian part-time college student and full-time social worker,
recalled:

> I stepped onto Brooklyn College's campus and thought that I was in line
> at the international terminal at JFK. Mad [a lot of] people was there
> from every country I could think of. But it was cool because most of us
> were immigrants or [our] parents were immigrants. In high school I was
> a little lost, but BC [Brooklyn College] was like Mecca. Other people
> who could understand what it was like to not fit in with any one group?
> Come on, man, you couldn't have asked for anything better than that.

The feeling of not completely belonging in either an immigrant world or
an American world was common among other second-generation immigrants. Through exposure to other ethnicities, however, as well as a critical
mass of other West Indians, the second generation would find the first opportunity to celebrate the dual parts of their identity.

Additionally, the second generation's conceptions of "blackness" and
"African American-ness" continued to crystallize as they came into constant
contact with black immigrants from the African continent and the Americas
in their college courses. The college-educated second generation spoke of taking classes that allowed them to explore various constructions of the black experience globally.

> A patron at Plantain Market reported that she specifically took a class in
> African American studies at Queens College because she wanted to learn
> about "them" and "their history." When asked about the "them" distinc-
> tion, the patron commented that while she was black, she was not
> African American and wanted to learn more about that particular group.
> (field notes, April 5, 1999)

In thinking about the importance of terminology, Justin, a twenty-three-
year-old Barbadian salesperson at a major retail store, eloquently articulated
the issue as he saw it:

We are all African Americans because we all come from Africa and now we are here in America. But that is not something I would call myself. Not that I have a problem with African Americans, it's just that they have a history . . . legacy . . . that I don't have and vice versa. I actually don't use "West Indian" that much either in describing myself unless I am talking to someone who is white or black folk not from New York, cuz I know that they probably won't understand what "Basian" [Barbadian] means. I consider myself to be a black Basian. I have to say "black" because there are a lot of different races in Barbados . . . and I have to say "Basian" because there are so many different kinds of black people in New York, and while we share a phenotype, that's all we got going on in common. Just ask my boy from Ghana.

Second-generation West Indians who moved away from home to attend college more often than not enrolled in predominantly white schools where they expected to be "one of a few West Indians." However, upon encountering a number of other second-generation West Indians within the black college community on campus, their identity formation followed a path similar to that of those who attended the predominantly minority CUNY system.[22] Interestingly, several people commented that predominantly white colleges fostered a kind of identity development among the second generation that was missing from majority minority institutions. Marlene, a twenty-seven-year-old Jamaican graduate student in sociology, remarked:

While there were not a lot of black people at UPenn, there were enough of us to survive. I was surprised to find out that many of the black students were West Indian or African. Of course, African Americans were the majority, but there were more of us than I thought there would be. I loved the fact that while we appreciated (and made fun of) each other's cultures, we could also come together along racial lines. There were a few incidents around campus while I was there that were clearly racial in nature, and all the black ethnic groups were able to form a unified front on how best to handle the situation. I think that is what is missing from New York. There are so many different groups there that coalition-building is damn near impossible. Don't get me wrong, I love the diversity in New York, but does it ever translate into anything substantive? We all have different backgrounds and identities, but which ones need to get back-burnered for the sake of the larger good? . . . Wow, I didn't realize how crucial my experiences at Penn were to how I view myself and other folks.

College gave many respondents the opportunity to learn more about their own ethnic backgrounds, along with other cultures. Respondents stated that college provided the space for an open forum to discuss some of the problems that had existed between the African American and West Indian communities and ways in which the two could, and should, work together. Interestingly, those respondents who had not yet finished college, or did not intend to fin-ish college, still viewed it as the site of positive reinforcement about their identities as racial and ethnic social beings.

CLASSIFYING RACE AND ETHNICITY

The intersection of race, ethnicity, and class plays a critical role in identity de-velopment for second-generation West Indians. A comparison of the middle-class and working-class West Indians in this study reveals that both socioeco-nomic groups identify ethnically, yet they have different ways of expressing their ethnic heritage. Since many of the working-class West Indians reside in predominantly West Indian neighborhoods in Brooklyn, their ethnicity goes undiscussed as they experience their culture in their everyday lives by fre-quenting West Indian businesses, hearing music from the Caribbean on the street, and seeing the flags from their parents' home country flying outside homes and on cars. However, for middle-class West Indians who reside in the more racially integrated neighborhoods in Queens, maintaining their ethnic identity takes a much more conscious effort.

Like Sara Lee (this volume) in her work on Koreans, I would argue that this class variance stems from the different ways in which working-class and middle-class West Indians relate to the collective definition of West Indian immigrants as a successful, upwardly mobile, "model" minority. Although working-class West Indians are aware of the model minority attitude, they also acknowledge the shift in that attitude in recent years as a result of the presence of large numbers of West Indians living in poverty in New York. They do not feel pressured to live up to the expected level of "success" because they see others who are also struggling to make ends meet. Paul, a thirty-one-year-old Trinidadian limousine driver, described his neighborhood:

> Everybody around here broke and just trying to make it. You know there are couple of families living in one apartment cuz they can't afford to live apart. East New York didn't used to be this run-down . . . but what you gonna do when you put a bunch of poor people in the same place? I re-member when we first moved here people talked about how bad Brownsville was with all the poor African Americans in there. . . . Damned if East New York isn't as bad if not worse . . . and its full of West Indians.

For middle-class West Indians who attend some of the top-ranking schools and procure prestigious jobs, there is less discrepancy between the "model" and their own lives.[23] They are proud of West Indian successes and more likely to believe that West Indian ethnic values lead to such accomplishments, which, in their minds, give West Indians a relatively high group status among immigrants. However, middle-class West Indians are also conscious of the ever-increasing presence of poor and working-class West Indians and are making clear distinctions between the two groups. For instance, Carmen gave voice to a sentiment shared by many of the middle-class respondents about the working-class second generation:

> You know, sometimes white people know what they are talking about. There are some serious shiftless people around here these days, and damn it if they all not black. They don't work, they don't know how to act, and they are not even trying to better themselves. Just chilling on the corner drinking and playing dominoes . . . and I'm talking about men and women. I'm always wondering where they get money for the drinks if they broke, but I can't be bothered to care. . . . I just need to get up out of here, away from these people. They just bring the neighborhood down.

Among many of the middle-class respondents and patrons, there was a definite sense of "us" and "them" when referring to poor and working-class West Indians. The middle class, "us," was typified by having manners, being educated (at the very least through high school), taking care of property—personal and public—being well spoken, attending church, and knowing how to dress appropriately for different occasions. Working-class West Indians, or "them," were automatically thought of as whatever the middle class was *not*.

It is important to note that the respondents did not always situate themselves in opposition to people from other classes in order to establish their own class identity. Hairstyling was frequently a hotbed of information about various West Indian functions going on throughout New York City generally, and in Queens specifically. For example, it was in Hairstyling that I first became privy to a parent-youth group in northern suburban New Jersey (and in Westchester County) that taught West Indian culture to its members by taking the kids to museums and plays and stressed community service. Many of the parents who frequented Hairstyling thought that the organization was a great idea for children not raised in predominantly West Indian neighborhoods and encouraged each other to "check it out."[24]

In talking to the patrons about this West Indian parent-child network in New Jersey, I was struck by how similar the mission of the group sounded to that of the national Jack & Jill organization for African Americans.[25] When I inquired as to why this group would be so attractive to both parents and their

children, Sheila, a thirty-one-year-old Jamaican investment banker, responded that the children "need to know who they are. They need to know
their black history, and they need to know their Caribbean history. They
won't be able to go anywhere if they do not know where they are from."

Given the saliency of ethnic identity among both working- and middle-
class second-generation West Indians, this research suggests that ethnic identity does not necessarily affect socioeconomic status, but that class position
facilitates a particular kind of maintenance of ethnic identity for different
groups.

INDEPENDENT WOMEN AND ENDANGERED BLACK MEN

Somewhat surprisingly, there was no overall difference between second-generation women and men in their identity construction. Both female and male
respondents commented that their gender did not determine how they identified themselves, but that it did affect how others viewed them. The women
revealed their struggle for independence from their patriarchal families and
what that meant for West Indian women in general. The men in the study
discussed blackness in terms of racial solidarity in the face of societal exclusion and disapproval.[26]

Consistent with the literature on societal gender roles, there were different
expectations for the women than for the men in the sample, and this had implications for how they saw themselves both individually and as a group. The
women at Hairstyling frequently commented on what they saw as the major
inequalities between West Indian men and women. Specifically, they spoke
about being put in submissive roles at home, yet they were raised to be independent individuals as they got older. One conversation was particularly
enlightening:

> A brother and sister, "J" and "Q," enter the shop arguing about some
> family function happening later in the day. "J" doesn't seem to under-
> stand why his sister doesn't want to go. "Q" then explains to no one in
> particular that she doesn't want to go because she is tired of not only hav-
> ing to serve all the men in the family, but also tired of being harassed for
> being unmarried at 33. She wonders why her marital status even matters
> considering everything else she has managed to accomplish in her life.
> "Q" says she is tired of all the unnecessary drama that comes with being
> a West Indian woman. She reveals that although she has a graduate de-
> gree and has a good job, when the family gets together, she is expected to
> turn into "wait-staff" waiting on the men "hand and foot," and that in-
> cludes her brother "J." "J's" comments indicate that not only is he not
> aware of what his sister has been going through with the family, but that
> he's not sure what has her so upset. Serving men in the family has been

going on for years, why would she start complaining now? "J" instructs his sister not to mess with a "good thing" and that she is just overreacting to nothing. It is important to note that while "J" is older than his sister and also single, family members don't comment on it. In fact, "J" never completed college and lives at home with his parents. (field notes, April 24, 1999)

The situation of "Q" here illustrates the fact that many second-generation West Indian women were encouraged, if not expected, to finish their education, get a good job, and then get married and have children. Most West Indian mothers insisted that their daughters be able to "take care of themselves without a man."[27] As a result of this pressure, second-generation West Indian women saw themselves as redefining what it meant to be a West Indian woman. Most of the West Indian women in my sample were single and declared that they would remain so until they found a mate who believed in "equal partnerships"—not one who would expect his wife to "make him a plate" and cater to his every need.

In contrast to second-generation West Indian women, who recounted their constant fight for independence within their families, second-generation men spoke at length about their experiences with racism and discrimination and were more concerned with their day-to-day survival, specifically when dealing with law enforcement. Leon, a twenty-eight-year-old Guyanese soca musician, voiced a frustration common to West Indian men:

> I am so tired of riding the train, walking down the street, or just standing still, and if cops are around, they will always ask me what I'm doing . . . like I'm bothering them. I would ask them why they are harassing me, but I know that they need very little motivation to shoot me. Giuliani has showed us over and over again that police have the right to shoot black men in open daylight for no reason and that they can get away with it.[28]

The men I interviewed would all agree with the respondent who said, "The black man's life is at stake, and the cops don't care where you come from." Sharing a conviction that the New York police regard all black men in the city as equally suspicious, regardless of ethnicity and class, these men have developed a sense of collective brotherhood across ethnic lines. Winston, a thirty-two-year-old Jamaican truck driver and part-time college student, noted:

> That is what separates us from the women. I know that they go through some things, but I don't think that they have a daily sense that their lives

are in danger like we do. Whether you're African American, Puerto Rican, Dominican, Jamaican, Haitian, or even a Filipino man, you know that this society reacts to you differently than they do other people. That's why boys will always be my boys. Cuz only they can truly understand what it's like being a colored man in America.

It is also important to note that the men in the study were fearful not only of being killed by law enforcement but also of being unjustly imprisoned. Winston's comments eloquently demonstrate that race and discrimination affect women and men of the second generation differently and that gender can lead to the saliency of one identity over another.

RACE, ETHNICITY, AND THE FUTURE OF IDENTITY WORK

The second-generation West Indians in this study demonstrate the complexity and saliency of their racial *and* ethnic identities in their everyday lives. Although one identity may be emphasized more than another, this difference is contextually based: racial and ethnic identity choices depend on the circumstances and the audience. It is evident from the research presented here that researchers must stop framing the question as a matter of second-generation West Indians choosing between racial and ethnic identities. That formulation mistakenly implies that the choice is dichotomous—that choosing to emphasize one identity is automatically to negate the other. Racial and ethnic identities are fluid categories, and the dichotomy conceptualization only exacerbates the misconception that racial and ethnic identities are fixed, or essential, in varying degrees. Second-generation West Indian immigrants embrace both their ethnic and racial identities without contradiction. Even more important, the research illustrates that the second generation understands and experiences their racial identification differently than African Americans do.

Although the second generation is not clearly "taught" their racial and ethnic identity in the same way that they are taught history and math in school, New York City is a venue in which they acquire a version of "the rules of racial classification" and of their own racial and ethnic identity (Omi and Winant 1994, 60). The boroughs of New York City, particularly Brooklyn and Queens, provide a unique setting because of their bounded geographic size, their substantial racial and ethnic diversity, and their relative racial and ethnic integration. As evidenced by the intergroup friendships and relationships among the second-generation West Indians presented here, many of New York City's racial and ethnic groups provide a context of extensive interracial and interethnic interaction among groups of color.

Not only does the racial and ethnic geography of New York City teach many racial lessons, but social institutions such as school and family also serve as a source of racial and ethnic information, a location (and means) for inter-racial interaction, and a means of both affirming and challenging racial attitudes and understandings. Second-generation West Indians have embraced the term "black" as one that encompasses the multitude of ethnicities present in New York City. Thus, I would argue that "African American" refers to a specific cultural and ethnic group that, while included in "black," does not accurately represent the experiences of second-generation West Indians. The second generation brings the importance of terminology to the discussion of identity and reminds us that "black" and "African American" are not interchangeable terms but ones that have specific references and legacies.

Socioeconomic status affects ethnic identity in a way that is understudied in the literature on second-generation immigrants. Middle- and working-class West Indians are expressing their ethnicity in divergent ways as a function of where they live, the racial and ethnic composition of their neighborhoods, and their own conceptions of "West Indian-ness." Scholars have been concerned with upwardly mobile West Indians and their propensity to use their ethnicity as a way to distance themselves from African Americans,[29] but it can also be argued that they are distancing themselves from all poor blacks, regardless of ethnicity.

An analysis of gender differentials in the second generation reveals how private and public space affect women and men differently. Second-generation women seek to renegotiate their identity as West Indian females within their families, while their male counterparts are literally in a fight for their lives within a racialized society.

Given the state of race relations in the United States, scholars have frequently argued that in order to prevent downward mobility, second-generation West Indians should not assimilate into African American culture. Not only does this theory ignore the impact of class status, but more important, it assumes that assimilation is unidirectional. I would argue that the proximity and integration of various immigrant communities in New York are fostering a new identity in the second generation that indicates bidirectional identity construction. This research reveals that immigrant culture in general is heavily influencing New York culture—to the point where people are adopting pan-Caribbean and pan-racial identities. Whether these pan-identities can alter or shift the color line that has divided this country since its inception remains to be seen.[30] We may in fact be simply moving to a white-nonwhite racial dichotomy, the ramifications of which would be disastrous for some and fortunate for others. However, what is clear is that immigrants and the identity choices they make will play a critical role in U.S. race relations for years to come.

NOTES

1. In this research I treat "race" and "ethnicity" as two distinct concepts. "Race" is defined as a socially constructed distinction based in physical appearance, while "ethnicity" is operationalized in distinctions based on national origin, language, religion, food, and other cultural markers.

2. This is not to say that Waters and other scholars of identity do not address the importance of context in their research. They do in fact take context into account in their studies. However, I am explicitly exploring how the changing context of New York City is fostering the changing nature of identity among second-generation West Indians.

3. I set the lower age limit also hoping to avoid those who might have still been attending high school full-time.

4. Almost half of the Panamanian immigrants to the United States are of Jamaican descent (Waters 1999).

5. I also included those respondents who immigrated to the United States before the age of twelve—the 1.5 generation, as defined by Rumbaut (1991).

6. Also referred to as "purposeful sampling" (Patton 1990), theoretical sampling is a strategy in which settings, persons, or events are selected deliberately in order to provide important information that could not be obtained as well using other strategies, such as convenience or probability sampling.

7. I chose these locations because they looked like places that catered to West Indian patrons from different generational backgrounds. For research purposes I felt that it was important to document generational dynamics between West Indians.

8. The names of the stores have been changed, with all other detail remaining factual.

9. West Indians of all racial and ethnic backgrounds frequented the store, including West Indian East Asians, Jamaican-descended Costa Ricans, and Belizeans. And though the owners were Korean, all of the six employees were West Indian.

10. The people running the bakery would often come to the Plantain Market for ingredients for their dishes.

11. Many patrons have been going to Hairstyling for five or more years and have referred others to the salon. In fact, many members of the same family frequent the salon.

12. The owner of Hairstyling is an African American woman from South Carolina, yet all her employees are West Indian—Jamaican, Haitian, St. Lucian, and Grenadian. The clientele at Hairstyling is predominantly West Indian, with a few African American customers.

13. Both the drugstore and the restaurant have an ethnically mixed clientele: African Americans, West Indians, whites, Puerto Ricans, and Dominicans.

14. The groups represented in the Queens neighborhood included African Americans, West Indians, Puerto Ricans, Dominicans, and native whites.

15. I found these statements particularly interesting considering that many West Indian immigrants are moving out of New York, specifically to Florida. When I raised this issue at Hairstyling, I was told that it was primarily the first generation moving to Florida and that many of those people had since relocated back to New York. In fact, this conversation spawned an argument in the shop about the "foolish" West Indians who would dare to move out of New York and then complain about it. A common response was, "What did they expect?"

16. Queens Village is located in Southeast Queens and borders Long Island.

17. This is not to say that everyone was mistreated by their teachers. Several people spoke of positive relationships with their elementary school teachers, but even in those relationships it was clear that race played a role. Teachers would tell the students that they would have to do better, and behave better, than the other students because they were black and other people would think less of them if they were not smart enough.

18. At some point the first generation went from trusting the school system to being proactive about their children's education, usually after communication within the ethnic networks had led them to realize that the schools did not always objectively operate on behalf of all students.

19. It is also important to note that several respondents were proactive about their own education and talked to teachers, guidance counselors, or older students about their options for high school. Without parental involvement, these respondents learned the necessary steps for admission into the schools of their choice and set to the task of gaining admission. Some respondents attended the local high school not out of choice but because their parents could not afford Catholic or private school and the students failed to win admission to the competitive high schools. However, many of the students who attended the local high school did so because their parents were under the mistaken impression that their children were much safer attending the local school because they would not have to travel on the subways or into neighborhoods that the parents were not familiar with.

20. When West Indian parents use the term "American," they are usually referring to the African American population.

21. Haitian immigrants had the worst reputation among all West Indian respondents, regardless of generation. No one could articulate where the dislike and the stereotypes came from, but everyone was clear that Haitians were the most oppressed and maligned ethnic group in New York City at that time.

22. Often the West Indians who left New York City still attended colleges that were not that far from the city. In fact, none of the respondents attended a college more than five hours away from New York by car. As happened when they chose a high school, West Indian parents often demanded that their children stay in New York for college. Once again, they assumed that their children would be "safer" and "do better" if they remained at home. Respondents who attended school outside of New York remarked that it was a member of the

school staff, a family member, or a family friend who impressed on the parents the merits of leaving home for college.

23. For the purposes of this research, I use the definition of "middle-class" put forth by Mary Pattillo-McCoy: "Economists use a measure called the *income-to-needs ratio* to identify class categories. The income-to-needs ratio divides total family income by the federal poverty level based on the family's size. The lower bound of the income-to-needs ratio for middle class status is frequently set at two; that is, if a family earns two times a poverty-level income, they are middle class (1999, 14–15). In addition, sociological conceptions of class include occupation and education along with measures of income (Blau and Duncan 1967). Studies of the black middle class in particular have used white-collar employment as the marker of middle-class position (Landry 1987; Oliver and Shapiro 1995; Wilson 1978, 1996). However, the strictest definition of middle-class is that it describes only those with a college degree, and it is this definition that I am utilizing in this research.

24. Although the majority of Hairstyling patrons resided in Queens, some customers lived on Long Island in areas where there were fewer West Indians than they had become accustomed to. This organization addressed issues that were more pressing for them than for other customers.

25. Jack & Jill is an organization for middle- and upper-class African American children that facilitates exposure to other African Americans through a variety of social and service activities. Admission is based on parental income, and there is a fee to become a member. Interestingly, this organization has come under fire within the larger African American community for being elitist and separatist.

26. Women also faced exclusion based on race, but differently than the men, who much more frequently felt at risk.

27. Several women in the sample were raised by single mothers, while others had fathers whom they described as extremely domineering.

28. Leon was referring to the fact that in all the fatal shootings that have occurred between the New York City police and innocent black victims, New York City mayor Rudolph Giuliani has excused the officers' behavior, and in one case the mayor attempted to justify the shooting by opening the victim's juvenile records to demonstrate that he had been a juvenile offender.

29. Scholars of West Indian immigration have discussed at great length the socioeconomic achievements of the first generation (see Bryce-Laporte 1972, 1987; Butcher 1994; Foner 1979, 1985, 1987; Kalmijn 1996; Kasinitz 1992; Laguerre 1984; Model 1991, 1995; Vickerman 1999; Waters 1991, 1994, 1999). However, due to the second generation just recently coming of age, there are few studies that examine the impact of class on this population.

30. The work of Portes and Rumbaut (2001) and Suarez-Orozco and Suarez-Orozco (2001) on the second generation living in other major immigrant cities also suggest that the color line may be shifting as a result of the contemporary immigration.

References

Blau, Peter M., and Otis Dudley Duncan. 1967. *The American Occupational Structure.* New York: Wiley.

Bryce-Laporte, Roy S. 1972. "Black Immigrants: The Experience of Invisibility and Inequality." *Journal of Black Studies* 3: 29–56.

———. 1987. "New York City and the New Caribbean Immigration: A Contextual Statement." In *Caribbean Life in New York City: Sociocultural Dimensions,* edited by Constance R. Sutton and Elsa M. Chaney. New York: Center for Migration Studies.

Butcher, Kristin F. 1994. "Black Immigrants in the United States: A Comparison with Native Blacks and Other Immigrants." *Industrial and Labor Relations Review* 47(2): 265–83.

Butterfield, Sherri-Ann. 2001. "Big Tings a Gwaan: Constructions of Racial and Ethnic Identity Among Second Generation West Indian Immigrants." Unpublished manuscript. University of Michigan, Department of Sociology.

Butterfield, Sherri-Ann, and Alex Trillo. 1999. "The Effects of Multi-ethnic Neighborhoods on the Construction of Racial and Ethnic Identities Among Second-Generation Immigrants." Paper presented to the annual meeting of the American Sociological Association. Chicago (August).

Foner, Nancy. 1979. "West Indians in New York City and London: A Comparative Analysis." *International Migration Review* 13: 284–313.

———. 1985. "Race and Color: Jamaican Migrants in London and New York City." *International Migration Review* 19: 708–27.

———. 1987. "The Jamaicans: Race and Ethnicity Among Migrants in New York City." In *New Immigrants in New York,* edited by Nancy Foner. New York: Columbia University Press.

———, ed. 2001. "West Indian Migration to New York: An Overview." In *Islands in the City: West Indian Migration to New York.* Berkeley: University of California Press.

Gans, Herbert J. 1992. "Second-Generation Decline: Scenarios for the Economic and Ethnic Futures of the Post-1965 American Immigrants." *Ethnic and Racial Studies* 15(2): 173–92.

Kalmijn, Matthijs. 1996. "The Socioeconomic Assimilation of Caribbean American Blacks." *Social Forces* 74: 911–30.

Kasinitz, Philip. 1992. *Caribbean New York: Black Immigrants and the Politics of Race.* Ithaca, N.Y.: Cornell University Press.

Laguerre, Michel S. 1984. *American Odyssey: Haitians in New York City.* Ithaca, N.Y.: Cornell University Press.

Landry, Bart. 1987. *The New Black Middle Class.* Berkeley: University of California Press.

Model, Suzanne. 1991. "Caribbean Immigrants: A Black Success Story?" *International Migration Review* 25: 248–76.

———. 1995. "West Indian Prosperity: Fact of Fiction?" *Social Problems* 42: 535–53.

Oliver, Melvin L., and Thomas M. Shapiro. 1995. *Black Wealth/White Wealth: A New Perspective on Racial Inequality.* New York: Routledge.

Omi, Michael, and Howard Winant. 1994. *Racial Formation in the United States: From the 1960s to the 1990s.* New York: Routledge.

Pattillo-McCoy, Mary. 1999. *Black Picket Fences: Privilege and Peril Among the Black Middle Class.* Chicago: University of Chicago Press.

Patton, Michael Q. 1990. *Qualitative Evaluation and Research Methods,* 2nd ed. Newbury Park, Calif.: Sage Publications.

Portes, Alejandro, and Rubén G. Rumbaut. 2001. *Legacies: The Story of the Immigrant Second Generation.* Berkeley, Calif., and New York: University of California Press and Russell Sage Foundation.

Rumbaut, Rubén G. 1991. "The Agony of Exile: A Comparative Study of Indochinese Refugee Adults and Children." In *Refugee Children: Theory, Research, and Services,* edited by Frederick L. Ahearn, Jr. and Jean L. Athey. Baltimore: The Johns Hopkins University Press.

Salvo, Joseph, and Ronald Ortiz. 1992. *The Newest New Yorkers: An Analysis of Immigration into New York City During the 1980s.* New York: Department of City Planning.

Stafford, Susan Buchanan. 1987. "The Haitians: The Cultural Meaning of Race and Ethnicity." In *New Immigrants in New York,* edited by Nancy Foner. New York: Columbia University Press.

Strauss, Anselm L. 1987. *Qualitative Analysis for Social Scientists.* Cambridge and New York: Cambridge University Press.

Suarez-Orozco, Carola, and Marcelo M. Suarez-Orozco. 2001. *Children of Immigration.* Cambridge, Mass.: Harvard University Press.

Vickerman, Milton. 1994. "The Response of West Indians to African Americans: Distancing and Identification." In *Research in Race and Ethnic Relations,* Vol. 7, edited by Rutledge Dennis. Greenwich, Conn.: JAI Press.

———. 1999. *Crosscurrents: West Indian Immigrants and Race.* New York: Oxford University Press.

Waters, Mary C. 1991. "The Role of Lineage in Identity Formation Among Black Americans." *Qualitative Sociology* 14: 57–77.

———. 1994. "Ethnic and Racial Identities of Second-Generation Black Immigrants in New York City." *International Migration Review* 28(4): 795–820.

———. 1996. "The Intersection of Gender, Race, and Ethnicity in Identity Development of Caribbean American Teens." In *Urban Adolescent Girls: Resisting Stereotypes,* edited by Bonnie Leadbeater and Niobe Way. New York: New York University Press.

———. 1999. *Black Identities: West Indian Immigrant Dreams and American Realities.* New York and Cambridge, Mass.: Russell Sage Foundation and Harvard University Press.

Wilson, William Julius. 1978. *The Declining Significance of Race: Blacks and Changing American Institutions.* Chicago: Chicago University Press.

———. 1996. *When Work Disappears: The World of the New Urban Poor.* New York: Alfred A. Knopf.

Woldemikael, Tekle. 1985. "Black Ethnics: A Case Study of Haitian Immigrants." *New England Journal of Black Studies* 5: 15–30.

———. 1989. *Becoming Black American: Haitians and American Institutions in Evanston, Illinois.* New York: AMS Press.

Chapter 11

Class Matters: Racial and Ethnic Identities of Working- and Middle-Class Second-Generation Korean Americans in New York City

Sara S. Lee

Asian americans comprise a diverse group of people with distinct cultural, historical, and social backgrounds and experiences. However, the American public and the popular press tend to perceive Asian Americans as a homogeneous group, comprised of people who share a common penchant for success. As members of a "model minority" group, Asian Americans are presumed to be smart, dependable, and industrious (Tuan 1998; Lee 2002).[1]

The second-generation Korean immigrants I interviewed for this study reacted in various ways to their ascribed "model minority" racial image. Some participants believed that the image accurately reflects the "true" characteristics of Korean Americans. For example, one participant said:

> Among the Koreans I know, all the Korean American families are doing well. . . . all the fathers are doctors. And, as far as I can see, they are all very happy; all the kids have gone to college, they are all working now, and it's like a picture-book happy family kind of thing.

Other participants saw their model minority image as a damaging stereotype and disdained it as an unrealistic myth that many Koreans find difficult to live up to:

> I realize that we have a model of what we want Korean Americans to be like, such as church-going, middle-class, hard-working, second-generation kids who do well in school and respect their parents. . . . But it's not

the case with a lot of Korean people. It just isn't true! But a lot of people who don't even live these lives believe that's what it means to be Korean American.

What factors or circumstances lead some second-generation Korean Americans to define their ethnic identities through the model minority lens and not others? Why do second-generation Korean Americans construct contrasting racial and ethnic identity meanings, and what consequences do these divergent identity meanings have in their lives?[2] In this chapter, I draw on sixty in-depth interviews with second-generation Korean Americans to examine the conditions that shape and influence the racial and ethnic identities of the immigrant second generation. The key factor here is social class.

Although almost all of the respondents interviewed for this study indicated that they had been stereotyped as a model minority, how they reacted to their stereotype typically varied according to social class. Middle-class Korean Americans, whose families had experienced upward mobility, extolled the model minority racial image as an accurate reflection of Korean and Asian American success writ large. In this regard, their ethnic identity did not clash with their ascribed racial identity, and their class privilege enabled them to see ethnicity as the fulcrum of their presumed group-wide success. Middle-class Korean Americans also felt proud of their ethnic identity, which drew further strength from their friendships with other middle-class co-ethnics, whom they met and networked with for the first time in college.

On the other hand, working-class Koreans who were fully aware of their working-class background and circumstances while growing up refuted the model minority as a falsely ascribed image. At the same time, however, the power of the model minority stereotype and the middle-class Korean community's unrealistically high academic and occupational expectations made working-class Korean Americans feel inadequate, ashamed, and ostracized from the co-ethnic community. They regarded themselves as an anomaly compared to their more numerous and "model," middle- and upper-class counterparts. Because of their low class status within the Korean American community, working-class Korean Americans also felt conflicted about their ethnic identity and interacted less with the Korean American community.

Much academic studies of second-generation identity have relied on survey data that ask respondents to pick or state one identity without giving them the option to expound what their identity means to them. This study compares the subjective racial and ethnic identities of working- and middle-class Korean Americans and reveals that ethnic identity is a specific marker for a complex reality: what the ethnic identity or identity label means to the individual is contingent on a multitude of interrelated and intersecting social identities (Tajfel 1981). Owing to the limited scope allotted, however, this particular chapter focuses specifically on the relationship between race, class, and ethnic identity and reserves other salient aspects of the Korean second generation's identity, such as gender, for forthcoming publications (see Lee 2004).

OVERVIEW OF THE LITERATURE

The descendants of earlier European immigrants, who now constitute the white majority, enjoy ethnicity as an option (Waters 1990). For them, ethnic identity is an outcome of "individual choice or selective personal and familial enjoyment of tradition," such as eating ethnic foods or attending ethnic festivals, that does not require any deep or extended commitment on their part (Waters 1990, 165). As Herbert Gans (1979) puts it, ethnic identity for whites is "symbolic"—it is mostly a feeling that comes at no cost and does not interfere with their behavior or lifestyle in any significant way. In contrast, the post-1965 immigrant children, because they are in majority a people of color, do not always have the option to assert or conceal their ethnicity at their discretion. For them, ethnic identity is often a reaction to an ascribed racial identity that is not of their own choosing (Waters 1999).

PAN-ASIAN AMERICAN IDENTITY

The pan-ethnicity theory predicts that Asian immigrant children will react to their common racial labeling by developing a pan-Asian American identity (Espiritu and Lopez 1990). Empirical studies show some support for this hypothesis. Interviews with second-generation Chinese and Korean immigrants reveal, for example, that many of them share a sense of "we-ness" with one another based on their common experiences of being identified racially by the larger society (Min and Kim 1999; Kibria 1997). Recent Asian American intermarriage rates also point to the growth of a pan-Asian identity among Asian Americans: increasingly, Asian Americans who intermarry are marrying inter-ethnically (for example, Korean Americans marrying Chinese Americans) rather than inter-racially (for example, Korean Americans marrying white Americans) (Shinagawa and Pang 1996; Lee and Fernandez 1998; Kibria 1997).

The pan-ethnic trend, however, cannot be generalized to all Asian Americans because most of the Asian identity research is based exclusively on a college-educated, middle-class sample (for exceptions, see Louie, this volume; Lew 2001). Middle-class Asian Americans are more likely than their working- or lower-class counterparts to develop a pan-Asian American identity because they attend big, four-year colleges and universities where Asian American studies courses and programs can provide Asian students with a shared framework for understanding and articulating their common racial status and history in the United States (Espiritu 1992). The increased numbers and interactions among middle-class Asian Americans on college campuses also add to their chances of developing a pan-ethnic identity by reducing their social and spatial distance (Shinagawa and Pang 1996). For these reasons, we do not know whether all Asian Americans are forming a pan-Asian identity, or whether pan-ethnicity is distinctively a middle-class phenomenon that results from their common "race-class" connection. This study seeks to better understand how class intersects with race and ethnicity for the Asian second generation, particularly for working-class Korean Americans whose experiences may diverge from, and even contradict, the "model minority" stereotype.

THE INTERSECTION OF RACE, CLASS, AND ETHNIC IDENTITY

The impact race has on second-generation identities varies from group to group, depending on the specific racial category and how those meanings are then interpreted by the group members themselves (Cornell and Hartmann 1998). Mary Waters (1999) argues that because racial identification carries class implications, the ways in which second-generation immigrants react and respond to their ascribed racial identities also vary according to social class backgrounds. Her study of racial and ethnic identities among West Indian youth living in New York City demonstrates this point well.

West Indian immigrants are ascribed with a racial stereotype that implies downward mobility and low status, but working- and middle-class West Indian youths construct different kinds of identities in response to their involuntarily ascribed identity. Waters finds that working-class West Indian Americans identify closely with African Americans because they have close residential, occupational, and social contact with them. Subsequently, working-class West Indians also adopt the "oppositional culture" that exists among urban African American youths, which subverts pro-mobility behaviors, such as doing well in school, and define these behaviors as "uncool" or as "acting white" (Ogbu 1990). Although the construction of this "oppositional identity" helps working-class youths to cope with their low status, it is a double-edged sword because their life chances and opportunities can be further eroded when they cast mobility as an act of selling out to the dominant white society (Waters 1999, 8). In contrast, middle-class West Indians try to distinguish themselves from African Americans and their negative stereotypes by asserting their ethnic or immigrant identities. They use their class resources to do this, mainly to facilitate more co-ethnic interaction, social capital, and cultural acquisition, which help them to counter their underclass stereotype. For example, some middle-class West Indian parents send their children to more racially integrated schools so as to create distance between their children from poor African American youths.

Waters's (1999) study helps us to understand the ways in which race, ethnicity, and class interact to shape the black second generation's identities and assimilation processes. However, the literature is largely silent about these interactions for the Asian second generation population.

RACE, ETHNICITY, AND CLASS FOR THE KOREAN SECOND GENERATION

Like many post-1965 immigrants from Taiwan, Hong Kong, India, and the Philippines who gained selective entry to the United States through the occupational preference system, most of the post-1965 Korean immigrants are middle-class professionals.[3] A 1979 survey of the Korean population in southern California shows, for example, that 75 percent of the Korean immigrants who entered the United States between 1966 and 1969 had worked as white-collar professionals in Korea (Hurh and Kim 1984). A more recent survey of the Korean immigrant population in the New York metropolitan area corroborates the middle-class skew of the Korean immigrant population. According to Dae Young Kim (2001), approximately 80 percent of the second-generation Koreans' fathers had at least some college experience, and 40 percent had graduate degrees.

In a co-ethnic community that is mostly middle-class, such as the Korean American community, does ethnicity trump class in the identities of the second generation? This study's incorporation of a conspicuously understudied segment of the second-generation Asian immigrant population—the Korean working class—enables us to finally examine the "flip side" of the race, ethnicity, and class interactions that have most commonly been studied to date. For example, what kind of identity issues do second-generation Korean immigrants confront as members of a racial group that is more commonly identified as a model minority than as an underclass?[4] More important, do working-class Korean Americans confront a unique set of identity dilemmas unknown to their middle-class counterparts because they are less likely to mirror their ascribed model minority image?

The Korean American community also seems to place an exceptionally high premium on higher education and prestigious occupations. According to research (Kim 1993; Lew 2001; Kim 2001), first-generation Korean immigrants define their prestige and status within their co-ethnic community through the academic achievement of their children. Many second-generation Koreans also equate being a good student and having a professional career with being Korean (Kim 1993; Lew 2001). Do working-class Korean Americans in New York share these exceptionally high expectations for academic and occupational achievement? If so, what are the resulting emotional costs or behavioral ramifications for the moderate- or low-achievers?

Finally, the Korean American case poses another unique and challenging question. Korean immigrants in New York do not have a traditional ethnic enclave. Manhattan's "Koreatown" is a small area in the vicinity of Thirty-second Street between Broadway and Fifth Avenue, but it is mainly a business district comprising restaurants, shops, various service providers, and international importing and wholesale businesses; it is not an ethnic residential neighborhood. Although downtown Flushing, Queens, is both a Korean American commercial center and a residential neighborhood, it is not a predominantly Korean enclave as it is teeming with other immigrants, such as the Chinese. In terms of residence, Korean immigrants tend to be dispersed throughout New York City. Thus, what is unique here is that working-class Korean Americans do not grow up or live in an ethnic enclave, as the working-class members of other immigrant groups do, such as the Chinese (Louie, this volume). Working-class Korean Americans also do not have an ethnic occupational niche that we know of. In this light, I ask: Do working-class Korean Americans have any immediate social or economic ties to the co-ethnic community? Or are they more likely to be assimilated and integrated into the general New York working-class population? Despite the absence of a residential Korean enclave, is there a common social space or a medium that creates a common, shared identity between working- and middle-class Korean Americans? If not, is there a significant social distance between the two groups?

METHODS

Between 1999 and 2001, I conducted sixty in-depth, open-ended interviews with working- and middle-class Korean Americans living in New York City. Most of the interviews were conducted in coffee shops and restaurants, but sometimes they took place in the respondent's home. The interviews covered the respondents' experiences in their neighborhoods, schools, and work-places, their friendships and families, and, if foreign-born, their experiences coming to the United States. I also asked about how these experiences related to their cultural values, behavior, and racial and ethnic identities.[5] All of the interviews lasted from one to four hours, with most of them lasting about two hours. They were tape-recorded and later transcribed verbatim.

SAMPLING

I recruited the participants for this study by first locating a sample cluster for each group, then "snowballing" the sample through their referrals. I recruited the middle-class sample cluster from a Korean American professional organization called the Young Korean American Network (Y-KAN). Y-KAN is a not-for-profit organization of approximately two hundred active and casual members, some of them intermittent. According to its mission statement, Y-KAN's purpose is to function as a social, cultural, and political bridge between the Korean American community and the broader communities of New York. Its activities range from social services, such as visiting a Korean American nursing home, to participation in broader New York community events, such as the Annual Staten Island Clean Up. Many members join Y-KAN, however, to network and socialize with other professional, second-generation Korean immigrants. During the early stages of my research, I attended a number of Y-KAN meetings and events to build rapport with the members and to recruit the initial cluster of five middle-class respondents for the study.

I recruited the working-class sample cluster from a police precinct located in Queens. Because more than 75 percent of the New York Korean population lives in Queens, I was able to identify and locate the highest number of Korean American police officers at this Queens precinct. I called and visited the precinct several times in order to identify the Korean American officers and recruit them for the study. In the end I was able to interview four Korean American police officers, and these officers introduced and referred me to their family, friends, and acquaintances, who were also from the working class.

THE SAMPLE

The sample for this study is not representative of the New York Korean American population. Rather, it is a purposive, or "criterion-based," sample that includes an even number of working- and middle-class, second-generation Korean immigrants, whose ages ranged between twenty-one and thirty-nine at the time of the interview. The median age of the sample was twenty-seven. The findings of this study therefore cannot be generalized to the wider Korean second-generation population in New York City or elsewhere.

I used two highly correlated indicators of class to define "working-class" and "middle-class": the respondent's father's education (to determine the respondent's class origin) and the respondent's occupation (to determine the respondent's class destination). Thus, the middle-class respondents in the sample were professionals whose fathers had college degrees. The working-class respondents were blue-collar or low-wage service workers whose fathers did not have college degrees. It is important to note here that all but one of the working-class respondents interviewed for this study either had a college degree or were attending college at the time of the interview. Although this may appear to be the result of a sample bias, a finding from a random, representative sample of Korean Americans in New York (Kim 2001) suggests that the present study's working-class sample, and their high rate of college attendance, resembles the larger Korean American working-class population. The survey found that irrespective of class background or status, about 86 percent of second-generation Korean Americans living in New York have attended college. Thus, both working- and middle-class Korean Americans appear to be attaining high levels of education. The reason for the exceptionally high rate of college attendance by working-class Korean Americans is discussed in the following section of this chapter.

FINDINGS

According to sociologist Milton Gordon (1964), members of the "ethclass," people who share the same intersection of ethnicity and social class, identify most strongly with one another because they share similar cultural behaviors and have frequent interactions. The interviews suggest that middle-class Korean Americans certainly feel the closest to other middle-class Korean Americans. However, their close identification with one another not only has to do with their opportunities to meet and interact with one another on college campuses, but also with their ability to construct a common narrative about the Korean American penchant for success, an idea that corresponds well with their own mobility experiences and the model minority image ascribed to them by the larger society. Contrary to what the "ethclass" hypothesis predicts, working-class Korean Americans do not have frequent interactions with one another because they grow up in isolation from their "ethclass" members and, unlike their middle-class counterparts, rarely have chances to meet and connect with one another. Because they are a minority within a predominantly middle-class, co-ethnic community, they are also disconnected from the larger Korean American community and even feel ostracized by it. Rather, working-class Korean Americans feel most strongly connected to and identify with other racial minority groups who have a history of racial and economic oppression here in the United States; their class-based connection to other minority groups cause them to regard ethnicity-based identity, particularly one that is based on what they regard as a false sense of group superiority, as ill-representative of their more complex and layered senses of self and subsequently, as politically stifling.

"THE JEWS OF THE EAST": MIDDLE-CLASS KOREAN AMERICANS
AND THEIR ETHNIC IDENTITY MEANINGS

Studies have found that some Asian Americans regard the model minority as
a positive and vital part of how they understand their own ethnicity (Kibria
1997; Tuan 1998; Lee 1996). For example, when I asked if race was ever a
significant factor at her work or to any of the people with whom she worked,
one of the middle-class respondents replied: "Being Asian is beneficial because Asians are looked upon as the model minority. People think that we're
all very smart, bright and studious, and [they think], 'If you want to get it
done, give it to that [Asian] person.' It's possible that I got my first job because my former boss thought that I would be that sort of person." In addition to such advantages in procuring jobs, some respondents indicated that in
general being Asian was an advantage because Asians are always given the
benefit of the doubt under uncertain circumstances.[6]

Middle-class Korean Americans also believed that their racially ascribed
model minority image accurately reflected the academic and economic accomplishments of Korean immigrants. Overall, they believed that Korean
Americans, as a group, "have done very well" in the United States. When
asked to describe the characteristics that they were most proud of about
Koreans, middle-class Korean Americans most frequently cited the academic accomplishments of Korean Americans and their tendency to become well-to-do, white-collar professionals, typically, doctors, lawyers, or
engineers. They also believed that Asians, especially Koreans, command a
lot of respect from the larger society as a result of their socioeconomic accomplishments.

Middle-class Korean Americans also felt no conflict in self-identifying and
being identified as Asian, as Korean American, and also as a model minority.
For them, ethnicity was the fulcrum of their presumed groupwide success and
thus a salient and proud aspect of their identity. They believed that Korean
immigrants experienced disproportionate mobility compared to other racial
and ethnic groups because of their ethnic values and characteristics, such as
diligence, perseverance, and an emphasis on education and the family. To illustrate this point, middle-class Korean Americans frequently referred to
themselves as the "Jews of the East."

The myth of Jewish success is one of the most widely acclaimed examples
of ethnic success in American history. According to Stephen Steinberg
(1981, 103), the convergence of several important historical, social, and economic factors explains the relatively rapid upward mobility of American
Jews:

Thus, in large measure Jewish success in America was a matter of historical timing. That is to say, there was a fortuitous match between the experience and skills of Jewish immigrants, on the one hand, and the man-power needs and opportunity structures, on the other. It is the remarkable convergence of factors that resulted in an unusual record of success.

However, the American public, the popular press, and social scientists have all attributed Jewish success to Jewish cultural values and characteristics, such as thrift, ambition, desire for education, and the ability to postpone gratification. By comparing themselves to American Jews, whom they regard as the quintessential model minority group, middle-class Korean Americans were asserting that they too had experienced disproportionate mobility because of their ethnic values.

Similar to the social class advantages (industrial experience and concrete occupational skills) that propelled turn-of-the-century Jewish immigrants into rapid mobility and large-scale entry into higher education (Steinberg 1981), human and social capital contributed greatly to the mobility of Korean immigrants as a whole. Although cultural difficulties and discrimination led many college-educated, middle-class Korean immigrants to experience downward mobility upon their arrival in the United States, their class resources and ensuing entrepreneurship enabled many of them to recover relatively quickly and achieve upward mobility (Abelmann and Lie 1995; Light and Bonacich 1988; Jennifer Lee 2002; Dae Young Kim, this volume). Many middle-class Koreans seemed unaware of their parents' class advantage. Instead, they believed that their parents immigrated to the United States with no resources but ultimately achieved success because of their hard work and desire to succeed—characteristics they attributed to being Korean. In interview after interview, middle-class Korean Americans indicated how proud they were of their parents for "pulling themselves up by their bootstraps" in ways, they believed, that other immigrants or minorities have not been able to do. For example, one respondent's father was a college-educated professional who had worked as an engineer in Korea. The respondent mainly attributed his father's success, however, to his efforts, because he had no money when he initially came to the United States:

> My dad came to America when he was thirty-three. He started from scratch, but achieved middle-class status and sent his kids to good schools. So I am very proud of them [first-generation Korean immigrants] because that's something that not many people have done. And I think a lot of kudos is deserved on their part.

Another common belief among middle-class Korean Americans was that their parents had left their home country, sacrificed their somewhat comfortable lives, and suffered hardships in the United States—all for the purpose of providing a better life for their children. Although a number of "push" factors motivated and led the Korean middle class to immigrate to the United States during the 1960s and the 1970s, such as the authoritarian military regime and restricted educational and career opportunities (Abelmann and Lie 1995), most middle-class Korean Americans I interviewed talked only about the sacrificial element of their parents' immigration:

> You hear the reasons why the Koreans came over—better education and better life. . . . The only concrete reason that my parents ever told me was for our education. "For you and your brother, so you can have a better life." We were pretty well off living in Korea so I don't see any other reason why they needed to move at that time.

Other middle-class respondents similarly guessed that their parents had left Korea for the sake of their children's future. One particular respondent told me, for example, that he had been puzzled as to why his father left a promising career at a prominent Korean company. Then one day a friend of his father's who lives in Korea told him, "It's a shame your father left [Korea], because if he had stayed he would have been our manager [at the company]. . . . Your father left because he wanted to make sure that you guys didn't experience any unpleasantries [*sic*]."[7]

These notions of parental sacrifice and triumphant economic success despite hardships lent a poignancy to middle-class Korean ethnic pride and provided a powerful marker of their ethnic identity. Most middle-class Korean Americans saw their family's success as a result of their parents' sacrifice and ethnic values, and hence they regarded their ethnic identity as salient and important in their lives. I do not argue that any part of this first-generation experience is untrue. Rather, I argue that the narratives of sacrifice and self-made success among the Korean second generation have become their "symbolic repertoires." According to Stephen Cornell and Douglas Hartmann (1998, 222): "Symbolic repertoires are ways of representing the group to itself—and, at times, to others—so as to establish or reinforce the sense among group members of sharing something special—a history, a way of being, a particular set of beliefs—that captures the essence of their peoplehoods." This narrative of Korean American sacrifice and self-made success gave professional Korean Americans a sense of "we-ness" as a people and reinforced the Korean ethnic boundary by extolling the Koreans' "model" success and their pride in this accomplishment. What they failed to recognize was that this was the experience of a particular cohort of middle-class Korean immigrants.

SHARING THE NARRATIVE

One of the most important means through which middle-class Korean Americans connect with the collective narrative of Korean immigrants is through their co-ethnic friendships. Co-ethnic friendships play a critical role in forging an ethnic identity because these friendships provide an invaluable opportunity to share racial and ethnic experiences with someone who identifies with such experiences.

For middle-class Korean Americans, who typically grew up in predominantly white, middle-class neighborhoods, college was often the first time they had seen a critical mass of Korean American or Asian American students.[8] Many of the prestigious and large four-year universities that middle-class Korean students attended also had various ethnic studies programs and organizations that made them feel welcomed and comfortable about exploring their identity for the first time. Although not every Korean American student who attended college participated in ethnic organizations, the mere existence of such organizations provided them with the means and opportunity to meet and connect with second-generation Koreans whose background and experiences mirrored their own (Kibria 1997).

Middle-class Korean Americans gave several reasons why they felt closer to their co-ethnic friends than their non-Korean or non-Asian friends. These included sharing the experiences of growing up culturally American but being treated as a foreigner, being expected to have an ethnic identity, and being on the margins of both mainstream American society and the Korean American community. They also shared mutual understandings about certain aspects of the Korean culture. These common experiences that middle-class Korean Americans shared with their co-ethnic friends provided them with a sense of validation in their distinctive second-generation Korean immigrant identity. Understanding that they were not alone in feeling neither Korean nor American, they developed an emergent ethnic identity based on shared experiences of growing up Korean in America rather than as Koreans living in America per se.

Middle-class Korean Americans also said that they felt a unique sense of "comfort" with other Korean Americans:

> My friendships with Korean people are a lot different from the ones I developed back in high school [with non-Koreans]. It's more personal. And

we're not as fake or as careful about stepping on each other's toes, you know? We don't have to be as courteous. . . . We understand, so we joke around a lot, and we're really comfortable to say what we really think and are honest about it.

The sense of comfort they described had much to do with not having to explain every little thing that made them different from a "typical" American person or family. These differences included, for example, taking off their shoes inside the house and having parents who were strict and fervent about their educational performance:

[Being Korean American] means that a lot of my friends won't be able to relate to certain things that my parents do . . . or certain things that I say about my parents. [*Like what?*] Like when I told one particular friend that my parents are not satisfied with an A-, she was like, "Why can't they be happy with that?" They're just not, you know? I find that a lot more of my Chinese and Korean friends can relate better: "Oh, I understand. My parents are like that too." Whereas a lot of my American friends, they don't get it. They don't understand it at all.

These middle-class Korean Americans also felt that they did not have to worry about expressing some of their most personal feelings about race and discrimination to another Korean or an Asian American person.

The most salient and important commonalities that middle-class Korean Americans shared with one another, however, were their family backgrounds and their immigration history, experiences largely shaped by not only their ethnicity but also their class. The experiences of their well-educated parents in enduring downward mobility, operating small businesses, and overcoming financial hardship were shaped by their middle-class status and the opportunity structures that became available to them when they were shut out from mainstream avenues for mobility. When Korean Americans share their experiences, they validate their experiences by linking them to a larger historical narrative that gives them a sense of belonging and comfort about who they are and a recognition that their experiences did not take place in a historical vacuum.

LOOKING THROUGH THE WORKING-CLASS LENS: ETHNIC IDENTITIES OF WORKING-CLASS KOREAN AMERICANS

In stark contrast to middle-class Korean Americans, who rarely spoke of class, working-class Korean Americans saw class as a primary factor shaping their mobility chances and opportunity structures. Most of the working-class Korean Americans interviewed for this study grew up in the predominantly working-class neighborhoods of Queens, Brooklyn, and the Bronx with other working-class minorities including blacks, Hispanics, and white ethnics. The close social proximity and frequent interaction with a non-ethnically exclusive working-class community enabled the working-class Korean Americans to interpret the Korean collective group experience using a broader framework than ethnicity.

Unlike their middle-class counterparts, working-class Korean Americans did not subscribe to a collective narrative that defined the Korean immigrant experience as success achieved by the first generation's hard work and sacrifice. They also did not believe that the widespread academic and economic success of Korean Americans was the result of their industriousness. Instead, working-class Korean Americans viewed and interpreted their academic and professional achievements explicitly through a class lens. For example, middle-class respondents touted ethnicity as the reason for their academic success, but many working-class respondents recognized that the type of college they attended and their limited academic success had much to do with their family's financial circumstances. For one thing, some working-class respondents did not have the option of going away to college because their families could not afford to lose their income: "A part of me had an obligation to stay home and help out my parents' business because at that time they owned a small grocery store. So I stayed nearby our home. Also, at the time, I had that other job working as a mover, so I didn't want to go away."

These respondents also recognized that financial matters not only dictated the *type* of school they attended but affected the *quality* of their college education. While it is common for college students to hold part-time jobs, working-class college students often have to work full-time and attend school part-time to make ends meet. Many working-class respondents indicated that they worked full-time or long hours during school and that their work schedule often interfered with their studies and caused them to attend school intermittently:

> I worked all kinds of jobs while I went to school—one semester full-time, one semester part-time. And I didn't take a cent from my parents from the age of eighteen until now. But for that, I ended up taking much longer to finish school. I worked as a bank teller, like from nine to four, and took night classes. It was physically draining. My grades weren't the best. And it was the worst that I've done academically in my whole life. By then, I sort of gave up. I thought, Why am I trying to do well? For what? I never had focus. I didn't know what I wanted to do. . . . And once you get used to making a certain amount of money at an early age, you become enticed by that and you get greedy and make more money. And so school [has] less priority.

To her chagrin, however, the respondent later realized that she had not prioritized school because no one in her social network informed her about how critical education was for mobility:

> But if someone were to have explained to me, "If you take this mentality, you'll just be struggling, and you'll remain working as a blue-collar laborer for the rest of your life, but if you invest some time in studying, you don't have to physically toil as much later on," I might have studied harder. But nobody explained that to me!

Thus, a part of the class disadvantage that working-class Korean Americans acknowledged was the lack of vital information and resources crucial to mobility among their parents and the people in their social networks. Another working-class respondent said, for example, that although she received "excellent" grades in high school and could have attended a better college, she did not because she "did not know any better":

> Nobody talked about colleges or schools to me, so I went to wherever I knew someone went. My sister went there, so I went there. . . . My parents had no clue as to how to guide us. We had no guidance whatsoever. It's bad enough if you don't have money, but if your parents don't have the skills to guide you, because they were never taught the skills themselves, it's such a sad situation. And so when I think about my situation, it's a real deprived way of growing up. And it's nobody's fault. It's just circumstances.

Working-class Korean Americans saw that their class position and limited social networks also limited their occupational mobility. One respondent who was working as a sales representative at an upscale department store articulated this point particularly well. When I asked whether she had ever experienced discrimination or unfair treatment at her job, she stated:

> Yes, [but] it wasn't like a sexual or a racial glass ceiling; it was more like a money glass ceiling. In my area, it helps if you came from big money and if you had style. But obviously, I don't have money, I don't hang out in posh places, or I can't buy Prada or Gucci. So I couldn't move up even though I was a better worker than somebody else. But obviously, that tied into the racial issues too, because me being Asian, I wasn't exposed to the white, Upper East Side crowd.

Working-class Korean Americans clearly saw that class intersects with ethnicity, which means that they did not necessarily have much in common with their co-ethnic counterparts. In fact, they often made very clear distinctions between them and their middle-class co-ethnic counterparts. A twenty-two-year-old woman who worked two jobs to pay for college differentiated her work ethic from those of the Korean American college students who attended her Korean church:

> Like I said, I've been working ever since I was twelve. And a lot of my [non-Korean] friends work too. But then there's the [Korean] kids at church. They don't really work. I don't know what they do. They go home and watch *Dawson's Creek.*[9] Like that was a lot of the people I bumped into. I mean, my mom pays for stuff. I obviously don't pay my mom rent. I obviously don't have to pay the bills. But at the same time, I'm not carrying a phone, a two-way pager, this and that, you know? My parents worked hard just to keep us fed and to keep the house and everything. It might be class resentment, but it's like, gosh, I think about how much they had to work and how hard I had to work, and they just had everything just kind of given. That bugs me.

Working-class respondents often disagreed strongly with what they regarded as the Korean people's need to own and flaunt their material wealth. They preferred not to associate with Korean Americans, whom they characterized as "rich, spoiled, upper-class people."

"YOU HAVE TO DO SOMETHING TO BE KOREAN": BLURRING THE ETHNIC BOUNDARY

Working-class Korean Americans who interpreted their experiences and identity explicitly through the class framework identified more closely with working-class people of color than with co-ethnics. The "others" of a society are the individuals who stand at its margins, the kind of people who remind the society's "core" of its boundaries and provide them with the ideological justification to oppress (Collins 1991, 68). Working-class Korean Americans formed a pan-other identity that linked the fate of Korean immigrants to those of other minorities who also experienced oppression and discrimination at the hands of the more powerful people: "[Koreans] have a history of being oppressed in Korea and here, so we should understand that other people face oppression. Being Korean American means that we see the social and economic injustices and that we try to be a part of the social change in this country."

A couple of other participants brought up Korea's history of colonization by the Japanese to underscore the common colonial status of Koreans and other minorities living in the United States. Other working-class respondents attributed Korean immigrant success to the accomplishments of African Americans and their civil rights efforts. For example, when asked whether Korean Americans as a group have been successful in the United States, one working-class respondent replied: "Successful? I think we [Korean Americans] have been very lucky in a sense that we arrived here [in the] post-civil rights era, after the African American civil rights movement. The African Americans basically paved the road for all the minorities here in America, and we have reaped the successes of their efforts."

Working-class Korean Americans also tended to define their racial or ethnic identity as a political identity. To them, being Korean American meant being politically active and involved in efforts to improve the lives of the oppressed and of marginalized peoples (that is, the "other"). One working-class male explained, for example, that it was "a political identification" when he identified himself as a Korean. He elaborated:

> I think people see the identification of Korean to be more about blood and language and where you were born and who your parents are. But I feel that to be a Korean in the United States is a more active type of identity. Meaning, I feel you have to do something to be Korean. I don't think anyone is born a Korean. I don't think speaking Korean or having Korean parents make you automatically Korean. I think people have to actively identify themselves as Korean through their community work. So to me, it is a broader definition. . . . For me, ethnic identity is constructed through people's activism.

In this regard, the ethnic identities of many working-class Korean Americans were reactive—formed in response to their unique circumstances of being working-class and Korean in the United States, not through the cultural values, norms, and behaviors they inherited from their parents. However, working-class Koreans' acute understanding of how class structures people's lives enabled them to engage in active "boundary blurring" (Alba and Nee 2003, 61): they challenged the middle-class Korean ethnic boundary and asserted their own ways to define their identities to make them more meaningful and salient to them.

"I'M NOT REALLY KOREAN BECAUSE I DON'T STUDY HARD": THE PROBLEM WITH BEING KOREAN AND WORKING-CLASS

Although many working-class Korean Americans made efforts to blur the Korean ethnic boundary defined in model minority terms, many of them were also simultaneously influenced by it because it clashed severely with their working-class status.

The Korean American community, including the second generation, possesses strikingly high expectations for "success" (Kim 1993). The respondents I interviewed indicated, for example, that they considered college to be the minimum level of educational attainment for a Korean person. More important, they indicated that the prestige of the school one attended (for example, private versus public, Ivy versus non-Ivy, and so on) determined the degree of "success" and status one maintained among Korean Americans. According to these high standards for success, many working-class Koreans (who have achieved moderate levels of success) did not view themselves as a typical or average Korean American. A nineteen-year-old working-class respondent who dropped out of college said, for example, "There is nothing Korean about me because I don't really study hard." According to the respondent, education is one of Koreans' most revered values. But because he was not as fanatic about education as most Koreans, he concluded that he was not very Korean. According to him, Koreans usually care "too much about who goes to what school and how well they are performing in school," and he did not identify with that.

Working-class Korean Americans also reported that other Koreans frequently "looked down" on them because of their poor academic credentials. One twenty-five-year-old male whose bouts of jail time had kept him from completing college said, defiantly, that he would still like to go back to school and complete his degree. When asked why finishing school mattered so much to him, he replied:

> A lot of it has to do with reputation. I can't fight it, you know. It's so hard to kick back education. Education is a form of power. Even my boss, who is not all that great, looks down on me like those other people. [*Those people who look down on you, are they mostly Koreans or non-Koreans?*] They are all Koreans! My non-Korean friends would never do that. Koreans have a habit of acting like they're the best. Koreans, they think they're all that.

The respondent's drive to finish his college education stemmed from his need to "save face" among co-ethnics. In some extreme cases, the fear of losing face loomed so large that those who did not complete college were extremely reluctant to disclose the fact. The following example demonstrates the shame that some working-class Korean Americans felt about not having a college degree. "Can I tell you something honestly if you never mention my name?" a respondent asked me during one interview. "Of course," I replied, as she began to tell me her big secret:

> I never graduated. I never graduated from school. [*What happened?*] I was waitressing at the time at this Japanese restaurant, and the money

was really good, you know? At the time I was like, "Why the heck do I need to go to college when I can be making all this money?" So I dropped out. . . . Now, whenever I'm around Korean people, I just feel like a big old loser.

Working-class Korean Americans whose jobs were not typical Korean jobs, such as law, medicine, or engineering, also experienced feelings of deep shame. The nonprofessional respondents indicated that they felt ashamed to talk about their jobs with other Koreans because they felt like the other Koreans looked down upon them: "[My job] shouldn't matter, but I think I'm a shallow person. It's tough when I talk to my friends. When we're out, I really don't like to talk about my job. Those things are kind of tough because my friends ask, 'So, what are you up to?' [I say,] 'Oh, I just work for . . . I just do nothing.'" They also feared that other Koreans would think that they were not smart enough or did not study hard enough in school because they did not have professional jobs. One respondent who works as a professional mover told me, for example, that he feels embarrassed when he wears his "workman's clothes" because he thinks that other people will judge him and think that he did not study hard in school. In comparison to their middle-class counterparts, who seemed to be attending prestigious schools and working in high-prestige jobs, he and other working-class Korean Americans saw themselves as "failures."[10]

The extent of the shame working-class Korean Americans felt about their academic and professional shortcomings ran deep because often these feelings of shame came from their parents. One respondent told me, for example, that her father repeatedly made her feel ashamed because she did not attend what he considered a "good college." Similarly, another respondent who attends a city college told me that her mother lied about the school she attended:

My mother lies about where I go to college. . . . She says I go to NYU and that I'll be going to Yale. . . . Obviously, a lot of parents do this, but the way my mom lies about the school I go to, or the way my dad doesn't want me to go visit my cousins because he thinks I'm not going to a certain school or whatever, things like that bug me. Why should that have to be an issue? Why should I be ashamed?

The respondent could not understand why her parents felt they had to save face by lying about the school she attended. As an American, she disagreed with her parents' Korean pretense and concern about what other Korean people might think. Despite her ideological rejection of her parents' values, the respondent's feelings of shame led her to intense self-blame and disparagement:

> But nonetheless, I do get ashamed now. So when I go to these [Korean] functions, I just lie. I lie too. I tell them I go to NYU, just like my mom said. I'm thinking, "I know what my mom's already told them," and I don't want to hear, "Oh, you don't go to, like, Cornell, Barnard, Columbia?" I don't want to have to deal with it at all! So I save my mom's face and save my face [by lying], which I hate myself for doing. It's so annoying!

For many working-class Korean Americans, being Korean American did not have a positive impact on their lives or give them a sense of pride. Rather, working-class Korean Americans often attributed whatever was negative about their lives to their ethnic identity. One respondent stated, for example, that her Korean identity was "hidden underneath all these blankets" and that it did "not come out too often," because she thought of her father's alcoholism as a Korean trait:

> I have a father who is a drunk. And I do think it gave me a really bad impression of Korean men in general. [My father] was the Korean that I knew the most intimately, the only Korean idea that I had, since I had not a whole lot of Koreans to compare it with. And I figured that the Americans were not like that, so I think it really did shape a lot of my Korean values. A lot of it. A lot of it.

Later, when I asked her if being a Korean American was significant to her in any way, she replied the following way: "Everything Korean represented my father, and my father represented obstacles. So why the hell would I want obstacles in my life?"

CONCLUSION

Studies on earlier European immigrants show that poor or working-class immigrants were typically concentrated into residential and occupational niches that segregated and isolated them from the mainstream (Steinberg 1981, 261; Gans 1962, 1979; Sandberg 1974; Crispino 1980). This limited their interaction with the mainstream and made ethnic community involvement a part of their daily life. It also made their ethnic identity more resilient. In contrast, economic mobility functioned to weaken ethnic ties and community life for middle-class immigrants (Steinberg 1981; Gans 1962, 1979; Alba and Nee 2003; Sandberg 1974). Because middle-class immigrants were residentially and occupationally dispersed, they shed their ethnic ties and identities more quickly. A recent study of working- and middle-class Chinese Americans in New York City also finds that the lives of the working-class Chinese Americans are much more infused with their ethnicity than the lives of their middle-class counterparts because they grew up and continued to live in a Chinese enclave (see Louie 2001 and this volume).

The findings in this chapter, however, contradict the previously found relationships between class and ethnic identity. Working-class Korean Americans appeared to be shedding their ethnic identity more quickly and willingly than their middle-class counterparts. Because working-class Koreans grew up with few ties to the co-ethnic community, they not only had few opportunities to meet other Korean Americans like themselves but also felt that they did not necessarily share anything in common with other Korean Americans. Instead, they felt closer to the other working-class minorities, such as African Americans, with whom they grew up, attended schools, and worked.

Working-class Korean Americans also disassociated themselves from other Korean Americans because they wanted to escape the negative social status their class conferred in the context of the Korean American community. When compared with their more "successful" cohort of second-generation Korean immigrants, they felt as if they were "underachievers." In light of the extremely high standard for success set by the Korean American community, they came to regard themselves as Korean anomalies and felt that they did not belong to the Korean American community. They downplayed their ethnicity as much as possible, refrained from co-ethnic interaction, and often rejected their ethnic identity altogether.

Middle-class Korean Americans, on the other hand, saw their parents' and their own successes largely as results of their parents' sacrifice and the ethnic values they maintained—most notably, their emphasis on hard work, education, and family. They saw their "ethnic values" as the fulcrum of their model minority success and took great pride in their ethnic identity. Although their ethnic pride was largely symbolic and did not result in any significant behavioral changes (Lee 2002), it did affect the primary group relationships of the second generation: they valued friendship with their "ethclass" more than any other kind.

Since the early 1980s, the Korean American population has increasingly become more heterogeneous in terms of class.[11] How the changing class dynamics and ratios of the Korean American communities across the United States affect the Korean second generation and their identities remains to be seen and deserves more scholarly attention. If the power of the model minority myth sustains, the stereotype can become a self-fulfilling prophecy. As W. I. Thomas's (Thomas and Thomas 1928, 572) "definition of the situation" states, "If men define situation as real, they are real in their consequences." If Korean Americans continue to make socioeconomic status a marker of their ethnic boundary, their definition of "Korean American" can become the reality. In other words, if only the successful members self-identify as Korean American and the less successful members do not—and consequently, "drop out," of the Korean American community—it may begin to appear as if ethnicity is indeed the fulcrum of their success. However, if working-class Korean Americans continue to resist and challenge the model minority group myth and articulate the common structural problems and concerns they share with other racial and ethnic minorities, their identity-work can improve inter-minority group relations and provide basis for a pan-minority political action toward collective economic progress.

This research was supported by the International Migration Program of the Social Science Research Council, the National Science Foundation (grant SES-0000267), and the Korea Foundation. The author would like to thank Herbert J. Gans, Philip Kasinitz, Jennifer Lee, Miliann Kang, Pawan Dhingra, and the anonymous reviewers at the Russell Sage Foundation for their comments on an earlier draft of this chapter.

NOTES

1. Another common Asian American stereotype is that of a "foreigner."
2. For the purpose of this study, I define "second-generation Korean Americans" as those whose parents were Korean immigrants and who were either born in the United States or came to the United States by age six. I use a cutoff age of six because I want to distinguish the "true" second generation from a population commonly known as the "1.5 generation"—immigrant children who were born in their parents' home country and had lived experiences there (through school attendance, for example) and whose primary language therefore is Korean rather than English. The sample age is capped at forty-one because a six-year-old child born to post-1965 immigrants would have been forty-one years old in the year 2000. See Mollenkopf, Waters, and Kasinitz (1997), for example, who use the same logic to establish the capping age of their second-generation sample.
3. The first wave of Korean immigrants comprised approximately 7,200 Korean male contract laborers who immigrated to Hawaii between 1903 and 1905. The second wave comprised approximately 15,000 Koreans, mostly the wives of U.S. servicemen and war orphans adopted by American citizens, who entered the United States between 1950 and 1964 (Min 1996).
4. Gans (1990, 1) uses the term "underclass" to refer to the growing number of persistently poor and jobless Americans. He also notes, however, that the term is often misused and becomes a value-laden, pejorative, catchall phrase for the "undeserving poor."
5. The study's interview questionnaire drew extensively from Waters (1990) and

Mollenkopf, Kasinitz, and Waters (1997). I also designed a number of questions to cater specifically to a Korean American sample.

6. The benefits of the model minority image even extend beyond the boundaries of work. The respondents indicated that in New York City's competitive rental housing market, landlords favor Asian tenants because they are perceived as clean, quiet ("less prone to throwing big parties"), and financially responsible ("good at getting their rent payments in on time").

7. By "unpleasantries" the speaker was referring to the extreme economic and social competition that restricts opportunities for the middle class in Korea. In Korea college admission, for example, is extremely difficult. According to Meery Lee and Reed Larson (2000), the Korean governement mandates a rigorous college entrance examination. Unlike the American SAT examination, which tests scholastic aptitude, Korean college entrance exams test all subjects studied in high school, including the subject of an individual's desired major. Additionally, college admission is severely limited: only one out of four applicants gains admission. This competitiveness persists despite the fact that only a small group of the top-ranked high school students take college entrance exams. Even among the college-educated, the nepotism prevalent in the Korean business culture restricts upward mobility to a select group.

8. Some middle-class respondents said that their families initially lived in more "working-class" neighborhoods, such as Flushing and Elmhurst, but eventually moved out to the wealthier suburbs when their parents could afford to do so.

9. *Dawson's Creek* is a television show about a group of teenagers who live in a middle-class, white suburban community.

10. Korean "working-class shame" contributed significantly to my efforts to recruit working-class Koreans for this study. When I asked for referrals from working-class Korean Americans in order to "snowball" my sample, they often wanted to introduce me to someone who they thought would make a "better" interview candidate—a more "typical" Korean person, that is, someone with impressive credentials such as a prestigious university degree or a lucrative job. Once I realized that the working-class second generation saw themselves as "atypical" Koreans, I tried to explain to them that I found their experiences to be quite interesting. I then asked whether they could introduce me to other Korean Americans who had similar life experiences or came from the same socioeconomic background as they did. The respondents usually said, enthusiastically, that they would try to think of someone, but they ultimately came back to me and said either that they could not think of anyone or that the person they thought of refused to be interviewed. Because many of the working-class Korean Americans I interviewed did not associate with Koreans other than family, many of them often did not know anyone they could introduce me to. However, I suspect that just as many were rather reluctant to do so owing to their class shame.

11. The increasing class diversity in the Korean immigrant community is evident in the fact that the percentage of professional Koreans immigrating to the United

States dropped from 26 percent during the late 1960s (1965 to 1969) to 16 percent during the early 1970s (1970 to 1974). During the late 1970s the percentage dropped further, to 8.6 percent. Similarly, the percentage of people with four or more years of college education decreased almost by half from 1965 to 1980. While 44 percent of Koreans who immigrated between 1965 and 1969 had completed four or more years of college, 31.7 percent of those who entered between 1970 and 1974 and 25.7 percent of those who entered between 1975 and 1980 had done so (Hurh and Kim 1984).

REFERENCES

Abelmann, Nancy, and John Lie. 1995. *Blue Dreams: Korean Americans and the Los Angeles Riots.* Cambridge, Mass.: Harvard University Press.

Alba, Richard, and Victor Nee. 2003. *Remaking the American Mainstream: Assimilation and Contemporary Immigration.* Cambridge, Mass.: Harvard University Press.

Collins, Patricia Hill. 1991. *Black Feminist Thought: Knowledge, Consciousness, and the Politics of Empowerment.* New York: Routledge.

Cornell, Stephen, and Douglas Hartmann. 1998. *Ethnicity and Race: Making Identities in a Changing World.* Thousand Oaks, Calif.: Pine Forge Press.

Crispino, James A. 1980. *The Assimilation of Ethnic Groups: The Italian Case.* Staten Island, N.Y.: Center for Migration Studies.

Espiritu, Yen Le. 1992. *Asian American Pan-ethnicity: Bridging Institutions and Identities.* Philadelphia: Temple University Press.

Espiritu, Yen, and David Lopez. 1990. "Pan-ethnicity in the United States: A Theoretical Framework." *Ethnic and Racial Studies* 13(2): 198–224.

Gans, Herbert J. 1962. *The Urban Villagers: Group and Class in the Life of Italian Americans.* New York: Free Press.

———. 1979. "Symbolic Ethnicity: The Future of Ethnic Groups and Culture in America." *Ethnic and Racial Studies* 2(1): 1–19.

———. 1990. "Deconstructing the Underclass." *Journal of the American Planning Association* 56(3): 271–78.

Gordon, Milton M. 1964. *Assimilation in American Life: The Role of Race, Religion, and National Origins.* New York: Oxford University Press.

Hurh, Won Moo, and Kwang Chung Kim. 1984. *Korean Immigrants in America: A Structural Analysis of Ethnic Confinement and Adhesive Adaptation.* Rutherford, N.J.: Fairleigh Dickinson University.

Kibria, Nazli. 1997. "The Construction of 'Asian American': Reflections on Intermarriage and Ethnic Identity Among Second-Generation Chinese and Korean Americans." *Ethnic and Racial Studies* 20(3): 522–44.

Kim, Dae Young. 2001. "Immigrant Entrepreneurship and Intergenerational Mobility Among Second-Generation Korean Americans in New York." Ph.D. diss., City University of New York.

Kim, Eun-Young. 1993. "Career Choice Among Second-Generation Korean Americans: Reflections of a Cultural Model of Success." *Anthropology and Education Quarterly* 24(3): 224–48.

Kim, Ilsoo. 1981. *New Urban Immigrants: The Korean Community in New York.* Princeton, N.J.: Princeton University Press.

Lee, Jennifer. 2002. *Civility in the City: Blacks, Jews, and Koreans in Urban America.* Cambridge, Mass.: Harvard University Press.

Lee, Meery, and Reed Larson. 2000. "The Korean 'Examination Hell': Long Hours of Studying, Distress, and Depression." *Journal of Youth and Adolescence* (April 2000): 249–71.

Lee, Sara S. 2002. "Racial and Ethnic Identities of Second-Generation Korean Immigrants in New York City." Ph.D. diss., Columbia University.

———. 2004. "Marriage Dilemmas: Partner Choices and Constraints for Korean Americans in New York City." In *Asian American Youth: Culture, Identity, and Ethnicity*, edited by Jennifer Lee and Min Zhou. New York: Routledge.

Lee, Sharon, and Marilyn Fernandez. 1998. "Trends in Asian American Racial/Ethnic Intermarriage: A Comparison of 1980 and 1990 Census Data." *Sociological Perspectives* 41(2): 323–42.

Lee, Stacey J. 1996. *Unraveling the "Model Minority" Stereotype: Listening to Asian American Youth.* New York: Teachers College Press.

Lew, Jamie. 2001. "Post-1965 Second-Generation Korean Americans: A Contemporary Study of Ethnic Capital." Ph.D. diss., Columbia University.

Light, Ivan, and Edna Bonacich. 1988. *Immigrant Entrepreneurs: Koreans in Los Angeles 1965–1982.* Berkeley: University of California Press.

Louie, Vivian. 2001. "The Difference Between Being and Becoming Chinese American: A Look at Class-Based Racial and Ethnic Identities Among the 1.5 and 2nd Generations." In *Social Science Research Council Conference on American Identities, Transnational Lives.* San Diego, Calif.: Social Science Research Council.

Merton, Robert K. 1967. *Social Theory and Social Structure.* New York: Free Press.

Min, Pyong Gap. 1996. *Caught in the Middle: Korean Merchants in America's Multiethnic Cities.* Berkeley: University of California Press.

Min, Pyong Gap, and Rose Kim. 1999. *Struggle for Ethnic Identity: Narratives by Asian American Professionals.* Walnut Creek, Calif.: Alta Mira Press.

Mollenkopf, John, Philip Kasinitz, and Mary Waters. 1997. "The Immigrant Second Generation in Metropolitan New York." Proposal to the Russell Sage Foundation, New York.

Neckerman, Kathryn, Jennifer Lee, and Prudence Carter. 1999. "Segmented Assimilation and Minority Cultures of Mobility." *Ethnic and Racial Studies* 22(6): 945–66.

Ogbu, John. 1990. "Minority Status and Literacy in Comparative Perspective." *Daedalus* 119(2): 141–68.

Phinney, Jean S. 1990. "Ethnic Identity in Adolescents and Adults: Review of Research." *Psychological Bulletin* 108: 499–514.

Rumbaut, Rubén. 1994. "The Crucible Within: Ethnic Identity, Self-esteem, and

Segmented Assimilation Among Children of Immigrants." *International Migration Review* 28(4): 748–94.

Sandberg, Neil C. 1974. *Ethnic Identity and Assimilation: The Polish-American Community: Case Study of Metropolitan Los Angeles*. New York: Praeger.

Shinagawa, Larry Hajime, and Gin Yong Pang. 1996. "Asian American Pan-ethnicity and Intermarriage." *Amerasia Journal* 22: 127–52.

Steinberg, Stephen. 1981. *The Ethnic Myth: Race, Ethnicity, and Class in America*. Boston: Beacon Press.

Tajfel, Henri. 1981. *Human Groups and Social Categories: Studies in Social Psychology*. Cambridge: Cambridge University Press.

Thomas, William I., and Dorothy Swaine Thomas. 1928. *The Child in America*. New York: Alfred A. Knopf.

Tuan, Mia. 1998. *Forever Foreigners or Honorary Whites*. New Brunswick, N.J.: Rutgers University Press.

Waters, Mary C. 1990. *Ethnic Options: Choosing Identities in America*. Berkeley: University of California Press.

———. 1999. *Black Identities: West Indian Immigrant Dreams and American Realities*. New York: Russell Sage Foundation.

Zhou, Min. 1997. "Growing Up American: The Challenge Confronting Immigrant Children and Children of Immigrants." *Annual Review of Sociology* 23: 63–95.

CHAPTER 12

AFFINITIES AND AFFILIATIONS: THE MANY WAYS OF BEING A RUSSIAN JEWISH AMERICAN*

AVIVA ZELTZER-ZUBIDA

RECENT census data suggest that there are about 300,000 immigrants from the former Soviet Union and their children living in the New York metropolitan area (March 1998 Current Population Survey). Most of those who left the Soviet Union since the early 1970s immigrated to Israel, where they received immediate citizenship under the "law of return" and extensive "absorption" and resettlement services. Those who chose to immigrate to the United States were assisted by Hebrew Immigrant Aid Society (HAIS) agents in Vienna—which was the first stop for all immigrants from the former Soviet Union—and flown to Rome, where they were housed, sheltered, and offered classes in English while their applications to immigrate to the United States were processed. The vast majority of those who landed in New York stayed in the city and were aided by the New York Association for New Americans (NYANA), which offered preliminary resettlement services. After studying the city, NYANA identified several neighborhoods that had relatively cheap and available housing, easy access to transportation, and an established Eastern European Jewish community, which the agency hoped would ease the newcomers' transition and resettlement in the new country (Orleck 1987). The majority of this immigrant group settled in Brooklyn, making Brighton Beach the largest Soviet immigrant community in the United States. Others settled in Queens, Staten Island, Long Island, and parts of New Jersey, forming vibrant ethnic neighborhoods there as well.[1]

The children of the latest immigration wave from the former Soviet Union—the children of the refuseniks who came in the mid-1970s and of those who came in the 1990s seeking a better life—are now coming of age as

* All names of individuals reported throughout the chapter are pseudonyms.

339

they negotiate their identity and place in American society. Drawing on data from the Immigrant Second Generation in Metropolitan New York Study, this chapter explores the process of identity construction among these young Russian Jewish Americans.[2]

Susan Emley Keefe (1992) describes ethnic identity as (1) the perception of differences between ethnic groups, (2) the feelings of attachment to and pride in one's ethnic group and cultural heritage, and (3) the perception of prejudice and discrimination against one's own group.[3] Nevertheless, ethnic identity is not manifested in or constructed from only what people say or perceive themselves to be but also from what they do (Ogbu 1990). Ethnic identity is constructed through interpersonal and intergroup relations (Alba 1985; Waters 1990), and as with other social identities, contact with and opposition to "the other" is a key element in defining the boundaries between "us" and "them" (Sales 1999). Ethnic identity is constructed through, and at the same time has implications for, people's and groups' relationships with others, their actions, and their behavior (Hurtado, Gurin, and Peng 1994). Hence, the general theoretical framework that informs this chapter views the formation of ethnic identity as a multifaceted and contingent process subject to various negotiations with an interactive social, institutional, and structural context (Nagel 1994). Thus, ethnic identity is understood as having symbolic aspects (Gans 1979; Alba 1990), as well as real implications for individuals' life chances and trajectories (Nagel 1994).

There is no simple answer as to who these children of Russian Jewish immigrants are, and what they may become. The truth is that many of the second-generation Russian Jews are ambivalent about the different dimensions of their identity and many of them find it difficult to define who they are. We might say that they are ambivalently "American," ambivalently "Russian," and ambivalently "Jewish" as they adopt existing identities or construct and negotiate new ones. For example, drawing on their parents' experiences in the former Soviet Union, some might view Jewishness as a primordial category that carries few behavioral attributes but has a deep cultural meaning. Others may adopt the common Jewish American identity that has an ethnic character. Embracing the Jewish Orthodox identity and way of life is another possibility that may appeal to some. And those who find it hard to assume existing identities can construct eclectic identities that are a little bit of many things at the same time, fusing Russian-ness, Jewishness, and American-ness in new and creative ways. Although these identities are not necessarily mutually exclusive and tend to fluctuate over time, they are derived from different experiences, based on different ideologies and beliefs, and imply different lifestyles (as reflected, for example, in residential patterns, marital and familial patterns, and occupational and career patterns).

The factors that seem to influence and shape the ethnic identities of young Russian Jewish Americans are their perception of the past, their experiences in the present, and their expectations of the future. The past is embodied in collective memories and family legacies about the pogroms and the Holocaust, about the discrimination and anti-Semitism in the Soviet Union, and about the immigration experience. The present is characterized by their daily experiences and interactions in schools and colleges, in neighborhoods, at work sites, and in other social contexts, such as contact with American Jewish institutions in the United States and with family and relatives in Israel. The future is represented by their stance toward the United States as their new home—a home where they can flourish and prosper.

To shed more light on the process of ethnic identity construction among young Russian Jewish Americans, I have organized the rest of this chapter into five sections. The first section describes some demographic and socioeconomic characteristics of the community in general and of the sample that is the subject of this chapter. The next section presents an insightful life story of a young Russian Jewish American woman as a way to gauge the complexity and richness of forging one's identity. The third section describes in more detail the content of some identity options that young Russian Jews adopt and construct. The fourth section elaborates the discussion about identity-shaping factors, and the last section offers some concluding remarks.

Socioeconomic Background

The socioeconomic context in which the children of Russian Jewish immigrants are constructing their ethnic identity is advantageous for several reasons. First, most of the immigrants from the former Soviet Union arrived in the United States under refugee status, which entitled them to many financial and other forms of aid that made immigration and resettlement less difficult. Second, most of the immigrants came to the United States well educated—many of them are engineers, doctors, teachers, or members of the managerial and professional classes. And finally, unlike many other immigrant groups that become racialized in the United States, Russian Jews (who were a deprived minority in the former Soviet Union) became part of the dominant racial group upon arrival in the United States. Since they are perceived as being "white," they can lose their accents and simply become "Americans" (or more precisely, "white Americans").[4]

Table 12.1 provides a description of the age, gender, and immigrant generation of the Russian Jewish sample.[5] As the table suggests, this is a relatively young and recently arrived group. More than half of the respondents were twenty-two or younger at the time of the interview, and 14.5 percent

TABLE 12.1   BASIC CHARACTERISTICS OF RUSSIAN JEWISH AMERICANS

	Number	Percentage
Age		
Eighteen to twenty-two	175	56.4%
Twenty-three to twenty-seven	91	29.1
Twenty-eight to thirty-two	45	14.5
Total	311	100.0
Gender		
Male	156	50.3
Female	155	49.7
Total	311	100.0
Generation		
Second	42	13.7
1.5 (ages one to twelve)	189	61.0
1.75 (ages twelve to eighteen)	78	25.3
Total	310	100.0

Source: Author's compilation.

were twenty-eight to thirty-two years old. This is not surprising given the relatively recent arrival of much of this population, particularly the larger upsurge of immigrants after the collapse of the former Soviet Union in 1989. The table also suggests that the sample is gender-balanced, with half male and half female respondents. Furthermore, table 12.1 shows that 13.7 percent of the sample (forty-two respondents) were born in the United States—the "true" second generation, about 60 percent arrived before the age of twelve and about one-quarter arrived between the ages of twelve and eighteen.

Table 12.2 presents data on parental education and household income patterns as a way to understand the socioeconomic background of second-generation Russian Jews. Despite the severe limitations put on Jewish educational achievement in the former Soviet Union since the 1950s (see Gold 1995), 82.3 percent of the respondents reported that at least one of their parents had a college degree. In 61 percent of the cases both parents were college graduates, while fewer than 20 percent reported that neither of their parents had a college education. Moreover, based on information reported by the respondents, 60 percent of them lived in households where both parents worked most of the time, while about 20 percent reported that at least one of their parents did not work most of the time. These data indicate that most of the children of Russian Jewish immigrants lived in

TABLE 12.2   PARENTAL BACKGROUND OF RUSSIAN JEWISH AMERICANS

	Number	Percentage
Parental college education		
Neither parent has college education	47	17.6%
One parent has college education	57	21.3
Both parents have college education	164	61.0
Total	269	100.0
Number of adult earners		
Both parents did not work most of the time	2	0.6
One parent worked some of the time	19	6.4
One parent worked most of the time	35	11.8
Both parents worked at least some of the time	62	20.9
Both parents worked most of the time	180	60.4
Total	298	100.0

Source: Author's compilation.

households with two incomes of college-educated workers. Even if we consider the status loss associated with immigration, table 12.2 suggests that the Russian Jewish immigrant community is generally well educated and financially stable.

Table 12.3 presents the educational attainment of second-generation Russian Jews by age. The data presented in the table suggest that they were following their parents' footsteps and pursuing postsecondary education. Among the youngest group, eighteen- to twenty-two-year-olds, about two-thirds had some college education. The majority of this group were enrolled in college at the time of interview. Among the twenty-three- to twenty-seven-year-olds, more than 60 percent had at least a bachelor's degree at the time of interview, about one-quarter had some college education, and only 2.2 percent of this age group had dropped out of high school. The oldest respondents in this group, twenty-eight- to thirty-two-year-olds, are obviously the most educated, with 31.7 percent reporting a graduate education and only 10.8 percent having less than some college education.

The fact that children of Russian Jewish immigrants are considered to be white, that they have high educational attainment, and that most of them come from well-educated and economically stable families has significant effects on the way they think of themselves and their community. These factors shape their path toward incorporation into American society as they navigate their lives and forge their futures in the New York of the twenty-first century. The next section presents one such story.

TABLE 12.3 EDUCATIONAL ATTAINMENT OF RUSSIAN JEWISH AMERICANS, BY AGE

	Less than High School		High School or GED		Some College		B.A. Degree		More than B.A. Degree		Total	
	Number	Percentage	Number	Percentage	Number	Percentage	Number	Percentage	Number	Percentage	Number	Percentage
Eighteen to twenty-two	21	11.9%	28	16.2%	112	63.7%	14	7.8%	1	0.5%	175	100%
Twenty-three to twenty-seven	2	2.2	10	11.4	22	24.3	43	47.4	13	14.8	91	100
Twenty-eight to thirty-two	1	2.5	4	8.3	13	29.8	12	27.8	14	31.7	44	100
Total	24	7.7	42	13.6	147	47.3	69	22.2	28	9.1	310	100

Source: Author's compilation.

"I FEEL FORTUNATE, I HAVE TWO CULTURES": ONE STORY, MANY INSIGHTS

Marina is a high-spirited thirty-two-year-old who works in the fashion industry. She emigrated with her family from the former Soviet Union in 1979. Her parents decided to emigrate "because [the Russians] were prejudiced against the Jews and so that we would be better off financially." The family settled in Brighton Beach. "It was okay," she said, "because, not knowing English, it was easier just getting around, particularly for the parents." Only in the United States did Marina realize that being Jewish "is both a religion and a nationality." "In Russia," she explained, "we were defined as Jews and that's that. Here we always have to distinguish—you are a Russian Jew. So while we were growing up with no religion in Russia, we knew we were different because we looked different."

In Russia Marina's family did not practice Judaism, although her grandmother had lingering childhood memories of some of the holidays. One time Marina came across a golden Star of David that her father had hidden in the house and did not dare to wear. Once when she was eleven, she remembered, "I was playing with my friends, and we started drawing different flags of different countries, and one of my friends asked me, 'What's a Jewish flag look like?' And I had no idea. I'd never seen one. I remember feeling very sad. 'Well, that's odd. I'm Jewish and I don't know it.' And I remember then going to my grandmother [and] she didn't know either. So that made me feel even sadder, and kind of odd. And [I thought to myself], Like, don't we have one?"

After immigrating to the United States, Marina's parents felt free to embrace Judaism and attended a Reform synagogue that catered to the Russian Jewish community. Although Marina did not attend synagogue as a teenager, she celebrated the holidays with her parents at home. "And even when I was married and my husband was not Jewish," she said, "we came to my parents for Jewish holidays to celebrate. Now that I am divorced and by myself, I also try to celebrate them."

Like many other children of immigrants, what was a comforting haven for parents could be a stifling ghetto for their children. From the beginning Marina aimed her sights outward, toward a larger, more diverse America. Living in the Russian community—where everybody knows everybody else and has an opinion about how young people dress, whom they date, and how much money they make—can be annoying at times. For young adults trying to figure out their way in life, being a part of a close-knit community can lead to too much control, too much pressure, and very limited exposure to, or participation in, New York, one of the most exciting cities in the world.

Marina's first encounter with American diversity was bittersweet. Starting at a local junior high school soon after arriving, she learned the gritty lessons of American pluralism from the mélange of Hispanics, African Americans, Chinese, Pakistanis, a lot of Russians like herself, and "some Americans," as Marina put it. Her classmates, she recalled, "didn't like it if you were Russian." The kids mocked the Russians for being immigrants, for not speaking English, and for not dressing like "an updated American kid. Everybody teased us." They were pushed and kicked in the hall.

Mixing had a flip side: in homeroom Marina sat next to a black boy, and "we really hit it off. I remember thinking he was cute," she said. By eighth grade most of her girl friends were black and Spanish, and once, after she and a Russian girl got in a dispute and the Russian girl threatened to "kick my ass, the black girls from my block took care of her—they roughed her up, and the Russian girl apologized to me. How could I not like these people?" By ninth grade things were much better "because we spoke more English, we were more American." Going to a specialized high school in the Chelsea section of Manhattan, the School of Fashion and Design, offered a taste of freedom. "Attitudes were very different. Kids there are a lot more cultured, and it was just fun." In high school her grades improved, in part because her English was much better and in part because she was "a lot more adapted to American culture."

Around this time Marina got into the punk scene and began hanging out in Washington Square, going to punk clubs, and dancing to new wave music. She spiked her hair glossy black, sometimes silver, and wore black lipstick and nail polish. "We dressed androgynous, or mostly in black, maybe gray, and everything layered. Actually, what they now call Gothic."

Exploring punk offered an opportunity to break free of the controls of Brighton Beach, a chance to be "American" and experience the excitement of life. Inevitably, Marina's explorations led to generational tensions. Her parents would tell her, "How come I don't look like a real girl, how come my hair's weird, what am I in to, why do I stay out so late? If I keep dressing like that, no guy will take me seriously and I will never get married."

Even now Marina chalked up her experience with punk to more then rebellion. She couldn't relate to "that whole Russian lifestyle. Russian people are very much into designer clothes, designer living, and status. My parents weren't like that. We weren't wealthy in Russia or in America, they wanted to make an honest living. They taught me, 'What's really important is to be a decent human being to get through life.'" Most of the Russian Jewish kids she knew didn't meet that ideal, and Marina found herself thinking, she said, "Oh my God, how boring, how disgusting, you found the lifestyle exactly of your parents. I remember thinking, Where's your own individuality?"

As Marina grew older, she became closer to the Russian Jewish community and identified proudly as a Russian Jew. She lived in a predominantly Russian Jewish section of Brooklyn on King's Highway. Most of her friends were now also Russian Jews. "It became more important because you have more things in common, as far as childhood and background." Her Russian improved. "There was a nail salon near my house that was owned by young Russian people. We started hanging out, and they would start telling jokes and anecdotes, and I really did not understand, so I started speaking Russian with them."

Nevertheless, when it came to a future marriage partner, Marina said, "I pretty much prefer people of black or Latin descent." Part of that preference was based in simple chemistry that went beyond romance. In almost every school or workplace setting, she had ended up with black friends because that was who she was comfortable with. She had been told that "one of the reasons black girls like me is that I'm not trying to be black. I think I am a very upfront and down-to-earth person, and I can be sarcastic and feel comfortable enough to make fun of myself. I think that's part of black and Latin culture."

There was still more to that connection. She had always been stirred by black literature and history. Maybe it had something to do with her experience of prejudice in Russia, maybe it was bound up in the humanitarian "Aquarian" part of her. She loved Maya Angelou, especially the poem "Phenomenal Woman." She recalled that in Angelou's autobiography, *All God's Children Need Traveling Shoes,*

> there's one line that really touched her, and she can remember crying. The author had left her African husband and moved to one of the countries on the West Coast of Africa. I think it was Liberia, Marina continues, and she and her son both said out loud they noticed that everybody was black and that's when they felt this is their country and they shed a tear. That was how I felt when I went to Israel for the first time, I stopped one day and looked around and thought, Oh my God, everybody's Jewish here. I understood how a black person could feel that way.

Marina's onetime plan to move to Israel, where her parents settled a few years ago, had been discarded. Her decision was based in part on practical considerations, such as the burden of learning Hebrew, a difficult language. Or maybe it was just that she had become too "American" to leave. "What can I tell you?" she asked with a devilish, self-bemused laugh. "I'm a shame to my Jewish countrymen. I'm too lazy to learn Hebrew, but not to learn Spanish, which appeals more to me."

In a sense, Marina's musical taste perfectly reflected the richness of her identity. When asked whether she listened to Russian music or Russian television, she emphatically said no. She did not mean to deny her affection for certain sentimental Russian love songs, or even the Russian pop she listened to as a twelve-year-old back in the former Soviet Union. But her real passion was for new wave, reggae, rap, and Latin music. She did not see this life of fusion as a burden, a prescription for confusion. She thought she was a richer person for it. Marina planned to teach her children someday about Russian as well as Jewish history and traditions. And she fully intended to raise them in a manner that would combine the Russian Jewish immigrants' way, which is "more involved" and keeps the family united, "so you know that no matter what you do you have your family's support," with the American way, which gives more freedom to the children. Straddling many cultures had been a kind of blessing. "I feel fortunate I have two cultures," Marina said.

ETHNIC OPTIONS: THE MANY WAYS OF BEING A RUSSIAN JEWISH AMERICAN

Unlike Marina, who seemed to live happily with the many complexities of her identity and viewed them as enriching and complementing experiences, many of the second-generation Russian Jews in the study were ambivalent and confused about the different dimensions of their identity, and many found it difficult to define who they were.

Although most second-generation Russian Jews felt that they were part of American society—they perceived the United States as home and intended to stay here—they were aware and proud of the fact that their values and way of life marked them as different from most other Americans. They tended to stay close to the community, the family, and the culture and intended to carry that culture over to the next generation. Those who attended college usually lived at home and went to nearby colleges, and those who were out of college also lived either with their parents or close by. They were proud to be Jews, and most of them engaged in some of the religious practices. Nevertheless, they did not consider themselves to be religious and perceived their Jewishness as a cultural and ethnic heritage, not a religious one. Many of them commented on the unwillingness of the community to "assimilate," but at the same time they stressed the importance of maintaining their Russian Jewish identity.

With regard to the issue of choosing a marriage partner, for example, the general sentiment was that it was very important to marry a fellow Jew. They spoke about the importance of making it easy for the families to get along, about not wanting to assimilate, and about having their partner understand them better. As this twenty-five-year-old man from Queens noted:

I guess I feel that I should marry a Jewish woman. [Why?] Well, because you know, everybody complains about assimilation, and I don't want to be a part of it. It's sort of like doing the dishonorable thing, you know. It feels like, if I marry a non-Jewish girl, I'm going to go into assimilation, cross that line. And even though I shouldn't really care, I should care what I want, maybe there's some things higher than what I want, you know? I guess some higher goals [are] beyond just [one] individual.

One respondent, a U.S.-born man from New Jersey, had married a non-Jew. His mother requested that the ceremony be conducted under the chuppah. They did that, and they also broke the glass at the end of the ceremony. He said they did it more "for fun" than as a matter of religion. With the birth of his son, however, he was becoming more and more interested in the cultural and historical dimensions of Jewishness—but also of Russian-ness.

When asked about their ethnicity, some simply said that they were Russian or Russian Jews or American. Others, like this twenty-nine-year-old man, were confused by the question. Replying that he had always considered his ethnicity to be "a question mark," he added:

I'm very intrigued in this, especially since my son was born, because I want to know so that we can chat about it. I asked one of my coworkers, who is a Hasidic Jew, to tell me about the history of ethnicity among Jewish people, and I received a very long, complicated answer, and he told me that this may not even have really been an answer. So I am very intrigued in really knowing, if it is possible, who I am ethnically, because I have no idea. What Eastern European, what Middle Eastern, what Western European genes have mixed to produce me—I really don't know.

When his American friends called him Russian, he would correct them: "According to them, that's what they just see, and at times I make the correction that I'm a Russian Jew. But what does that mean? Well, I don't know what that means. So that is an excellent question."

Back in the Soviet Union, Jews were a persecuted ethnic-national minority. The letter "J," standing for "Jewish," was printed in people's passports (the main identification in the former Soviet Union) under the "nationality" rubric and was usually experienced in terms of fear and blunt discrimination. Many of the respondents recalled discrimination against themselves and their families in the former Soviet Union, where Jews were not allowed into medical school and other high-prestige institutions and were constantly afraid of becoming the victims of violence. As a reaction to discrimination, many Jews opposed the government, often tacitly by not belonging to "the Party" or not fully participating in its activities (Gold 1995; Orleck 1999). Being Jewish meant being "smart" and educated. It also meant "knowing how to work the system"—negotiating the elaborate labyrinth of Communist bureaucracy and dealing with suspicious Gentiles. It was their Jewishness, which was an obstacle and a source of hardship that many wished to hide, that later turned into a great resource, allowing them and their families to leave the former Soviet Union.

Jewish identification had carried little intrinsic cultural or religious content in the former Soviet Union (mainly because Judaism was prohibited by the government); in the United States, on the other hand, Russian Jewish immigrants and their children were faced with many religious and secular forms of Jewish culture and a large and organized Jewish community that provided them with most of the resettlement services they received.

A small segment of immigrants became observant and joined the Orthodox community. Though welcomed, not all of them felt entirely accepted. Eighteen-year-old Rachel was born in the United States, shortly after her parents emigrated from Russia. After her birth, her mother had become increasingly observant, and now the family was part of the Orthodox community.

> [My mom] wanted me to get a Jewish education because in Russia she was not able to. The Jewish schools wanted a woman who was religious, who kept all the laws, who covered her hair. So my mother conformed a little bit . . . just so I can go to a Jewish school. Then, as I went along, I would ask, "Why don't you do this? Why don't you do that?" and eventually they started doing it. I don't know if they are doing it for the kids or they are doing it because they want to. But I think they would have stopped by now [if they did not like it].

All this Judaic renewal did not utterly vanquish a distinctively ethnic Russian identity. As she mulled her future partner, Rachel said she would definitely marry a religious person, but also someone from a Russian background, "so the parents can get along and they can meet in each other's houses. [My parents] feel that every American guy that goes out with me will always consider them Russian, will always look at them as lower."

More than paranoia, such sentiments were earned from hard experience. "There was this one guy who I knew his parents would not let me go out with him if they found out my parents were Russian . . . so I hid it. I did not say my parents were from Russia, I said that we muddled around in there." Rachel was troubled by the fact that she and her family could not fully feel a part of the Orthodox community and that her Russian background was considered a disadvantage, but she could do nothing about it besides trying even harder to blend in.

Most immigrants found the Orthodox way of life profoundly foreign and were intimidated by its rigorous demands. Typically, after the restraints of Russian life, they looked to America as a place of freedom, and they were reluctant to ghettoize themselves within the Orthodox community. Joining the mainstream Reform and Conservative communities appealed to some, since doing so gave heightened meaning to their Jewishness without being burdensome. Others expressed their Jewishness in "creative" ways—such as having a large family gathering and daylong feast on Yom Kippur (the most important fasting day in the Jewish religion). In general terms, second-generation Russian Jews can be described as ambivalently Jewish. That is to say, there was an overwhelming degree of pride among second-generation Russian Jews in being Jewish, and also some degree of religious practice. Nevertheless, the interpretation that most of them gave to their activities was more cultural and ethnic in character than religious.

Stan, a twenty-four-year-old real estate broker, came to the United States in his early teens and settled with his family in Bensonhurst, Brooklyn. His family and other immigrant families in the community were approached by an Orthodox rabbi who became a central personality in that community. Even after they moved to a different neighborhood, Stan and his family maintained close contacts with the rabbi and continued to attend services at his synagogue. Stan had the following opinions about Judaism:

Q: You consider yourself to be Jewish?

A: Yes.

Q: What does that mean to you?

A: The million-dollar question. I am Jewish. I'm not observant. It means support of a community for me personally. I think the Orthodoxy is the right thing. The fact that I am not observing is my personal thing rather than what I would say . . . the correct form is. I would say Orthodoxy is correct, but I'm not there.

Q: How often do you go to services?

A: I would say two or three times a month.

Q: You said you're not observant. What do you practice? Do you fast on Yom Kippur?

A: Definitely, yes.

Q: Do you observe holidays?

A: Yes.

Q: Is it practiced at home?

A: Definitely Yom Kippur. Rosh Hashanah and Passover to a limited extent. No bread.

Q: No bread on the first day?

A: No bread at all. . . . There could be not-kosher stuff, but no bread.

Lana, now thirty-two, came to the United States at the age of three. For her, "Judaism is more than a religion. You don't have to be observant to be a Jew." Lana, who fasts on Yom Kippur, said tentatively, "I guess it's symbolic. I light candles on Hanukkah because I think it is pretty. It's fun. I had dinner at my parents' house for Rosh Hashanah, but I don't go to shul."

Even those who were not practicing often expressed a strong, albeit clearly "ethnic" rather than religious, sense of Jewishness. For many respondents, being Jewish was very meaningful. It generally had a positive affective connotation. There was a sense of pride or belonging and of history and culture. The following are some examples of respondents' sentiments about "being Jewish":

> For me, it is primarily ethnic and cultural. A level of history that I completely accept and adopt. It doesn't extend to religion for me. I think that you can be just as Jewish without being religious at all. (a twenty-five-year-old male)

> It's not just being religious. Because people could be not religious and still be Jewish so—that kind of thing. A lot of people who are not Jewish and not Russian have a difficult time understanding that, and I get that a lot. (a twenty-six-year-old male)

> I still associate myself with the Jews and the heritage and background and what Jewish people have gone through, and my family, and so, yes, I definitely feel a sense of belonging. It's just the religious aspect that I don't partake in. (a twenty-three-year-old female)

Indeed, at least one respondent took chauvinistic pride in Jewishness in spite of, not because of, Judaism being a religion:

> I consider myself to be Jewish because I consider relative to all the other nationalities and ethnicities Jewish people are more smarter from my experience. And that's the main reason I consider myself lucky. And religious aspects of it are not as bad as some of the other religious aspects. Like, they don't make you feel as guilty. I don't think they ever teach you're going to go to hell if you do this. They are not as strict, and they don't have as many stupid things in the religion as other religions. If you're not religious, what else does being Jewish mean? It's like I said, it's part of a group where over the long run of hundreds and maybe thousands of years, I believe the Jewish religion inhibited people less than other religions. It lets people grow mostly intellectually, much better than in other religions. It limits you less. (a twenty-six-year-old male)

There was an alternative for those who were loath to give up all ethnic distinctiveness but felt uncomfortable with becoming just Jewish Americans. People whose parents were never fully accepted as Russians in the former Soviet Union could become "real" Russians in Brooklyn—living within the boundaries of the Russian-speaking community, which consists of many cultural, social, and economic institutions. One could find Russian-speaking businesses to fill practically any need—Russian delis and restaurants with exotic foods, insurance or travel agencies, day care, health or legal services, and home care services.

There is a thriving cultural industry in the Russian Jewish community that is manifested in the publication of books and newspapers in the Russian language, such as *Vicherny New York* (Evening New York) and the established *Novoya Ruskaya Slova* (New Russian Word), in Russian television channels (which broadcast locally produced Russian sitcoms, music videos, and talk shows as well as programs from Russia), and in a local music industry.

The identity of community members is largely Russo-centric, derived from their Russian as well as their Jewish heritage, while borrowing from contemporary American life. For some Russian Jewish Americans, emigration enabled them to rediscover a sense of Russian-ness. They celebrated Russian language and culture and stressed the importance of having *Russian* Jewish friends. Some chose to participate in school or university activities based on the presence of other Russian immigrants. For example, one respondent joined the Russian Club at Yeshiva University, where he and his fellow members would gather for social activities, such as attending a Broadway show. "I really enjoyed it," he recalled. "It is important, because they understand you much better than anybody else."

Although some people were critical of the oppressive government and poor living conditions that they or their parents had experienced in "the old country," they were often nostalgic about their old life, comparing the warmth of friendships in the old country to those in the United States, where everything seemed to them to be about money. Nevertheless, those who went back to visit returned to the States with very strong but mixed emotions associated with "connecting with their roots," on the one hand, but also with feelings of estrangement and confusion about their identity, on the other. Gene, a twenty-year-old college student, commented on his visit to his hometown ten years after immigrating to the United States:

> I visited my old school. I was a little bit nostalgic. Otherwise, I felt like it was a little bit confusing, because I realized that I have changed, or they have changed, so much that I can't get along with them, or there was an imprint of a different society on me, that I can't really communi-

cate with them and I have different interests and points of view. So it was a little bit harsh, I would say, getting together with my old friends and trying to find our common language. So that was the last time I went.

IDENTITY-SHAPING FACTORS

Feelings of discrimination and fear of violence are central in shaping the identity of Jews in the former Soviet Union. Viga, a twenty-one-year-old woman who came to the United States at the age of ten and was currently a graduate student at NYU, had a very emotional reply to the question: "What does being a Russian Jew mean to you?"

> It's an ethnicity. It carries some background. . . . It carries some cultural stuff. [Russian Jews] were so thoroughly deracialized because you see a mommy, daddy being shot, and you don't want to speak Yiddish anymore. That's what my grandma went through. Her parents were shot by the Russian pogromists before her very eyes. Never again did she so much as hint (of being Jewish). She married a Ukrainian man, which was a big defection from the Jewish tradition. They don't marry other people, especially Ukrainians, who are known for their anti-Semitism. That was a very bad thing. The only Jewishness that came through was the obsession with education. Higher education and books. . . . I have my grandma's last name. I took it when I got naturalized. She had a tremendous influence in my life. I didn't want that last name to die with her. . . . So that's the only thing about Jewishness, there was no religion.

Discrimination and fear were also the main reasons Jews decided to leave the former Soviet Union, seeking a safer way of life and better opportunities for themselves and their children. Alla, a twenty-year-old college student who came to the United States at the age of eight, described what triggered her family's decision to immigrate:

> I guess it was when my mom worked for a computer company in Russia and they were getting imports from out of Russia. The whole computer [center] of Ukraine was there in our little town, and she was one of the head people, and they were making a group to go to Italy for some project. And then they told her since she was Jewish she cannot go. And this was a last-minute thing. And my parents just got furious.

Respondents' connection to Jewishness often had a lot to do with family relationships and parents' attitudes. One respondent rejected religion because he had a conflictual relationship with his father, who had forced it on him. Another respondent, who had a good relationship with her parents and whose family tried to preserve religious rituals even before immigration, became involved with a synagogue and was actively observant. Yet another respondent, a twenty-eight-year-old male, rejected religion but had a strong feeling of pride about being Jewish owing to his mother's influence:

> She sent me to yeshiva, to the Jewish school. And she liked me to understand . . . where my heritage comes from, and she liked to be Jewish, is very proud of being Jewish. She wanted me to have some understanding of it. She didn't want to, nor could she, turn me into a person that's completely religious, but she gave me a bar mitzvah and stuff.

Another important factor shaped the Jewish sentiment of the second-generation Russian Jews—their attitudes toward and attachments to Israel. Attitudes toward Israel were an important source of Jewish identity, mainly for those who did not have a strong religious identity. About one-third of the respondents had visited Israel at least once, and most of those who had not visited Israel wanted or intended to do so.

Those who had been to Israel described it as a wonderful experience. They recalled the gorgeous places they had been to and the wonderful people they had met. Most of them also described their strong spiritual experiences in Israel and the profound feeling of "longing" and "fascination" they had being for the first time in a place "where everybody is Jewish."

> Well, it's sort of a fascination, almost like a longing. Maybe it's the original—a homeland . . . because I could never feel America as a homeland. Because it's not like I was born here. And actually, I can't say Israel is my homeland, because I wasn't born there either, but it's a very complicated thing, I don't understand all of it myself. (a twenty-three-year-old female)

> It was this incredible feeling of spirituality in the air, and I'm not a religious person, so to have this overpowering feeling of—these are our roots—it was great. [We] went to Jerusalem, did all the sights. [We] went to the Wailing Wall, but then we also went, like, scuba diving, so they really, like, had everything packed into the trip. So it was great. (a twenty-five-year-old female)

Several respondents stated that, if needed, they would actively support Jews and the state of Israel.

> On a daily, humdrum basis, I don't feel any responsibility, but when push comes to shove, of course I do. If there was a major riot about the state of Israel, I would participate in support of what I would feel about the situation. I would feel responsible. But on a daily basis, no. And to

date, I have not done this at all. That's the track record. (a twenty-two-year-old male)

Well, like, for example, if there would be, like, riots against Jews, like a war where Israel was in danger of annihilation, I think I would do as much as I can. (a twenty-four-year-old male)

Although most respondents shared the feeling that Israel was the country of the Jewish people and the source of their pride, they also perceived it as a dangerous country (because of the national security situation, the terrorist attacks, and the mandatory army service) and one that offers fewer economic opportunities and less mobility. One respondent noticed that her relatives in Israel seemed to have smaller houses and cars than the family in the United States, even though they had "good jobs." Such perceptions led respondents to view Israel as a symbolic home and homeland, but not as a place they would consider settling and living in.

Another important factor in the process of ethnic identity formation among second-generation Russian Jews was their contact with the main institutions of their "proximal host" (Mittelberg and Waters 1992)– the American Jewish community.[6] As in the case of the Israeli immigrants described by David Mittelberg and Mary Waters (1992), there is a disjuncture between the elements that Russian Jews use to define ethnicity and those used by the American Jewish community. This disjuncture was the underlying cause of the ambivalence that Russian Jewish Americans felt toward their Jewishness and its interpretation.

And indeed, the issue of Jewish identity and its manifestation was a point of contention between the established Jewish American community and the Russian Jews who had come since 1965. The relationship between the two groups has been a major factor in Russian Jews' construction of an ethnic identity in the United States in cultural as well as structural terms. It was the established Jewish community that was responsible for lobbying the U.S. government to let Russian Jews into the country and grant them refugee status. They were also responsible for providing their "lost Jewish cousins" with resettlement and social services and allocating government resources to them. American Jews expected and in many cases insisted that the new immigrants "assimilate" into the community and adhere to its cultural norms and organizational structure. The Russian Jews in turn felt that they were being forced to adopt an identity that was unfamiliar to them, while at the same time being alienated and excluded from decisionmaking positions within the community and its organizations (Orleck 1999).

Most immigrants came from Russia knowing very little about Judaism and its religious practices. It was usually some form of Jewish educational program (such as yeshivas, day camps, after-school programs, or Hebrew school) that exposed them and their children to Jewish culture, tradition, and practice as it was constructed in the United States. It is important to note that even though most second-generation Russian Jews did not consider themselves religious, they reported relatively high levels of participation in Jewish ceremonies (such as having a bar mitzvah and lighting candles on Hanukkah). This was mostly a result of their exposure and participation in the American Jewish institutional context, which highlighted the centrality of the social structure to the construction of identity and its content.

For many immigrant families, the first contact with religion was through the yeshiva. Afraid of the unfamiliar public schools, many Russian immigrants sent their children to yeshivas, which were controlled by equally unfamiliar Orthodox Jews. The Russians saw the yeshiva as a way to satisfy a preeminently secular desire to shield their kids from "undesirable influences," such as drugs and crime. Orthodox institutions made great efforts to reach out to the Russian Jews through social services and subsidized education; in return, they expected the immigrants to become part of the Orthodox community.

The yeshiva experience was not always a happy one, and often the disappointment was mutual. The Orthodox were dismayed when the Russian Jews did not take to Orthodoxy, and the Russians chafed at the condescending and disrespectful manner in which they were treated by the Orthodox. Natalie, a twenty-five-year-old lawyer, was six when her family migrated to the United States. She went to a Jewish day school that had made Russian Jews their "project." "They were sort of disappointed in us," she said wryly. "They watched all these things on television about refuseniks and these poor Russian Jews wanting so desperately to study Torah and weren't being allowed to—so now they will [be able to]." But, she added with a smile, "we did not want to study Torah, and they were not happy with us."

The demands for observance placed on the children frequently caused tension with parents who were not observant or not observant enough. "It was traumatic, for me and for my parents," recalled Lana, a twenty-nine-year-old who attended yeshivas from first grade until graduation from high school. "[My parents] did not want to be religious. They explained that they have been this way for this long and were not going to change [and become more observant]. They said that when I grow up and have my own house I could do whatever I wanted, but that I am not going to change their life."

Since Russian Jews are unwilling to fully assimilate into their proximal host group of Jewish Americans and are not willing to return to their country of origin, they are left, according to Mittelberg and Waters (1992, 430), with only two other options. They can create a separate community based on a

Russian Jewish American ethnicity that does not revolve around religion, or they can evolve into a symbolic ethnicity and retain only loose ties with either a Russian or a Jewish ethnicity.

CONCLUSIONS: "MY HOME IS AMERICA"

The discourse about Jewishness as well as Russian-ness among young Russian Jewish Americans illuminates the three important factors that Keefe (1992) describes as associated with the construction of ethnic identity. First is the perception of differences between Jews and non-Jews. This boundary is twofold in that it aligns Russian Jewish Americans with other Jews in the United States, and elsewhere, while at the same time pointing to the difference between Jews and non-Jews within the Russian community. Second, the pride in Jewish and Russian heritage, history, culture, and tradition is very central in the discourse about identity and its meaning. And third, the collective as well as the personal memories and narratives regarding discrimination and persecution in the former Soviet Union are central factors shaping the ethnic identity of Russian Jewish Americans. Nevertheless, there are other factors that influence their ethnic identity, such as class and race as well as attitudes toward Israel and contact with Jewish American institutions.

But whatever else they may be, the children of Russian Jewish immigrants are sure of one thing—they are becoming Americans. Their parents may still be foreigners, but they are not:

> I would definitely identify myself as an American New Yorker. So within that, it's like being able to eat in every restaurant, every kind of food that is available to you and communicates so much about culture. I think that speaks for itself volumes. I can have incredible Ethiopian food for lunch and then have a wonderful Korean dinner. And that's what being an American is. With all the liberties to express how you feel about that, as you wish. . . . All discarded into a disposable plastic bag. (a twenty-one-year-old woman)

Only a few expressed any interest in returning to the former Soviet Union, even for a visit. Although most wanted to visit Israel, only a minority would consider settling there permanently. Most of the respondents were somewhat confused and ambivalent about the different components of their ethnic identity and their meanings and manifestations, but at the same time they were reluctant to give up that identity; they did not feel that being a Russian Jew was at odds with becoming American. For better or for worse, America, and particularly New York, was home. And most of them liked it that way. They were very happy to live in the United States—the "land of opportunity," or more specifically, in New York the city of "cultural diversity"—and they intended to seize all of the opportunities, freedoms, and cultural richness it had to offer. If you asked them, there was nothing to stop them from pursuing the American Dream except their own will and hard work. In a way it seems that constructing a unique Russian Jewish identity was part of becoming American—or more specifically, white middle-class American.

I am greatly indebted to Philip Kasinitz, Yehouda Shenhav, Anat Liebler, Jennifer Holdaway, and especially to Hani Zubida for their candid and unwavering support, and for their valuable suggestions and thoughtful comments on earlier drafts.

NOTES

1. According to most estimates, 80 percent of the immigrants and their children are Jewish, at least in the broadest sense of the term.
2. The Immigrant Second Generation in Metropolitan New York Study, from which data for this chapter were collected, was supervised by Philip Kasinitz, John Mollenkopf, and Mary C. Waters. The study looked at young adults, ages eighteen to thirty-two, whose parents are from five immigrant groups: Dominicans, Chinese, West Indians, South Americans, and Russian Jews, and who had lived in the United States for at least six years, as well as three "native" groups— native whites of native parentage, native African Americans of native parentage, and Puerto Ricans—for comparison. The two elements of the study were a multistage household telephone survey in New York City and its suburbs, with interviews lasting about forty minutes, and in-depth, loosely structured in-person interviews with a 10 percent subsample of the telephone respondents. These follow-up interviews each lasted between one and a half and four hours. Through these interviews extensive information was gathered about respondents' family backgrounds, the neighborhoods in which they grew up, the schools they attended, their experiences with various institutional settings, their labor market outcomes, and their political and social participation.

    The statistics reported later are based on 311 phone surveys, and the quotations are taken from 40 in-depth interviews (most of which I conducted myself) with second-generation Russian Jews. The selection criteria for this group are based on a very broad definition of religion; thus, any respondent in the appropriate age group who self-identified as Jewish, or who lived in a household where any of the members self-identified as Jewish, was qualified to participate in the research.
3. I would like to expand the last proposition to include perceptions of not only discrimination but also of favoritism.
4. See, for example, Brodkin's (1998) argument.

5. For a full description of the Russian Jewish sample, see Kasinitz, Zeltzer-Zubida, and Zoya Simakhodskaya (2001).
6. The proximate host is the group to which the receiving society assigns immigrants—the waiting category in the minds of the individuals in the receiving society.

REFERENCES

Alba, Richard. 1985. "The Twilight of Ethnicity Among Americans of European Ancestry: The Case of Italians." *Ethnic and Racial Studies* 8: 134–58.
————. 1990. *Ethnic Identity: The Transformation of White America.* New Haven, Conn.: Yale University Press.
Brodkin, Karen. 1998. *How the Jews Became White Folks and What That Says About Race in America.* New Brunswick, N.J.: Rutgers University Press.
Gans, Herbert. 1979. "Symbolic Ethnicity: The Future of Ethnic Groups and Cultures in America." *Ethnic and Racial Studies* 2(1): 1–20.
Gold, Steven J. 1995. *From the Workers' State to the Golden State: Jews from the Former Soviet Union in California.* Boston: Allyn and Bacon.
Hurtado, Aida, Patricia Gurin, and Timothy Peng. 1994. "Social Identities: A Framework for Studying the Adaptations of Immigrants and Ethnics: The Adaptation of Mexicans in the United States." *Social Problems* 41: 129–51.
Kasinitz Philip, Aviva Zeltzer-Zubida, and Zoya Simakhodskaya. 2001. "The Next Generation: Russian Jewish Young Adults in Contemporary New York." Working paper 178. New York: Russell Sage Foundation.
Keefe, Susan Emley 1992. "Ethnic Identity: The Domain of Perceptions of and Attachment to Ethnic Groups and Cultures." *Human Organization* 51: 35–43.
Mittelberg, David, and Mary Waters. 1992. "The Process of Ethnogenesis Among Haitian and Israeli Immigrants in the United States." *Ethnic and Racial Studies* 15(3): 412–35.
Nagel, Joane. 1994. "Constructing Ethnicity: Creating and Recreating Ethnic Identity." *Social Problems* 41(1): 152–76.
Ogbu, John U. 1990. "Cultural Model, Identity, and Literacy." In *Cultural Psychology: Essays on Comparative Human Development*, edited by James W. Stingler, Richard A. Shweder, and Gilbert Herdt. Cambridge: Cambridge University Press.
Orleck, Annelise. 1987. "The Soviet Jews: Life in Brighton Beach, Brooklyn." In *New Immigrants in New York*, edited by Nancy Foner. New York: Columbia University Press.
————. 1999. *The Soviet Jewish Americans.* Westport, Conn.: Greenwood Press.
Sales, Teresa. 1999. "Constructing an Ethnic Identity: Brazilian Immigrants in Boston, Mass." *Migration World Magazine* 27: 15–21.
Waters, Mary C. 1990. *Ethnic Options: Choosing Identities in America.* Berkeley: University of California Press.

CHAPTER 13

COSMOPOLITAN ETHNICITY: SECOND-GENERATION INDO-CARIBBEAN IDENTITIES

NATASHA WARIKOO

If the applicant is a white person within the meaning of this section he is entitled to naturalization; otherwise not. . . . A high caste Hindu, of full Indian blood, born at Amritsar, Punjab, India, is not a "white person."
—*U.S. Supreme Court decision in* U.S. v. Bhagat Singh Thind, *1923*

DURING the 1920s, Bhagat Singh Thind, an Indian immigrant to the United States, attempted to become a naturalized citizen under a law that gave the right of naturalization to "white" residents. The U.S. Supreme Court eventually denied Thind's right to citizenship, based on his nonwhite status, in spite of arguments that scientific racial classification systems at the time placed northern Indians in the category of "Caucasian."

Since the time of Bhagat Singh Thind, race has had a strong impact on the experiences of immigrants, although today's immigrants have less interest in pushing for identification as "white" in all spheres of their lives. Arturo Vargas, the executive director of the National Association of Latino Elected and Appointed Officials, suggests that, "to the extent that being white means being American, we [Latinos] are white. But at the same time, we don't have to deny being Latino as much as before because we've had a significant civil rights movement, and politically we're still one block" (quoted in Moore and Fields 2002). In this chapter, I explore the relationship between race and ethnic identity through the experiences of second-generation Indo-Caribbean teenagers. I ask: What happens to the identities of second-generation youth who do not fit into American white or black categories, who are not easily identified racially, and who live in neighborhoods in which no ethno-racial group dominates?

I used second-generation Indo-Caribbean teenagers as a case study in an attempt to answer this question. Indo-Caribbeans hail mostly from Guyana and Trinidad. Their ancestors came to the West Indies during the nineteenth and early twentieth centuries as indentured servants from India to work on sugar plantations. Through in-depth interviews with thirty-one teenagers in the New York City metropolitan area and a school ethnography in Queens, I explored the identities of second-generation Indo-Caribbean teenagers, who are South Asian by race, West Indian by ethnicity, American by nationality, and Hindu, Christian, and Muslim by religious background. The interviews discussed self-definitions of identity; tastes in music, dress, and Hindi movies; and social networks. I found that Indo-Caribbean youth had multivalent, "thick," and fluid identities that could not be categorized simply. This *cosmopolitan ethnicity*, as I call it, was thick, like black racial identity in the United States, because it influenced all aspects of life.[1] Thickness, or salience, in this context describes the presence and expectation of ethno-racial identity rather than the weight of particular identities.[2]

Simultaneously, cosmopolitan ethnicity is chosen and multifaceted, like the symbolic ethnicity of white ethnic communities (Gans 1979; Waters 1990; Alba 1990). Its cosmopolitanness stems from the influence and presence of cultural forms and individuals from a diversity of ethnic and racial groups. Four main factors led to cosmopolitan ethnicity: cultural backgrounds in multi-ethnic societies; the multi-ethnic environments in which Indo-Caribbean youth lived and attended school; an absence of economic competition to solidify ethnic boundaries; and a race that was neither black nor white. Finally, gender strongly influenced the ethnicity choices made by the Indo-Caribbean youth I interviewed.

CONCEPTUALIZING RACE AND ETHNICITY

Stephen Cornell and Douglas Hartmann (1998) recognize that race and ethnicity are socially constructed categories, and they distinguish race and ethnicity in three main ways: ethnicity is based on claims of shared history, symbols, and descent, whereas race is based on perceived physical differences; ethnicity is usually self-asserted, whereas race is usually assigned by others; and race more commonly reflects unequal power relations. In this study, I focused on ethnicity by exploring teenagers' self-described identities as well as their social and cultural habits. I recognize, however, that racial assignment often influences ethnicity as well. Indo-Caribbeans are racially South Asian yet ethnically West Indian, and this complexity was evident in how they discussed their identities.[3]

Cornell and Hartmann (1998, 82) also look at the thickness versus thinness of identities, or "the degree to which an ethnic or racial identity organizes the social life of the group." This notion of the depth of ethnic or racial identity is relevant to my research as well, although I used thickness to mean the thick presence and expectation of ethnic identity assertion in general rather than the thickness of particular identities. I found that thick identity does not necessarily parallel racial assignment. That is, my respondents had thick identities that were more asserted and multivalent than assigned and unitary.

THEORIES OF IDENTITY

In *Ethnic Options*, Mary Waters finds that white suburban Catholics who are second-generation or higher have "symbolic ethnicity": ethnic identity that is chosen and can be turned off or on according to convenience or cultural trends or for any other reasons (Waters 1990; Gans 1979).[4] This group fits the traditional straight-line assimilation model, meaning that by the third generation the community has become part of mainstream white America in its social networks, culture, and economic status. The white suburban Catholics of Waters's study choose to display their ethnicities only sometimes, such as during ethnic holidays. Because no racial differences with dominant American society mark white Catholics, they are able to choose when to take on an ethnic identity—for example, displaying Irish identity on St. Patrick's Day— and when to simply be "American" with no hyphen. Thus, for Americans whose ascriptive identities do not mark them as marginalized, ethnicity is optional (Waters 1990; Appiah 1996). What happens, then, to ethnic communities that are not white?

In *Black Identities*, Waters (1999) describes the identities of black West Indian New Yorkers. She finds three modes of identity for the children of black West Indian immigrants: African American identity, largely associated with living in poor or working-class African American neighborhoods and with oppositional identity; ethnic identity, largely associated with living in mostly white suburbs and involving a distancing from African Americans by emphasizing ethnic identity; and immigrant identity, largely associated with recently arrived immigrants. Waters argues that the racial hierarchy of the United States quickly subsumes the ways in which immigrant and second-generation black youth identify and that the master status of black racial identity quickly affects their self-conceptions. Although race defines a strong identity for second-generation black West Indians, within black identity the youth still make choices about *how* they construct a black identity, shaped largely by the environment in which they live.

Although Chinese, Mexican, and Indian immigrants have come to the United States since the nineteenth century, discussions of race in America have traditionally focused on the black-white racial divide of the urban Northeast. On the one hand, if we think that racism affects blacks more significantly than other groups, especially with respect to interpersonal discrimination and residential segregation (Massey and Denton 1993), then we might expect nonblack minorities to be less affected by their nonwhite status and in general to show less desire to create an explicit, strong identification with one group, as is the case with the white ethnics in Waters's *Ethnic Options* (1990). On the other hand, individuals who are neither black nor white often elicit assumptions of foreignness, even if they are second-generation or higher (Tuan 1998). This may prevent them from moving into a mainstream "American" culture—whether black or white—and hence they may cling to what Waters (1999) calls an immigrant identity, even in the second generation and beyond. The effect of a multi-ethnic environment, however, might be quite different.

MULTI-ETHNICITY

What happens in the multi-ethnic environment? This question is motivated by the increasing preponderance of multi-ethnic neighborhoods in certain urban areas, such as New York City, Los Angeles, and Miami (Alba et al. 1995; Frey and Farley 1996).[5] Richard Alba and his colleagues (1995) found that between 1970 and 1990 the New York City metropolitan area experienced a sharp increase in multi-ethnic census tracts and a decline in all-white tracts. In fact, the most frequent racial combination found by these authors was mixed neighborhoods of whites, blacks, Hispanics, and Asians. Sixty percent of residents in the New York metropolitan area lived in one of these neighborhoods or in one that was white-Hispanic-Asian.[6] Consequently, public schools in urban America, especially in immigrant-receiving cities such as New York and Los Angeles, serve an increasingly diverse student body. Gary Orfield and John Yun (1999) report an increase in the number of schools with three or more racial groups and an increase in the diversity of the schools that students of color attend. Multi-ethnicity creates a situation in which no one "American" or "ethnic" way of being predominates over others. Many of the chapters in this volume vividly describe multi-ethnic environments in New York City (see Karen Chai Kim, Foerster, Malkin, Marwell, and Trillo). An interest in understanding the effects of the multi-ethnic environment on teenagers' constructions of ethnic and racial identity motivates this study.

THE CASE OF INDO-CARIBBEANS

I chose to use second-generation Indo-Caribbean youth in New York City as a case study to understand how nonblack and nonwhite immigrants understand themselves as Americans in a multi-ethnic environment. Because a sizable second-generation South Asian community exists in New York City, I could observe whether Indo-Caribbean youth identify with other South Asians, with Asian Americans more broadly, with black West Indians and by association African Americans, or with all or none of the above. We might expect, given South Asians' status in the United States (Indians have the highest median income, and the model minority stereotype is often applied to South Asians),[7] that the second generation would have an incentive to move into the South Asian community, which is very similar to Indo-Caribbean society in the West Indies but also very different. Also, if ascriptive race continues to dominate American society, we would expect Indo-Caribbeans to identify most with the South Asian diaspora. On the other hand, if ethnicity predominates, Indo-Caribbeans might identify more strongly with West Indians as a whole. I look at self-identifications as well as at how identity manifests itself in consumption and taste preferences and in social networks.

INDO-CARIBBEAN HISTORY

Indians have a long and complicated history in the West Indies. The relationships of Caribbean Indians with India have at times and in certain aspects been strong, and at other times quite tenuous. After slavery was abolished in 1833 in the West Indies, companies began importing indentured laborers from India (as well as from other countries) to meet the labor needs of plantations formerly run by slave labor, mostly in Guyana and Trinidad. The last boat of indentured servants from India arrived in the Caribbean in 1917 (Vertovec 1992). By 1924 300,000 Indians had arrived in Guyana and Trinidad, roughly 80 percent of whom stayed in the Caribbean (Williams 1970; Vertovec 1992). Another 100,000 settled on other Caribbean islands (Birbalsingh 1993). Black-Indian strife sometimes erupted, a result of colonial attempts to divide and conquer people along racial and religious lines (Prashad 2001). Planters often used Indian workers to undercut the demands of black workers, and in Trinidad planters and colonial rulers organized the economy so that blacks lived largely in urban areas and Indians in rural areas (Kale 1995; Prashad 2001). Culturally, Indo-Caribbeans blended their diverse Indian cultures and eliminated the solid caste system of their Indian heritage (Vertovec 1992).

Some points of interracial and interreligious solidarity existed between former slaves and indentured servants. For example, Hindu, Muslim, and Afro-Trinidadian working people all participated in Trinidad's *hosay* festival, which originated in a Muslim festival commemorating the death of Hussain, the grandson of Mohammed (Prashad 2001). By the late nineteenth century, however, colonial rulers had cracked down on the hosay festival and begun a policy of "cultural development" by inviting orthodox Hindu and Muslim leaders from abroad to Trinidad in attempts to break solidarity between Indian Muslim, Hindu, and (largely Christian) black Trinidadians. Furthermore, as many Caribbean Indians bought land from emancipated slaves, they gradually became a land-owning class and hence attracted resentment from Afro-Caribbeans, especially in Guyana. Thus, a somewhat contentious history between Afro- and Indo-Caribbeans began many years ago and was fueled in part by colonial desires to divide the people of Guyana and Trinidad. This history led to the current makeups of Guyana and Trinidad, where 51 percent and 40 percent of the populations, respectively, are of Indian descent.

Political strife in Guyana and the 1983 economic recession in Trinidad led large numbers of West Indians, including those of Indian descent, to migrate to the United States, three-fourths of whom settled in New York City (Foner 2000; Vertovec 1992). Today, Richmond Hill, Queens, has become a common destination for Indo-Caribbean families. Accurate statistical information on this community remains elusive, owing to the lack of an obvious category on census race and ancestry questions.[8] One indicator of the scale of Indo-Caribbean migration to the United States is the fact that about 240,000 Guyanese and Trinidadian immigrants live in New York State, according to the 2000 census. Overall, however, slightly more than 10 percent of them mark "Asian Indian" as their racial identity. If the second generation is the size of the first generation (as is the case for the United States as a whole), then at least 50,000 Indo-Caribbeans live in New York State (U.S. Department of Commerce 2000).

METHODOLOGY

In addition to a month-long ethnography at Harrison High School in Queens, I conducted thirty-one in-depth interviews.[9] I met approximately half of my respondents through contacts with community leaders and a subsequent snowball sample. The other half were students recruited at the high school of my ethnographic research. Nineteen respondents were second-generation, four were 1.5-generation (immigrants who came to the United States before age twelve), and eight were more recently arrived immigrants. I interviewed fifteen young men and sixteen young women. All lived in Manhattan, Queens, Brooklyn, or Jersey City. All but two respondents ranged in age from fifteen to nineteen. The two exceptions were thirteen and twenty. Finally, I visited many community organizations, including a campaign office, religious institutions, and youth groups. The interviews focused on teenagers' constructions of their identities, both through how they understood themselves and through their behaviors. I used two main aspects of behavior to illuminate the acculturation process: taste or cultural preferences and social networks.

RESEARCH CONTEXT

> *We're from Guyana, my neighbors are from—some are from Africa, some are from Puerto Rico, I believe someone's from China, down the street, so when we all come together we talk about our cultures and our differences. If we have a religious function, a jundi [the Indo-Caribbean term for a Hindu religious service], we invite all the neighbors over because they're very interested in seeing what we do and the beliefs that we have. And if they have a function, we'll go over there [to] see their cultural background.*

I call the neighborhood in which Harrison High School is located Ethnictown. As discussed earlier, new trends in immigrant residential patterns, especially in port cities such as New York, have led to a rise in multi-ethnic environments. Ethnictown was once a largely Italian and Irish middle-class neighborhood. Recently, middle-class Indo-Caribbeans, first from Guyana and now increasingly also from Trinidad, are moving into Ethnictown, many from a neighboring and more predominantly Indo-Caribbean neighborhood.[10] The neighborhood's census tract indicates a mixed community: 15 percent of the residents are non-Hispanic white, 10 percent are black, 19 percent are Asian Indian, and 25 percent are Hispanic (U.S. Department of Commerce 2000).[11] My anecdotal experience suggests that the vast majority of the Asian Indians by race in the neighborhood are ethnically West Indian.[12] The other Asian Indians are more recent immigrants from South Asia, most of them Punjabi Sikhs. The area is middle-class, with row houses along the residential streets, many with American flags alongside flags from Puerto Rico, Guyana, Trinidad, Jamaica, and many other countries, as well as West Indian Hindu prayer flags. Along one of the main avenues of the neighborhood lie shops that cater to the Indo-Caribbean community, selling West Indian meat pies, curries, *rotis*, *saris*, and all sorts of music (especially Hindi film songs, *soca*, *chutney soca*, reggae, Hindi remixed music, and Punjabi *bhangra*).[13]

Harrison High School is also diverse. According to the New York City Board of Education's statistics, in 2001 Harrison High's student body was 12 percent non-Hispanic white, 31 percent non-Hispanic black, 31 percent Hispanic, and 26 percent Asian and other, largely mirroring the surrounding neighborhood. The school has a reputation for being safe and secure, and indeed some students explained that safety was the reason they had moved to the school after feeling unsafe in other Queens and Brooklyn high schools. The school was vastly over-crowded; at close to four thousand students, the school operated at 170 percent of its capacity. The school principal identified this as the school's number-one problem, and one that pervaded every aspect of student life, from classroom overcrowding to no lunch breaks to difficult extracurricular scheduling. There had been a sharp increase in the number of poor children attending Harrison High School. In 1998 only 11 percent of the student body was eligible for fed-erally subsidized free lunch at school. By 2000 that percentage had grown to 34 percent, including 58 percent of the entering ninth- and tenth-grade students. Thus, the school was in a state of transition, trying to deal with overcrowding and to manage a student body that hailed from fifty-seven different countries.

FINDINGS

In the following sections, teens insightfully describe the multiple aspects of their identities.

IDENTITY

> *If you're Guyanese Indian, you're not really Indian. . . . I never really felt like I fit in with groups of just Indian kids. . . . But at the same time, you're not exactly Caribbean, just because you have that Indian background, so it's a very unique kind of other thing.*

When asked about their identities, second-generation Indo-Caribbean youth gave quite diverse answers.[14] Individuals reported giving different answers de-pending on the specific question asked, who was asking, and where they were in New York City when asked (see also Butterfield, this volume). It is inter-esting to note, however, that none said simply, "American." Race and ethnic-ity clearly play important roles in the lives of these youth. The multi-ethnic environment seemed to create a situation in which individuals were expected to have some kind of ethnicity, although the lack of a dominant ethno-racial group allowed for less rigidity in the color line.

Because of the contextual nature of identity, questions about religion, na-tionality, culture, race, and so on elicited quite different responses from these young people. One second-generation Guyanese young man, age eighteen, said explicitly:

> I say I am American as far as my nationality would go. But if anyone asks, "I am Indian," or, "My parents are from Guyana." I consider my-self West Indian. . . . Different contact, different question, different an-

swer. If it was "Where are you from?" I would say, "Here." Or "Where are your parents from?" I would say, "Guyana." "What are you?" I would say, "Indian," obviously, because I have a Hindu background.

This young man, as well as others with similar responses, expressed little to no confusion, consternation, or conflict with the multiple aspects of his identity. Responses also changed depending on who was asking the question. Chris, age sixteen, had a Guyanese mother and a mixed white father:

> When I'm hanging out with the Indian kids, I say I'm white, but when I'm hanging out with the white kids, I say I'm Indian. . . . If anybody makes fun of white people, I be like, "Hey, I'm Indian, look at me, I'm Indian!" Or if they start making fun of Indian people, I say, "I'm white! Don't you see my father?" . . . I can choose, I can kind of choose.

In addition to different responses for different questions and different situations, teens recognized that their self-definitions also changed over time. Rich, a nineteen-year-old recent immigrant from Trinidad, put it succinctly: "When I was in Trinidad I was considered . . . Indian. Now it's, like . . . people come up to me asking if I'm from the Middle East, from India . . . so it's, like, your identity changes. Your identity is affected by other people . . . people's views on your identity."

Rich no longer thought of himself as Indian, in part because others associated Indians and Middle Eastern immigrants with negative behaviors. That is, his ascriptive identity changed when his environment changed. Surveys that ask closed-ended questions about ethnic identity miss this dynamic aspect of ethnic identity. Many studies do acknowledge the changing nature of ethnic identity over time (see Portes and Rumbaut 2001; Waters 1999), but not across contexts within the same individual (for an exception, see Harris and Sim 2002).

Although most teens seemed comfortable in their multiple, contextual identities, many did describe frustration with others' attempts to categorize them. For example, when I met Roma, she wore a summer dress, an Indian *bindi* on her forehead, and had long, painted nails with designs on them, a style made popular in New York City by African American women. A recent high school graduate, she exuded self-confidence and a strong sense of identity; she also had strong feelings about others' attempts to categorize her:

> Just to make things easier for people, I'll be like, "Yeah, I'm West Indian." They'll be like, "What island are you from?" I'm like, "I'm not from an island, I'm from part of South America." They're like, "Oh, you're Hispanic," and I'm like, "No, I'm not Hispanic, I'm Indian," and

they're like, "Oh, you're from India," and I'm like, "No, I'm not from India. I'm Indian, but I'm from South America!"

Roma's frustration stemmed from others' inability to allow for a flexible, multivalent identity, not her own confusion. In fact, she later said, "I consider myself to be more Indian than West Indian. Because West Indians are more like Trinidad, Jamaica, you know? The islands, that's West Indian. We're not West Indian." Although Roma was American by birth and citizenship, people frequently asked about her background, and she was often mistaken for Latina. Like Asians and Hispanics, who are seen as neither black nor white, Roma fell into a category of perceived foreigner, even though she was born in the United States.

Denise, a tenth-grade student, reported having to explain the difference between East and West Indians.[15] When asked how she responds to questions about her background, she said:

> I say "Indian," and then I say "West Indian." Some of them don't even know. As soon as they hear "Indian," they think from the Middle East and Pakistan and India, things like that. So I tell them "West Indian." Then they know from the Caribbean, Trinidad. . . . Some of them don't know the difference between Indians, East and West.

Denise patiently taught others about the different "kinds" of Indians. Similarly, one thirteen-year-old respondent who lived in Jersey City, which has a much smaller West Indian population than Ethnictown's, had a teacher say to her, " 'No, you're not [Indian].' I was like, 'Yes, I am! How are you going to tell me that I'm not Indian?' And he goes, 'Um, well, Guyana is in South America, and India is, you know, in Asia.' I was like, dude, he's just closed-minded, he doesn't really know anything." It seems that she had to teach her teacher about West Indian history for him to accept her asserted identity. The older sister of this young woman once was forced to call herself "Hispanic" on a school form by a teacher when the teacher heard that Guyana is located in South America. Respondents stubbornly maintained their asserted boundaries of identity, even when frustrated by others' assignments to different identities.

Race, then, did not play the same role for these youth that it does for many black youth, whose ascriptive racial identity pervades most aspects of life through strong assumptions and prejudices about black youth in the larger society. In contrast, finding a box in which they can place Indo-Caribbean youth is often confusing to others. Indo-Caribbeans cannot easily be pegged with an ascriptive racial identity (although clearly many do try!). When others try to box them in racially, many youth resist those racial assignments.

Thus, Indo-Caribbean identity cannot be easily understood as a discrete ethnic or racial category with solid boundaries. Second-generation youth comfortably move in and out of multiple aspects of their identities, they adopt different aspects of their identities in different contexts, and they resist others' ascriptive definitions. This was true of both the young men and the young women I interviewed.[16]

A look at taste and consumption practices may help us develop a deeper understanding of the ways in which Indo-Caribbean youth overtly express their identities.

CONSUMPTION AND TASTE: MUSIC, DRESS, AND MOVIES

Sociologists have discussed the use of consumption as a means of social differentiation or a marker of social status (Veblen 1912; Bourdieu 1984). Consumption may be multimotivational rather than based simply on a desire for social distinction, conspicuous consumption, or rational choice (Friedman 1994). A person's consumption patterns can help us understand his habitus and ethnic identity (Lipsitz 1994). The choices that youth make are not necessary outcomes of their ethnic backgrounds, nor do all individuals of the same background make the same cultural choices (Appiah 1996). However, taste and cultural patterns provide another lens through which to understand the construction of ethnic identity and cultural forces. Indeed, respondents linked their cultural interests to their identities. For example: "The type of music that I listen to has something to do with my identity, like especially the Indian music, you know. That's who I am, and that music helps me relate to who I am. . . . And then my American music helps me realize that I'm also an American."

The cultural taste and consumption patterns of second-generation Indo-Caribbean youth demonstrated a facility and comfort with myriad cultural forms. Music most commonly provided a forum in which youth could dabble in multiple styles and even create new forms by mixing different genres. This fluidity reflected the multi-ethnic environment in which respondents lived, as well as the multi-ethnic societies in the West Indies from which their parents came. In terms of ethnic Indian clothing and Hindi movies, girls expressed much stronger interests than boys, possibly reflecting the fact that in American culture South Asian female cultural styles—such as henna tattoos, bindis, and sari fabrics—have become popular in mainstream culture. In contrast, South Asian males are stereotyped as cab drivers and newspaper sellers and have become common targets of racial profiling since the World Trade Center attacks.

Music   The nature of music provides for the most flexibility in terms of taste and consumption. Music production is cheaper than movies, perhaps providing more room for hybridity and new, unconventional styles. Diverse radio stations in New York City provide a forum in which to hear many different styles of music easily. African American, second-generation, and immigrant New Yorkers exchange music, language, and dance styles to both participate in diverse musical scenes and create new hybrid forms (Kasinitz, Mollenkopf, and Waters 2002). Most of my respondents had quite diverse musical tastes. One respondent "listen[ed] to hip-hop and Indian music, and a little bit of soca and reggae. And maybe Spanish, maybe salsa." Another respondent mixed Indian and West Indian music (soca) while changing it slightly, creating something altogether new: "Me and my brother, we have a CD mixer, so we put beats into the Indian music to make it fun and stuff. . . . Indian music with beats at the back. . . . You can add a little soca, soca beats."

With this hybrid music, neither racial nor ethnic identity dominated, yet both had a strong influence on teens' musical interests. Generally, respondents listened to all kinds of East Indian and West Indian genres of music. They thus created a boundary—albeit quite fuzzy—around diasporic South Asian and West Indian musical styles through their musical interests.[17] The Day Jam that I attended exemplified this boundary. An Indo-Caribbean dance club in Queens organized alcohol- and smoke-free parties for high school students on weekdays when there was no school. On the day I attended a Day Jam, the vast majority of music that I heard was soca, calypso, Hindi film songs, bhangra, and reggae. I also heard some hip-hop tracks, however, and the typical shoulder moves of Punjabi bhangra dancing melded into the hip-hop moves that are not so different. East Indian and West Indian music styles loomed large in the everyday lives of these youth, yet no *single* type of music defined their musical tastes; what defined their tastes, in a sense, was diversity, fluidity, remixing, and a lot of choosing.[18]

Parents influence the diverse musical interests of youth. Indo-Caribbean immigrants come from societies where calypso, soca, Hindi film songs, and chutney soca (Hindi lyrics over soca beats) are all popular. Stacey, a seventeen-year-old living in Manhattan, heard many types of music at family parties: "Indian music or reggae . . . Spanish music too." The family get-togethers Stacey attended were on her Guyanese mother's side. Her white father listened to techno, another favorite of hers. After September 11, Stacey organized a dance performance in which she and her friends dressed up in red, white, and blue *langas* (an ethnic Indian outfit) and danced to Indian music while carrying an American flag. Stacey's family environment was one that made it possible to blend American patriotism with popular Indian culture. For these Indo-Caribbean youth, music generally seemed to take on the expression of a diasporic sense of self, which in some ways was part of being a New Yorker, especially in multi-ethnic Queens.

Movies and Clothing   When I began my research in Queens, I quickly found out that DVDs have led to an increased interest in Hindi movies in the Indo-Caribbean community. More careful probing, however, suggested a gendered pattern of interest in things Indian with respect to clothing and movies. Teenagers' taste for ethnic Indian clothing paralleled their interest in popular Indian movies—girls more commonly and more enthusiastically reported an interest in and preference for Hindi films as well as ethnic Indian clothing than did their male peers. Perhaps this difference is due to the film content, since most Indian movies are epic love stories, with lots of drama and songs interspersed.[19] Regardless of the origin of this gender difference, it influenced cultural identity. Girls generally described their interest in Hindi movies as stemming in part from a desire to learn about their "culture." For example, one girl, when asked to explain her interest in Hindi movies, said:

> I guess lately I've grown more into the culture, I don't know why. . . . I've come to appreciate it more now than when I was younger. . . . [In the past my parents] would listen and watch their movies and we'd be laughing at them. And then a few years later *I'm* the one who's watching the movies, *I'm* the one who wants to dress up, *I'm* the one who wants to go out and get Indian CDs.

Another explained that "Even though these stories are made up, a lot of them have a lot of cultural value. As in Pardes, it showed like how women were brought up, how women were, you know . . . how they were supposed to be respected, in certain areas that a lot of women nowadays don't grow up. . . . [They] brought a lot of light into my culture." Even the daughter of the founder of a Hindu church reported learning about Hinduism and Indian culture through Hindi movies.[20] Teenage girls' equation of culture and Bollywood (as the Hindi film industry is known, named for its center in Bombay) looks to an Indian culture based in India rather than in the Caribbean for "authentic" Indian-ness.

Hindi movies suggest normative guidelines for behavior for young women, who are expected in many ethnic communities to maintain culture for their future families (Kurien 1999; Khan 1995; Suarez-Orozco and Suarez-Orozco 2001; Maira 2002). Indo-Caribbean youth had picked up on gendered ideas about culture and tradition, even if they resisted them. Tasha, a fifteen-year-old Guyanese American, disliked watching Hindi films with her parents because her parents used the films as lessons in behavior:

> [One movie] was about family ties, and how the girl was really close to her parents, and then she made her parents ashamed and then tried to climb back up to that ladder to be with her parents. So, I watched that with my parents, and my parents were like, "So you see how close families are? You see how this is?" I'm like, "Yes, Mom, yes, Dad."

Boys reinforced traditional notions of Indian womanhood found in Bollywood movies. For example, when asked to explain her statement that boys like "more traditional" girls as girlfriends, Katherine told me: "Guys are supposed to have this macho attitude . . . and being traditional is more sensitive. . . . They expect us to be traditional in our culture . . . and guys are supposed to be hard."

In terms of ethnic clothing, only Hindu respondents reported having Indian clothes, which were worn to church, weddings, and other religious occasions. Among Hindus, girls much more commonly had Indian clothes. Moreover, many young women reported gaining their sense of style in Indian clothes from Hindi movies. Bollywood clearly influenced these young women's taste in Indian clothes.

Boys, on the other hand, often distanced themselves from Indian cultural forms outside of music. Asha compared herself to her thirteen-year-old younger brother: "When I go to functions, when my parents have prayers . . . is when I wear Indian clothes. . . . But my brother, forget it, as soon as the religious function is over, he goes and changes as quickly as possible. He doesn't want to be . . . seen in that."

Asha, a second-generation Trinidadian, later told me that if she and her mother began to watch a Hindi movie at home, her father would join them only on occasion, and her brother would leave the room right away. A few boys did report having worn ethnic clothes as young boys, but not anymore: "Teenaged guys usually wear khaki pants and a white shirt [to the mandir]. . . . Young little kids will wear the *kurta* and stuff, but teenagers, they don't."

One eighteen-year-old young man I met, Henry, sported a large gold cross around his neck, baggy jeans, and Timberland boots, a style made popular by African American hip-hop artists.[21] He spoke with an urban black cadence, explaining that:

> It's hard for an Indian to say he's Indian. . . . Because a lot of people down being Indian, because a lot of Indians are cab drivers, you know, a lot of

them own convenience stores. . . . I have no problem with them personally, but a lot of people do. . . . I think people get a kick out of the way
Indians are, the way they speak. . . . [Do you ever face any kind of racism
or discrimination?] Sometimes, but that's because they think I'm either,
they think I'm Indian . . . and they discriminate against Indians . . . I'm
different. I dress differently. I pretty much give it away that I'm not Indian . . . but what I don't like is if they call you Indian, then they mock
Indian.

When asked about his background, Henry identified as Trinidadian, and
sometimes West Indian, but never Indian. Indian identity seemed quite problematic for him, and he seemed to notice a larger cultural association of Indian male identity with low-status work like driving a taxi or running a convenience store. He made it a point, then, to set his boundary to exclude
"Indians," in part through his style of dress. Generally, male respondents
tended to adopt more urban black cultural styles than their female counterparts. In her research with South Asian American young adults in New York
City, Maira (2002, 58–59) also found that, "for many second-generation
men, hip-hop style connotes a certain image of racialized hypermasculinity
that is the ultimate definition of cool. . . . A male body that exudes toughness
might well counter . . . stereotypes of Indian Americans." This distancing is
perhaps exacerbated by the increasing incidence of racial targeting of South
Asian–looking men since the World Trade Center attacks. Many young men
reported some kind of racial harassment in direct response to September 11.

Thus, Indo-Caribbean young women created a boundary around being
Indian with respect to clothing and movies, whereas Indo-Caribbean young
men disidentified with "Indian" in these cultural realms, recognizing the lack
of "subcultural capital" associated with Indian male cultural identity in contemporary America.[22] Indo-Caribbean youth live in a cultural milieu in which
it is fashionable and a source of subcultural capital to be a South Asian
woman, but to be a South Asian male is to be seen simultaneously as a terrorist and as a worker in a position of low power, such as convenience store
owner or taxi driver (La Ferla 2002). This environment pushes females—often seen as keepers of culture and tradition in any community—to identify
strongly with things Indian, and males to have weaker identification with Indian cultural forms and to prefer urban African American cultural identity.

SOCIAL NETWORKS

In addition to taste and consumption, social networks reflect a community's
mode of adaptation to a new environment. Milton Gordon (1964) described
incorporation into the dominant society's social networks as structural assim-

ilation, suggesting that this type of assimilation takes much longer than cultural assimilation. His further distinction between primary ties and secondary relationships is akin to Mark Granovetter's (1973) distinction between strong and weak ties. In this model, integration with the host community in primary relationships indicates more structural assimilation, often associated with social mobility (Gordon 1964). Weak ties lead to more dispersed networks that, for example, provide individuals with access to job prospects that they would not be able to secure from strong ties (Granovetter 1973). Here I explore who Indo-Caribbean youth define as their "in-group," and the degree to which their peer relationships are ethnically integrated.

Social networks tell a story of identity different from the one told by taste and consumption. When describing their closest friends, respondents invariably identified Indo-Caribbean peers. Also, seven of the ten teens in dating relationships at the time of our interview were dating other Indo-Caribbean youth.[23] The others dated a diverse group of peers, although no one's partner had an East Indian or Afro-Caribbean parent. When asked whether it was important to him or his family that he date or marry a particular type of person, one young man responded that, because his parents "want to keep their culture, and the trend of Indian and Guyanese going," he felt that he could date or marry another "Indian Guyanese" only, not a black Guyanese or an Indian from India. Clearly, "Indian Guyanese" holds strong meaning in the family of this boy, regardless of his future partner. Most respondents, however, had quite ethnically diverse friends in their secondary relationships. For example, when asked whether he had any South Asian friends whose families were from the Subcontinent, one young man said: "I have pretty much friends from every background. Puerto Rican, Dominican, Jamaican, Indian, Arabic, Chinese, Vietnamese, European, everything."

Another young woman explained that she had one best friend, a fellow Indo-Guyanese girl, and many diverse friends with whom she socialized but did not share her deepest thoughts:

> I have a lot of friends. . . . But she [her best friend] is someone that I trust, tell everything to. . . . The other friends I like to go shopping, I'll go have lunch with them, clubbing and stuff. . . . [They're] West Indian, mixed Spanish, and they're also black, and Indians from India.

Thus, for second-generation Indo-Caribbean teenagers, the boundary for primary relationships included only Indo-Caribbean peers, but secondary relationships came from all ethnic groups.

At Harrison High School, many respondents reported that although there were many ethnic social circles at school, they themselves hung out with all the groups and did not stick to one. Chris, who had a white American father and a first-generation Guyanese mother, explained the situation:

> The Spanish kids hang out with the Spanish kids, the Indian kids hang out with the Indian kids. Usually, they all stick together. Like, after school you see one corner, they'll have all Spanish kids, the next corner will have black kids, you know, they don't really mix around too much. . . . As soon as the periods change you walk through the hallway you already know "Oh, all the Spanish kids are gonna be over here, all the Indian kids are gonna be over there, the black kids are gonna be over there." Usually I'm by myself, but I have Spanish friends and black friends also. . . . Like, on my way to class I go to each group, "What's going on," and stuff.

I often spotted Chris wandering the halls between classes, indeed chatting with kids of diverse races, styles, and dispositions. This seeming contradiction makes sense if we think of ethnic cliques as loosely formed circles of friends whose boundaries are fluid and dynamic. Perhaps the multi-ethnic environment enabled youth to take pride in this diversity of relationships.

Some tension did exist between Indo-Caribbeans and East Indians whose families had recently arrived from India, Bangladesh, or Pakistan. One young man explained: "You got the real India, India-India people, then you have us Guyanese and Trini or whatever. We separated like that. . . . We don't really mess with them, you know, we're not too fond of them."

East Indian students also kept Indo-Caribbeans at a distance. After seeing many girls dance to Hindi songs at the school talent show, I sat down to lunch with some East Indian students. I asked them who the girls in the talent show were, and I was confidently told by Virender, a Punjabi Sikh who grew up in Kuwait until age fourteen: "They're not Indian. They're West Indian." "How do you know? Are you sure?" I asked. "Yeah, we're sure," replied Mona, Virender's Bangladeshi friend. Virender then explained: "The [East] Indian girls are more . . . well, shy." From the tone of Virender's and Mona's voices, I understood that they expected good, morally upstanding girls to be shy. Karen Leonard (2000) finds a similarly antagonistic relationship between descendants of Punjabi immigrants to California from the early twentieth century and more recent immigrants from South Asia. Early Punjabis' identities as "Hindu" included Sikhs, Hindus, and Muslims as well as the descendants of mixed Mexican-Punjabi couples. South Asian immigrants arriving in California in the post-1965 wave, however, challenged the former group's claims of Hindu identity, suggesting that the descendants of the early immigrants were not "authentically" Hindu. The two communities remain largely separated. Similarly, the Indian identification I saw with Indo-Caribbean girls' consumption and all teens' music tastes did not carry over to Indo-Caribbean teenagers' social networks, which generally did not include East Indians.

Discussion

Unlike many Afro-Caribbean immigrants in New York City who take on either a distinctly African American or distinctly West Indian identity (Waters 1999), Indo-Caribbean youth in New York City did not take on a unique, unitary identity. However, Indo-Caribbean youth's identities as immigrants and sometimes as East Indians were stronger than the symbolic ethnicity of white suburban ethnics (Waters 1990), in part because they were keenly aware of their nonwhite status. Indo-Caribbean youth developed *cosmopolitan ethnicity*: fluid, multidimensional, and thick identities. Perhaps a blend of Gordon's (1964) melting pot and cultural pluralism best describes ethnic identity in this context. Indian music played over hip-hop and soca beats, a diversity of secondary friendships with intra-ethnic primary ties, Indian dances to the recent hip-hop hit "Addictive" alongside spoken word and traditional rock at the high school talent show—these are just a few illustrations of this fluidity. These multiple identities manifested themselves in different ways and in different contexts for Indo-Caribbean youth, who generally felt comfortable moving among myriad cultural influences and identities.

I see four factors that prompt this fluidity of identity: having a cultural background in West Indian multi-ethnic societies; living in a multi-ethnic New York environment with limited local exposure to South Asians from the Subcontinent; lacking economic incentives to identify with one single ethnic group; and being of a race that is neither black nor white and not easily categorized by others.[24] Gendered stereotypes of South Asians in the larger U.S. context led to different manifestations of this cosmopolitan ethnicity for Indo-Caribbean boys and girls.

MULTI-ETHNIC CULTURAL BACKGROUNDS

The families of my respondents came from Guyana and Trinidad, both of which have roughly equal numbers of ethnic Indians and blacks (in addition to descendants of laborers of other countries, including Portugal and China). Steven, an immigrant who was now in eleventh grade, told me that he liked Ethnictown's diversity because it's almost like home, because back in Trinidad the culture was, like, everything was diverse, cosmopolitan. . . . There's, like, the different celebrations that they have, like Divali [a Hindu holiday], like Eid [the Muslim holidays], they have the African celebrations. Everyone, even though you're Indian, you're black, you're Chinese, you take part in the celebration and everyone in the whole [town], they're celebrating.

Another told me that her mother wore a sari and then a white wedding gown at her Hindu wedding. Having a background in the West Indies had given the parents of these teenagers a facility in navigating multiple ethnic traditions, and their children learned quickly from them and their surroundings.

Religious intermarriage among respondents' parents was quite common, and at least half of my respondents reported more than one faith in their families, most commonly through intermarriage (of ethnic Indians of different faiths) but also through conversion. One family had three children and four faiths: the Trinidadian mother's background was Muslim, but the fathers of her children were Christian, Hindu, and Sikh; all were Indo-Trinidadian except the Sikh man, who was an Indian immigrant. The Hindu child, Meena, reported:

I have so many different religions. . . . I go to Catholic school . . . my father is Hindu, half my family is Muslim, I've been to Hindu temples, I've been to Sikh gurdwaras, I've been to the Catholic church, I've been to the mosque. . . . I fasted during Ramadan, I fasted during the Hindu holy month, I fasted the Christian month. I'm faced with so many different religions and races. It's cool. . . . I like it like that.

Surely such cultural mobility creates an environment in which children develop skills to move easily between cultures and identities. Boundaries appear to have been redrawn; in South Asia, both during the nineteenth century (when most Indo-Caribbeans' ancestors arrived from India) and today, religious intermarriage has been uncommon and has brought great social stigma. In contrast, Indo-Caribbean families quite frequently and comfortably have interfaith marriages. Perhaps the boundary line of identity shifted from religious identity in India (to the exclusion of other religions) to Indian identity in the West Indies (to the exclusion of blacks). The secondary migration to the United States appears to have led to a second boundary shift, such that race is no longer as essential as it is in the West Indies.

MULTI-ETHNIC NEIGHBORHOOD AND SCHOOL ENVIRONMENT

As described earlier, urban America's population is increasingly diverse. The populations of Ethnictown and many neighborhoods like it in New York City are multi-ethnic, and no ethnic or racial group constitutes a majority. One tenth-grade student who explained that she had gone to multi-ethnic schools all her life described her neighborhood:

> Well, we're Trini [Trinidadian]. I have a neighbor that's Guyanese on one side and Spanish, Mexican on the other side. So it's pretty diverse. I have Italians across the street. I have Indians around the corner. They're all mixed, like Mexican and Venezuelan and Portuguese all in one household, and Puerto Ricans and Dominicans and Guyanese Indians. Yeah, they're all mixed.

Thus, there is no obvious neighborhood group into which Indo-Caribbeans might be expected to assimilate.

Although in the United States there are 1.8 million ethnic Indians and fewer than 100,000 Indo-Caribbeans, Harrison High School's neighborhood has many more Indo-Caribbeans than East Indians. This leads to a situation in which some East Indian immigrants in the school are mistaken for West Indian, as reported by many East Indian immigrant students (much to their chagrin). Generally, a weak South Asian identity in the United States makes for a less obvious American racial group with whom Indo-Caribbean youth can identify.

The multi-ethnic environment has two important effects. First, it makes for a more accepting environment in which residents and peers generally tolerate diversity; no one group is able to dominate the environment over others. One Hispanic young man I met at Harrison High School told me that he transferred to the school from a predominantly black school. Because he was one of a small minority of Hispanic students at his former school, he experienced frequent racial harassment and eventually requested a safety transfer to Harrison, where his average shot from 65 to 93. The young man attributed the safety at Harrison to no one group being in the majority, so that no group could dominate and pick on minorities. He was careful not to single out black students for blame at his old school, however, pointing out that, "when whites were in the majority, they did the same thing to black kids."

Second, the multi-ethnic urban environment creates avenues for the expression of ethnicity and a simultaneous expectation of it. That is, the environment encourages individuals to assert their chosen ethnic identities, although it does not force these choices to be simple or static. An example provides a good illustration of the thickness of ethnicity in the multi-ethnic environment. One day at Harrison High School I met an Italian American young woman hanging out with two Hispanic friends. She told me about her Hispanic boyfriend and then asked her friends for the latest Spanish songs they were listening to through their headphones. The young woman's hairstyle was similar to those of many Hispanic girls in the school, and she discussed the Spanish she was trying hard to learn with them and in Spanish class at school. She embodied the need for ethnicity in the multi-ethnic environment. Ethnicity for her, however, needed a group to identify with, and since very few ethnic Italians attended her school, she was adopting a Hispanic ethnicity.

THE ABSENCE OF AN ETHNIC NICHE

Susan Olzak (1983, 355) describes ethnic mobilization as "the process by which groups organize around some feature of ethnic identity . . . in pursuit of collective ends." This mobilization often results when ethnic groups occupy particular niches in a job market such that competition for jobs becomes tied to ethnic identity (Bonacich 1972; Patterson 1975; Waldinger 1996). My research suggests that there is no ethnic job niche for Indo-Caribbeans. Of the respondents who gave their parents' occupations, no more than two reported any occupation aside from mothers who worked in the health industry, mostly as nurses. Even so, fewer than one-third of respondents' mothers worked in health-related occupations. Unlike their Afro-Caribbean counterparts, Indo-Caribbean immigrants have not occupied a strong ethnic job niche, perhaps owing to their small numbers, in spite of having an ethnic business enclave. With no clear economic incentive to mobilize and consequently cling strongly to one identity, Indo-Caribbeans have moved toward a cosmopolitan ethnicity.

BETWEEN BLACK AND WHITE

> *I think we're in the middle of white and black. We're right in the middle. I don't know. I guess we're considered black, because there's only white and black in the world.*
>
> —*Junior, age 17*

With an ascriptive racial identity that is neither white nor black, Indo-Caribbean youth have neither the privileges that come with whiteness nor the master status of blackness in American society. Moreover, others could not easily categorize the Indo-Caribbeans I interviewed—they were often mistaken for Arabs, Latinos, or East Indians. As Junior suggested, if there is only black and white in the world, then he is black, or a person of color. But he began by placing himself between black and white. Indo-Caribbean youth did report instances of racial discrimination, especially in largely white areas, and in response to the World Trade Center attacks. Yet race did not define every aspect of their identities, as demonstrated by their contextual accounts of how they identified.

I argue that Indo-Caribbean youths' racial identity in contemporary America lies between white ethnics, who have thin asserted identities, and African Americans, who have thick identities that are largely assigned. The presence of ethnicity in the lives of Indo-Caribbeans is thicker than the symbolic ethnicity that Waters finds in second-generation white Catholics, in part because they are assigned a nonwhite racial identity. In its nonwhite status, Indo-Caribbean identity is assigned. In this respect, Indo-Caribbeans share experiences in the United States with many Latinos, Arab Americans, and East Indian Americans, whose racial identities are not obvious to most outsiders and who consequently do not experience the strong ascription of black racial identity, yet who are also clearly assigned nonwhite racial identity. However, one stable identity does not pervade every aspect of Indo-Caribbean life, and indeed, a defining characteristic is the fluidity of the boundaries of identity for this community with cosmopolitan ethnicity.

GENDER AND SOUTH ASIAN IDENTITY

Gendered stereotypes in the American popular imagination also affect Indo-Caribbean identities. Some of my male respondents linked Indian identity to powerlessness and the negative stereotypes associated with Indian male identity in the United States. Many told me that the Indian (meaning Sikh) students in their school were often picked on because of their turbans.[25] After September 11, the young men with whom I spoke frequently cited incidents of being targeted as suspected terrorists—quite the opposite stereotype of the weak, bullied teenager, but a negative image nonetheless.

These negative associations contrast sharply with the increasing popularity of "Indo-chic" in women's fashion, including henna tattoos, sari fabrics, bindis, and more (La Ferla 2002; Maira 2002). Orlando Patterson (1975) suggests that the context of reception and the economic structure affect the way in which ethnic communities choose to incorporate in new environments. Although Patterson's argument applies to economic conditions in the host country, we can think more generally of contextual influences in the host country, which would include media representations, neighborhood makeup, the school environment, and more. Mainstream popularity and subcultural capital give young women greater incentive than young men to identify as Indian. Maira (2002, 123) points out that invitations to South Asian American club parties in New York City often request "proper or elegant attire" for men and "ethnic attire" for women. More generally, women in diasporic communities often are expected to maintain cultural identities within the home, while men focus on the work world or the public sphere (see Butterfield, this volume). Nancy López (this volume) describes the ways in which the public school environment racializes second-generation Dominican men and women quite differently as well.

CONCLUSIONS

In this chapter, I have described the formation of a new type of ethnic identity, which I call cosmopolitan ethnicity. The second-generation Indo-Caribbean teenagers I met crafted their multidimensional identities through their self-identifications; their tastes in music, ethnic Indian clothing, and Hindi films; and their social networks. I found that most teens expressed interest in multiple types of East Indian, West Indian, and American music. Their tastes in ethnic clothing and Hindi films were gendered—girls expressed more interest in things Indian. Finally, primary social networks remained in the Indo-Caribbean community, while secondary relationships were quite diverse. Four main influences lead to these cosmopolitan ethnicities: family backgrounds in multi-ethnic societies; multi-ethnic school and neighborhood environments; an absence of ethnic niches in the job market; and racial identity that is neither black nor white. Different degrees of subcultural capital associated with Indian male and Indian female identity in contemporary America influence the manifestation of cosmopolitan ethnicity for boys and girls.

Cosmopolitan ethnicity has emerged alongside the breakdown of the binary schema of race in black and white that has dominated racial politics in America. Scholars have already begun to look at ethnic enclaves as alternative spaces to black and white neighborhoods. Specifically, segmented assimilation theory predicts assimilation patterns based on residence in middle-class, largely white neighborhoods, poor and largely black neighborhoods, or ethnic enclaves (Portes and Zhou 1993). However, the assumption that youth choose one group to which they will assimilate, based on a homogenous residential environment, no longer holds weight for many children of immigrants, for two reasons. First, when no majority group dominates an immigrant's neighborhood, assimilation can move in many different directions, so that the old question of "assimilation to what" takes on new meaning. Also youth in the multi-ethnic environment make many different choices and are influenced not only by neighborhood peers but also by media images, popular culture, and dominant gender roles in their communities and the larger society. Second, unlike the outcomes suggested by segmented assimilation theory, the cultural forms to which an ethnic group assimilates may or may not mirror the social networks, identities, or even values of the group. The different social processes may unfold quite differently, as they do for Indo-Caribbean youth. Choice is important, but individuals no longer necessarily choose *between* but *among* different ethnicities; moreover, choices are fluid, dynamic, and contextual.

Hence, when studying the incorporation of immigrants' children, researchers should disaggregate culture, identity, values, and social networks, rather than assume that the different realms always mirror one another. Each unique lens tells us something about the available scripts for a community. For example, social networks tell us more about the local environment and the choices available to youth, whereas consumption involves popular culture and media images in addition to the local environment. Also, unlike what segmented assimilation theory suggests, a young person's taste for hip-hop music need not signal assimilation to an oppositional culture and its values.

We are likely to witness an increase in cosmopolitan ethnicity, owing to the changing urban landscape in immigrant receiving areas; increasing interest in Third World culture, especially in fashion and popular culture; and increasing numbers of immigrants arriving in the United States from multi-ethnic societies such as the West Indies and Brazil. This new form of ethnicity suggests a need to reevaluate former notions of identity. I posit three shifts: ethnic identity is not unitary; individuals exert choice with respect to identity; and identity can be simultaneously symbolic and thick.

First, if youth no longer feel compelled to cling to one aspect of their identities, then we no longer need to think of identity as unitary and definitive of the individual. Perhaps identities then become part of the different roles and faces that individuals take on in different performances in a Goffman-like dramaturgical model of social interaction (Goffman 1959). That is, given that the youth I studied expressed security and no "identity crisis" with their multifaceted identities, we should question the notion of ethnic identity as one coherent, essential core of the individual.

Second, individuals choose different types of identity in different realms of their lives, as I observed in the differences between Indo-Caribbean young men and women, as well as in the differences in individual identities in different situations and realms of life. The element of choice, however, should not blind us to the hegemonic power of the dominant society outside of the local context that youth encounter. The dominant American society still privileges white, native status, although the power in this identity is shifting, especially at the margins.

Third, ethnic identity need not be either symbolic or thick—it can be both simultaneously, as it was with my respondents. That is, the importance and salience of ethnic identity does not preclude an individual expressing different identities in different contexts. This is especially true of nonblack minorities, whose racial identities matter in the larger society in that they are marked as nonwhite, but whose racial statuses are more ambiguous and hence less strongly ascribed than those of black Americans. Beyond their status as racial minorities, they can and often do choose to construct multidimensional identities.

Today's multi-ethnic environments encourage the development of multivalent ethnic identities rather than assimilation into either a unitary American culture or an ethnic identity. Immigrants to the United States and their children increasingly encounter diverse cultural forms and ethnic identities, and a dialectic between existing ethnic boundaries and the new environment ensues. I argue for the careful study of multi-ethnic environments for a better understanding of contemporary immigrant incorporation and would suggest that the multi-ethnic environment shapes ethnic identity in new ways. Finally, my empirical observations of cosmopolitan ethnicity suggest a more normative question: how *should* we think about identity to allow for maximal individual self-actualization?

Anthony Appiah (1996, 104) suggests that "racial identity can be the basis of resistance to racism; but even as we struggle against racism . . . let us not let our racial identities subject us to new tyrannies." In other words, we should not limit any group, whether defined by ethnicity, race, gender, religion, or other affiliation, to a particular set of cultural scripts traditionally associated with that group—for example, jazz or hip-hop for African Americans, or Hindi movies for South Asians. Rather, we should allow for the fluidity, contingency, and fracture of identities (Appiah 1996). Similarly, David Hollinger (1995) suggests a "postethnic" perspective on the future of ethnic boundaries in America, situated between pluralism's inherited boundaries and the voluntary, multifaceted dynamism of "cosmopolitanism."[26] Like Hollinger and Appiah, I feel optimistic that these rich environments will promote immigrant incorporation and self-actualization in ways that greatly enrich American society and its newcomers.

I hope that future research will explore the influence of the multi-ethnic environment on the identities of other nonblack minorities, such as Southeast Asian Americans, Latinos, and Arab Americans who do not identify as white or black. I suspect that a similarly cosmopolitan ethnicity will emerge. The perceptions and ethno-racial ascriptions of peers and community members would provide yet another understanding and perspective on the construction and negotiation of identities in the multi-ethnic environment.

I am grateful for comments and guidance on this research from Mary Waters, Gwen Dordick, Orlando Patterson, and Philip Kasinitz. I have also benefited from the helpful comments of participants in the Multi-disciplinary Program in Inequality and Social Policy at Harvard University, funded by the National Science Foundation.

NOTES

1. David Hollinger (1995) uses the concept of cosmopolitanism to mean something quite different. He distinguishes cosmopolitanism—voluntary, multiple identities that recognize the dynamism of groups and new cultural combinations—from pluralism—identities shaped by inherited boundaries that attempt to protect and perpetuate existing cultures. He suggests that a postethnic identity, somewhere between the two, signals a "critical renewal of cosmopolitanism in the context of today's greater sensitivity to roots" (5). Postethnicity resonates with my notion of cosmopolitan ethnicity in its recognition of fluid, changing, asserted boundaries amid strong roots in inherited ethnic boundaries. Postethnicity, however, is more normative than descriptive and suggests somewhat weaker ethnic roots than what I am describing.
2. This definition of "thickness" or "salience" is slightly different from Cornell and Hartmann's (1998) and Stryker's (1968). Cosmopolitan ethnicity involves a thickness or salience of ethnic identities overall rather than the thickness of a particular ethnicity. In other words, individuals are expected by their peers to invoke an ethnic identity when making social and cultural choices about, for example, music, religion, and dating.
3. Although official census categories do not include "South Asian" as a race, I would argue that in American society today ascriptive racialization causes Indo-Caribbeans to be seen as Asian Indian—or more generally, South Asian.
4. Catholic Americans have not always been seen as white in American society. For example, during the second wave of immigration to the United States, the Irish and many Italians were seen as a different race from mainstream Anglo-Saxons. By 1965, however, the racial line was drawn between "Caucasians," including Irish, and "blacks" (Jacobson 1998).
5. Alba and his colleagues (1995) define a multi-ethnic neighborhood as one with a presence of two or more racial groups; presence of a racial group is defined as at least one hundred members of that group in the neighborhood, as reported by the census. William Frey and Reynolds Farley (1996) define a multi-ethnic area as one "in which two or more of the three minority groups (Latinos, Asians, blacks) make up a greater share of the metropolitan area's population than of the national population." According to this definition, in 1990 there were thirty-seven multi-ethnic metropolitan areas in the United States.
6. Some research suggests that this trend is specific to traditional immigrant-receiving cities. Frey (1996) finds that low-income, less-skilled domestic mi-

grants often leave large port-of-entry cities (such as New York, Boston, or Los Angeles) for cities such as Atlanta, Seattle, or Orlando. Thus, port-of-entry cities are becoming increasingly multicultural and younger, while cities that draw internal migrants—mostly in the Rocky Mountain area, the Southwest, and the South—may not have the same multiculturalism.

7. The South Asian community, however, is bifurcated. Earlier immigrants tended to be middle- and upper-middle-class professionals. Today South Asian immigrants come as both professionals and low-skilled workers. The segment of the community interacting with urban youth tends to be those of lower socioeconomic status.

8. For example, we might expect Indo-Caribbeans to mark "Asian Indian" for race and a West Indian category as one of their ancestry choices. However, the 2000 census shows that there were more immigrants born in the West Indies who identified racially as Asian Indian than there were individuals who indicated anywhere in the West Indies as part of their ancestry who identified racially as Asian Indian, suggesting that some Indo-Caribbeans did not mark a West Indian category for their ancestry, and others did not mark Asian Indian for their race. Thus, there is no accurate way to measure the size of the community using census data (U.S. Department of Commerce 2000).

9. I have changed the names of the high school, its surrounding neighborhood, and my respondents, in the interest of confidentiality.

10. Note that the relationship between the Italian establishment and the more recently arrived Indo-Caribbeans in Ethnictown has sometimes been contentious. In a much publicized 1998 incident, an Indo-Caribbean teenager was beaten unconscious by a group of Italian youths shouting racial epithets (Sengupta 1998).

11. Another 29 percent identified with either more than one race or "other" on the 2000 census.

12. Note that Indo-Caribbeans most commonly mark "Asian" and "Asian Indian" in the race census category, but many also mark the "other" category. Some of my respondents reported being instructed by community leaders to call themselves Asian when asked about race, indicating that the choice was not obvious. Thus, even though these statistics give some sense of the demographics, they probably do not accurately portray the exact makeups.

13. Soca is a blend of West Indian calypso and soul. Chutney soca is a mix of soca and Hindi film and folk songs. Bhangra is traditional Punjabi folk music that has become quite popular in the young South Asian American community.

14. Specifically, I asked, "When others ask, 'What are you?' what do you tell them?" All understood this to be a question about ethno-racial identity.

15. By "West Indian" I mean anyone who has a parent born in the West Indies. By "East Indian" I mean anyone who has a parent born in South Asia—India, Pakistan, Bangladesh, Nepal, Bhutan, or Sri Lanka.

16. Other research on gender and second-generation identity (López 2002; Rumbaut 1996; Waters 1996) suggests that girls more commonly and more successfully maintain bicultural identities than their male peers.

17. Fredrik Barth (1969, 6) first introduced the notion of boundary maintenance in ethnic identity, suggesting that "ethnicity is a matter of social organization above and beyond questions of empirical cultural differences: it is about 'the social organization of culture difference.'" In other words, because ethnic groups distinguish themselves by maintaining boundaries between each other, boundaries are the salient markers of ethnicity rather than the cultural contents within those boundaries.

18. Also interesting was the diversity of youth who attended the Day Jam, which included significant numbers of Afro-Caribbeans, Indo-Caribbeans, East Indians, and whites.

19. A video store owner in Richmond Hill confirmed that girls more commonly rented and bought Hindi movies than boys, and one respondent observed that even in Trinidad mostly girls watched Indian movies. However, this is not the whole story: cinema audiences in India are largely male.

20. Although "temple" is most commonly used in the United States to refer to Hindu religious institutions, most Hindu respondents used the terms *mandir* (the Hindi word for a Hindu place of worship) or "church" to refer to their places of worship.

21. Note that identification with African American culture did not necessarily entail identification with or even acceptance of African American people, which I address in the section on social networks. Indeed, Sunaina Maira (2002) finds that East Indian American youth appropriate black cultural styles while maintaining a sense of superiority toward African Americans.

22. I take the notion of "subcultural capital" from Sarah Thornton (1996), who defines it as "hipness," akin to Bourdieu's (1984) cultural capital but within youth cultures.

23. This figure resonates with the national figure of 70 percent of Asians in the United States marrying other Asians (Waters 2000).

24. Note that not all four factors are necessary for a cosmopolitan ethnicity. Rather, each increases the likelihood that such an ethnicity will develop. Further studies will compare the relative importance of each of these variables.

25. Ethnictown's East Indian population is dominated by Punjabi Sikhs. In addition, there are families from Bangladesh and a smaller number from Pakistan and other parts of India.

26. As mentioned earlier, Hollinger's (1995) use of the term *cosmopolitanism* differs from my own definition of *cosmopolitan ethnicity*. Cosmopolitanism suggests a lack of roots in particular ethnicities and personal histories, unlike cosmopolitan ethnicity.

REFERENCES

Alba, Richard. 1990. *Ethnic Identity: The Transformation of White America.* New Haven, Conn.: Yale University Press.

Alba, Richard D., Nancy A. Denton, Shu-yin J. Leung, and John R. Logan. 1995.

"Neighborhood Change Under Conditions of Mass Immigration: The New York City Region, 1970–1990." *International Migration Review* 29(3, Autumn): 625–56.

Appiah, K. Anthony. 1996. "Race, Culture, Identity: Misunderstood Connections." In *Color Conscious: The Political Morality of Race*, edited by K. Anthony Appiah and Amy Gutmann. Princeton, N.J.: Princeton University Press.

Barth, Fredrik. 1969. "Introduction." In *Ethnic Groups and Boundaries: The Social Organization of Culture Difference*, edited by Fredrik Barth. Prospect Heights, Ill.: Waveland.

Birbalsingh, Frank. 1993. "Introduction." In *Indo-Caribbean Resistance*, edited by Frank Birbalsingh. Toronto: TSAR.

Bonacich, Edna. 1972. "A Theory of Ethnic Antagonism: The Split Labor Market." *American Sociological Review* 37: 547–59.

Bourdieu, Pierre. 1984. *Distinction: A Social Critique of the Judgment of Taste*. Translated by Richard Nice. Cambridge, Mass.: Harvard University Press.

Cornell, Stephen, and Douglas Hartmann. 1998. *Ethnicity and Race: Making Identities in a Changing World*. Thousand Oaks, Calif.: Pine Forge Press.

Foner, Nancy. 2000. *From Ellis Island to JFK: New York's Two Great Waves of Immigration*. New Haven, Conn.: Yale University Press.

Frey, William H. 1996. "Immigration, Domestic Migration, and Demographic Balkanization in America: New Evidence for the 1990s." *Population and Development Review* 22(4, December): 741–63.

Frey, William H., and Reynolds Farley. 1996. "Latino, Asian, and Black Segregation in U.S. Metropolitan Areas: Are Multi-ethnic Metros Different?" *Demography* 33(1, February): 35–50.

Friedman, Jonathan. 1994. "Introduction." In *Consumption and Identity*, edited by Jonathan Friedman. Chur, Switz.: Harwood.

Gans, Herbert J. 1979. "Symbolic Ethnicity: The Future of Ethnic Groups and Cultures in America." *Ethnic and Racial Studies* 2(January): 1–20.

Goffman, Erving. 1959. *The Presentation of Self in Everyday Life*. New York: Doubleday.

Gordon, Milton. 1964. *Assimilation in American Life: The Role of Race, Religion, and National Origins*. New York: Oxford University Press.

Granovetter, Mark S. 1973. "The Strength of Weak Ties." *American Journal of Sociology* 78(6): 1360–80.

Harris, David R., and Jeremiah J. Sim. 2002. "Who Is Multiracial? Assessing the Complexity of Lived Race." *American Sociological Review* 67: 614–27.

Hollinger, David. 1995. *Postethnic America: Beyond Multiculturalism*. New York: Basic Books.

Jacobson, Matthew Frye. 1998. *Whiteness of a Different Color: European Immigrants and the Alchemy of Race*. Cambridge, Mass.: Harvard University Press.

Kale, Madhavi. 1995. "Projecting Identities: Empire and Indentured Labor Migration from India to Trinidad and British Guiana, 1836–1885." In *Nation and Migration: The Politics of Space in the South Asian Diaspora*, edited by Peter van der Veer. Philadelphia: University of Pennsylvania Press.

Kasinitz, Philip, John Mollenkopf, and Mary C. Waters. 2002. "Becoming American/Becoming New Yorkers: Immigrant Incorporation in a Majority Minority City." *International Migration Review* 36(4, Winter): 1020–37.

Khan, Aisha. 1995. "Homeland, Motherland: Authenticity, Legitimacy, and Ideologies of Place Among Muslims in Trinidad." In *Nation and Migration: The Politics of Space in the South Asian Diaspora*, edited by Peter van der Veer. Philadelphia: University of Pennsylvania Press.

Kurien, Prema. 1999. "Gendered Ethnicity: Creating a Hindu Indian Identity in the United States." *American Behavioral Scientist* 42(4): 648–70.

La Ferla, Ruth. 2002. "Kitsch with a Niche: Bollywood Chic Finds a Home." *New York Times*, May 5.

Leonard, Karen. 2000. "Punjabi Mexican American Experiences of Multi-ethnicity." In *We Are a People: Narrative and Multiplicity in Constructing Ethnic Identity*, edited by Paul Spickard and W. Jeffrey Burroughs. Philadelphia: Temple University Press.

Lipsitz, George. 1994. *Dangerous Crossroads: Popular Music, Postmodernism, and the Poetics of Place*. New York: Verso.

López, Nancy. 2002. *Hopeful Girls, Troubled Boys: Race and Gender Disparity in Urban Education*. New York: Routledge.

Maira, Sunaina. 2002. *Desis in the House: Indian American Youth Culture in New York City*. Philadelphia: Temple University Press.

Massey, Douglas S., and Nancy A. Denton. 1993. *American Apartheid: Segregation and the Making of the Underclass*. Cambridge, Mass.: Harvard University Press.

Moore, Solomon, and Robin Fields. 2002. "The Great 'White' Influx." *Los Angeles Times*, July 31.

Olzak, Susan. 1983. "Contemporary Ethnic Mobilization." *Annual Review of Sociology* 9: 355–74.

Orfield, Gary, and John T. Yun. 1999. "Resegregation in American Schools." Cambridge: Civil Rights Project, Harvard University (June).

Patterson, Orlando. 1975. "Context and Choice in Ethnic Allegiance: A Theoretical Framework and Caribbean Case Study." In *Ethnicity: Theory and Experience*, edited by Nathan Glazer and Daniel P. Moynihan. Cambridge, Mass.: Harvard University Press.

Portes, Alejandro, and Rubén Rumbaut. 2001. *Legacies: The Story of the Immigrant Second Generation*. New York: Russell Sage Foundation.

Portes, Alejandro, and Min Zhou. 1993. "The New Second Generation: Segmented Assimilation and Its Variants." *Annals of the American Academy* 530: 74–96.

Prashad, Vijay. 2001. *Everybody Was Kung Fu Fighting: Afro-Asian Connections and the Myth of Cultural Purity*. Boston: Beacon Press.

Rumbaut, Rubén G. 1996. "The Crucible Within: Ethnic Identity, Self-esteem, and Segmented Assimilation Among Children of Immigrants." In *The New Second Generation*, edited by Alejandro Portes. New York: Russell Sage Foundation.

Sengupta, Somini. 1998. "United Ethnically, and by an Assault: Two Groups of East Indians Are Brought Closer, for Now." *New York Times*, October 7, pp. B1–2.

Stryker, Sheldon. 1968. "Identity Salience and Role Performance: The Relevance of Symbolic Interaction Theory for Family Research." *Journal of Marriage and the Family* 30(4): 558–64.

Suarez-Orozco, Carola, and Marcelo M. Suarez-Orozco. 2001. *Children of Immigration*. Cambridge, Mass.: Harvard University Press.

Thornton, Sarah. 1996. *Club Cultures: Music, Media, and Subcultural Capital*. Hanover: University Press of New England.

Tuan, Mia. 1998. *Forever Foreigners or Honorary Whites? The Asian Ethnic Experience Today*. New Brunswick, N.J.: Rutgers University Press.

U.S. Department of Commerce. U.S. Census Bureau. 2000. *Integrated Public-Use Microdata Series 2.0, 1 Percent Sample*. Available at: www.ipums.org.

Veblen, Thorstein. 1912. *The Theory of the Leisure Class*. New York: Macmillan.

Vertovec, Steven. 1992. *Hindu Trinidad: Religion, Ethnicity, and Socioeconomic Change*. London: Macmillan.

Waldinger, Roger. 1996. *Still the Promised City? African Americans and New Immigrants in Postindustrial New York*. Cambridge, Mass.: Harvard University Press.

Waters, Mary C. 1990. *Ethnic Options: Choosing Identities in America*. Berkeley: University of California Press.

———. 1996. "The Intersection of Gender, Race, and Ethnicity in Identity Development of Caribbean American Teens." In *Urban Girls: Resisting Stereotypes, Creating Identities*, edited by Bonnie J. Ross Leadbeater and Niobe Way. New York: New York University Press.

———. 1999. *Black Identities: West Indian Immigrant Dreams and American Realities*. Cambridge, Mass.: Harvard University Press.

———. 2000. "Immigration, Intermarriage, and the Challenges of Measuring Racial-Ethnic Identities." *American Journal of Public Health* 90(11, November): 1735–37.

Williams, Eric. 1970. *From Columbus to Castro: The History of the Caribbean 1492–1969*. New York: Vintage.

CHILDREN OF IMMIGRANTS,
CHILDREN OF AMERICA

Nathan Glazer and Daniel Patrick Moynihan's 1963 classic *Beyond the Melting Pot* marked a paradigm shift in the study of assimilation. They argued that the Jews, Italians, Irish, African Americans, and Puerto Ricans of New York City had not and would not melt into a homogeneous mass but rather had become distinct ethnic groups—different from their immigrant parents, but still self-consciously organized as distinct interest groups with strong ethnic identities. In so doing, these ethnic groups altered previous expectations about the later stages of assimilation. Glazer and Moynihan challenged the inevitability, advisability, and even possibility that ethnic distinctions would totally disappear, even while outlining a story of New York City and America as a greenhouse for stimulating the growth of the ethnic politics and identities created in the welter of New York politics and street life.

What Glazer and Moynihan did not fully appreciate in 1963 was that New York and the nation were poised on the edge of a profound political, social, and demographic transformation. The civil rights revolution and the reopening of America as a destination for immigrants from around the globe were just on the horizon. Within a few years these events would alter our understandings of New York's ethnic scene in two fundamental ways. In a new preface to the second edition of the book published in 1970, Glazer and Moynihan pondered the first of these changes: the meaning of the explosion of racial conflict in the 1960s for their analysis of New York's African American population. Clearly shaken by the riots, calls for a black separatist politics, and scholarly arguments that nonwhites should be considered internally colonized peoples rather than ethnics, Glazer and Moynihan (1963/1970, viii) wrote that "race has exploded to swallow up all other distinctions, or so it would appear at the moment."

The importance of immigration was less clear in 1970. Glazer and Moynihan mentioned the city's growing Chinese and Cuban populations but did not see that the "new immigration" would transform the system of racial and ethnic distinctions in the city. They wondered about whether then-resurgent working-class Irish and Italian ethnic identities would become more prominent—a phenomenon that in retrospect seems more a last gasp than a future trend—and they debated whether African Americans and Puerto Ricans would choose ethnic group status or racial separatism, ruling out assimilation as an option for them. From a twenty-first-century vantage point, their discussion of Puerto Ricans seems particularly dated, since they predicted that this group would be absorbed into the larger "Catholic group" of Italians and Irish and did not foresee the development of a "Hispanic" or "Latino" category that by the mid-1970s would be seen as a virtual "race."

With the clarity of hindsight, we now know that those with European-born grandparents or even more distant European ancestors *did* assimilate, even as they reshaped that mainstream and created new meanings for their ethnic ancestries (Gans 1979; Waters 1990; Alba and Nee 2003). For them, ethnicity became optional, voluntary, enjoyable, and ultimately less about social distinction than about individual identities, lifestyle choices, family histories, and group rituals. The same cannot yet be said for the nonwhite groups.

The confluence of rising immigration from non-European sources and the persistence of racial difference in urban America has again prompted scholars to focus on the question of how the new Asian, Latin American, and Caribbean immigrant groups will fit into the supposedly alternative choices of assimilation into the (white) mainstream, ethnicization as distinct groups among many others, and racialization as a subordinate category. The possibility (and hope) that many of the new groups will avoid the last fate has once more raised the notion of assimilation to a higher level even than when Glazer and Moynihan published the second edition of *Beyond the Melting Pot*.

As Rogers Brubaker (2001) and others have noted, assimilation has been revived in a new form. Brubaker distinguishes between a general increase in similarity, which does not imply only one direction of change and sees outcomes as a matter of degree, and a more specific meaning of "to make similar" that implies that the majority will coerce a minority toward an all-or-nothing outcome. Critics have discredited only this latter meaning, while Richard Alba and Victor Nee have rehabilitated the former in their major new book, *Remaking the American Mainstream* (2003). Yet both uses of the term posit changes in the arriving population while begging the question of how much the receiving population will also be changed by the process of incorporating immigrants—that is to say, the question of "assimilation into what?"

Brubaker (2001, 542) highlights the importance of this issue: "Recent accounts are sensitive to the possibility of different rhythms and trajectories of assimilation or dissimilation in different domains. . . . On current understandings, assimilation is always domain-specific and relative to a particular reference population; and the normative stance one takes toward it will also depend on the particular domain and reference population." This shift in the understanding of assimilation has led scholars to change the questions they ask about what is happening—"a shift from the mono-dimensional question, 'how much assimilation?' to the multidimensional question, 'assimilation in what respect, over what period of time, and to what reference population?'" (544).

Segmented assimilation theory attempts to provide answers to these questions. The theory, formulated by Alejandro Portes and Min Zhou (1993) and elaborated and tested empirically by Portes and Rubén Rumbaut (2001), argues that the children of immigrants may take one of three paths, depending on their situation: assimilating into a mainstream American (white) middle-class culture, remaining within an ethnic or immigrant enclave culture, or embracing a native minority oppositional culture and identity. They see the first two paths as leading to upward mobility and generally positive outcomes for the second generation. The last path leads to downward mobility, with attendant antisocial behavior. Segmented assimilation thus accepts that American racial categories remain rigidly placed within what David Hollinger (1995) has disparagingly called the "ethno-racial pentagon." It is ironic that segmented assimilation theory, which posits that a small range of identity paths determines socioeconomic outcomes, has developed at the same time that the social constructionist turn in ethnic theorizing emphasizes fluid identities, malleable boundaries, and situationally derived meanings of identities.

Concern that a significant portion of today's second generation might be experiencing downward mobility relative to their immigrant parents was an important motive for our study. We wanted to know whether they would end up swelling the ranks of the most impoverished part of New York's racial "minority" population. The chapters in this volume provide some grounds for this concern, as in Nancy López's description of how poorer parts of the Dominican and West Indian populations find themselves stuck in some of the city's worst educational institutions. But we feel that a different problem is actually a greater cause for alarm. The relatively successful incorporation of many children of immigrants into the city's native-born "black" and "Hispanic" populations may be obscuring just how badly many native children of native African American and Puerto Rican parents are now doing.

No one second-generation experience emerges from the pages of this book as the predominant trajectory for the children of immigrants. They are following different paths shaped by different circumstances. Some of those perceived as "closest" to native minorities (who may also come to perceive themselves that way) are being incorporated into the most disadvantaged parts of American society. These immigrant children are indeed being assimilated into a "segment" of society. Yet many other cases presented in this volume counter both the notion of second-generation decline relative to immigrant parents and the notion of forestalling that outcome by clinging to a parental ethnic enclave. By and large, these young people are joining—while also profoundly reshaping—the economic, cultural, and social mainstream.

To be sure, "black" and "Hispanic" immigrant groups face challenges that those seen as "white" or "Asian" do not. They are indeed becoming part of black and Hispanic America and wear their "African American" or "Latino" identities in an easy and unconflicted manner. Butterfield's and Trillo's respondents, for example, show much less ambivalence about and distancing from native minorities than studies often reveal among their parents (see Waters 1999; Vickerman 1999; Kasinitz 1992; 2004.). Yet even these groups are not becoming part of and diversifying an urban "underclass." Rather, they are reshaping the black, Hispanic, and minority categories.

The civil rights era helped make this possible. These categories no longer mean what they did to Glazer and Moynihan in 1970: the institutions and procedures of affirmative action have provided many entry points into important institutions (Kasinitz 2004). Demographic change has played a part as well. In New York "black" no longer means *native* African American and "Hispanic" no longer means "Puerto Rican." Among young adult blacks, African Americans with native parents are now a minority in New York, while New York–born Puerto Ricans are a minority among Hispanics.

Finally, these case studies have convinced us that the discussion of oppositional culture among the children of immigrants confuses style for substance. Many black and Hispanic children, whether they have immigrant or native parents, listen to hip-hop music and affect a "ghetto" presentation of self (often incorrectly attributed to native minority roots, given the large number of immigrant children involved in producing hip-hop culture) *without* being criminals or gang members. (For more on the multicultural roots of hip-hop, see Rivera 2003; Hinds 2002.) So do the children of Asian immigrants, white immigrants, and white natives! For many young people, hip-hop *is* the mainstream, and being drawn to it is hardly evidence of joining a subordinated "segment" of society that engages in self-defeating behavior. A young man wearing baggy clothes and ostentatious jewelry and blasting gangsta rap from the oversized speakers in his car will certainly draw an adverse reaction from authority figures—notably the police—if his skin is dark, whether his parents are immigrants or tenth-generation descendants of American slaves. But sharing a taste for the music and clothing popular among native black youngsters in poor neighborhoods does not necessarily mean that the children of immigrants will share their educational outcomes or labor market position.

While these case studies show that young people from different immigrant backgrounds are likely to have different life experiences, it is equally important to note that ethnicity is not always the most central category in their lives. The logic of survey data may make it too easy to compare how Dominicans are doing relative to South Americans or Chinese compared to native whites. It creates the danger of becoming overly focused on ethnicity. The ethnographic approach taken by the authors in this volume enables us to see how such factors as gender and class become elements in young people's lives that are just as important as their race or ethnicity, and sometimes more important.

In short, these chapters give the striking impression that their subjects rarely fit into one of the three boxes posited by segmented assimilation theory: white mainstream, ethnic enclave, or native minority. These young people *do* have reference populations—Jews for the Russians, African Americans for the West Indians, and Puerto Ricans for the Dominicans and South Americans. Yet they live in far more diverse worlds than segmented assimilation theories postulate.

A NEW YORK STORY?

On balance, these chapters tell a story that should lead the reader to be cautiously optimistic, with an eye toward a few dark clouds visible on the horizon. They present a story of social and economic inclusion, advances in education and occupational opportunities, cultural and social intermixing, and the creation of a vibrant youth culture in a city of enormous diversity and largely unacknowledged competence. The groups have achieved, if not perfect harmony, a widespread rough-and-tumble tolerance for each other.

In these pages, the city and its institutions seem surprisingly open to including the second generation, perhaps more so than for the children of native minority groups. Although these young people feel the sting of disadvantage and discrimination, they move in a world where being from "somewhere else" is the norm. For them, being a New Yorker is being *both* ethnic and American, both different from whites and different from their immigrant parents. In contrast to the tortured searches for identity undertaken by students on elite college campuses, these young people do not seem to feel any particular need to give up their cultures or identities to become successful and accepted. The only young adults who felt pressure to be less ethnic were the working-class Koreans studied by Sara Lee.

This inclusive environment may stem not only from New York's long history of absorbing immigrants but from the local successes of the civil rights movement. The relative harmony and acceptance reported by these young people may also reflect the particular moment when our ethnographers were in the field—the affluent end of the 1990s. This was a period of plentiful jobs, if not always good ones. After years of starvation budgets and malaise, the city's huge system of public colleges, generally seen as on an upswing, provided a safety net of second chances for many young people. More recently, the city has experienced a significant recession, and it has become more costly to attend a public college. Whether this period will also lead to more ethnic conflict and actual or perceived discrimination is as yet uncertain.

Yet in bad times as well as good, the city remains a place formed by centuries of absorbing new immigrants. As Glazer and Moynihan put it in 1963:

> New York is not Chicago, Detroit, or Los Angeles. It is a city in which the dominant racial group has been marked by ethnic variety and all ethnic groups have experienced ethnic diversity. Any one ethnic group can count on seeing its position and power wax and wane and none has become accustomed to long term domination, though each may be influential in a given area or domain. None can find challenges from new groups unexpected or outrageous. While this has not necessarily produced a reservoir of good feeling for groups different from one's own, the evolving system of inter-group relations permits accommodation, change, and the rise of new groups. (Glazer and Moynihan 1963/1970, xiii)

This adaptability has persisted despite the nonwhite origins of most new immigrant groups. No doubt New York City still has an entrenched white establishment that can trace its roots in the United States back many generations. But the new second generation rarely encounters such people on the job, in the unions, or around the neighborhoods, schools, and subways of New York. Instead, they see a continuum of "whites" who trace their origins to Italy, Ireland, Germany, Russia, Poland, Greece, or Israel. If Italians are yesterday's newcomers and today's establishment, then maybe Colombians are the new Italians and, potentially, tomorrow's establishment. New Yorkers, old and new, are happy to tell themselves this story. It may not be completely true, but the fact that they tell it, and believe it, is significant and may help make it come true.

New York's racial divides also do not have the sharp boundaries of exclusion and permanency that they may take on elsewhere in the country. The native blacks who led the union that Amy Foerster studied had inherited the union from Jews but still saw themselves as upstarts and outsiders even though they had become an entrenched old guard in the eyes of their West Indian members, some of whom were doubtless poised to make their own bid for leadership. In recent years, New York saw a new, highly visible leader emerge in the powerful Transit Workers Union (TWU). Roger Toussaint hails from Trinidad and gained his first political experience as a high school student activist in that country's near-uprising in 1970. He won the union presidency with support from a multi-ethnic and largely second-generation immigrant coalition, displacing African American leaders, who had themselves displaced an Irish American leadership decades earlier. The New York press immediately began to draw parallels between Toussaint and Mike Quill, the colorful Irish onetime revolutionary who led the TWU in the midtwentieth century. For New Yorkers facing a potentially crippling transit strike, this should not have been a comforting analogy, for Quill led some of the bitterest public employee strikes in the city's history. Yet the analogy is strangely comforting nevertheless: its subtext is that the accent may be new, but the story is familiar.

When it comes to race, however, some aspects of the story have decidedly changed. Dark-skinned immigrants and their children clearly face discriminatory barriers that others do not, but post–civil rights New York also gives them access to programs, institutions, and rights unheard of in earlier eras. The new groups are reaping advantages as well as disadvantages from being classified as "racial minorities." While African Americans and Puerto Ricans, joined by the descendants of earlier West Indian immigrants, struggled to create institutions, today the children of nonwhite immigrants are often in a better position to take advantage of them. The educational programs for Spanish-speaking students studied by Trillo, the public college studied by Louie, the political organizations studied by Marwell, and the union studied by Foerster, all are examples of institutions shaped by the civil rights movement, and they all provide real opportunities for immigrant and second-generation populations. Counter to the segmented assimilation model, qualifying as black or Hispanic does not have wholly negative consequences. Although we do not doubt that some second-generation members and many of their parents believe that it is important to distance themselves from native minorities, the studies in this book convince us that becoming a native minority can have positive as well as negative aspects in a post–civil rights world.

THE QUESTION OF GENERATION

Finally, these ethnographies call into question whether "second generation" is a concept that ordinary people think about in the course of everyday life. Though it has been the main analytical descriptor for us, for the most part it does not seem very important to the people we studied or to the institutions that serve them. Race, gender, ethnicity, class, color, and occupation are all factors that these young people said affect their lives. For the most part, they were not self-conscious about being the children of immigrants or about constituting a "second generation." It is not a category, however, employed by the public schools, the workplace, or the advertising or retail worlds.

The term's salience is greatest in the Korean and Chinese communities. The churches that Karen Chai Kim studied tailor their programs for this group, and Dae Young Kim reports that Korean Americans have even more specific terms than first and second generation: 1.25, 1.5, and 1.75 generation. But for most other groups and a great many Chinese and Koreans, generation, in the sense of "distance from the old country," does not seem to be the defining characteristic that many social scientists believe it to be.

Scholars who study ethnicity have used the term "generation" in at least three ways: to measure distance from the old country, to measure exposure to American society, and to define a specific age cohort that moves through historical time together. In studies of the great wave of European immigrants who arrived in New York and elsewhere in the United States between 1880 and 1924, historical circumstances created a close linkage between these three notions of generation. For example, 60 percent of the total Italian immigration to the United States after 1820 occurred between 1900 and 1914. These young adults had children in the 1920s who came of age during the 1940s and had children of their own, the third generation, in the 1950s. The young adulthoods of each of these cohorts occurred at a time of national economic expansion, producing group upward mobility, as Richard Alba (1988) has pointed out.

The editors of this book include a third-generation Irish American (Mary Waters), a third-generation Jewish American (Philip Kasinitz), and a mongrel third-generation German American (John Mollenkopf). The respective worlds of our second-generation parents, who grew up in or near New York City, were ethnically homogenous but also very much tied to generation. Our Jewish, Irish, and German American fathers grew up in neighborhoods where most of the members of their parents' generation had been born abroad and virtually everyone their own age was born in the United States. (In the 1920s, of course, national legislation cut off further immigration.) The intersection of cohort, immigrant generation, and their own age made "second generation" a lived reality for them, and indeed for many other residents of New York City at that time. It stood for having achieved a certain distance from their immigrant parents and the old country, while still not quite being part of American society, but it also meant sharing the historical experience of becoming American. Like other Americans born in the 1920s and 1930s, they experienced the Depression, World War II, and the prosperity and suburbanization of the 1950s. It is hard to say how much of what they experienced and who they became can be attributed to their immigrant parents and how much to having been born in a particular historical moment. The decline of immigration in the late 1920s and the onset of depression and war prevented the emergence of newer waves of first- and second-generation youngsters to whom we might compare them. Nonetheless, they saw their "second-generation" distinctiveness from their immigrant parents *and* from the American mainstream as a natural and important feature of their lives. The other young people with whom they shared their ethnic neighborhoods, the city streets, their classrooms, and their workplaces were in the same boat.

When Marcus Lee Hansen wrote his famous essay on "Third Generation Return" in 1938, he described a psychology that is not at all evident among the young people we studied in 2000:

> The sons and daughters of the immigrants were really in a most uncomfortable position. They were subjected to the criticism and taunts of the native Americans and to the criticism and taunts of their elders as well. All who exercised any authority over them found fault with the response. . . . The delinquency of the second generation was talked about so incessantly that finally little Fritz and little Hans became convinced that they were not like the children from the other side of the tracks. They were not slow in comprehending the source of all their woes: it lay in the strange dualism into which they had been born. . . . Whereas in the schoolroom they were too foreign, at home they were too American. . . . The gap between the two generations was widened and the family spirit was embittered by repeated misunderstanding. How to inhabit two worlds at the same time was the problem of the second generation. . . . The problem was solved by escape. . . . He wanted to forget everything: the foreign language that left an unmistakable trace in his English speech, the religion that continually recalled childhood struggles, the family customs that should have been the happiest of memories. He wanted to be away from all physical reminders of early days, in an environment so different, so American, that all associates naturally assumed that he was as American as they. (Hansen 1938/1990, 205)

Of course this describes an era when Anglo-conformity, not multiculturalism, was the predominant motif. Yet it conveys the concept of generation as a sharp or bright boundary (Alba, forthcoming). Today generation appears to be more of a blurred boundary. With the continuing arrival of younger and older immigrants, being of a certain age is no longer as tightly correlated with being a given immigrant generation. In Trillo's community college study, a newly arrived Dominican immigrant can sit next to a second-generation Dominican who has never been to the Dominican Republic or next to someone born in the United States who has lived for long stretches of time with his grandmother in the DR. What does this mean for assimilation? The newly arrived immigrant quickly learns about American life from her classmates, facilitating her incorporation into American society. Yet she also replenishes the ethnic raw materials that enable her second-generation peers to keep up their

Spanish skills and learn about the latest music and cultural practices "back home." The transnational person complicates the sociologist's task because her generational status may not tell us much about either her exposure to American society (she may know less about it than someone born in the DR who came to New York as a child and never went back) or her distance from her parents' country. She acts as a bridge between the youth cultures of the Dominican Republic and the United States, influencing Dominicans who will never set foot in this country (Levitt 2001, 2002).

Although the concept of generation is clearly not as useful a descriptor as it was for our parents' generation, it remains an important analytical concept. As ethnographers who listen to our subjects, we hear the message that the new second generation is sending in this book: they are not lost between two worlds, but move easily between them and among each other. They do not strive to be American, but feel that they are American just by being who they are. They may be impatient with how their parents do things (what twenty-year-old is not?), but they are not ashamed of their parents. And while we do not know who they will be in twenty years, or what their children will be like, they have clearly found a home in America as citizens of that complex and endlessly fascinating world, New York City.

REFERENCES

Alba, Richard. 1988. "Cohorts and the Dynamics of Ethnic Change." In *Social Structures and Human Lives*, edited by Matilda White Riley, Bettina J. Huber, and Beth B. Hess. Newbury Park, Calif.: Sage Publications.

————. Forthcoming. "Bright Versus Blurred Boundaries: Second-Generation Assimilation and Exclusion in France, Germany, and the United States." *Ethnic and Racial Studies*.

Alba, Richard, and Victor Nee. 2003. *Remaking the American Mainstream: Assimilation and Contemporary Immigration*. Cambridge, Mass.: Harvard University Press.

Brubaker, Rogers. 2001. "The Return of Assimilation? Changing Perspectives on Immigration and Its Sequels in France, Germany, and the United States." *Ethnic and Racial Studies* 24(4, July): 531–48.

Gans, Herbert. 1979. "Symbolic Ethnicity: The Future of Ethnic Groups and Cultures in America." *Ethnic and Racial Studies* 2(1): 1–20.

Glazer, Nathan, and Daniel Patrick Moynihan. 1963/1970. *Beyond the Melting Pot: The Negroes, Puerto Ricans, Jews, Italians, and Irish of New York City*. Cambridge, Mass.: MIT Press.

Hansen, Marcus Lee. 1938/1990. "The Problem of the Third-Generation Immigrant." In *American Immigrants and Their Generations*, edited by Peter Kivisto and Dag Blanck. Urbana: University of Illinois Press. (Orig. pub. in *Augustana Historical Society Publications*.)

Hinds, Selwyn Seyfu. 2002. *Gunshots in My Cookup: Bits and Bites from a Hip-Hop Caribbean Life*. New York: Altira Press.

Hollinger, David. 1995. *Postethnic America: Beyond Multiculturalism*. New York: Basic Books.

Kasinitz, Philip. 1992. *Caribbean New York: Black Immigrants and the Politics of Race*. Ithaca, N.Y.: Cornell University Press.

———. 2004. "Race, Assimilation, and Second Generations, Past and Present." In *Not Just Black and White: Historical and Contemporary Perspectives on Immigration, Race, and Ethnicity in the United States*, edited by Nancy Foner and George Fredrickson. New York: Russell Sage Foundation.

Levitt, Peggy. 2001. *The Transnational Villagers*. Berkeley: University of California Press.

———. 2002. "The Ties That Change: Relations to the Ancestral Home over the Life Cycle." In *The Changing Face of Home: The Transnational Lives of the Second Generation*, edited by Peggy Levitt and Mary C. Waters. New York: Russell Sage Foundation.

Portes, Alejandro, and Rubén G. Rumbaut. 2001. *Legacies: The Story of the Immigrant Second Generation*. Berkeley: University of California Press.

———. 2004. "Race, Assimilation, and 'Second Generations,' Past and Present." In *Not Just Black and White: Historical and Contemporary Perspectives on Immigration, Race, and Ethnicity in the United States*. New York: Russell Sage Foundation.

Portes, Alejandro, and Min Zhou. 1993. "The New Second Generation: Segmented Assimilation and Its Variants." *Annals of the American Academy of Political and Social Science* 530: 74–97.

Rivera, Raquel Z. 2003. *New York Ricans from the Hip-Hop Zone*. New York: Palgrave Macmillan.

Vickerman, Milton. 1999. *Crosscurrents: West Indian Immigrants and Race*. New York: Oxford University Press.

Waters, Mary C. 1990. *Ethnic Options: Choosing Identities in America*. Berkeley: University of California Press.

———. 1999. *Black Identities: West Indian Immigrant Dreams and American Realities*. Cambridge, Mass.: Harvard University Press.

INDEX

Boldface numbers refer to figures and tables.

F 128.9 .A1 B33 2004

Becoming New Yorkers